The Lessons
of Recent Wars
in the Third World,
Volume I

The Lessons
of Recent Wars
in the Third World,
Volume I

Approaches and Case Studies

Edited by

Robert E. Harkavy
The Pennsylvania State University

Stephanie G. Neuman
Columbia University

Lexington Books
D.C. Heath and Company/Lexington, Massachusetts/Toronto

Library of Congress Cataloging in Publication Data
Main entry under title:

The Lessons of recent wars in the Third World.

  Includes bibliographies and index.
  Contents: v. 1. Approaches and case studies.
  1. Military art and science—Developing countries—History—20th century—Addresses,
essays, lectures. 2. Military history, Modern—20th century—Addresses, essays, lectures. 3.
World politics—1975–1985—Addresses, essays, lectures. 4. Developing countries—Armed
Forces—Addresses, essays, lectures. I. Harkavy, Robert E. II. Neuman, Stephanie G.
U43.D48L47 1985   355'.009172'4   83-47912
ISBN 0-669-06765-2 (v. 1: alk. paper)

Published simultaneously in Canada
Printed in the United States of America on acid-free paper
International Standard Book Number: 0-669-06765-2
Library of Congress Catalog Card Number: 83-47912

Contents

Introduction

T his volume is the first of two that grew out of a research project devoted to the study of recent wars. The aims of the study are threefold: to examine and compare the ways in which recent wars have been fought; to determine what factors are associated with the success or failure of the combatants; and to discover how the lessons learned might be applied in the future. In general, the focus has been on the forms that armed conflict has taken, the elements that have affected their outcome, and their impact on the combatants and other actors in the international system.

This first volume discusses some methodological approaches to the subject, and presents case studies of eight recent wars. In the first chapter, Robert Harkavy provides a broad conceptual outline of the issues and questions to be dealt with in the subsequent chapters. Several authors then discuss a variety of possible analytical approaches. In chapter 2, Harvey Starr and Benjamin Most focus on the ways in which quantitative comparative macroanalyses of recent conflicts can improve our understanding of them. In chapter 3, Jay Luvaas advocates the study of military history to better comprehend today's wars, but cautions us about the inherent difficulties in deriving lessons from that study. Concentrating on the microlevel of analysis, T.N. Dupuy argues in chapter 4 for the combined application of quantitative and historical methods to the study of individual wars. He demonstrates their compatibility and utility with his own quantified judgement model (QJM).

The focus of attention then moves to the wars themselves. Arranged chronologically, five conventional and three unconventional armed conflicts are described and analyzed. William H. Lewis discusses the struggle between Ethiopia and Somalia over the Ogaden Province in chapter 5, and the hostilities between the Moroccans and the Polisario over the Western Sahara in chapter 6. The invasion of Vietnam by the People's Republic of China is examined by Harlan Jencks in chapter 7. In chapter 8, Caesar Sereseres investigates insurgencies in Central America, and the vicissitudes of the guerrilla war in Afghanistan are detailed by Joseph Collins in chapter 9. In chapter 10, William Staudenmaier describes the tactics and strategies of the Iran-Iraq war, and, in chapter 11, Harlan

Ullman reviews the military encounter between Great Britain and Argentina over the Falkland Islands. Finally, in chapter 12, Seth Carus investigates the technological significance of the war in Lebanon. Chapter 13 provides a summary of the questions, ideas, and tentative conclusions reached by the contributors.

The idea for research on lessons from recent wars was conceived by the editors late one snowy night in New York in 1983. Our interest was aroused by the frequency of and terrible costs associated with regional wars and the relative lack of solid, systematic information about them. Media treatment has been sporadic at best. Its quality and quantity are usually dictated by the policies of press control on the part of the combatants; the accessibility of the disputed region; the availability of a reporter to cover the story; the intelligence of the journalist; and the cognizant editor's assessment as to the newsworthiness of the war itself. As a rule, the longer the combat, the more erratic the reporting.

In addition, academics and policy researchers, since the end of World War II, have focused primarily on the theoretical possibility of war—particularly nuclear war—in Central Europe, concentrating their considerable analytical abilities on likely scenarios that might precipitate such a conflict, its probable outcome, and the ways of dealing with it. In comparison, with the possible exception of the Vietnam conflict, only peripheral theoretical attention has been given to the wars that have actually been fought. What little analytical work does exist concentrates on the causes of war and ways of deterring it. The analysis of war itself—how it is fought and what determines its outcome—has been left to the professional military.

The Lessons from Recent Wars project, then, was born out of the editors' curiosity about and excitement over a subject of mutual interest, theoretical significance, and policy relevance which, in our view, has been neglected by nonmilitary analysts. By bringing together academic, military, and policy-making professionals from a variety of disciplines to describe, analyze, and compare the course of recent wars, we saw an opportunity to begin bridging some of the conceptual gaps of the past and to broaden our understanding of organized human violence.

Once born, the idea was welcomed, nurtured, and supported by the Strategic Studies Institute of the U.S. Army War College, Carlisle Barracks, Pa. A conference was held at Carlisle, September 20–22, 1984, at which initial versions of the papers written for the upcoming volume II were presented. In the light of those discussions, the authors revised their papers and the chapters took the form in which they will be presented in volume II.

Robert Harkavy and I warmly thank the U.S. Army War College for its support and for the organization of the conference. We also acknowledge with gratitude the support of the Department of Defense for four papers that will appear in volume II. The Alexander von Humboldt Foundation and the Institute of Political Science of the Christian-Albrechts-Universität, Kiel, West Germany, provided assistance by granting support and hospitality to Robert Harkavy during the summers of 1983 and 1984 while this project was under way. Marjean Knokey of the Research Institute on International Change, Columbia University, deserves many thanks for the many services she provided throughout this undertaking. Dawit Toga, a Ph.D. candidate at Columbia University, deserves thanks for his cheerful help with the production of both volumes.

Finally, we would like to add a word of appreciation to Jaime Welch-Donahue, our editor at Lexington Books, who gave the moral support and cooperation necessary for achieving smooth, efficient, and rapid publication.

Stephanie G. Neuman

Part I
Background and
Methodological Problems

1

The Lessons of Recent Wars: Toward Comparative Analysis

Robert E. Harkavy

In 1982, the telescoped and nearly simultaneous wars in the Falklands, in Lebanon, and on the Iran-Iraq border seemed virtually to have spawned a new industry in academe and among media defense analysts. There was a prolific outburst of articles intended to divine the "lessons" learned from these wars, even as the last-named continued on unabated and a second—Lebanon—seemed hardly a subject for definitive postmortems. Then, too, the "low-intensity" conflicts in Afghanistan and Central America—and to a lesser degree those in Western Sahara, Chad, and Namibia—provided still another milieu for "lessons learned," involving near-ritual, though unavoidable, comparisons with Vietnam and with a chain of precursors stretching back through Malaya and the Philippines.

In a pure sense, of course, there was nothing remarkable about attempts to ascertain the lessons of contemporaneous wars. That tradition goes back through the centuries; indeed, as Jay Luvaas points out in chapter 3, the divining of lessons was institutionalized by the German general staff in the nineteenth century. Much closer to our time, both the Vietnam War and the Middle Eastern wars of 1967 and 1973 spawned their own instant histories replete with lessons, including some produced in almost indecent haste to capture hungry public readerships.

It might be argued that the burgeoning interest in the purely military aspects of these wars might well be interpreted, in part, as reflecting conservative political currents in the West: Reaganism, Thatcherism, and their counterparts elsewhere. In addition, geopolitics had again become fashionable; ROTC enrollments were back up. Thus, the zeitgeist of the early 1980s was really more conducive to the study of war than had been the case a decade earlier.[1]

Furthermore, the shift in scholarly attention back to war-fighting seemed to convey a certain sense of the earlier overplaying of the now-familiar concatenation of civil-military relations, arms control, conflict theories, and other such gentle and essentially reformist manifestations of modern security studies.

The shift in attention back to war-fighting and away from the preparations for war was anticipated by military historian John Keegan, who, ironically, was a scholar known for having speculated aloud about the possible "abolition of battle" in the face of its overwhelming contemporary horrors. He states:

> War, the good quartermaster's opportunity, the bad quartermaster's bane, is the institutional military historian's irritant. It forces him, whose urge is to generalize and dissect, to qualify and particularize and above all to combine analysis with narrative—the most difficult of all the historian's arts. Hence, his preference paradoxically for the study of armed forces in peacetime. But, as Mr. Michael Howard concluded at the end of a long, very painstaking and generally warm review, "The trouble with this sort of book is that it loses sight of what armies are *for!*" Armies, he implied, are for fighting. Military history, we may infer, must in the last resort be about battle. That certainly reflects Clausewitz's view. In an economic analogy, which delighted Engels and has helped to ensure this Prussian (admittedly vaguely Hegelian) general an unobtrusive niche in the Marxist *Temple du Genie,* he suggested that "fighting is to war" (the paraphrase is Engels') "what cash payment is to trade, for however rarely it may be necessary for it actually to occur, everything is directed towards it, and eventually it must take place all the same and be decisive."[2]

In turn—and here, I think, one is on less speculative ground—this directs attention to the abnormally wide gulf that has long existed between the discipline of military history and the endeavors of political scientists and other social scientists that fall variously under such rubrics as security studies, arms control, comparative strategy, peace studies, and the like. Michael Howard earlier stated the matter as follows:

> The military historian today is bound to wonder whether "military history" still exists, or should exist, as a distinct field of study. Fifty years ago neither in the United States nor in the United Kingdom would anybody have seriously raised the question. Everyone knew what military history was. It was the history of the armed forces and of military operations. Its subject-matter occupied an insulated arena, with little if any political or social context.
>
> This kind of combat and unit history still serves a most valuable function both in training the professional officer and in providing essential raw material for the more general historian. To write it effectively calls for exceptional experience and skills. But it is not surprising that so limited a function attracted very few historians of the first rank. It is more surprising that so many historians of the first rank, for so many years, thought it possible to describe the evolution of society without making any serious study of the part played in it by the incidence of international conflict and the influence of armed forces. So long as military history was regarded as a thing apart, it could not itself creatively develop, and general historical studies remained by that much the poorer.[3]

Howard's more recent optimism to the contrary, there would appear to be only scant evidence that this gulf has been bridged of late in American academe.[4]

Indeed, there is a sense that it may have widened anew in recent years, after the passing of what some came to refer to as "the golden age of strategy."[5] It is to the bridging of that gap that this volume is addressed.

Lessons Learned: Some Conceptual and Methodological Issues

The effort to draw lessons from the comparative study of war involves a complex tangle of methodological and philosophical issues that are laden with ideological disputes and tightly held disciplinary perspectives. What is involved is, of course, merely a subset of the more broadly based arguments fought over the whole terrain of the social sciences.[6] Those arguments involve questions about the limits of comparative analysis (wars as sui generis versus wars as illustrations of types); about keeping things in the perspective of statistical additivity (apples and oranges);[7] about the primacy of various levels of analysis or analytical vantage points; about the necessity for or tolerance of moralizing or prescriptive applications; and about more subtle related issues of style, tone, and mood.[8] By and large, historians tend to deny the possibilities of theory and insist, rather, on limiting themselves to halting analogies, if not mere flat description. Hence, we have Luvaas's subtle preference for "insights gained" rather than "lessons learned." Social scientists—who are more given to normative and prescriptive analysis— claim that theory is necessary to understanding, to reading some order into chaos.

These vital and arcane arguments aside, a substantial number of important methodological or conceptual issues appear to be involved in the study of lessons learned. For the most part, these issues can be seen as various dimensions of the familiar "levels of analysis" problem, listed as follows and subsequently elaborated upon:

Various time perspectives or temporal vantage points—the value of hindsight and the associated issue (never fully resolved) of revisionist writings;

Differing national perspectives on lessons learned—that is, U.S., Soviet, British, and various less-developed countries' (LDCs) perspectives, and the perspectives of combatant and noncombatant nations;

Differing subnational perspectives—the analytical and political context of bureaucratic rivalries and the role of intraservice disputes as applied to lessons learned;

A spectrum running from macro- to microlevel approaches to lessons learned—grand strategy, grand tactics, operational levels, small unit tactics, and so on;

Disciplinary perspectives on lessons learned (anthropology, political science, and so on) as they correlate with the aforementioned spectrum of macro- to-micro levels;

Ideological perspectives—Marxist, liberal, conservative, developed and underdeveloped "worlds";

The uses of lessons learned for strictly analytical purposes versus as a propaganda vehicle (which may involve the issue of conscious versus subconscious uses);

Losers' perspectives and winners' perspectives—either way, they both fight the last war;

Negative versus positive lessons—what not to do again and what to do again;

The direction of inferences—lessons applicable to a potential big-power war in Central Europe, to other Third World wars, and lessons applicable to the conduct of war versus those applicable merely to the diplomacy of warfare;

The role of leadership and the depersonalization or bureaucratization of warfare as a historical datum;

The application of "time-tested principles"—for instance, the use of Clausewitz as checklist.

Some important conceptual issues will be omitted from discussion here, simply because they are covered in one or another of the subsequent chapters dealing with approaches to lessons learned. For instance, Dupuy, in chapter 4, and Starr and Most, in chapter 2, deal with various issues of quantification, ranging from a microlevel (indices of comparative combat effectiveness) to a macrolevel (trends in types and incidence of wars in the postwar period).

Starr and Most have also provided another methodological angle. In the broadest sense, they demonstrate that lessons learned can be approached from any of three distinct angles: case studies, comparative analysis, and longitudinal analysis. This volume consists primarily of case studies; the forthcoming second volume will deal with the various comparative dimensions enumerated later in this chapter. In this context, longitudinal analysis is somewhat less germane, since the number of roughly applicable (in a nonempirical sense) cases is small—the several Arab-Israeli wars, the India-Pakistan wars, and perhaps the Ethiopia-Somalia conflict.

The problem of time lags or the amount of hindsight required for validly ascertaining lessons is a daunting one that may ultimately be unresolvable. One is reminded of the common claim, not entirely facetious, that a Metternich or a Bismarck could be adjudged "good" or "bad" (successful or unsuccessful) diplomats depending on which later—even *much* later—retrospective vantage points are used. The 1967 Arab-Israeli war offers an excellent example of this problem. Widely considered an unambiguous triumph for Israel until well after 1967, it is now viewed—even by strong Israeli supporters—as a mixed blessing, to the extent that it exacerbated Arab feelings of humiliation and produced additional irredentist claims and political problems.

In terms of lessons of recent wars, this problem of vantage point is particularly acute.[9] After all, several of these wars are still ongoing, and their immediate outcomes are very much in doubt. (Afghanistan, Central America, Western Sahara, and Iran-Iraq fall into this category.) Others have "ended" in ways that may later be perceived as mere truces or breathing spells; that is, there may yet be additional rounds whose conduct and outcomes may greatly alter perceptions of the lessons of earlier rounds that have been the subjects of numerous instant histories (Lebanon, the Horn of Africa, and perhaps China-Vietnam or the Falklands).

The uncertainties apply not only to predominantly politico-military lessons but perhaps also to strictly military ones (that is, tactical or doctrinal). If Argentina were to be more successful with submarines or air-to-ship missiles in a new round, or if Syrian surface-to-air missiles (SAMs), even if manned by Russians, were to be more effective in a Lebanon round 2—particularly if such wars were to take place soon—perceptions of the first rounds' lessons would surely be altered or at least rendered very ephemeral.[10] Certainly, from the vantage point of 1984, the lessons of 1973 have been modified by the broader perspective provided by the lessons of 1982—perhaps with a natural overall centripetal tendency toward perception of more even, incremental change.[11]

There are numerous external vantage points, of course, from which lessons may be read from Third World wars. There is an American view, a French view, a Soviet view, a Chinese view, and many others, including those of numerous watchful LDCs that are themselves in situations of potential conflict. The Falklands war, for instance, may have been read by U.S. naval experts primarily in the context of the ongoing debate between respective advocates of large and small carriers (which also illustrates the role of "lessons" in interservice and even intraservice doctrinal and budgetary battles). In the USSR, however, the ease with which British nuclear attack submarines rendered the Argentine surface fleet useless may have been seen as the most instructive lesson.[12] There is also the rather murky, not easily answered question of what lessons are read into war outcomes by the relevant Third World military planners themselves and how such lessons are then applied. Just such a division of perspectives would, for instance, impel one to question whether Egyptian military leaders' evaluations of the 1967 war were congruent with those of Western military historians and, if not, whether the differences would involve essentially "nonrational" factors—that is, a lack of sufficient detachment.[13]

The continuum from macro- to microlevel—running from the broadest pos-

sible politico-military considerations to those such as the proper attack formations of an infantry squad or tank company—presents a particularly difficult
problem for comparative analysis of wars. It is not easy to handle all of these
levels simultaneously or in relation to one another.[14] The reader will note that
some of our case study analysts are more or less comfortable with one or the
other end of the spectrum, though this may derive from interpretations of what
is most important in given cases.

Here, too, one deals with the specific and differential contributions of the
various disciplines whose interests and expertise converge upon military strategy
and tactics. Political scientists—often profoundly ignorant of military technology, not to mention military history—tend to operate at the level of contextual
diplomacy; they are also interested in civil-military relations, the impact of internal political cleavages on the conduct of war, and so forth. Psychologists dwell
on problems of morale, battle fatigue, and the like, whereas anthropologists and
sociologists deal with the cultural foundations of small-unit social relations.[15]
Usually, it is only the military officers themselves—and perhaps a handful of
professional historians or social scientists—who can operate at the levels of
grand tactics and of even smaller-scale tactics and can provide insights into the
lessons derived from the performances of individual weapons systems. It is for
these reasons that comparative analysis of wars in the Third World is so difficult;
not unexpectedly, different scholars will prefer to focus on different levels, only
sometimes because it is in their own domains that the most salient, crucial lessons
are to be found.

Then there is the matter of sheer ideological perspectives. Americans often
think such matters are absent from conceptual debates in this country, or at any
rate are confined within the marginal nuances of a narrow liberal-conservative
spectrum. However, these matters, too, may involve perceptual differences applicable to "lessons"—sometimes in the most curious ways. (Could the "small is
beautiful" perspective on aircraft carriers be a reflection of broader political ideology?[16]) On a more global basis, one could talk, at least theoretically, of a
Maoist or Marxist "way of war" and hence such interpretations of its lessons,
begging the question of whether such theoretical contructs may ever really over-
ride more pragmatic factors and those of nationalism. For instance, could one
see Marxist-Leninist theory as substantially affecting Soviet perceptions of Third
World conflict? One writer, in attempting to assert this point, has averred that
"the central Soviet premise on war is a Leninist one," but that it borrows heavily
from Clausewitz, hence further complicating the relationship of war to
ideology.[17]

It is also worth remembering that the military doctrines of all of the major
European powers before World War I were heavily affected by the prevailing
philosophical climate of social Darwinism, with its emphasis on "will" and
"elan," feeding, in turn, into an emphasis on offensive strategies.

The facts of who has won or lost wars may have an important bearing on how those wars are adjudged regarding "lessons." The claim is sometimes made that a loss in one war, if not fatal, can prove an advantage in planning for the next one. The losers rethink tactics and strategies; also, they replace failed leaders and elevate those who performed well in a losing cause. Meanwhile, the winners tend to be locked into "proven" strategies, perhaps even to the point of intensifying or concentrating on previously successful tactics, even as the context defined by new weapons developments is altered, perhaps crucially. Hence, van Creveld notes Israel's increasing reliance on "King Tank" and its mass shock effect after 1967, even as new developments in antitank weapons were creating the need for a shift toward a more balanced-arms approach.[18] (This view is now subject, again, to new interpretation after 1982.) Pakistan's misreading of the approximate standoff it achieved against larger India in 1965 may have had a major influence on its disaster in 1971; in addition, Pakistan appeared prone to misapplying lessons it apparently thought it could apply from the intervening Israeli victory in 1967.[19] Jordan was apparently so overawed by the Israeli performance in 1967 and so dismayed by its own blunder in getting involved that it stayed out of the initial phases of the 1973 war, which may well have cost the Arabs a possible victory.

Roger Beaumont has pointed out, with considerable cogency, that the lessons of war (and, presumably, other categories of lessons) might be further divided into positive and negative lessons—that is, what to do again because it worked and what not to do again.[20] This distinction involves more than a clever verbal trick; indeed, it may provide fertile ground for theorizing in the context of the extensive literature on the psychological dimensions of decision making.[21] For instance, it may alert us to the link with the concept of satisficing (satisfactory decisions short of maximizing) and to generalizations about why decision makers instinctively concentrate on avoiding mistakes at the expense of more positive, risky, and aggressive aims. That is, it is possible that negative lessons ("Let's not repeat that blunder") may be more salient and may receive more attention than positive ones, even to the point of weighting overall analysis.

The matter of the direction of inferences—that is, their very purposes—from the lessons of recent Third World wars presents a very tricky problem. Most U.S. writings in this vein almost automatically interpret such lessons to the extent that they might apply to a later major conventional war in Central Europe. Other Third World analysts presumably derive their own lessons in a similarly parochial manner—that is, as they would apply to their own regional military contingencies. Even for U.S. defense planners, however, it is worth pointing out that not only strictly military (operational, tactical) lessons are germane. A number of these Third World wars—Iran-Iraq, Falklands, the Horn—should have provided lessons regarding, for instance, arms resupply policy—that is, lessons deriving from the diplomacy surrounding Third World warfare.

Jay Luvaas's chapter in this volume points out that in past centuries, lessons of war were determined primarily, if not wholly, at the level of individual generalship. The lessons learned were thus very personalized; the strategies of the "great captains"—Frederick, Wellington, Napoleon, and so forth—were the focus of most military analysis. Nowadays, the reader of Third World war reportage might scarcely ascertain even the names, much less the successes and failures, of respective foes' military leaders (British Admiral Sandy Woodward and Israel's Ariel Sharon might be partial exceptions). War leadership has become virtually faceless in its bureaucratization. Whether this is merely a curious academic point is hard to tell.

Finally, it is worth noting that some analysts choose to gauge lessons learned through rather structured checklists of evaluative criteria. Harry Summers has evaluated the U.S. performance in Vietnam according to one such checklist of hoary principles—in this case as offered up by the amazingly durable writings of Clausewitz.[22] Dupuy utilizes a quantitative scheme for comparing combat effectiveness, then offers advice on "how to fight outnumbered and win."[23] Summers and Dupuy thus illustrate, respectively, the nuanced distinction between a more broadly gauged politico-military orientation and one that is more closely pegged to an operational military level.

The Dimensions of Comparative Analysis

With some of the indicated caveats in mind, a number of areas would appear to be apt subjects for comparison. Some of the following subjects lean toward predominantly methodological issues, while others are more mundane and topical:

The conjunction of strategy, doctrine, tactics, and weapons;

Military geography—terrain, weather, number of fronts;

Cultural dimensions of the conduct of warfare;

The so-called human factor—the psychology of morale, comparative pain thresholds, possible trends regarding the human sustainability of combat;

Arms transfer patterns, arms resupply, and the war-fighting role of indigenous arms industries;

Great-power intervention—coercive diplomacy, surrogate forces, and the broader aspects of security assistance;

War termination and the nature of protracted, interminable conflicts;

The media, public opinion, and the management of war news;

The comparative economics of the conduct of Third World warfare.

Of course, not all of these dimensions can be examined with equal appropriateness to all of the recent wars. Some are more important in some cases than in others; compare, for instance, the role of news management (or its absence) in the Falklands and Lebanon cases with those of Vietnam-China or the Horn.

Then, too, there is the serious problem of the divide between conventional and unconventional (high- and low-intensity) warfare with respect to some dimensions that require vastly different modes of analysis. The analysis of arms transfers, for instance, proceeds along much different routes, as applied to conventional versus unconventional warfare. Indeed, although arms resupply to combatants in conventional wars seems normal and accepted in the competition among big powers, it must be conducted almost as a form of covert action in some unconventional wars (Afghanistan, Central America), where incumbent regimes beleaguered by insurgents are tied to one or another great power.

In some instances, attempting to generalize across both conventional and unconventional wars may involve peculiar contradictions, even tautologies. For instance, in discussing cultural perspectives on warfare, it might be conjectured that conventional warfare is really a part of the Western historical tradition, redolent of Clausewitz and the mystique of the decisive battle. The imagery is akin to chess and football or rugby (moving fronts, seeming momentum toward victory, a definitive ending or final whistle), whereas Maoist doctrines of unconventional warfare are often claimed to stem from another cultural tradition—one that is more comfortable with protracted, interminable warfare, inconclusive or nondecisions, and the absence of visible, definable fronts.[24] Hence, it is not surprising that in recent decades, U.S. military writings have seemed bifurcated between what have become almost two wholly separate strategic traditions: those of conventional land war and those of unconventional war or counterinsurgency.[25] The terminology is telling; conventional warfare is more often than not called *war,* whereas low-intensity cases are more often referred to as *conflicts.*[26] The distinctions also seem to reveal a lingering tendency in the United States to separate the military from the political—a tendency that has been used to characterize a peculiarly "American way of war."[27]

The Conjunction of Strategy, Tactics, Weapons, and Doctrine

At the very core of the standard, long-term military histories (Marathon to the Mitla Pass) are the crucial interrelationships of strategy, tactics, doctrines, and weapons.[28] Military history is portrayed therein as a never-ending developmental skein, an endless tale of action and reaction, with each new weapon and tactic eventually countered by another.[29]

Particularly germane here are the long-term cyclical ebbs and flows of advantage to offensive and defensive tactics and strategies, which, in turn, have been propelled by new weapons developments.[30] As discussed by numerous military historians, these factors tend to move in relatively long-term cycles, heretofore often spanning generations if not centuries and often punctuated by key watershed battles or campaigns in which the prevailing assumptions hitherto held by an era's military planners are shattered with finality. Van Creveld cites Marathon (490 B.C.), Adrianople (378 A.D.), Pavia (774), Hastings (1066), Crecy (1346), Valmy (1792), and Cambrai (1917) as examples of such watersheds.[31] (His choices might appear a bit Eurocentric or "Western".)

Quester, van Creveld, and others have attempted to theorize or to elaborate somewhat on the context of shifts between offensive and defensive advantages. Van Creveld has discerned a rhythmic, incessant variation through history of periodic shifts in advantage among three major elements of combat: mobility, firepower, and protection. Others—such as Luttwak, following, in turn, from the tradition of Liddell-Hart's writings on indirect strategy—prefer the terminology of attrition and "relational maneuver" (or mobility), roughly related, respectively, to defense and offense.[32] However, whereas some tend to see epochal phases of attrition and maneuver warfare dictated primarily by extant state-of-the-art weaponry, strategists such as Luttwak (often in the context of a "reformist" critique of the U.S. military) stress the discretionary nature of the distinction, particularly as applied to the common strategic dilemma of outnumbered nations that are perceived to depend utterly on compensating by relational/maneuver strategies.

The standard analysis of these factors, in the most general sense as they apply to the past century, is familiar enough. Both alliances prepared for wars of mobility before World War I (the Schlieffen Plan versus Foch's Plan XVII), with strategies philosophically underpinned by some intellectual currents of the late nineteenth century.[33] When those strategies failed in the trenches of northern France—and despite the advent of the tank, tactical aircraft, and poison gas in 1917–1918—the doctrinal result was the Maginot Line. The bogging down of the German blitzkrieg in the Russian snow and mud and the high attrition rates of numerous World War II battles subsequently inspired NATO's essentially static defensive strategy, further involving nuclear weapons. Israel's temporary debacle in 1973, however, was thought finally to have ended the era inaugurated by the German blitzkriegs of 1939–1940; antitank and antiaircraft missiles were thought to have permanently diminished the roles of armor and tactical aircraft. In 1982, however, the successful Israeli SAM-busting tactics and their newly regained successful use of armor were said to have already reversed the seeming watershed of 1973. By 1984, some analysts saw in the introduction of new Soviet SAM technology to Syria the possibilities of still another reversal.[34] Battle history had appeared to accelerate; the cycles were telescoped, and the seeming watersheds were following upon one another more quickly.

Clearly, the attribution of watersheds and of eras to weapons and tactics had normally been in connection with the leading military powers of a given period—

those on the cutting edge of technology. In retrospect, however, what appeared to be a startling shift of advantage to the defense in 1914 (machine guns, artillery, barbed wire) was later thought to have been anticipated (if not widely understood) by the U.S. Civil War, the Russo-Japanese war and perhaps the Boer War. A cutting edge may indeed exist, but the signs may sometimes be read elsewhere.

This, in turn, raises the question of what military lessons can be inferred—for whom and for what purpose—from the varied recent wars of the Third World. Answering this difficult question requires taking into account a variety of factors: the state of weaponry, the capacity of combatants to use weapons effectively, the terrain, and so on.

As indicated earlier, the recent Israeli-Arab wars appear foremost among those that have provided lessons regarding the nexus of weapons and tactics in the eyes of Western analysts. Hence, the technological developments from 1973 to 1982 were followed with enormous interest, particularly regarding the future roles of armor and tactical airpower. [35] Israel's use of weapons, in particular, has been widely interpreted as indicative of the state of the art at the superpower level, though some analysts have cautioned against pushing the inference too far, particularly because of the smaller space involved and (for air war) the lesser density of combat. In the face of similar questions, the naval war in the Falklands has drawn immense interest because of its possible implications for superpower maritime competition.[36]

It is important to point out, however, that the mixed and presumably related lessons of some of the other recent Third World conflicts may indicate just how difficult such generalizations can be. Iraq and Iran, fighting with many of the same weapons used in the central Middle Eastern conflict, have been locked in a nearly stationary slugfest for over four years, which has reminded some of World War I.[37] Indeed, the terrain in many areas is quite amenable to armored maneuver warfare, despite the mountains and marshes in some parts of the front. In 1971, India conducted a virtual blitzkrieg offensive in Bengal despite difficult riverine terrain, in a manner deemed by one military analyst "a classic example of the application of Liddell-Hart's theory of the expanding torrent."[38] The Somalia-Ethiopia war was pretty much one of maneuver (fought by nations one might consider inherently less able to conduct mobile, forward operations than Iraq or Iran),[39] whereas the onslaught by the People's Republic of China (PRC) against Vietnam in 1979 seemed to have had the character of a costly meatgrinder offensive across a broad front, albeit with some roadbound use of armor.[40] None of these wars appears to have interested Western observers in terms of possible lessons for Central Europe as had the 1973 war.

Two possible generalizations appear worthy of consideration here, and they are offered with caution. First, the skein from 1967 to 1973 to 1982 in the Middle East may indicate that generalizations about offensive and defensive advantages have become far more ephemeral and more subject to surprise. Generalizations (even arguable ones) that once were applicable for lengthy epochs have now been telescoped into a much shorter time frame. Second, it is possible that the lessons of recent wars make the argument for treating individual cases nearly sui generis because of geographical specifics (weather, frontal width of combat lines, mountain and river barriers) and because, at bottom, Israel and India may be one thing and Iran, Iraq, and Argentina another.

Of course, the conjunction of weapons, tactics, and doctrines in the arena of unconventional warfare may be seen to have its own imputed skein of development, and perhaps its own watersheds of sorts.[41] One might surmise that tactics might evolve more slowly, since the role of new, advanced technology might be thought less crucial or at least less likely to produce rapid qualitative changes. Generally, that appears to be the case. However, the U.S. innovations with helicopters in Vietnam—for moving troops about rapidly and as firing platforms—appear to have been followed by the USSR in Afghanistan, the ultimate outcome in Vietnam notwithstanding. And in the Western Sahara, with its relative lack of cover, both helicopters and fixed-wing aircraft have been used extensively for counterinsurgency operations.

Less clear are the lineal developments in low-intensity wars with respect to the tactics of counterinsurgency: search and destroy, scorched earth and free-fire zones, strategic hamlets, and fixed fortifications versus more mobile and aggressive tactics. Here, such "grand tactical" considerations must be judged in the context of geographical realities; the extent to which merciless, brutal suppressive activities are allowed for by domestic and external pressures; the extent of casualities and the duration of war sustainable by an incumbent power, and so forth. One way or another, the lessons provided by Vietnam, particularly for the Soviets in Afghanistan and for U.S. friends in Central America, have received a great deal of attention.

Military Geography

Perhaps simply because of the relentlessly idiosyncratic nature of the subject, the comparative aspects of military geography have received little attention in modern security studies; indeed, there is no recent full-length coverage of the subject.[42] One might surmise a parallel with the submergence of geopolitics as a field of study until very recently. Yet even a casual glance at the histories of recent wars in the Third World appears to reveal the crucial importance—in a comparative sense—of the traditional staples of military geography: topography or land features, depth and buffer zones for absorption of foes' initial thrusts, frontal width and channeling of avenues of attack, compartmentalization and cross-compartmentalization of avenues of attack, the weather, and the number of fronts with which a combatant must simultaneously cope (whether wholly separated or not).

The narrowness and ruggedness of the corridor leading from the Golan Heights toward Damascus was very advantageous to Syria's layered defenses in 1973, preventing Israel from using its preferred mobile armor tactics without violating Jordan's frontiers and virtually forcing it into an attrition slugfest in advancing toward the Syrian capital. The sandy deserts and the few passes through the mountains in western Sinai were critical tactical considerations there in 1956, 1967, and 1973. The mountains east of Baghdad have acted as a defensive barrier against Iranian offensives, hence also allowing Iraq to concentrate its main defensive forces farther to the south.[43] The mountains in Ethiopia flanking the Abyssinian plateau and the Rift Valley channeled the Somalian thrust in 1977–1978, giving Ethiopia time to regroup for a counteroffensive and to acquire external assistance. The rugged terrain in northern Vietnam was apparently helpful to Vietnam in blunting the PRC offensive in 1979, partially canceling the PRC's numerical advantage and reducing the usefulness of its armor.

The military histories are loaded with common generalizations regarding the nexus of military geography to weapons, tactics, and strategies. Flat and uncovered plains are commonly said to lend themselves to rapid armored movement, whereas mountain barriers are said to favor the defense (provision of high ground) and to restrict mechanized forces. Similarly, regions that are crisscrossed with water barriers or that contain swamplands are not considered good tank territory.

Yet the recent wars in the Third World provide some cautionary exceptions to these generalizations. Israel's armor moved rapidly across tough desert terrain in 1967 (some of it considered impassable for tanks), and it also advanced rapidly through rugged terrain in Lebanon in 1982. India, in the eastern zone of its 1971 war in Bengal, conducted rapid offensives across difficult riverine territory, against what was considered a competent professional army. Furthermore, although the Iran-Iraq frontier appears to provide good tank country, there has been a stalemated war with little in the way of rapid armored movement.

The standard generalizations about terrain may perhaps be more easily reflected in the experiences of recent unconventional wars. The thick cover in much of Vietnam and in Central America does appear to have rendered counterinsurgency warfare very difficult (obversely, it has favored "hit-and-run" insurgency tactics), even taking into account the morale and effectiveness of incumbent forces' regimes. In parts of the Western Sahara, open desert terrain and clear weather have indeed appeared to favor defensive forces, which were able to construct fixed lineal defenses and also to conduct counterinsurgency operations from the air; more rugged areas have provided sanctuaries for guerrilla forces. Afghanistan may provide mixed lessons, however, since the Afghan rebels have demonstrated the capacity to sustain guerrilla actions even without the aid of extensive cover, albeit they were favored by mountain terrain that inhibits Soviet ground-mobile operations.

The role of depth (involving primarily a nation's overall area but also the location of key cities, industries, and military strong points in relation to borders) has been much argued over. The standard illustration is Russia's use of its vast spaces to absorb and then defeat Charles XII, Napoleon, and Hitler. Space can be traded for time, often taking advantage of seasonal variations in weather. Iran in 1980 and Ethiopia in 1977 are some recent examples of successful absorption efforts. On the other hand some analyses of the Israel-Egypt conflicts of 1967 and 1973 have claimed that, in counterlogical fashion, Israel's less effective performance in 1973 was partly an ironic result of its having acquired the Sinai buffer, which also resulted in the degrading of its early-warning capability (regarding troop movements in Sinai) and—because of its normally low levels of deployment outside of actual war—left its forward positions precariously exposed.[44]

Israel and Iraq may still be considered to be laboring under a disadvantageous depth/locational problem. Iraq's capital, Baghdad, is much closer to the contested frontier areas than is Teheran, and this has been important, for instance, in forcing Iraq to maintain extensive defensive deployments between the border and the capital. The asymmetry also puts into serious question the Iraqi preventive war strategy of 1980, in that it could not easily have succeeded either in the destruction of the Iranian army or in the overrunning of the major Persian core areas; that, in combination with Iran's numerical advantage, was likely to be ultimately telling, barring complete collapse of the Teheran regime.

It must be noted that Syria and Jordan, too, labor under depth problems in relation to Israel; in Jordan's case, this was no doubt a compelling rationale for its effective abstention in 1973. In the Horn, Ethiopia's vast depth and the mountain barrier between the Ogaden plains and the Ethiopian plateau, containing the major urban centers of Addis Ababa and Harrar, were altogether decisive in explaining the war's outcome in 1978. As with Iraq, Somalia's preventive war strategy was to appear, retrospectively, as wholly inadequate to cope with this disadvantage, in the absense of a capability to strike decisively over long distances with ground forces. In addition, Somalia suffered from the absence of favorable defensive barriers to an Ethiopian counterattack into its own territories, which, had it not been for external restraints (the United States and the USSR jointly, apparently), might well have resulted in a total debacle.

The impact of space on the conduct of insurgency or counterinsurgency warfare has not received great attention, though some commentaries have remarked upon the smaller space of El Salvador and Guatemala relative to Vietnam as perhaps serving to ease the problem of counterinsurgency. The Soviets have clearly had problems coping with the vast reaches of Afghanistan with "only" some 110,000 troops, which virtually dictates a combined strategy of retaining secure control over only major cities, along with search and destroy tactics. In the Western Sahara, the emptiness and virtual economic irrelevance of much of that area's desert has allowed Morocco to concentrate defensively only on the areas inside its lengthy defensive berm.

The Cultural Dimensions of Conflict

During much of the postwar period—perhaps underpinned by the relentless ecumenical universalism of American academe—the subject of comparative cultural perspectives and their associated effects has been handled very cautiously. That has recently changed, however, perhaps only coincidentally along with the rise of sociobiology, geopolitics, and other theoretical interests associated (not necessarily logically) with a more conservative sensibility. Indeed, the recent past has witnessed academic works on a specifically Chinese style of warfare that is said to be derived from the game of wei'chi and others that examine the comparative cultural aspects of national strategy.[45] In addition, the Iranian revolution, the Iran-Iraq war, and the events in Lebanon have given rise to some scholarly and journalistic speculation about an "Islamic way of war."[46]

The term *comparative culture* is used loosely here; it can refer to the varied or mixed impacts of religion, ethnicity, race—indeed, any internalized cultural or other identity that one might associate with certain definable tendencies to conduct warfare in identifiable, unique ways.[47] It is also recognized that the differences may be less than stark, though sometimes crucial.

During and after the Vietnam War, and also harking back to the Chinese Civil War and the Korean War, much was written about identifiably Asian or Chinese modes of waging war. Westerners were claimed to be wedded to finite (time) wars, decisive set-piece battles, and visible moving fronts; Asians, by contrast, were claimed to have a more patient, long-term view that was amenable to protracted conflict and a spatial perspective allowing for fluid if not nonexistent fronts. Hence, it was claimed, Westerners could not easily cope with protracted guerrilla war nor, more broadly, with those having inconclusive endings.

The events of the late 1970s riveted attention to an Islamic way of war that was said to feature fanaticism, an indifference to death, a cult of martyrdom, the promise of paradise for heroes, and the like. Such imagery was made vivid in the West by the Iranian human-wave tactics at Bustan and Basra, the Sadat assassination, the kamikaze truck bombings in Lebanon, and so on. Providing one caution for such analyses were the occasional comparisons to the Japan of the 1930s and 1940s, with its banzai and kamikaze attacks, which emanated from a very distinct (from Islam) religious and social environment, albeit one that was also supportive of violent fanaticism.

The subject of pain thresholds—that is, the capacity to sustain casualties—is often discussed in these contexts; Vietnam and Iran-Iraq have raised some daunting questions for Western analysts.[48] Such discussions often shade into discussions of modes of rational or nonrational decision making, as adjudged through Western blinders. Non-Western "fatalism" is also sometimes discussed in connection with military grand strategy, for instance, in connection with the seemingly mysterious Egyptian decision making in 1967. (Japan's assault on Pearl Harbor was similarly questioned.[49])

Whether comparative culture deserves a separate niche here may be argued. Recent Arab and Argentinian actions might perhaps be as easily understood as the result of desperate, humiliated nationalism, and traumatic pasts, rather than of cultural characteristics such as Islamic fanaticism or Latin *machismo*.[50] There are also questions regarding whether the impact of such factors can be seen at the level of small-unit tactics or in terms of preferences for the use of certain weapons (or disdain for others).[51]

One other possibly relevant aspect of comparative culture as applied to war-fighting is perhaps more suitably discussed under the rubric of class structure and patterns of authority. After the 1967 war, Israeli commentators such as Y. Harkabi hypothesized that the dismal performance of the Egyptian forces was rooted in Egypt's class structure—specifically, its rigid, hierarchical military structure, which allegedly featured enormous social distance between officers and soldiers.[52] The result was claimed to be not only low morale, but the absence of any kind of autonomous decision making or initiative at small-unit levels, which was deemed a particular disadvantage in fast-moving maneuver warfare.

Similar characterizations have been offered in connection with the Iraqi army's performance, particularly at the outset of the war with Iran in 1980.[53] Indeed, similar questions have been posed with regard to the Soviet army. Particularly difficult to ascertain—if these speculations have any real merit—is whether the root cause is in indigenous class structure or otherwise in traditional authority patterns rooted in culture or, rather, whether it derives from the military organization and decision-making modes of major-power client states. Soviet military influence on Iraq and Egypt has been discussed in this manner, as has the combined impact of traditional culture and American influence on the South Vietnamese ARVN.

The Human Factor in War

A review of the recent literature on trends in warfare reveals a certain paradox or, certainly, some contradictory perceptions. On the one hand, some raw data appear to indicate that levels of inter- and intrastate violence are climbing. This trend is variously attributed to clashing nationalisms, religious and ideological hatreds, the frustrations of economic deprivation, and so forth. However, one also sees analyses—particularly those pegged upon the anticipation of increasing global interdependence and the development of new norms or regimes associated with international organizations—that posit a decrease in violence, even a growing irrelevance of military matters.[54]

At another level, the British historian John Keegan has postulated an impending "abolition of battle," with roots in an assumed increasing disinclination of soldiers of all nations to fight. Basically, his claim is that the increasing terror, brutality, and impersonality of modern battle (noise, viciously efficient killing weapons, absence of interpersonal combat encounters, and the like) make it more and more unlikely that many nations will be able to find persons who are able and willing to sustain combat for more than short periods.[55]

Whether these projections—clearly made with Central Europe in mind—are equally applicable to recent or future Third World conflicts is an interesting question. Surely, the ability of the Khomeini regime to find countless thousands of young men who were willing to martyrize themselves in exchange for a reserved spot in Paradise might seem to argue the contrary, unless the absence in that war of sustained periods of intense combat provides one explanation.[56] Similarly, the Chinese and Vietnamese armies appear to have sustained enormous casualties in their one-month war in 1979, without producing any audible postmortems about morale problems. Indeed, the subjects of battle fatigue and psychiatric breakdown seem to have risen mostly in connection with the U.S. and British experiences and now, also, with regard to Israel's quagmire in Lebanon (where van Creveld reports a higher incidence of battle fatigue than had been reported in previous Israeli wars).[57]

However, Keegan broaches another aspect of this subject that provides links to the historical trends concerning duration of war and, hence, the alternation of advantage between offense and defense, or alternating tendencies to attrition and maneuver warfare. He cites a U.S. report regarding the capacity of soldiers to sustain long periods of combat, as follows:

> There is no such thing as "getting used to combat." . . . Each moment of combat imposes a strain so great that men will break down in direct relation to the intensity and duration of their exposure. . . . psychiatric casualties are as inevitable as gunshot and shrapnel wounds in warfare. . . . Most men were ineffective after 180 or even 140 days. The general consensus was that a man reached his peak of effectiveness in the first 90 days of combat, that after that his efficiency began to fall off, and that he became steadily less valuable thereafter until he was completely useless. . . . The number of men on duty after 200 and 240 days of combat was small and their value to their units negligible. The fighting of the Second World War, in short, led to an infantryman's breakdown in a little under a year.[58]

These generalizations raise some important questions regarding warfare in the Third World. For instance, what might they portend for the possibility that Israel—despite its preemptive warfare doctrine—might one day find itself in a more protracted war? What do they mean in the context of the lengthy Iran-Iraq war, which, because of Iraq's much smaller population, may have required it to keep soldiers at the front in combat for precariously long periods? What, indeed, might they mean for the possible use of nuclear weapons in some later situations, if and when armies should disintegrate for the reasons cited by Keegan?

One other matter brought to prominence by the recent wars in the Third World is the comparative effectiveness of professional versus conscript armies, a matter perhaps related more than tangentially to the issues of morale and the capacity for sustained combat effectiveness.[59] Indeed, the literature has pointed to the apparent contradictions of some recent experiences: the British army's performance in the Falklands has been cited as proof of the value of a small, professional army with units based on tradition, whereas Israel's performance in

1982—as before—has been claimed to validate the preference for a conscripted "citizen's" army. Both the experiences of the United States in Vietnam and of Argentina in the Falklands have been used to illustrate the pitfalls of the latter type.

Arms Transfers, Arms Resupply, and the War-Fighting Utility of Indigenous Arms Industries

Virtually all of the recent wars in the Third World have been fought by nations or groups that were wholly or substantially dependent upon the major powers for their weapons. Indeed, arms transfer diplomacy may be said to have been a contributing factor to the onset of war in several instances. Furthermore, the ability of combatants to sustain those wars has been heavily affected by the major powers' willingness and capacity to resupply spare parts and replacement end-item systems.

In some instances, nations that were relatively assured of uninterrupted weapons supplies have appeared to initiate preventive—or, rather, "window of opportunity"—wars during periods when their rivals were in the middle of fundamental realignments of arms client relationships. Ethiopia in 1977 and Iran in 1980 (both far weightier nations than their regional rivals) were attacked under such circumstances when Somalia and Iraq, respectively, took advantage of their transitioning to new suppliers. Israel's attack in connection with the Suez crisis in 1956 may also be cited as an example of an assault predicated on the assumption that further arms supplies to rivals would fundamentally change the regional military power balance. That was a near textbook example of a preventive war.

Some wars, of course, have been so short-lived as to preclude the necessity for resupply. The Middle Eastern conflicts of 1967 and 1982 are examples, although in the latter instance, massive postwar Soviet resupply was crucial to the evolving military balance and associated diplomacy.

In lengthier, intense conflicts that involve extensive attrition of materiel, resupply has often been a major determinant of outcomes.[60] The 1973 conflict was a salient and much-publicized case that involved rival, competitive superpower airlifts and truly massive arms resupply. In the Horn war of 1977–1978 and in the Iran-Iraq war, both sides have been availed of multiple and often confusing sources of resupply that were not easily predicted by a simple "cold war" model of clientship, as had been the case in 1973. Iraq has been resupplied by France, Brazil, Italy, China, and the USSR (with extensive financing from Saudi Arabia and other Gulf States), while post-Shah Iran, cut off from its erstwhile U.S. source, has apparently relied at various times on North Korea, Libya, China, Syria, the USSR, Israel, and South Korea, supplemented by alleged and obscure "private" sources in Western Europe.[61]

Morocco's difficulties in acquiring U.S. arms early in its Western Sahara imbroglio, the Soviets' resupply operation on behalf of Vietnam in 1979, and Argentina's frantic quest for replacement weapons in 1982 (in Israel, South Africa,

Libya, Brazil, and Peru, among others) have all illustrated the importance of re-supply to the conduct of war. Generally, the USSR has responded consistently with massive arms resupply to its beleaguered clients, while the United States, often Hamlet-like in its ambivalence regarding client support versus arms control and "conflict termination," has exhibited a long and tortuous history of half-hearted and temporary embargoes, quarantines, nonlethal weapons support, and the like.[62] Meanwhile, both major powers and the various Third World combat-ants have been engaged in energetic diplomacy aimed at assuring access to air staging points and overflight rights, which would enable resupply operations should they be required. This diplomacy is engaged in during peacetime as well as ad hoc during wartime, as witness recent U.S. base negotiations with, among others, Spain, Portugal, Morocco, Egypt, and Oman.[63]

Not all Third World nations are totally dependent on major powers to sus-tain combat operations in war, although none are near independence. Israel and India, for instance, have built extensive indigenous arms industries that can greatly reduce the need for resupply during war, particularly with regard to con-sumables, such as ammunition, some spare parts, and so on. In 1982, Israel dis-played a range of indigenous combat equipment (albeit most of it with some U.S. or other component content)—electronic countermeasures; missiles for interdict-ing SAMs, drones, and remotely piloted vehicles (RPVs); innovative new tank armor, and the like—some of which apparently acquitted itself well.

Another question regarding arms transfers is whether choice of major sup-pliers—more often than not determined on the basis of ideological ties—has been a significant determinant of the outcome of wars. As noted, under most circum-stances, the Soviets appear more likely to come through with large-volume resup-ply during conflict, a function both of production and inventory data and a lesser inclination to be hamstrung by "idealistic" concerns over arms control or "con-flict control." However, quality also counts. After the 1973 war, the Egyptians complained that they had been disadvantaged relative to Israel's U.S. and other Western-source arms; indeed, that complaint may have been one major reason for Egypt's subsequent shift in diplomatic alignment.[64] Syria made similar com-plaints after 1982, impelling the then-humiliated Soviets to a massive rebuilding of Syria's forces, with an across-the-board introduction of qualitatively more modern weapons.[65] It is also worth recalling, however, that in the hands of the Vietnamese and the Ethiopians, Soviet arms have prevailed on the victors' side; in the Ethiopian case, however, it was against a foe that was also mostly armed by the USSR.

Intervention by the Major Powers

Arms transfers are but one element, albeit a crucial one, of security assistance. One could also point to other roles played by major powers: seconding of advi-sors, provision of surrogate forces—(sometimes in large-unit formations), assis-tance with intelligence information, coercive threats, and both external (long-range) and internal logistics. Generally, the weaker or smaller the powers involved in war, the more such conflicts are subject to crucial tilting on the basis of such external assistance—that is, the more easily a big power's role can be decisive.

The use of Cuban surrogate forces, transported and armed by the Soviets and operating at large-unit levels, was a crucial determinant of the outcomes in the Horn and Angola. Less vital have been the roles of Pakistani, North Korean, and other "volunteers" on the side of the Arabs in several wars with Israel. Soviet forces manning SAMs in Syria (and earlier in Egypt) are important not just because of their relative (to their hosts) technical competence, but also because of their obvious, intended roles as tripwires—an element of coercive diplomacy that may impose certain boundaries on the scope of fighting.

The startling development of satellite reconnaissance in the last twenty years has added a crucial new dimension to great-power roles in Third World conflicts. The USSR and the United States apparently aided the Arabs and Israel, respectively, in this way in 1973; it was claimed that Israel's lunge across Suez toward the end of the war was made possible by U.S. satellites' discovery of a gap in the Egyptian Suez defenses.[66] During the Falklands war, there were claims of U.S. and Soviet satellite reconnaissance aid, respectively, to the United Kingdom and Argentina; these claims were not publicly substantiated.[67]

More broadly, one may cite the efforts at coercive diplomacy by major powers as an important element in the outcomes of some wars. Soviet threats aborted what otherwise would have been a more decisive Israeli victory in 1973; U.S. threats, albeit milder, served to abort Israel's military success in 1982. U.S. threats in connection with the "Carter doctrine" as applied to the Persian Gulf may have constrained Iran, at least until recently, from interdicting oil commerce out of the Persian Gulf; those threats have even extended to potential Iranian retaliation for Exocet missile attacks on its oil installations and tankers. Soviet threats also held the ring for Vietnam in its war with the PRC, even as the latter tried to pressure Vietnam to relent in its military activities within Cambodia.

Sometimes, superpowers have exercised counteracting coercive threats; in other cases, such as late in the 1973 war, the coercion has been additive, if asymmetric, on one side. In still other cases, only one major power has been directly involved. These factors direct attention to a careful study of the comparative diplomatic leverage held by combatants, juxtaposed with the extant realities of ideologically based client relationships.

War Termination versus Protracted, Interminable Conflicts

As noted earlier, most of the recent major conflicts within the Third World do not appear to have been concluded with any finality—by a formal, meaningful peace treaty, by the creation of what would lead to a permanent peace (amounting to, in Karl Deutsch's terminology, a "security community"), or by the "final" annihilation of one of the combatants.[68]

Just as declarations of war have become rare in recent decades—signaling the vitiation of some older norms of international law—perhaps formal peace treaties are now rarely to be entered into.[69] Possibly, our assumptions about the normalcy of clearly demarcated beginnings and endings of war are derived from further assumptions about the normalcy of the European classical system of diplomacy, an inclination deemed both common and perhaps disorienting in the writings of older international relations scholars (according to some contemporary critics). The primordial hatreds and associated absence of converging norms of behavior evidenced in wars between ethnic, racial, religious, and ideological antagonists simply may not allow for conclusions based on handshakes or signed documents. In an era of total war and total diplomacy, protracted or sporadic serial wars are perhaps to be expected. Somewhat paradoxically, it might be claimed that weakly evolving norms of international organization that militate against warfare, along with the tendency of the superpowers to intervene to foreshorten Third World conflicts, may have rendered decisive, overwhelming military victories a rarer phenomenon. Not only the Arabs, but also Pakistan, Vietnam, and Somalia have been spared what otherwise could have been more devastating defeats because of external pressures.

However, the losers don't forget. Their defeats leave them stewing in humiliation and craving vengeance as they await the opportunity for a new round. Hence, so many of the recent conflicts appear to have taken on the character of mere episodes that end with the full expectation all around that war will one day be resumed (note the recent flare-ups between China and Vietnam, Ethiopia and Somalia).

To the extent that these characterizations of contemporary conflict diplomacy are correct, there may be profound effects on the planning and conduct of wars. "Underdog" nations—such as Egypt in 1973 and perhaps Iraq in 1980—may initiate wars with limited aims, reckoning that if things go awry (as is more or less expected), they will be rescued by outside forces rushing to hold the ring. Israel, virtually requiring preemption to avoid attrition war but wary of the impact of preemption on U.S. concerns about who "starts" wars, may thus feel safe in preempting only in every other war, or perhaps in two out of three.

The foregoing discussion applies primarily to conventional wars. Unconventional wars, while often protracted, paradoxically tend to have definitive endings, as note the denouements in Vietnam and perhaps Nicaragua, among many others.

The Media, News Management, and Public Opinion

Some events surrounding the Falklands and Lebanon wars in particular, but also the brief skirmish in Grenada—and with Vietnam as obvious background—have spotlighted the potentially important role played by the media and by governmental news management in determining the outcome of wars.

As has been discussed in numerous other places, supporters of the U.S. involvement in Vietnam claimed that the media—print and video—had sorely damaged the war effort, particularly with regard to the interpretation of the outcome of the 1968 Tet offensive.[70] There were some charges of ideologically inspired, deliberate slanting of news. It was also claimed that public support had been undercut by the very nature of contemporary war reporting, which daily brought vivid, bloody war scenes into the nation's living rooms. In 1982, pro-Israel supporters made similar charges—that is, that American and European reporting of the war, deliberately or not, had vastly exaggerated civilian casualties and refugee statistics along the Israeli invasion route toward Beirut, hence greatly affecting Western public opinion and prompting U.S. pressures that aborted Israel's opportunity to destroy the surrounded PLO in Beirut.[71] The media's role in Central America has also been hotly disputed.

Britain's successful control of the media in connection with the Falklands invasion—however eased by the obvious facts of geographical inaccessibility—was widely heralded, by contrast with Vietnam and Lebanon, as a "how to do it" model.[72] Hence, U.S. control over the media during the Grenada invasion was not surprising (and was widely considered one aspect of its success and was applauded as such by U.S. public opinion); it was also doubly ironic in view of the Pentagon's obvious anti-Israeli tilt in the summer of 1982.

In some of the other recent Third World wars, the role of the media has been less clear and, for the most part, seemingly less important. That, too, may be arguable, however, if only in a reversed form. There has been extensive criticism in some quarters in the United States of the failure by the American press to give full, sustained coverage of the war in Afghanistan, that failure further being assumed to have acted in the Soviets' favor. Meanwhile, both Iran and Iraq have exerted fairly strict controls over war coverage, so that a reader attempting to follow the war in the Western press is often forced to interpolate between the rivals' own war bulletins, which usually vary greatly. The Western Sahara war coverage has likewise been sporadic and not particularly informed; and coverage of the war between the PRC and Vietnam also had to be interpreted by sifting through grandiose rival propaganda claims.

The media's impact has also been important in affecting public opinion in the combatant nations themselves. The development of some antiwar sentiment in Israel in 1982 is an example of such an effect (although it is not entirely ascribed to the media). The postwar disillusionment with the reporting in Buenos Aires during the 1982 war was another example—one with important political ramifications. Just how these matters have worked out in Morocco, the Soviet Union (regarding Afghanistan), Iraq, Iran, Ethiopia, and Somalia is an important topic deserving of more extensive treatment.

The Comparative Economics of Third World Warfare

Partly because of the absence of even remotely reliable data, there has been almost no comparative analysis of the economics of war in the Third World. The subject may deserve some attention, however, because it is important to analyses of winning and losing; to the diplomacy surrounding conflicts; to war initiation and termination; and to the linkages with domestic policies and supports.

The Iraq-Iran war in particular has brought such comparative economics into focus. That lengthy and yet inconclusive struggle has clearly strained economies on both sides, each of which, at the war's outset, was considered an oil-rich state with a surfeit of cash. Each side has exerted itself politically and militarily to cut off oil exports from the other—Iraq by bombing Iranian oil facilities, Iran by persuading its ally, Syria, to shut off Iraqi oil exports transited by pipeline. Overall, Iraq appears to have been more greatly disadvantaged, and the result has been the request for massive infusions of aid from Saudi Arabia, Kuwait, and other Gulf oil states. Incidentally, the Saudi role as war financier has also been seen in connection with Egypt and Syria (the former cut off after Camp David), Morocco, and Somalia.[73]

Israel's always taut economic condition (and its crucial dependence on U.S. aid) has been one major reason for its traditional preemptive, short-war strategy. Its eschewing of preemption in 1973, whether or not because of U.S. pressure, led to a twenty-two-day war often assumed to have cost Israel the equivalent of nearly one year's GNP. Nowadays, the cost of the Lebanon occupation and the projected costs of another war with Syria constitute strong constraints on Israeli actions; the asymmetry relative to Syria with its Saudi backing is an important factor of Middle Eastern politics. Elsewhere in this volume, Jencks reports on the significant drain of the 1979 war with Vietnam on the PRC's economy—and that was a three-week war!

The post-Falklands debates over the economics of British naval losses (indeed, of the entire operation); the economic devastation of Argentina (hyperinflation and foreign debts) in the wake of that war; the drain on the Soviet economy caused by Afghanistan; the role of Soviet military and economic aid in Ethiopia's pursuit of victory in 1978 (apparently involving massive effective Soviet grant aid); and the role of war-induced debt to the USSR in propelling Egypt's diplomatic about-face after 1973 are all further examples, however difficult to measure, of the importance of economics to the conduct of these wars.[74]

Summary: Interrelationships among Comparative Dimensions

The main focus of this chapter has been a discussion of the various comparative dimensions of contemporary warfare in the Third World as discrete topics. It has provided a checklist of various angles of vision and levels of analysis; the subjects were presented in no particular order and in no hierarchy of relative importance.

However, the merely *seriatim* presentation of these dimensions may obscure some very important interrelationships between them, involving a complex web of reciprocal causation or correlation. In great measure, the other dimensions act as independent variables in relation to what might be considered a core variable—the domain of strategies, tactics, and weapons. As an example of two-way causation, however, one might point to the possibility that the now almost traditional role of the media may, in some cases, dictate preemptive, short-war strategies (on that point, the Israeli and American military staffs might agree). Otherwise, the relationships among these dimensions are legion. Cultural perspectives on warfare feed into those on war termination—who is more or less likely to surrender or sue for peace? Geographical factors often determine the duration of war (stalemates versus quick wars of annihilation) and, hence, their economics, if the variable of intensity is held constant. Economics, in turn, may dictate strategies and tactics—for example, preemptive gambits for the economically weak or attrition strategies for the economically strong. Economics may also determine arms resupply, particularly if outright aid from suppliers or friends is unavailable.

Some of these relationships may be unclear and debatable; for example, has the mountainous geography of Afghanistan been a historical determinant of culture, including cultural perspectives on war? Some may be reciprocally causal; for example, do certain strategies and tactics, such as attrition warfare, cause morale problems, or do morale problems dictate certain kinds of tactics? These are large and complex problems with no easy or ready solutions.

Notes

1. This thesis is conveyed indirectly in Richard Grenier, "The World's Favorite Movie Star," *Commentary* 77(April 1984): 61–67. In discussing Clint Eastwood's popularity, Grenier reminds us that traditional American patriotism is deeply rooted, particularly in the South and West and in small towns.

2. John Keegan, *The Face of Battle* (New York: Viking, 1976), p. 28.

3. Michael Howard, *Studies in War and Peace* (New York: Viking, 1959), p.184, in the introduction to an essay entitled "Strategy and Policy in Twentieth-Century Warfare." The same themes are addressed in greater detail in various selections in John E. Jessup, Jr., and Robert W. Coakley, *A Guide to the Study and Use of Military History* (Washington, D.C: Center for Military History, 1979).

4. See Jay Luvaas, "Military History: Is It Still Practicable?" *Parameters* 12(March 1982): 2–14; and Trevor Dupuy, "History and Modern Battle," *Army* 32(November 1982): 18–25.

5. This is discussed in Howard, *Studies in War and Peace,* and more briefly in Henry W. Bradsher, "Is the U.S. Surviving on Stale Strategic Concepts?" *Washington Star,* December 29, 1976, pp. 5–6. See also Walter Emil Kaegi, Jr., "The Crisis in Military

Historiography," *Armed Forces and Society* 7(Spring 1981): 299–316. Kaegi states that "the gap between historian and strategist has widened greatly in recent years, especially in the nuclear age, with the analyses of Bernard Brodie, Herman Kahn, and Henry Kissinger essentially arguing for a metahistorical approach to strategic realities in the post-1945 era" (p. 313).

6. As applied more broadly to comparative foreign policy, see, for instance, Wolfram Hanrieder, ed., *Comparative Foreign Policy: Theoretical Essays* (New York: David McKay, 1971); Edward Morse, *A Comparative Approach to the Study of Foreign Policy: Notes on Theorizing,* Research Monograph No. 36 (Princeton, N.J.: Center of International Studies, 1971); and Patrick McGowan and Howard Shapiro, *The Comparative Study of Foreign Policy* (Beverly Hills, Calif.: Sage, 1973).

7. These issues are addressed in chapter 2 of this volume, by Harvey Starr and Benjamin Most. For broader discussion, see the references cited in their note 1.

8. Regarding matters of tone and style as they affect actual analysis, see Keegan, *The Face of Battle,* pp. 35–45, on "the rhetoric of battle history."

9. A good example of the importance of taking these matters into account is the recent "revisionist" literature on the Vietnam War, which is appearing now that the immediate passions have faded. For a review and analysis of this recent literature, see Fox Butterfield, "The New Vietnam Scholarship," *New York Times Magazine,* February 13, 1983, p. 26ff.

10. See, for example, Lewis P. Young, "Further Thoughts on the Lessons of the Falklands Crisis," *Asian Defence Journal* 36(October 1982): 90–92; Edgar O'Ballance, "First Thoughts: The Falkland Islands Campaign," *National Defense* 67(September 1982): 34–39; Brenda R. Lewis, "The Falklands War—A Recap," *Army* 32(September 1982): 22–29; Simon Durwen, "Lessons of the Falklands Conflict," *Asian Defence Journal* 36(September 1982): 80–86; and Anthony Cordesman, "The Falklands War: Emerging Lessons for Power Projection and Force Planning," *Armed Forces Journal International* 120(September 1982): 29–46.

11. See William S. Lind, "Simple Tanks Would Suffice," *Harper's,* September 1982, pp. 22–24; Anthony Cordesman, "The Sixth Arab-Israeli Conflict—Military Lessons for American Defense Planning," *Armed Forces Journal International* 120(August 1982): 29–31; "Lessons of Lebanon," *Defense Attache,* no. 4 (1982), pp. 23–35; and "Killer Electronic Wizardry," *Business Week,* September 20, 1982, pp. 74–84.

12. For an analysis of the imputed Soviet view of the Falklands war, see, for example, Schuyler Foerster, "Clients and Conflict: Soviet Perspectives on the Limited Wars of 1982," in James Brown and William P. Snyder, *The Regionalization of Warfare* (New Brunswick, N.J.: Transaction, 1984).

13. See, for instance, Saad Shazli, *The Crossing of the Suez* (San Francisco: Mideast Research, 1980), especially chapter 3.

14. These distinctions are dealt with in John Collins, *Grand Strategy: Principles and Practices* (Annapolis, Md.: Naval Institute Press, 1973), especially chapter 1; and E.J. Kingston-McLoughry, *The Spectrum of Strategy* (London: Jonathan Cape, 1964), especially chapters IV and V. From Edward Luttwak, "On the Meaning of Victory," *Washington Quarterly,* Autumn 1982, pp. 17–24:

"Much more serious is the multiplicity of contexts and facets in warfare. When we contemplate the most intricate of human mass activities, we see not merely through a glass darkly but rather though the dazzling refraction of a diamond. We see one truth tactically and another technically, while an operational view may yield yet another result, and the higher levels of strategy several more. (p. 20)

15. See the various selections in the special issue, "Combat Readiness for a Deterrent Strategy," *Armed Forces and Society* 6(Winter 1980), especially Anne Hoiberg, "Military Effectiveness of Navy Men during and after Vietnam," pp. 232–246, which references much of the relevant literature to that point, particularly regarding mental health problems associated with the Vietnam War. See also Peter Watson, *War on the Mind: The Military Uses and Abuses of Psychology* (New York: Basic Books, 1978).

16. This point, which perhaps may be dismissed too easily as merely cute or flippant, actually derives from the theory of cognitive dissonance, most closely associated with Leon Festinger, which alerts one to the likelihood of "politically consistent" cognitive structures across a broad swathe of intellectual domains.

17. See Foerster, "Clients and Conflict," p. 4. For background, see Sigmund Neumann, "Engels and Marx: Military Concepts of the Social Revolutionaries," in E.M. Earle, ed., *Makers of Modern Strategy* (Princeton: Princeton University Press, 1943) chapter 7. Here, Engels is reported to have been heavily influenced by Clausewitz.

18. Martin van Creveld, *Military Lessons of the Yom Kippur War: Historical Perspectives,* Washington Papers No. 24 (Washington, D.C.: Georgetown Center for Strategic and International Studies, 1975). Arguing against the too-early assumption of the demise of the tank was Avraham Adan, *On the Banks of Suez* (Novato, Calif.: Presidio Press, 1980), chapter 35.

19. Gen. D. Palit, *The Lightning Campaign: The Indo-Pakistan War, 1971* (Salisbury: Compton Press, 1972), p. 77, claims that "the Pakistani High Command has for a number of years nursed a pipedream about launching a massive, surprise offensive deep into Indian territory spearheaded by armored formations, a la Moshe Dayan."

20. Roger Beaumont, "Guidepost or Guesses?: Is the Lesson of War Concept Valid?" In Brown and Snyder, *The Regionalization of Warfare.*

21. See, for example, Joseph de Rivera, *The Psychological Dimension of Foreign Policy* (Columbus, Ohio: Charles E. Merrill, 1968), especially the material in chapter 5 on "risk-taking"; and Irving Janis, *Group Think: Psychological Studies of Policy Decisions and Fiascos,* 2nd ed. (Boston: Houghton Mifflin, 1983).

22. Harry Summers, *On Strategy: The Vietnam War in Context* (Novato Calif.: Presidio Press, 1982).

23. See T.N. Dupuy, "Let's Get Serious About Multipliers," *Army* 33(May 1983): 18–25.

24. Scott A. Boorman, *The Protracted Game: A Wei'-chi'i Interpretation of Maoist Revolutionary Strategy* (New York: Oxford University Press, 1969).

25. At the "lower" end, the terminology becomes confusing, as *guerilla warfare, revolutionary warfare,* and *low-intensity warfare* often are used interchangeably, though some attribute distinct characteristics to them. A recent Hudson Institute conference in Washington, "Terrorism and Low Order Warfare," hinted at still another category, presumably inspired by the U.S. experience in Lebanon.

26. This point is made in J. Dougherty and R. Pfaltzgraff, *Contending Theories of International Relations,* 2nd ed. (New York: Harper & Row, 1981), pp. 181–188.

27. See Lincoln P. Bloomfield, "American Approaches to Military Strategy, Arms

Control, and Disarmament: A Critique of the Postwar Experience," in R. Harkavy and E.A. Kolodziej, eds., *American Security Policy and Policy-Making* (Lexington, Mass.: Lexington Books, D.C. Heath, 1980), chapter 14.

28. See, for example, B.H. Liddell Hart, *The Decisive Wars of History: A Study in Strategy* (Boston: Little, Brown, 1929); B.H. Liddell Hart, *Strategy* (New York: Praeger, 1967); J.F.C. Fuller, *The Decisive Battles of the Western World and Their Influence Upon History*, 3 vols. (London: Eyre and Spottiswoode, 1954–1956); and J.F.C. Fuller, *Armament and History* (London: Eyre and Spottiswoode, 1946).

29. See Neville Brown, "The Changing Face of Non-Nuclear War," *Survival* 24(September–October 1982): 211–219.

30. George Quester, *Offense and Defense in the International System* (New York: Wiley, 1977). See also John J. Mearsheimer, *Conventional Deterrence* (Ithaca, N.Y.: Cornell University Press, 1983), especially chapter 2; and Jack Levy, "The Offensive/Defensive Balance of Military Technology: A Theoretical and Historical Analysis," *International Studies Quarterly* 28(June 1984): 219–238.

31. van Creveld, *Military Lessons of the Yom Kippur War*, p. 6. See also Martin van Creveld, "Turning Points in Twentieth Century War," *Washington Quarterly* 4(Summer 1981): 3–8.

32. Edward Luttwak, "Notes on Low-Intensity Warfare," *Parameters* 13(December 1983): 11–18.

33. These intellectual currents are discussed in, among other sources, Alfred Vagts, *A History of Militarism* (New York: Norton, 1937), chapters VII–VIII.

34. See "U.S. Analysts Upgrade Opinion of Syrian Units," *New York Times*, December 5, 1983, p. A12; and "Black Clouds in Middle East," *New York Times*, October 8, 1983, p. A1.

35. A good summary of these arguments is contained in Edward Luttwak, "Commentary: Defense Planning in Israel: A Brief Retrospective," in Stephanie Neuman, ed., *Defense Planning in Less-Industrialized States* (Lexington, Mass.: Lexington Books, 1984). pp. 131–144.

36. In addition to sources cited elsewhere in this chapter, see the following chapters in Brown and Snyder, *The Regionalization of Warfare:* John F. Guilmartin, "The South Atlantic War: Lessons and Analytical Guideposts, A Military Historian's Perspective"; Dov S. Zakheim, "The South Atlantic: Evaluating the Lessons"; and Maj. Gen. T.A. Boam, "Lessons from the 1982 Falklands Campaign."

37. In addition to sources cited elsewhere in this chapter, see Anthony Cordesman, "Lessons of the Iran-Iraq War: Tactics, Technology, and Training," *Armed Forces Journal International* 119(June 1982): 68–83.

38. See Michael Carver, *War Since 1945* (London: Weidenfeld and Nicolson, 1980), p. 233.

39. See *Strategic Survey: 1978* (London: International Institute for Strategic Studies, 1979), pp. 94–99; James Mayall, "The Battle for the Horn," *World Today*, September 1978, pp. 336–345; and several articles in the *New York Times*, February 12 and 13, 1978.

40. See *Strategic Survey: 1979* (London: International Institute for Strategic Studies, 1979), pp. 56–60; Li Man Kin, *The Sino-Vietnamese War* (Hong Kong: Kingsway International, 1982); and Harlan Jencks, "China's 'Punitive' War in Vietnam: A Military Assessment," *Asian Survey* 19(August 1979): 801–815.

41. See, for example, Edward Luttwak, "Notes on Low-Intensity Warfare," in Rich-

ard Hunt and Richard Shultz, eds., *Lessons from an Unconventional War: Reassessing U.S. Strategies for Future Conflicts* (New York: Pergamon, 1982); Bard O'Neill, William Heaton, and Donald Alberts, eds., *Insurgency in the Modern World* (Boulder, Colo.: Westview Press, 1982); and Sam Sarkesian and William Scully, eds., *U.S. Policy and Low-Intensity Conflict: Potentials for Military Struggles in the 1980s* (New Brunswick, N.J.: Transaction, 1981).

42. Though somewhat dated, an exception is Louis C. Peltier and G. Etzel Pearcy, *Military Geography* (Princeton, N.J.: Van Nostrand, 1966). This work is pegged closer to the grand strategic than the operational level. More recently, see Patrick O'Sullivan and Jesse W. Miller, Jr., *The Geography of Warfare* (London: Croom, Helm, 1983).

43. In addition to the chapter in this volume by William Staudenmaier (chapter 11), see his "Military Policy and Strategy in the Gulf War," *Parameters* 12(June 1982): pp. 25–35; and "War Between Iran and Iraq," in *Strategic Survey: 1980–81* (London: International Institute for Strategic Studies, 1980), pp. 49–52.

44. This point is made in Insight Team of the London Sunday Times, *The Yom Kippur War* (New York: Doubleday, 1974), pp. 165–166.

45. Boorman, *The Protracted Game*. For more general coverage, see Ken Booth, *Strategy and Ethnocentrism* (New York: Holmes and Meier, 1979); Adda Bozeman, *Politics and Culture in International History* (Princeton, N.J.: Princeton University Press, 1960); Colin Gray, *Strategic Studies: A Critical Assessment* (Westport, Conn.: Greenwood Press, 1982), chapter 5, in the section "Strategy and Culture," which is devoted primarily to "strategic cultures" within the context of the U.S.–Soviet nuclear competition; and Stephen Wilson, "For a Socio-Historical Approach to the Study of Western Military Culture," *Armed Forces and Society* 6(Summer 1980): 527–552.

46. See Richard D. Lyons, "Who Are These Smiling Killers?" *New York Times,* December 18, 1983, section 4, p. 1; "Roots of Assassins: Hashish and the Year 1090," *New York Times,* December 14, 1983, p. 12; and "Tangled Wars of Code Names and Allegiances in Beirut," *Washington Post,* February 1, 1984, p. A1.

47. Such cultural perspectives may perhaps also be "inherited" or passed on, even despite massive long-term political changes and revolutions. See, for instance, Steven D. Stinemetz, "Clausewitz or Khan? The Mongol Method of Military Success," *Parameters* 45(Spring 1984): 71–80. According to Stinemetz: "Like many other armies past and present, the Soviet military cannot be analyzed aside from the web of social values that holds it together. . . . In this respect, the Soviet Army resembles its distant antecedent, the Mongol horde."

48. See, for example, the pathfinding analysis in John E. Mueller, "The Search for the 'Breaking Point' in Vietnam," *International Studies Quarterly* 24(December 1980): 497–519, and the subsequent critiques by Richard Betts and Frederick Z. Brown in the same issue.

49. John Toland, *The Rising Sun*, vol. I (New York: Random House, 1970), especially chapters 3 and 6. With regard to cultural determinants of strategic thought, Toland points not only to Japanese fatalism but also to an ingrained attraction to sudden, surprise blows:

> The concept of achieving decisive victory by one surprise blow lay deep in the Japanese character. Their favorite literary form was the *Haiku,* a poem combining sensual imagery and intuitive evocation in a brief seventeen syllables, a ra-

pier thrust that expressed, with discipline, the illumination sought in the Japanese form of Buddhism. Similarly, the outcome in Judo, sumo [wrestling] and kendo [fencing with bamboo staves], after long preliminaries, was settled by a sudden stroke. [p. 191]

50. For an illustration of this point, see the excellent article by Thomas L. Friedman, "Rise of Militancy by Moslems Threatens Stability of Egypt," *New York Times,* October 27, 1981, pp. A1, A10, Friedman states:

Tallal's depression and subsequent turn toward a more fundamental belief in Islam after the 1967 war is, by all accounts, not uncommon. Many people feel that the resurgence of Islamic militancy in Egypt dates to that overwhelming defeat . . . everyone was questioning themselves after the war . . . they kept asking what it was about our society, our culture, our political system that could pave the way for such a defeat.

51. Some analyses posit a nearly nonrational attraction for *machismo* in the Israeli army as a way of compensating for centuries of helplessness and passivity. Hence, as stated in Insight Team, *The Yom Kippur War:* "Dayan valued Sharon because in the fifties Dayan was trying to create an officer corps whose philosophy would be to take any objective by frontal attack, paying for it with lives. . . . Dayan's aim was to exorcise Jewish cleverness from the Israeli army" (p. 325).

52. Yehoshafat Harkabi, "Basic Factors in the Arab Collapse during the Six Day War," *Orbis* 11(Fall 1967): 677–691.

53. See Seth Carus, "Defense Planning in Iraq," in Neuman, *Defense Planning in Less-Industrialized States*, pp. 29–51.

54. A brief critique of this thesis is provided in Edward Kolodziej and Robert Harkavy, "Developing States and the International Security System," *Journal of International Affairs* 34(Spring/Summer 1980): 59–87.

55. Keegan, *The Face of Battle*, pp. 340–341.

56. See, for example, "Iraq Leaves Dead Iranians to Display to Reporters," *New York Times,* March 6, 1984, p. A6.

57. Martin van Creveld, "The War: A Questioning Look" *Jerusalem Post, International Edition*, December 12–18, 1982, pp. 12–13. He correlates psychiatric casualties with low morale on the basis of the Israeli experience in Lebanon in 1982 and also discusses the role of technology in a manner somewhat distinct from Keegan's, concentrating on the impact of increasing military specialization.

58. Keegan, *The Face of Battle*, pp. 355–336.

59. For example, see David R. Segal and Katherine Swift Gravino, "The Empire Strikes Back: Military Professionalism in the South Atlantic War," in Brown and Snyder, *The Regionalization of Warfare*.

60. A fuller coverage of the subject of arms resupply is provided in R.E. Harkavy, "Arms Resupply During Conflict: A Framework for Analysis", *Jerusalem Journal of International Relations*, forthcoming.

61. See, for example, "Iran Said to Get Large-Scale Arms from Israel, Soviet, and Europeans," *New York Times,* March 8, 1982, p. A1.

62. Regarding the Carter administration in this connection—that is, the ill-fated PD-

13 restraints policy and the aborted Conventional Arms Transfer (CAT) talks, see P. Hammond, D. Louscher, M. Salamone, and N. Graham, *The Reluctant Supplier* (Cambridge, Mass.: Oelgeschlager, Gunn and Hain, 1983), especially chapter 6.

63. See Robert E. Harkavy, *Great Power Competition for Overseas Bases* (New York: Pergamon, 1982), chapter 5.

64. See, for example, Insight Team, *The Yom Kippur War,* pp. 370–371, which is especially valuable regarding comparisons of tanks.

65. See, for instance, "Syrian Army Said to Be Stronger Than Ever, Thanks to Soviet," *New York Times,* March 21, 1983, p. A4; and "Soviets Reportedly Replace Syria's Summer Weapons Losses," *New York Times,* December 3, 1982, p. A1.

66. This is hinted at by way of accusation in Mohammed Heikal, *The Road to Ramadan* (London: Collins, 1975), p. 251; also, on p. 229, there is a related reference to "American reconnaissance planes based in Greece."

67. See Jack Anderson's column, *Centre Daily Times,* January 16, 1984, p. A4:

> At the time of the Falklands invasion, the Soviets were so eager to win Argentina's friendship that they sent two spy satellites up and relayed information to the right-wing military government in Buenos Aires. Intelligence sources say the Soviets continued to provide updates on British activities in the Falklands to Argentina at least as late as last summer.

Regarding U.S. help to the United Kingdom, see "Argentina Holding U.S. Responsible for Upsets," *New York Times,* May 30, 1982, p. 16.

68. Karl Deutsch, *Political Community and the North Atlantic Area* (Princeton, N.J.: Princeton University Press, 1957), chapter II.

69. This possibility is discussed in Brian Jenkins, "New Modes of Conflict," RAND/R-3009-DNA, (Santa Monica, Calif.: Rand Corporation, 1983). Jenkins ventures projections about the future of armed conflict.

70. See, for example, Peter Braestrup, *Big Story: How the American Press and Television Reported and Interpreted in the Crisis of Tet 1968 in Vietnam and Washington* (Boulder, Colo.: Westview Press, 1977); and Michael Mandelbaum, "Vietnam: The Television War," *Parameters* 13(March 1983): 89–97.

71. See, for example, Edward Alexander, *NBC's War in Lebanon: The Distorting Mirror* (New York: Americans for a Safe Israel, 1983).

72. See Boam, "Lessons from the 1982 Falklands Campaign."

73. See Adeed Dawisha, *Saudi Arabia's Search for Security,* Adelphi Paper No. 158 (London: International Institute for Strategic Studies, 1980), especially pp. 17–31.

74. Some insights into the comparative economics of recent wars may be gleaned from the various contributions to "Special Issue: The Economic Foundations of War," *International Studies Quarterly* 27(December 1983).

2
Patterns of Conflict: Quantitative Analysis and the Comparative Lessons of Third World Wars

Harvey Starr
Benjamin A. Most

The focus of this chapter is the lessons that can be drawn from quantitative comparative analyses of the trends, patterns, and relationships in recent Third World conflicts. Each Third World conflict provides its own lessons—lessons idiosyncratic to the special circumstances and conditions of that conflict. It is possible, however, to identify a set of factors, or variables, that are applicable to a wider sampling of such conflicts. The population of Third World conflicts may be summarized, or modeled, in terms of these variables to describe the aggregate lessons of wars in the Third World that have occurred in the post-1945 period.

In this chapter we will be taking such an aggregate, or comparative, perspective on the lessons of conflict. We wish to employ the basic notions of a comparative approach by comparing and contrasting across a number of cases and looking for patterns of similarities. This will permit us to make more general statements concerning conflict in the international system—statements that not only point out similarities but also permit us to identify significant differences. By creating a statistical baseline, we will have a starting point from which to judge the lessons presented in the following case studies and understand how unique or "normal" each case actually is.

We must make clear that the following discussion is intended to be a descriptive general introduction to the patterns of post–World War II conflict. Focusing on violent conflict in the Third World by no means implies that actual and potential violent conflict in other areas of the world is insignificant. However, the great preponderance of violence in the contemporary international system has erupted in Third World areas—either as internal violence or as cross-border war. This

Support for the research reported herein has been provided by the National Science Foundation under grants SES 82-08779 and SES 82-08815. An earlier version of this chapter was presented at the Indiana Consortium for Security Studies Workshop, "Complex Challenges of National Security in the 1980s: Emerging Patterns of Conflict," Bloomington, Indiana, June 1980.

leads us to a second use of *context* in the discussion of patterns of Third World conflict. In addition to a general context of lessons to aid in the understanding and utility of case studies, the patterns discussed here provide an important context for each state or any international actor in the system. Simply, each nation-state is embedded in an international system that constrains its possible and probable behavior. Violent conflict in the Third World constitutes at least one important element in the environment of states in other areas of the world. Insofar as it has the actual or potential capability of affecting those other states, Third World conflict constitutes a phenomenon that other states (as well as Third World states) must understand and may need to take into account in their foreign policy formulation and execution.

In this chapter, we will specifically be looking at the forms, levels, locales, and overall effects of Third World conflict. These variables will have an impact on the parties and forces involved, the strategies they follow, the possibility of outside intervention, the expansion of the war, and the like. In turn, these questions of strategy, intervention, and expansion will affect questions of war termination, military and political payoffs, and costs.

Before moving to the analyses, we will provide a brief consideration of the validity of the quantitative comparative approach and its utility for drawing lessons that are policy-relevant.

The Validity and Utility of the Comparative Approach[1]

Consider for a moment just what we mean by the term *lesson*. In our view, the word is most commonly connected with the drawing of inferences or the making of generalizations; something has happened, presumably for some reason, which we believe we can specify, and we wish to generalize to other possible future occurrences. Sometimes we wish to avoid the reappearance of the event altogether; in other instances, we want to alter the outcome should similar situations develop in the future, or we may wish to understand why an occurrence turned out the way it did, so that we can reproduce that result in the future. We might want to understand what has happened so that we can better learn to anticipate or recognize problems while they are still in their early phases of development or to understand the effects of previous policies.

Other lessons might be sought; this listing is by no means exhaustive. The point is that efforts to specify or delineate lessons seem closely related to the drawing of inferences and the making of generalizations from the study of a number of cases of conflict in the Third World. To do this, however, we must determine what evidence, analyzed in what ways or developed using what types of research designs and approaches provides an adequate basis for drawing inferences. Should one, for example, use historical or experiential evidence from a single case—or would one be better advised to be as systematic as possible, specifying each step in the analysis, developing quantitative data, and assessing them across large numbers of cases or within a given case across time?

No one way of proceeding is always appropriate; analysts and interpreters need to figure out what they want to say and select the methods appropriate to those ends. Such methods should be seen as tools, and the question we must ask continually is whether they are useful or not useful given the task at hand.

If *lessons* means (in a minimal sense) learning the relationships between variables in one case to be able to understand those relationships in another case, one must compare cases. Using theoretical or conceptual frameworks, a small set of "important" variables is selected for such comparison. This is necessary because it would be impossible to compare cases if the totality (if one could indeed construct such a thing) of those cases was used; each case is truly unique. For a number of reasons relating to the logic of research design, efforts to draw lessons seem likely to be best advanced by studies that utilize a variant of two basic comparative research designs: cross-sectional and time-series. The former involves looking across a large number of cases at one point in time; the latter involves looking at a single case across a large number of time points. In both cases, one is comparing cases on a theoretically selected set of variables, a set much smaller than that used in a case study.

One can perhaps begin to understand the reasoning behind these research designs by noting, first, that each datum, "fact," or variable can be defined on three dimensions: it is only one of many possible variables; it is selected from a particular polity or case; and it is drawn from a specific point in time. Taken together, these three dimensions may be understood to define a hypothetical cube that encompasses all of the "facts" in the world (see figure 2–1, a).

In parts b, c, and d of figure 2–1, three different ways of "slicing" reality are demonstrated. A case study approach focuses on the relationships among a large number of variables in one case at a single point in time. A cross-sectional (or synchronic) design focuses on the relationships among variables in a large number of cases at a single point in time. Finally, a time-series (or diachronic) design focuses on the relationships that hold through a large number of points in time in a single case.

To summarize a lengthy and complex set of arguments found in the literature (see note 1), the case study approach, as a rule, is likely to produce complete explanations and yield lessons that have a demonstrated applicability to only one case and an unspecified generalizability across space and through time (but see note 1 for works that indicate the *potential* comparative utility of case studies). The output of a case study is generally difficult to evaluate (because of the generally low degree of explicitness) and is likely to yield findings that are difficult to explain to decision makers because of their complexity and detail. To the extent that proponents of case studies stress that the unique and idiosyncratic nature of the world dictates their approach, they implicitly embrace the comparative perspective when they attempt to apply the lessons learned in a case study to current

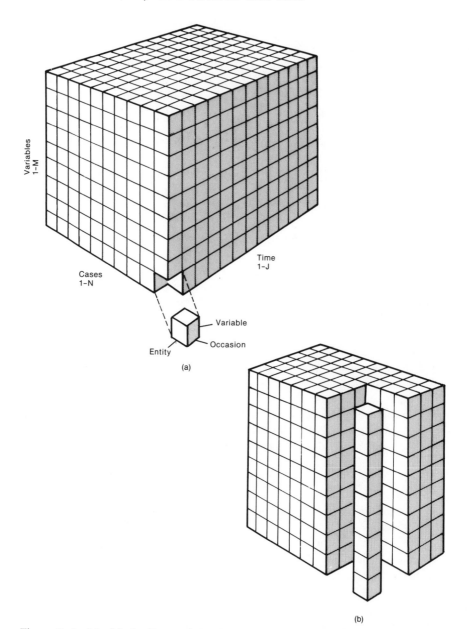

Figure 2–1. Models for Research Design: (a) hypothetical cube encompassing all of the "facts" in the world; (b) case study approach—one entity, one point in time, many variables; (c) cross-sectional design—one to *N* entities analyzed simultaneously, one point in time, few variables; (d) time-series design—one entity, up to an infinite number of time points *J*, few variables.

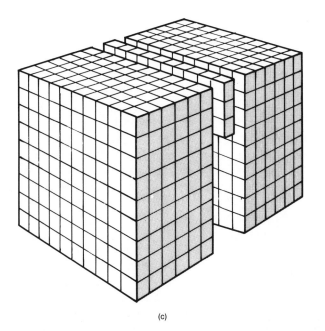

(c)

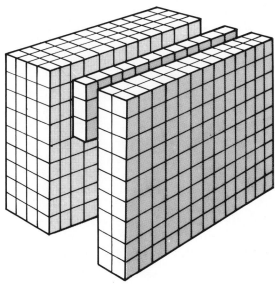

(d)

Source: An earlier version of this figure appears in Benjamin A. Most, *Points of Departure: An Introduction to the Systematic Study of Public Policy* (Cambridge, Mass.: Schenkman, forthcoming). That figure, in turn, is based on a figure in John V. Gillespie, "An Introduction to Macro–Cross National Research," in John V. Gillespie and Betty Nesvold, eds., *Macro-Quantitative Analysis* (Beverly Hills, Calif.: Sage, 1971).

problems; this necessarily involves making at least implicit comparisons. Thus, they reason like comparativists but adopt none of the systematic rigor and precision of the comparative approach.

The cross-sectional design, in contrast, is capable of producing relatively simple and partial (that is, somewhat inaccurate) explanations that have some demonstrated generality and the potential for greater generalizability across additional cases. Because analysts who use the cross-sectional design tend to be more explicit about their initial assumptions, biases, and expectations, about how they operationalize their concepts, about how they select and manipulate their data and weigh their evidence, and about the predictions they wish to make and the evidence that would refute those predictions, readers will be better able to evaluate the quality of their work. While this type of comparative design thus has certain advantages, it is by no means a cure-all. It limits one to static views and correlational findings. The results from the analysis may or may not be generalizable to different points in time.[2]

The attributes of the time-series design are somewhat similar to those of the cross-sectional approach insofar as it, too, is likely to yield simple and partial explanations. In this instance, however, the demonstrated generality is through time within a given case; the likely potential for further generalizability is to more time points in that case. Time-series research has the potential for yielding dynamic findings. Unfortunately, the time-series approach leaves unexplored the question of whether or not the lessons are generalizable across space to other cases. It is therefore less well suited than the cross-sectional design for isolating patterns and tendencies that hold across a number of cases.

Analysts typically compensate for limitations in the cross-sectional and time-series designs by selecting independent and dependent variables from different time slices, or by executing a "comparative statics" design in which separate cross-sectional analyses are conducted on several slices of time. Although this solves many of the problems of each approach, there is no assurance that the comparative method will necessarily enable the investigator to identify cause and effect. However, it is logically impossible to identify cause-and-effect relationships and to sort out genuine linkages from those that are the result of happenstance unless one adopts an explicitly comparative approach. The case study method alone will not and cannot suffice. The comparative method is logically necessary—though admittedly not sufficient—for drawing the types of lessons in which we are often interested.

Patterns and Trends in Third World Conflicts

Forms of Conflict

Few concepts in the study of international relations and foreign policy are neat and precise. The concepts of violent conflict and war are not exceptions. Conceptualizations, measurement criteria, and operational indicators vary markedly across different war data sets and from one research project to another.[3]

Some of these distinctions are reflected in the major studies that have focused on wars since the Napoleonic period. Quincy Wright stressed the "legalist" notion that war was a special state of international law that took place between legally similar entities (that is, states) and that was bounded by such legal activities as declarations of war, peace treaties, declarations of neutrality, and the like. Lewis F. Richardson, another pioneer in the systematic study of war, based his study on "deadliness." His primary criterion was death caused by violence, from one death up to magnitudes of deadliness in the 6.5 to 7.5 range (3,162,278 to 31,622,777 deaths). The Correlates of War Project has primarily used criteria that tap the large-scale, organized quality of war, combining aspects of both Wright's and Richardson's approaches. Wars must have at least one state taking part (interstate wars require at least one state on each side) and must cause at least 1000 battle deaths.[4]

Studies that have investigated only the post–World War II period have used less stringent criteria for war. Istvan Kende, for example, uses the following guidelines: (1) there must be activities of regular armed forces on at least one side; (2) there must be a certain degree of organization and organized fighting on both sides; and (3) there must be a certain continuity between armed clashes.[5] Events-data sets for all or some of the postwar systems have also attempted to categorize conflictual interactions. The Conflict and Peace Data Bank (COPDAB), for example, has created a fifteen-point cooperation–conflict scale, using events in the three "most conflictual" categories to create a conflict data set.[6]

Although these studies make many distinctions, and could be compared in a variety of ways, one primary distinction is between interstate war and other forms such as civil war, colonial war, or extrasystemic war. Until World War II, when most observers thought of war, it was of the type called "interstate" (Correlates of War), "balance of power" (Wright), "border" (Kende), or "international" (Azar). Indeed, before World War II, this was the predominant form of violent international conflict. Wright's war data for 1900–1941 show that 80 percent were interstate wars.

Since World War II, however, that trend has been reversed. Kende's study of armed conflicts during the 1945–1976 period (120 such events are reported) indicates that only 15 percent of them were interstate, while the remaining 85 percent were some form of internal war. Thus, in contrast to earlier trends, most contemporary wars are being fought either between colonial powers and rebel groups or *within* the territory of a single state.[7] Increasingly since World War II, moreover, we have seen the legal trappings of war being dropped; that is, wars have been fought without any declaration of the state of hostilities.

Although most of the legal aspect of war has been dispensed with, however, the somatic consequences of war—people dying—have continued to characterize war in this era. Indeed, two different compilations of casualties caused by post-

1945 civil/internal wars indicate that the loss of life has been quite large. The Correlates of War Project, using a rigorous and highly specified set of criteria for inclusion, identify thirty civil wars between 1945 and 1980. These thirty conflicts lasted a total of 1,268 months, with an average duration of 3.5 years. It is not surprising that such protracted conflict would produce more than 3,830,000 battle-related deaths (an average of 127,700 deaths per civil war). Ruth Leger Sivard presents a list of wars between 1945 and 1983 from which eighty-six cases of civil war, civil strife, and colonial wars of independence can be identified. Sivard estimates a total of more than 11,750,000 military and civilian deaths resulting from these violent conflicts during this period. This staggering total averages out to more than 136,700 per case (not greatly discrepant from the Correlates of War average for military-related deaths).[8] In line with past analyses of civil and international war, the civil wars of the contemporary era have tended to be long and deadly.

Two additional patterns discovered by Kende should also be noted. Focusing on three categories of war—internal antiregime, internal tribal, and border wars, all of which are coded as having occurred with or without foreign intervention—Kende observes that the principal form of conflict during the 1945–1976 era was internal antiregime with foreign participation. Somewhat surprisingly, however, internal tribal wars accounted for 30 percent of the conflicts between 1967 and 1976, up from 15.5 percent during the 1945–1970 period. Thus, many of the challenges to Third World governments seem *not* to be arising directly from foreign sources, although outside elements may play a role. Rather, threats increasingly appear to result from internal tribal and ethnic cleavages. Because of the heterogeneous nature of many Third World states—such as Lebanon—it seems fair to presume that this trend will continue.[9]

The pattern that Kende observes in connection with the sources of foreign intervention in Third World conflict is also of interest. In the last ten years, Western involvement has dropped, but there has been more Third World and Socialist participation in the world's internal conflicts (again, Lebanon and Central America are good examples). It is no longer a matter of having a few-excolonial powers ceasing to intervene. Rather, the trend indicates that regional intervention is increasing in frequency. In Africa, for instance, local armies have increased in size to the point where external use is now plausible (for example, the Tanzanian activity in Uganda). Although they are still small compared to the armies of other regions and as a ratio of population, the use of these local armies as a foreign policy tool for intervention is now an option.[10]

The trend of regional intervention also highlights the changing roles of the United Nations and regional organizations in the management of local conflict. Recent research has indicated that referrals of conflicts to both the United Nations and regional organizations fell to a low point in the mid-1970s but rose again in 1980 to a level comparable to that of the early 1960s. However, the rates of success in "managing" conflicts for the United Nations (10 percent) and regional organizations (15 percent) in 1980 were the lowest for the entire 1945–1980 period.[11]

It is also important to note that changes in the form of Third World conflicts have been accompanied in many instances by alterations in the nature of conflicts that are being waged. Put simply, the internal conflict that now characterizes most of the fighting in the Third World is highly politicized. This politicization derives from the fact that it is revolutionary conflict that challenges governments. This challenge may be motivated by ideological, political, economic, or ethnic goals. What we have, however, are governments being challenged by nonstate actors who wish to seize power (often wanting to change the entire institutional structure of the governing system) or to break off part of the state into a separate political entity. This challenge to governments is the heart of the growing politicization of conflict. Wars are fought to win the support of people and/or to alienate the people from the existing government. One can see this especially in Lebanon and Central America, but it is also apparent in the Spanish Sahara and the Horn of Africa.

Political factors, then, very often take precedence over strictly military ones. Revolutionary forms of war, such as guerilla warfare (or violence such as terrorism), predominate. For a variety of reasons, they have become internationalized—for example, through proxy wars of the superpowers, through what Pierre Hassner has called "international civil war" (supporting those rebelling against one's opponent), or through "holy alliance" (supporting the governments of friends against their rebels).[12] One very basic lesson that emerges from all of this should therefore be clear: A very different type of conflict has evolved in the post–World War II era. A related set of lessons seems implicit in the fact that the need for international organization has apparently increased at the same time that there has been a trend toward decay of the post–World War II conflict management regime. The increasing incidence of internal war in the Third World poses the familiar question of whether or not outside parties should intervene, and on which side. This, in turn, relates to questions of the role and activity of international organizations dedicated to order and conflict resolution.

Reviewing the outcomes of conflict, however, one lesson may be that it is still difficult to topple governments, especially if there is outside intervention to support the government. Looking at the Correlates of War civil war list, and removing the four cases that are still ongoing, governments have won in seventeen of twenty-six cases (65.4 percent); the opposition has won in nine cases (34.6 percent). In the eight cases in which there was intervention on the government's side, the government won six times (75 percent).

Thus, the international context within which states must act will be made much more complex by the changing forms of international conflict. Most Third World conflicts, internal in form, create ambiguity regarding the policy responses of outside powers (and often produce strange bedfellows, as in the Biafran war or even in the more traditional interstate war between Iraq and Iran). Policy responses of specific states become entangled with the increasingly complicated issues of international law and the responses of international organizations. Internal war directly impinges on questions of the recognition of governments, the identification of the "legitimate" or "legal" government, more general issues of identification of the parties to conflict and their standing as legal international actors, legal strictures against intervention in the internal affairs of sovereign states, and equally explicit norms regarding the rights of self-determination and autonomy.

The United States and the Soviet Union, as superpowers with extensive alliance systems, spheres of interest, and, by definition, global concerns, will be more affected than most states by this complexity. How should states deal with aggression? What is aggression in this context, particularly given the ambiguity of the UN definition of aggression (Resolution on the Definition of Aggression, December 14, 1974, UNGA Res.3314 [XXIX]) and its inability to handle internal conflict? Closely related to aggression is the question of whether or not the superpowers, especially the United States, should support the governments of friends and allies. Which ones require such support? Which ones deserve it? The internal nature of Third World conflict makes discrimination in the support of allies both more crucial and more difficult. The lessons of such conflicts force policymakers to confront the same questions of priorities that George Kennan posed a quarter of a century ago: Which areas of the world are of central interest to American policy and warrant possible intervention?[13]

In sum, the changing nature of the forms of international conflict in the Third World creates a more ambiguous and complex environment for the foreign policy of states. The next two sections present variations on this theme, concerning the increase or decrease of international violence and the location of that violence.

Increase and Decrease in International Violence

Because of the evolution in the dominant forms of international conflict, some observers have claimed that the world is more warlike since World War II, while others claim it is less so. For the latter group, this appears to be so because of the growing infrequency of cross-border international wars. The former group points to both the increasing number of internal wars and the enormous loss of life since 1945: the total figure for Correlates of War international war and civil war is 7,205,000 battle deaths; Sivard claims a world total of 16,359 military and civilian deaths.

What have the longer-run and short-run trends been in international conflict? A number of researchers, including Wright, Richardson, and the Correlates of War Project,[14] have found cycles of international violence; that is, aggregating the amount of international violence in the system as a whole, alternating periods of peace and war have been found. The war–peace cycles discovered have usually

Table 2–1
Average Number of Wars, 1945–1976

Time Period	Average Number of Armed Conflicts
1945–1948	6.3
1949–1952	6.6
1953–1956	8.3
1957–1960	9.6
1961–1964	13.3
1965–1968	20.1
1969–1972	17.1
1973–1976	11.1

Source: Istvan Kende, "Twenty-Five Years of Local Wars," *Journal of Peace Research* 8(1971): 5–27; and "Wars of Ten Years (1967–1976)," *Journal of Peace Research* 15(1978): p. 228.

been in the twenty- to thirty-year range. These studies have investigated the international system since the Napoleonic wars, although Wright's data cover the period from 1480 to 1965. The cyclical nature of the occurrence of war does not seem to have demonstrated any long-term increase or decrease in international conflict.

Richardson, using a variety of statistical and mathematical techniques, found that wars are distributed randomly in time, and he uncovered no evidence that war was becoming either more or less frequent. The Correlates of War Project, with a different set of wars but covering approximately the same time period (1816–1965, later updated to 1980), also found that interstate war was neither waxing nor waning; no trend could be discovered. This research did, however, find that extra-systemic war, between states and nonstate actors, was increasing during this period. Kende's first study seemed to support such a finding in the postwar period. His findings indicated that there was an increase, but mostly in internal war with outside intervention, not in the classic interstate border war.

Table 2–1 shows the steady increase in the average number of armed conflicts occurring during four-year time periods. The average rises from 6.3 in 1945–1948 to over 20 during 1965–1968. Kende's original study, which stopped in 1968, indicated an upward trend since World War II. However, as Kende's later study indicates, this trend began to reverse itself at the end of the 1960s, as the last two time periods in table 2–1 show. The average number of wars for 1973–1976 is approximately the same as the average for the whole 1945–1976 period. Thus, instead of finding a major upward trend, it appears that we have another cycle. This finding is supported by the COPDAB data set, which reveals an average of twenty-five conflicts per year during the 1965–1970 period. This falls to an average of fourteen for 1971–1975 and fifteen for 1976–1979.

One possible lesson of this pattern in the rate of warfare during the 1945–1980 period is that, *contrary* to allegations that the Soviet Union has increasingly supported revolutionary movements, that it has done so with increasing (some seem to assume "invariable") success, and *despite* the dramatic increase in the number of nations in the international system that could be involved in war and the general trend toward "nationalism," *there has not been an uninterrupted trend* in the overall rate of warfare.[15]

The increase and decrease in the frequency of international conflict since World War II is closely related to both the change in the forms of conflict and the change in the location of and participants to conflict. Although the states are not faced with an ever more conflictual world, they must try to understand where and why and how international conflict is taking place and the prospects for the continuation of such trends.

Location of and Parties to Conflict

Before World War II, the majority of wars took place in Europe (or close by) and were fought by European powers. This reflects the Eurocentricity of an international system dominated by European technology and colonization. Yet a simple but striking fact is that since the end of World War II, very little violent conflict has taken place in Europe. War has taken place almost entirely on the territory of Asian, African, and Latin American countries. The arena of war has been the Third World, with the occurrence of internal wars that have been internationalized by external intervention.

As shown in table 2–2, part A, only 5 of Kende's 120 armed conflicts (4 percent) during the 1945–1976 period occurred in Europe. For that period, the Middle East and Asia led the world in violent conflict (with 30 percent and 29 percent, respectively). The Third World as the arena for conflict is also confirmed by analyses using nation-years of war rather than simple frequency. As a measure of intensity, nation-years tap the length of conflict and the number of states involved. Europe still contributed the fewest nation-years of war from 1945 to 1976, with only 3.8 percent. Using this measure, Asia ranked first, with 40.7 percent, and Africa moved into second place, with 25.5 percent. This reflects the short, sharp interstate wars in the Middle East in contrast to the many protracted, internal anticolonial and guerrilla wars of Asia and Africa.

One of the more important trends to note is the increasing occurrence of armed conflict in Africa. Part A of table 2–2 also indicates the distribution of wars over the 1967–1976 period. The largest rise during this period was in Africa, with 17.5 percent during the whole 1945–1976 period but 28.6 percent during the last ten years of that period. This is particularly evident when using the nation-years measure of intensity of conflict; Africa accounts for 35 percent of nation-years of war over the 1967–1976 period. This appears to be related to the aforementioned increase in tribal/ethnic-based antiregime activity, but it is

Table 2–2
Distribution of International Conflicts in the Postwar System

A. Geographic Distribution of Wars

	Number of Wars		Nation-Years of War	
	1945–1976	*1967–1976*	*1945–1976*	*1967–1976*
Europe	5 (4%)	1 (0.02%)	3.8%	4.7%
Asia	35 (29%)	12 (24.5%)	40.7%	33.9%
Middle East	36 (30%)	17 (34.7%)	19.4%	17.4%
Africa	21 (17.5%)	14 (28.6%)	25.5%	35.0%
Latin America	23 (19%)	5 (10.2%)	10.7%	9.0%

B. COPDAB Data on Interventions

Intervening Parties	1965–1970	1971–1975	1976–1979	Total
Developed West	58	21	2	81
Third World	8	21	13	42
Communist states	3	1	8	12

C. Locations of Terrorist Incidents, 1968–1975

Location	Number of Incidents
Atlantic community	572 (49%)
Middle East	159 (13.6%)
Asia	102 (8.7%)
East Europe	18 (1.5%)
Latin America	282 (24%)
Africa	37 (3.2%)

Sources: Part A: Istvan Kende, "Wars of Ten Years (1967–1976)," *Journal of Peace Research* 15(1978): 229. Part B: William Eckhardt and Edward Azar, "Major World Conflicts and Interventions, 1945 to 1975," *International Interactions* 5(1978): 75–109. Part C: Edward Mickolus, "Trends in Transnational Terrorism," in M. H. Livingston, ed., *International Terrorism in the Contemporary World* (Westport, Conn.: Greenwood Press, 1978).

also at least partially a result of the conflict directed against white-dominated rule in the former Portuguese colonies, Rhodesia and South Africa. In addition, the tacit U.S.–Soviet agreement not to intervene in Africa appears to have broken down, beginning with Soviet activities in Angola. This latter point, as well as the multiethnic nature of most African states and the increasing willingness by regional powers to intervene, indicates that Africa should continue to see high levels of violent conflict.[16]

As noted, many internal conflicts were fought with some external intervention. Kende observes that for the whole 1945–1976 period, 38 percent of the armed conflicts were fought with foreign participation; for the 1967–1976 period, 40 percent were fought with foreign participation. The Center for Defense Information study notes that foreign combat troops were involved in eight (20 percent) of the forty violent conflicts occurring in 1983. Kende's data and the COPDAB data agree that the Western powers were the major interveners until the early 1970s. Kende's first study had the United States as the most frequent intervener (in twenty-six of ninety-seven armed conflicts), followed by Britain with nineteen and France with twelve. The COPDAB data in part B of table 2–2 also indicate that the developed West was the major intervention force during the 1965–1970 period.

Both Kende and COPDAB also demonstrate that Western intervention has decreased. Kende notes that, from 1945 to 1966, developed capitalist countries intervened forty-four times, whereas the Third World and Socialist countries each had three interventions. In the 1967–1976 period, the Western interventions numbered only twenty, compared to fourteen from Third World countries and three from Socialist countries. The COPDAB data in part B also indicate that Third World interventions matched Western activity in the 1971–1975 period, and both Third World and Communist activity surpassed Western interventions during 1976–1979. For 1983, six of the eight interventions involving combat troops identified by the Center for Defense Information came from Socialist countries (for example, Vietnam in Cambodia), one such intervention was Third World (Syria in Lebanon), and one was Western (United States). Eckhardt and Azar note simply: "The era of Western imperialism in terms of military intervention would seem to have come to an end."[17] Although we may not want to go that far, there has certainly been a change in the nature of interventionary states. This, too, makes for a more complex international environment.

We have noted that intervention on behalf of the government appears to favor that side in civil conflict, but there are still many confounding factors in predicting the outcomes of conflict involving Third World states (either internal or cross-border wars). One lesson of the postwar period is that simple preponderance in military capability does not ensure victory. As Andrew Mack has pointed out, large, developed states fighting local wars are caught in an asymmetry that militates against success; just because they are large and their survival is not threatened, they cannot mobilize the will or the resources needed to defeat a smaller opponent whose survival *is* at stake.[18] This model of power as the willingness to suffer was most clearly demonstrated in the Vietnam conflict. North Vietnam was willing to suffer—to not be defeated—in order to win. The losses accepted were considerably beyond those that forced states to concede in other modern wars.[19]

The location of contemporary conflict is clearly of importance, both for theory and for policy. A brief discussion of some of the reasons for this distribution may highlight reasons for its continuance. First, there is the general opportunity for the occurrence of these forms of conflict. There are presently more than 160 states in the system, most of them Third World states that have attained independence since 1945 and very few of which are internally homogeneous. Various subcultural cleavages tear at the fabric of these societies. At the same time, most of these states are less developed and are struggling to improve economically and create the infrastructure of the modern state. The challenges and problems they face are enormous, creating much internal turmoil and instability. In addition, they are states without the habit and precedent of peaceful change.[20] Many lack mechanisms for a regular or peaceful change of government or transfer of political power. Many, such as in the Horn of Africa or the Spanish Sahara, have also inherited border conflicts as a result of the artificial boundaries drawn by the colonial powers, which both exacerbate tribal or ethnic cleavages and provide further opportunities for internal and external conflict.[21] Finally, such vulnerable states exist in a world where two superpowers espouse conflicting ideologies and economic and governmental systems and where a call for aid will be heard by one and the other will move to aid the opponent, whether government or challenger. All of these factors tend to reinforce the patterns of Third World conflict described here.

Internal problems also make many states targets for external "penetration," to use Rosenau's term. The growing economic and ecological interdependence of the system makes such penetration more likely. Conflict and intervention are possible consequences of the sensitivity and vulnerability that come with interdependence.[22] The relationship between internal conflict and the internationalization of conflict could also be reversed, however. Government leaders, recognizing the problems sketched out here, could try various strategies at "nation-building"—the drawing together of diverse peoples into one group with nationalist feelings of group identity. Early nation-builders, such as Sukarno, Nkrumah, and Nasser, often used the existence of external opponents as a means to attempt to bring about internal cohesion. The possible relationship between external threat and internal unity has been developed by sociologists such as Simmel and Coser.[23] Conditions for the success of such a strategy are not easy or automatic. This strategy may lead to external intervention in one's affairs or to interstate conflicts. Idi Amin's miscalculation regarding Tanzania led to a war that looked very much like a standard interstate war. However, the Tanzanian goal was simply to remove Amin and aid his internal opponents, so it could also be classified as external intervention. The point in this example, however, was how external enemies were used for internal purposes (on the part of Amin) and how this strategy could lead to international conflict.

Another lesson concerning terrorism may be found by investigating the location of transnational terrorist activity and other forms of armed violence. Part C of table 2–2 shows the geographic distribution of 1,170 transnational terrorist incidents studied by Mickolus.[24] Note that the West (the Atlantic community) serves as the location for most of the activity, while Africa has the least. Transnational terrorism appears to occur where other forms of international violence do not appear. The reasons for this provide a useful contrast between war—especially the various forms of internal, guerrilla war—and terrorism.

Clearly, if one is at war to overthrow a specific government, then terrorism (the "weapon of the weakest") is not necessary for its purposes of propaganda, highlighting a cause, or discomforting the government. Where there is internal war, there is no need for terrorism. If, however, the government is so strong that internal war is out of the question, then the terrorist weapon is more appropriate. The states of the Atlantic community, which, for a variety of reasons, have not experienced war, have thus been the location of terrorist activity. More important, these states are also democracies. If "terrorism is theater," as suggested by Brian Jenkins, then terrorists require media that will focus attention on their acts. The free mass media of democracy provide the best environment for terrorist activities; the figures reported for Eastern Europe, for example, comprise only 1.5 percent of the total terrorist activities identified by Mickolus.

Although there are some similarities between terrorism and guerrilla war activities, this comparison of location highlights the great differences between the two forms of violence and the very different lessons each provides. The character of the states and situations in which each form occurs says much about the utility and purposes of each. There are also clues here to the manner in which states could or should respond to these forms of conflict in the international environment.

Contagion and Diffusion: Do Dominoes Fall?

Returning to the question of the opportunity for conflict, it should be noted that research on the relationship between borders and war has indicated that small nations' numbers of borders are correlated with their war involvements.[25] More important, perhaps, is the consistent finding across several data sets, samples of nations, and time frames that countries with warring states on their borders, in contrast to countries whose neighbors are at peace, are significantly more likely to experience conflicts of their own. Although additional investigations are in progress, the preliminary evidence suggests—as many U.S. national security policymakers have argued—that some types of "first" wars, under at least certain conditions, do have a potential for destabilizing nations and areas beyond the arena in which the conflict initially erupts.

The increase in the number of states, especially in Africa but throughout the Third World, the resulting increase in the aggregate number of international frontiers, and the concomitant expansion in the number of nations that could trigger diffusion processes or be affected by them, suggest a likely continuation of these trends. The populations that can initiate or receive the "war disease" is growing. For a variety of reasons, both external (for example, numbers of borders and dependent status) and internal (for example, ethnic or tribal divisions and low degrees of government institutionalization), more and more of that population seems vulnerable to catching the disease.[26]

This does not mean that Communism will spread from one nation to another in the Third World, as some analysts and observers have contended. Work on diffusion and contagion has focused to date on the spread of war occurrences, not on the outcomes of the wars. Thus, it does not really demonstrate that "dominoes" actually "fall." Nevertheless, the lesson from this work is that there is at least some validity to one aspect of the domino theory. If the analyses to date are correct, one consequence of war is more war. Thus, the outbreak of conflict in one nation or between one pair of nations should indeed alert decision makers to the possibility that other, neighboring nations could soon experience similar events.

Conclusion

We have presented a number of patterns and trends derived from cross-sectional studies employing different data sets of war and violent conflict since 1945. The description of the international system presented here, which derives from an analysis of the total population of conflicts identified by these data sets, indicates that there are still decision makers, states, and nonstate actors willing to use violence to achieve their goals.

Although most of these conflicts are internal, the utility of violence between states is also quite evident—producing, according to Correlates of War data, over three million battle casualties in the post–World War II era (with the Iraq-Iran war being the most prominent contemporary example). The data indicate that organized violence continues to destroy large numbers of human beings and that this violence is occurring in the Third World. It has demonstrated a tendency to diffuse across space, so that the occurrence of violent conflict is dangerous to neighboring states as well (even if the conflict is internal or civil). This is in line with identified short-term trends indicating an increase in violence between states and nonstate actors.

The patterns and trends outlined here also indicate that conflict in the Third World is highly politicized and largely internal, with revolutionary conflict subjected to intervention from external sources. The pool of possible sites for conflict and possible intervenors is extensive, drawing upon most of the global system, not just Western "imperialists." The internal nature of these Third World conflicts muddies up and makes much more complex the interpretation of the guidelines offered by traditional views of security, by international law concerning behavior during war, and by norms concerning intervention in the internal affairs of sovereign states (at a time when it appears that the international conflict management regime is in decline). Although Quincy Wright attempted to define war as a special legal situation between two actors of equal legal status, contemporary conflict often deals with actors of unequal legal status and raises issues of sovereignty and intervention in internal affairs.

Although this brief conclusion summarizes the major points developed in this chapter, a number of other generalizations could be presented. Our point is simply that such a characterization of the contemporary system (and the two contexts discussed at the beginning of the chapter) could be developed only by a systematic survey of the total universe of conflict as identified in the various data sets. As noted, whereas the case studies presented later in this volume will provide rich detail on each particular conflict, we have attempted here to provide a broader context within which to place those studies.

Notes

1. The arguments in this section are drawn primarily from Benjamin A. Most, *Points of Departure: An Introduction to the Systematic Study of Public Policy* (Cambridge, Mass.: Schenkman, forthcoming); Gregory A. Raymond, "Introduction: Comparative Analysis and Nomological Explanation," in Charles W. Kegley, Gregory Raymond, Robert Rood, and Richard Skinner, eds., *International Events and the Comparative Analysis of Public Policy* (Columbia: University of South Carolina Press, 1975); and John V. Gillespie, "An Introduction to Macro–Cross National Research," in John V. Gillespie and Betty Nesvold, eds., *Macro-Quantitative Analysis* (Beverly Hills, Calif.: Sage, 1971). See these sources also for more complete discussions of the comparative approach, the debate between traditionalists and behavioralists in political science, and attendant issues. For a discussion of the utility of case studies for systematic inquiry, see Bruce M. Russett, "International Behavior Research: Case Studies and Cumulation," in Michael Haas and Henry Kariel, eds., *Approaches to the Study of Political Science* (San Francisco: Chandler, 1970). See also Richard Smoke, *War: Controlling Escalation* (Cambridge, Mass.: Harvard University Press, 1977) for a good example of the use of focused comparison and case studies.

2. Analysts and interpreters of many cases simply cannot spend the time necessary to develop the rich contextual data that it is possible to build into case studies. Thus, although the case study approach maximizes depth, the cross-sectional approach sacrifices depth for breadth. The cross-sectional design is likely to yield less detailed and less complete explanations, but the demonstrated generality and the potential generalizability of those results is greater.

3. See also Benjamin A. Most and Harvey Starr, "Conceptualizing 'War': Consequences for Theory and Research," *Journal of Conflict Resolution* 27(1983): 137–159, for a fuller discussion of conceptualization and operationalization issues in regard to war.

4. See Quincy Wright, *A Study of War*, rev. ed. (Chicago: University of Chicago Press, 1965); Lewis Fry Richardson, *Statistics of Deadly Quarrels* (Chicago: Quadrangle Books, 1960); J. David Singer and Melvin Small, *The Wages of War, 1816–1965* (New York: Wiley, 1972); and Melvin Small and J. David Singer, *Resort to Arms: International and Civil Wars, 1816–1980* (Beverly Hills, Calif.: Sage, 1982).

5. Istvan Kende, "Twenty-Five Years of Local Wars," *Journal of Peace Research* 8(1971): 5–27; and "Wars of Ten Years (1967–1976)," *Journal of Peace Research* 15(1978): 227–241.

6. See, for example, William Eckhardt and Edward Azar, "Major World Conflicts and Interventions, 1945 to 1975," *International Interactions* 5(1978): 75–109; and Edward E. Azar, "The Conflict and Peace Data Bank (COPDAB) Project," *Journal of Conflict Resolution* 24(1980): 143–152. The three most conflictual categories are #13—subversion, small air or border clashes, skirmishes, or blockades; #14—limited hostile acts with minor costs; and #15—very hostile war actions, territorial occupations, and many deaths.

7. Of 265 conflict situations identified by COPDAB, only 25 percent could be called international. Even the Correlates of War data set, which is weighted toward interstate conflicts, finds that only 35 percent of 57 "wars" from 1946 to 1977 were interstate.

8. See Small and Singer, *Resort to Arms*, table 13.2; and Ruth Leger Sivard, *World Military and Social Expenditures, 1983* (Washington, D.C.: World Priorities, 1983), p. 21.

9. Indeed, there is even an increasing movement by ethnic and regional groups in the developed states for the assertion of autonomy.

10. See, for example, Henry Bienen, "Armed Forces and National Modernization: Continuing the Debate," Paper prepared for the First Wharangdae Symposium on Armed Forces National Development, Seoul, Korea, September 1981.

11. See Ernst B. Haas, "Regime Decay: Conflict Management and International Organizations, 1945–1981," *International Organization* 37(1983): 189–256.

12. See Pierre Hassner, "Civil Violence and the Pattern of International Power," in *Civil Violence in the International System, Part II,* ADELPHI PAPERS No. 83, (London: International Institute for Strategic Studies, 1971).

13. See George F. Kennan, *Memoirs* (Boston: Little, Brown, 1967), chapter 15, especially pp. 378–379, for commentary on this point as presented in the Mr. "X" article.

14. See also Frank Denton, "Some Regularities in International Conflict, 1820–1949," *Background* 9(1966): 283–296; and Frank Denton and Warren Phillips, "Some Patterns in the History of Violence," *Journal of Conflict Resolution* 12(1968): 182–195.

15. The potentially complex interplay between nationalism and interethnic conflict and increasing international interdependence has recently been discussed in K.J. Holsti, "Change in the International System: Interdependence, Integration, and Fragmentation," in Ole Holsti, Randolph M. Siverson, and Alexander George, eds., *Change in the International System* (Boulder, Colo.: Westview Press, 1980), pp. 23–53.

16. A compilation by the Center for Defense Information, describing ongoing violent conflict during 1983, indicates that Africa remains an important site for violent conflict, but not the dominant one. Of the forty conflicts identified, ten are in Africa, ten in Asia, ten in the Middle East/Persian Gulf, seven in Latin America, and, as to be expected, only three in Europe. Again in support of the previously noted trends, thirty-five of the forty conflicts are described as "internal"—guerrilla or civil wars. In 1983, the five interstate conflicts were Iraq-Iran, Ethiopia-Somalia, North and South Yemen, North and South Korea, and China-Vietnam. See *Defense Monitor* 12, no. 1 (1983).

17. Eckhardt and Azar, "Major World Conflicts," p. 75.

18. Andrew Mack, "Why Big Nations Lose Small Wars: The Politics of Asymmetric Conflict," *World Politics* 27(1975): 175–200.

19. See Steven Rosen, "A Model of War and Alliance," in J. Friedman, C. Bladen, and S. Rosen, eds., *Alliance in International Politics* (Boston: Allyn and Bacon, 1970); and Steven Rosen, "War Power and the Willingness to Suffer," in B.M. Russett, ed., *Peace, War, and Numbers* (Beverly Hills, Calif.: Sage, 1972). Concerning Vietnam, see John

Mueller, "The Search for the 'Breaking Point' in Vietnam: The Statistic of a Deadly Quarrel," *International Studies Quarterly* 24(1980): 497–519.

20. One observer of factors involved in the development of African conflict includes "the lack of *strong* cultural prohibitions against conflict." See Maria C. Papadakis, "Applying International Relations Theory to Regional Conflict: An African Study," Paper presented at the Midwest Political Science Association annual meeting, Milwaukee, 1982.

21. See Harvey Starr and Benjamin A. Most, "Contagion and Border Effects on Contemporary African Conflict," *Comparative Political Studies* 16(1983): 92–117.

22. See Robert Keohane and Joseph Nye, *Power and Interdependence* (Boston: Little, Brown, 1977), chapters 1 and 2.

23. See Lewis Coser, *The Functions of Social Conflict* (New York: Free Press, 1956) for summary and analysis of Simmel's theses; and Arthur Stein, "Conflict and Cohesion: A Review of the Literature," *Journal of Conflict Resolution* 20(1976): 143–172.

24. Edward Mickolus, "Trends in Transnational Terrorism," in M.H. Livingston, ed., *International Terrorism in the Contemporary World* (Westport, Conn.: Greenwood Press, 1978).

25. See Harvey Starr and Benjamin A. Most: "The Substance and Study of Borders in International Relations Research," *International Studies Quarterly* 20(1976): 581–620; "A Return Journey: Richardson, 'Frontiers' and War in the 1946–1965 Era," *Journal of Conflict Resolution* 22(1978): 441–467; and Starr and Most, "Contagion and Border Effects."

26. See Benjamin A. Most and Harvey Starr, "Diffusion, Reinforcement, Geopolitics and the Spread of War," *American Political Science Review* 74(1980): 932–946; and Starr and Most, "Contagion and Border Effects."

3
Lessons and Lessons Learned: A Historical Perspective

Jay Luvaas

Throughout history, and especially during the past two centuries, serious soldiers have essentially learned their grim trade in one of two ways—from their own experience or by studying the experiences of others. Until the wars of the mid-nineteenth century, the experiences of others were captured more often by studying military history than by sending missions to report on possible changes in the organization, tactics, and equipment of rival armies.

Indeed, before the French Revolution, thoughtful soldiers perhaps learned as many lessons from the Greeks and Romans as from their own contemporaries, which is scarcely surprising if one remembers the role of the classics in all formal education. Prominent among the "great captains" serving as role models were Alexander, Hannibal, and Caesar, and the controversy over line versus column that raged in military circles throughout most of the eighteenth century grew out of the Chevalier de Folard's exhaustive study of the Greek phalanx. Frederick the Great's innovative oblique order was regarded by many contemporaries as the revival of a tactic used by Epaminondas at Leuctra in 371 B.C., perhaps because it was known that among his military retinue on campaign was Captain Guichard, a noted authority on classical warfare. In his own writings, Frederick asserted that much could still be learned from the *Commentary of Polybius*, the source of Folard's massive studies, and some idea of the fast pace of change in military tactics in the eighteenth century is suggested by Frederick's assertion that "it would further human knowledge if instead of writing new books, we would apply ourselves to making decent extracts from those already in existence."[1]

The foremost theorists who emerged from the Napoleonic Wars, Carl von Clausewitz and Baron de Jomini, both based their theories exclusively on the study of modern history. Clausewitz viewed military theory as an analytical tool to be applied to the systematic study of recent history, while Jomini derived his principles from a detailed study of campaigns of Frederick and Napoleon.[2]

Not until the acceleration of the Industrial Revolution, in fact, did military men begin to think in terms of innovational change in waging wars. Increasingly, the professional soldier studied his art, tinkered with his organization, equipment, and doctrine, and scrutinized potential adversaries in the hope of enjoying advantage in some future battle. No longer were armies necessarily similar in organization, tactics, and weaponry, and the introduction of new means of communication and transportation, improved fire power, and the mass army challenged familiar assumptions and prodded military men everywhere to study recent developments in their crafts. Consequently, official observers flocked to the United States to learn what they could from the American Civil War, and the general introduction of military attaches about the same time reflects new concern for lessons to be learned from neighboring armies nearer home. With each major improvement in weaponry, the lessons of history became increasingly blurred. Writing in the 1820s, Clausewitz maintained that any war fought after 1740, when most European armies were armed with the flintlock musket, was "close enough to modern warfare to be instructive." German officers studying his theories at the end of the century assumed that "when it becomes a question of obtaining practical hints for our own strategy and tactics . . . we must not go farther back than 1866." World War I monopolized the attention of the next generation of soldiers, and a decade after World War II, no less an authority than Walter Millis suggested that "the advent of the nuclear arsenals has at least seemed to render most of the military history of the Second War as outdated and inapplicable as the history of the War with Mexico."[3]

Today, even the term *lesson* has become obsolete; *lessons learned* is the current catch-phrase for the inevitable lists of observations that accompany most accounts of the latest military endeavor as the gaze of soldiers everywhere shifts from one war to the next, trying desperately to keep pace with the relentless march of technology and unstable conditions the world over.

Living in an age when material progress was not yet claimed to be our most important product, when it was widely assumed that human nature was constant and that the universe was governed by fixed rules that had only to be discovered, the typical officer—if he studied his profession at all—did not expect to learn specific lessons in tactics or strategy. To him, the lessons consisted in arriving at a better understanding of how the art of war was practiced by some successful commander or "great captain."

Frederick the Great is a case in point. While accompanying the Prussian contingent with the Imperial Army commanded by Prince Eugene when the French invaded the Rhineland in 1733, the crowning lesson Frederick learned in frequent conversations with the most famous general of his day was how the prince had mastered the art of war. Always place yourself in your opponent's shoes, Eugene had advised, and years later, when Frederick urged his own officers to study the campaigns of "the greatest warrior of this century," he stressed that they must work especially hard to examine his views "to learn how to think in the same way." Frederick's favorite military memoir, Feuquieres's *Memoirs Historical and Military*, was instructive for the same reason. He reminded his own junior officers:

That harsh critic has related minutely all the mistakes that generals committed in his day. . . . developed the anatomy of campaigns that he witnessed by showing the causes of success and the reasons for failure . . . [and] indicated the road that must be followed if one desires to instruct himself, and by which researches the first truths, which are the basis of the art, are discovered.[4]

The causes of success and the reasons for failure were the most important lessons a soldier could learn—and if ever a general learned from his own successes and failures, it was Frederick. Consequently, when he wrote his own history of his campaigns, it was primarily intended to help educate his successors by instructing them in "the reasons that had impelled him to act, his limited resources, and the traps prepared for him by his enemies." Frederick insisted:

The success of any war depends greatly on the capacity of the general; on a knowledge of the places he occupies, and on the art with which he may derive advantage from his situation, either in preventing the enemy from taking such posts as might favor his purpose or in choosing himself those most conducive to success.

Frederick believed that if one studied his opponents carefully, it would be possible to "learn his mannerisms and penetrate his intentions by the way he acts." Austrian commanders usually had their soldiers cook on marching days, "so if you notice much smoke between five and eight o'clock in the morning you can safely assume that they will make a movement that day." Whenever an Austrian intended to give battle, he usually recalled all large detachments of light troops. Even more, one learned from his own mistakes, and in this sense Frederick viewed the 1744 Bohemian campaign as his own school in the art of war and the victorious Austrian Marshal Traun "as his preceptor." Admitting that no general had ever committed more faults than he had during this ill-fated invasion of Bohemia, Frederick catalogued every one of his mistakes in his published memoirs.[5]

This was the way most military men in the eighteenth century learned their lessons. They were mainly interested in the nuances of their trade, the stratagems of their opponents, and the experiences of their predecessors. Because armies in the eighteenth century were pretty much alike in the way they were recruited, formed, armed, and drilled, no one army enjoyed a particular advantage over another. The difference was usually determined by the skill of the commanders.

However, soldiers then, like many soldiers now, were anxious to discern the secrets of an army that, like Frederick's Prussians, had managed often "to fight outnumbered and win," and—with his lopsided victories at Hohenfriedburg, Soor, and Leuthen—foreign officers began to scrutinize Prussian methods for instructive lessons in tactics. Inevitably, they focused attention on Frederick's "oblique order" and the attack *en echelon*, which refer to Frederick's practice of striking the extremity of his adversary's line either by extending one flank beyond that of the enemy and advancing in an oblique direction, rolling up the enemy's flank, or by advancing with his battalions in echelon, each a couple of hundred paces to the rear of the other so as to strike the enemy's flank with the foremost echelon. Foreign officers studied both maneuvers diligently on the drill ground at Potsdam, not appreciating that the secret of the Prussian success was not in any particular formation, but in the superior discipline and mobility of the infantry and in Frederick's own genius. "Old Frederick laughed in his sleeve at the Potsdam parades," Napoleon snorted, "when he perceived young French, English and Austrian officers so infatuated with the maneuvers that in themselves were fit only for gaining a reputation for a few adjutant majors."[6]

If Frederick was indeed chuckling, perhaps it was at his own naiveté when he was their age; in his first battle, Frederick had endeavored to offset his own inferiority in cavalry by placing two battalions of grenadiers between the cavalry squadrons of each wing. "This was the disposition made by Gustavus Adolphus at the battle of Lutzen," he explained to his successors, noting that "according to all appearances," this particular tactic "will never more be practiced."[7] One of Frederick's first lessons in tactics, apparently, was to learn not to rely on formations simply because they had seemed to work in another place and at another time.

Similarly, Baron von Steuben, who had learned his art of war under Frederick, appreciated that the solution to a military problem in one set of circumstances would be no guarantee of success in another. Whereas Frederick controlled his army, which had largely been recruited forcibly among the dregs of society, through fear and harsh discipline, Steuben quickly understood that the shivering soldiers at Valley Forge seemed to be motivated primarily by devotion to their cause. This placed different requirements on leadership, and Steuben's published *Regulations* departed in many details from the famed Prussian drill, even in matters such as the introduction of the two-rank line and the importance attached to light infantry. Had Washington sent a commission to Europe to report on Prussian methods, and had the members been no more perceptive than many European contemporaries, the results at Valley Forge could have been disastrous.[8]

In the armies of France and England, the new military manuals stressed Prussian formations, often confusing form with substance. Two discerning French observers, however, did not make this common error. The Comte de Guibert analyzed the Prussian system and pointed out that techniques that had worked well in Prussia would be less successful elsewhere. The Comte de Mirabeau agreed and went so far as to predict that Prussian military power would soon evaporate under a less capable successor. Both attributed the secret of Frederick's successes to the superior mobility, discipline, and drill of his troops.[9]

They were correct. "Good fortune," Frederick had written, "is often more fatal to princes than adversity." After his death, the Prussian army grew stagnant while French military leaders, smarting from their humiliating defeats during the Seven Years' War, embarked upon a series of reforms in military administration and the tactical instruction of the army, especially the artillery. Thus, Guibert, DuTeil, Mesnil-Durand, and other military writers laid the groundwork for changes that would soon come during the wars of the French Revolution and Napoleon:

> Thus on the eve of the Revolution the army was well organized and well trained. Its drill books had been repeatedly revised and represented the best military thought of the day. A series of camps of instruction had rendered the troops proficient in evolutions suited for war. . . . The cavalry was well mounted. The artillery . . . was the best in Europe.[10]

The French army had learned not so much from the Prussian successes as from their own failures, which had forced thoughtful soldiers to think creatively about their entire military system.

The French Revolution of 1789 shattered traditional social structure, gave birth to a virulent nationalism that made possible the new mass citizen army, and ultimately involved Europe in nearly two decades of war. Although many elements of the old military system survived, circumstances gave fresh impetus to mobility, flexibility, and individual initiative. No tactical innovator himself, Napoleon skillfully orchestrated the recent reforms and many of the new practices of the armies of the Republic.

Napoleon's major innovations were in the realm of strategy, enabling both Clausewitz and Jomini to devote their lifetimes to explaining what was new about his methods and why they had so often succeeded. He excelled as an administrator. He introduced the concept of the army corps, reorganized the military transport service, and created a logistical system that enabled him—to use one of his favorite phrases—"to maneuver according to circumstances." Napoleon substituted the two-rank line for the normal line of three ranks—not because he had read about this temporary British expedient during the American Revolution, but because he had gradually become convinced that the third rank was of little use, and he was beginning to run low on manpower. He instructed his minister of war to compile studies of French sieges in Germany and Spain, he advocated a special chair of history to study ways in which the French frontiers had been defended over the ages, and he urged historians to undertake the study of recent campaigns. Because "no historian gets to our own days," there was always, according to Napoleon, a significant gap in the historical knowledge of young officers that made it difficult to link past events to those of the present. Consequently, "all of our young men find it easier to learn about the Punic Wars than the war of the American Revolution," while the wars of the French Revolution would be no less "fertile in lessons."[11] Later, Napoleon even proposed the publication of military manuscripts in the Imperial Library to establish the documentary foundation for such historical studies.[12]

Inevitably, Napoleon's victories forced changes in other armies. The British army developed fresh interest in light infantry that could hold the French *tirailleurs* at bay while cooperating closely with infantry of the line; Austria and Russia increased the number of light troops and adopted the French battalion column; and Prussia, humiliated by the defeat at Jena in 1806, went beyond adopting specific practices to introduce limited political and social reforms that would offer a rejuvenated army a cause to fight for what was similar to that which had motivated French soldiers.[13] It would be no exaggeration to state that after the end of the Napoleonic Wars, most military lessons were conducted in French.

The Crimean War of 1854–1856 demonstrates, among other things, how little professional soldiers in Russia, England, and France had advanced in their thinking since 1815, despite the introduction of the Minié rifle, which trebled the effective range of infantry weapons, and the conversion of some artillery into rifled guns. The celebrated "charge of the light brigade" demonstrated the failure of traditional cavalry tactics, although no cavalryman in the world would have conceded the point in public before the lesson was taught again during the American Civil War. For infantrymen, the war was barren of any new lessons; the British maintained their traditional "thin red line," the French fought with a modified cloud of skirmishers backed by columns, and the Russians employed their customary dense masses. Only in military engineering were there new lessons to be pondered, and here there was professional disagreement. In the first attempt at official military history in the British army, engineers and artillerymen could not agree upon the obvious. To the engineers, the superiority of earthen parapets over masonry "was fully and clearly shown" in the stubborn Russian defense of Sebastopol, whereas the history of artillery operations during the siege pointed to the opposite conclusion—that "earthworks, however laboriously and skillfully constructed, cannot successfully withstand a heavy and continuous artillery fire."[14] One is reminded of Melville's commentary on nature, wherein each man, "selecting and combining as he pleases . . . reads his own peculiar lesson."[15]

There was, however, one lesson about which nearly all military men could agree—the potential danger posed by newspaper correspondents. The dispatches of William Russell of *The Times*, with his vivid pen-portraits of suffering and inefficiency in the siege lines before Sebastopol, had exposed the outmoded military system and had aroused public opinion; although this was never openly treated within the army as a lesson to be learned, the army became fully alerted to this new danger. After the war, in a practical handbook for staff officers, the adjutant general included a section on dealing with the press. He warned:

> As long as the British public's craze for sensational news remains as it is now, the English General must accept the position. Only newspapers of importance . . . should be allowed to have a correspondent with the army, and only one correspondent be allowed for each paper. It is most desirable they should be carefully selected men . . . known for the honesty with which they report news.[16]

It was a lesson well learned by the army. For the rest of the Victorian age, most news from distant colonial campaigns would come either from newspapermen known to be friendly to the army or, in many cases, from serving officers who, with permission from the commander, contracted with respectable newspapers to send occasional accounts from the front.

The American Civil War was the first great conflict waged with the products of the Industrial Revolution, the first in which steam and iron were used by both sides to transport and supply armies over rails and in which ships of wood and sail gave way to the ironclad. This reemergence of a rough symmetry in technology forced tactical innovation. The Minié rifle and rifled artillery put a bloody end to Napoleonic tactics. No longer were massed infantry assaults and mounted cavalry charges feasible in the face of modern firepower. Eventually, the Napoleonic line and column yielded to looser and more extended formations and to advance by rushes, and by 1863 field entrenchments could be found on practically every field of battle. Cavalry quickly learned to fight dismounted, with carbines rather than traditional lance and saber, and the horse became essentially a means of conveyance, enabling enterprising cavalry leaders like Jeb Stuart and Nathan Bedford Forrest to "get there first with the most."

One would think that such obvious changes would have attracted the attention of the European military observers who flocked to the scene; surprisingly, however, few carried back these basic tactical lessons, and no European army officially paid them any attention. Nor did European armies learn anything that was new about strategy, although several individuals commented that Sherman's campaigns revealed an unusual mastery of logistics. A French observer even went so far as to cite Sherman's Atlanta campaign as a masterpiece of turning and outflanking maneuvers, worthy of serious study "by any soldier who is interested in his profession."[17] Except for a few officers who happened to be interested in the subject, however, there is nothing to indicate that Sherman's maneuvers were studied by professional soldiers in Europe. Sherman himself learned valuable lessons, which he summarized in his *Memoirs,* suggesting that, more often than not, the best teacher of "lessons learned" is experience. According to Sherman, this was beyond doubt the "dearest school on earth."[18]

Why did European armies thus ignore the obvious? The reasons are instructive. First, it should be pointed out that they *did* learn a number of lessons from the Civil War, most particularly in the military use of railroads, coastal defenses, the performance of new rifled artillery, military sanitation, and fortification. They learned lessons in these areas precisely because this is what they had been directed to observe and report upon.

No responsible military leader in Europe assumed for a minute, however, that the American improvised armies could teach much in tactics or that American generals—however much they might try to emulate him—could ever improve upon Napoleon. Moreover, the American terrain was totally unlike that of Western Europe; the distances involved, the relatively sparse population, the vast forests and swamps, and even the mountainous areas bore little resemblance to what strategists and tacticians could expect to encounter. Furthermore, the war had not been fought between regular armies trained and disciplined in the European manner. It would have been too much to expect of human nature for any European officer to have set aside his own convictions, traditions, and the habits of a lifetime in analyzing the Civil War experience. Except for a few individuals— most notably, Colonel G.F.R. Henderson of the British Staff College—it was not until the 1914–1918 war that European soldiers were willing to reassess the lessons of the American Civil War, when it clearly became a signpost that had been missed.

Then, too, the German wars for unification in 1866 and 1870 quickly eclipsed the Civil War. Now there was evidence—much closer to home and in campaigns between regular armies—of the impact of the breechloader and rifled artillery on tactics, of the efficient military use of railroads, of the vital importance of military mobilization (an area in which the American experience could offer only negative lessons), and of the importance of a trained general staff. Even though the Prussian company columns had tended to dissolve into a swarm of skirmishers, as the conventional Civil War battle lines had tended to do by 1863, and even though mounted shock tactics of cavalry usually ended in failure, as had also been the case in the Civil War, the lessons learned by European soldiers ignored practically everything that had occurred prior to the universal introduction of breechloaders in 1866. German uniforms, tactics, organization, and military terminology became the vogue in every army, and in practically every Western nation except Britain and the United States, German models of national conscription, mobilization, and officer education were slavishly imitated. Although American soldiers continued to cling to the lessons they had learned from the Civil War, the influence of German tactical doctrine and instruction was such that a lecturer at Leavenworth in 1907 could legitimately complain that "von Moltke teaches us our strategy, Griepenkerl writes our orders, while Von der Goltz tells us how they should be executed."[19]

We can learn something about the nature of lessons learned by following a couple of Royal Engineers as they poked around the battlefields of 1870 shortly after the war. Here again, to paraphrase Melville, the two officers selected and combined their information to read their "own peculiar lesson." Naturally interested in hasty entrenchments, the two engineers inspected the French positions at Gravelotte to determine "the extent and nature" of the only entrenchments they could find on the field—a few slight shelter trenches. Their conclusions ran counter to the lessons learned by nearly everyone else. "So far from being questioned as desirable by the results of this war," they reported, from the effect produced in the one portion of the only battle where breastworks had been "fairly tried . . . it would be madness to deliberately neglect" such measures in the future. Gravelotte "proves as decisively as one example can that musketry trenches, judiciously placed, may, though slight, prove a most formidable addition to a defensive position." Had the French thrown up similar works at Wissenburg and Woerth, it would have been "absolutely impossible," according to these observers, "for the Prussians to have assaulted successfully up the long slope in the face of the Chassepot rifle."[20]

Perhaps in considering what were the exemplary lessons of the Franco-Prussian War, we would do well to remember the observation, made half a century earlier by the well-known Prussian theorist Carl von Clausewitz, that "where a new or debatable point of view is concerned, a single thoroughly detailed event is more instructive than ten that are only touched on."[21] He was referring specifically to examples from history, but the professional interests of these two Royal Engineers enabled them to see Gravelotte as the exception that proved the rule. The rest of the military world—if they noticed the shelter trenches at all—merely dismissed them as exceptions.

The wars at the turn of the century in South Africa, Cuba, the Philippines, and Manchuria more nearly resembled the Civil War than they did the successful Prussian campaigns. Smokeless powder, the machine gun, modern artillery with high explosives, and the extensive use of entrenchments forced an extension of the battle lines and made existing tactical forms largely obsolete. But this was not the lesson learned by most observers. Again, as in 1861–1865, professional soldiers tended to discount the significance of wars that were not waged by regular armies under conditions that would prevail in Europe. Neither the Spanish army nor the U.S. Army was taken seriously; the Boers had no regular military establishment; the Russians had revealed serious internal weaknesses in recent wars with the Turks; and, although the Germans had trained the modern Japanese army, few Western observers at the time could have set aside prevailing notions of white supremacy. Moreover, in each instance, the terrain differed markedly from that in Europe, which was more heavily populated and enjoyed a good transportation network. Thus, although individual observers noted most of the tactical and technical lessons that these wars had to teach, thanks to the special conditions involved, their elaborately detailed reports had little impact on armies in Europe.[22]

In large measure, this was due to the controlling influence of doctrine, which by the end of the century had evolved in most of the armies in Europe. Though indispensable to a modern army, doctrine can nonetheless impose blinders on the vision of military observers and official historians. It can dictate the questions in the mind of each observer, and—as true of military operations as of any historical materials—no document answers questions that are never asked. Doctrine also tends to form the basis for judgment and to provide the context for evaluating information; here again, it has often unwittingly contributed to distortion.

This is seen clearly in the German Staff history, *The War in South Africa*, a patronizing work in which the officers of the Historical Section of the Great General Staff showed a remarkable tendency to judge events in the light of their own predilections. Thus, "the fighting at Paardeberg strikingly exemplifies the whole significance of the principle underlying the German infantry regulations, namely, that the preliminaries to success in the modern infantry attack are great depth of formation and a limited extent of front at first." The British, it was asserted, had failed in the early battles because they had rigidly adhered to outward forms; and when, as a result, British leaders "sought refuge principally in new forms," the German official history was openly contemptuous. It was not the doctrine that was in error, but its application.[23]

In Manchuria several years later, the Japanese victory convinced German official historians once again of the superiority of their doctrine. They did not ask many searching questions about possible existing differences in the discipline, morale, training, and leadership of the two armies, nor did they inquire whether the Japanese cavalry was victorious because of superior doctrine based on shock tactics or simply because it was better disciplined and better led. Yet it is questions such as these that should determine any valid lessons learned. It was enough for most European officers that the Russian concept of mounted infantry had succumbed to the shock tactics of the Japanese cavalry. Even American cavalrymen turned their backs on the lessons of the Civil War as they applied to their army, for in 1911 it was officially decreed that, henceforth, mounted action was to be "the main role" of American cavalry, and its organization, armament, and instruction "should be with a view to rendering it effective in such action." Cavalrymen who protested the change grumbled, "No matter what our cavalry accomplished in the Civil War, no matter what the tactics we inherited from that war teach, the Germans have long held as a valuable tradition that shock tactics is the main thing so we will adopt it."[24]

The influence of doctrine on official history is indicated by one of the criticisms of the British *Official History of the Russo-Japanese War:* "If the comments in the *Official History* are to have any value for the Army they must be in consonance with the doctrine of war which the General Staff is teaching."[25] The reverse side of this coin is seen in the comment of a distinguished British officer who was attached to the Japanese army throughout the war: "On the actual day of battle naked truths may be picked up for the asking; by the following morning they have already begun to get into their uniforms."[26]

The armies that rushed headlong into war in 1914 ignored the lessons of the Russo-Japanese War. Once the fronts became entrenched, they remained basically static, although new techniques, weapons, and tactics evolved in every army. Aside from the introduction of the tank and military aircraft, probably the most important single innovations were in German tactical doctrine, particularly the elastic defense that had evolved by 1916 and the new Hutier or infiltration tactics that nearly achieved a breakthrough on the Western front in the spring of 1918. This concept for offensive operations was initially proposed, in fact, by a French captain in 1915, but it attracted no support in high places, and so it remained for the Germans, who had captured his pamphlet in a trench raid, to apply the basic ideas. One might ask why it was the Germans "who were the better learners from the common experience." The answer applies also to those who would learn lessons from any war:

> Methodology was a factor in German success. No tactical concept remained in the isolation of pure theory. The better German tacticians judged ideas according to the actual environment in which they would be applied. . . . No tactical concept was a thing-in-itself with inherent strength; concepts crossed the gap from theory to reality.[27]

German Supreme Headquarters directed talented officers, including men of all ranks, to derive principles from recent combat experiences, and the General Staff provided both the organization and the atmosphere that enabled the army to capitalize upon the hard lessons of experience. As Crown Prince Rupprecht acknowledged: "There is no panacea. A formula is harmful. Everything must be applied according to the situation."[28]

Probably no war in history has been more closely scrutinized than World War I. It dominated the psyche of that vast community of sufferers who survived the attrition in trenches, and it served as the basis for all kinds of postwar studies that dealt with everything from the human dimension in combat to mobilization, the influence of technical science, and the political and economic factors in total war. Caught pretty much by surprise in 1914, soldiers who survived the war tried to learn what it could teach about leadership, weaponry, tactics, strategy, and coalition warfare.

The literature varies from such technical works as Baron von Freytag-Loringhoven's *Deductions from the World War* and Commandant Bouvard's *Les Lecons militaires de la guerre* to more specific and generally more useful studies, such as Sir Frederick Maurice's *Lessons of Allied Co-operation: Naval, Military and Air, 1914–1918,* General DeGaulle's *The Army of the Future,* and the future Field Marshal Erwin Rommel's *Attacks.* The war was analyzed in the military schools of every army, where it provided numerous historical examples in minor tactics and troop leading.

Because World War I provided a universal experience, with trench conditions much the same on every front and tactical problems that defied any apparent solution, one might reasonably have expected general agreement about the lessons to be learned from that conflict. Opinion remained sharply divided, however, particularly over the future of new weapons such as the tank and the airplane. To the like of Guilio Douhet, Billy Mitchell, B.H. Liddell Hart, and J.F.C. Fuller, the limited experience with these revolutionary new weapons pointed to a revolution in warfare. For them, the war contained special lessons that more conventional minds failed to fathom. In reading their suggestive books, however, one should keep in mind the observation of a Dutch historian that "however solemnly some people may talk about the lessons of History, the historian is after all only a man sitting at his desk."[29]

The general staffs, too, were selective. The Germans seemed intent on returning to their strategic tradition by stressing the need for "highly mobile and well-trained striking forces to carry out the strategy of decisive manoeuvre," whereas postwar French doctrine increasingly reflected an emphasis on the defensive and methodical battle and firepower. The experience in England underscores Sir Ian Hamilton's assertion that truths on the battlefield quickly don uniforms and march away—in step. In 1932, the chief of the Imperial General Staff formed a War Office committee to examine the lessons of the war by analyzing the official histories to determine whether the army's training manuals were adequately reflecting experience. The experience of this committee illustrates the irreverent definition of doctrine as "the opinion of the senior officer present," for the senior officer in the British army, the new chief of the Imperial General Staff, quickly moved to suppress the report. He was upset because the lessons that the committee had recommended to British soldiers bore a suspicious resemblance to the writings of his anathema, the military reformer and theorist Captain B.H. Liddell Hart. The report, concluding that the instructive lessons of the war "are largely the mistakes of Command," had stressed the following:

> . . . the essential need for surprise, and the means of achieving it; the development of night attacks; the conversion of a 'break-in' into a 'breakthrough' by an accelerated technique of exploitation—employing a completely mechanized force, supported by assault aircraft, and applying quickened means of intercommunication, fuller development of wireless, more forward command . . . less elaborate orders . . . the need for developing the technique of, and training in, the counter-attack and counter-offensive; the need to lighten the infantryman's load and equip him as an athlete; the need to simplify infantry drill and modernise it to accord with modern tactics.[30]

This tendency of each army to select, combine, and read its "own peculiar lesson" continued throughout the interwar years. French soldiers, for example, saw in the Spanish Civil War a confirmation of their doctrine that stressed a tightly controlled battle with tanks employed on a wide front in mass, supported by the artillery and infantry. To a British pioneer in armored warfare, however, the lesson was that the tanks employed in Spain were too small. From Germany, General Heinz Guderian insisted that false lessons were being learned in Spain—too few tanks had been employed at any one time, the Spanish soldiers were poorly trained, and the terrain imposed difficulties.[31]

So wedded was the French army to its own doctrines that it dismissed the obvious lessons of the Polish campaign in 1939. Whereas the Germans closely examined their performance to improve upon their own doctrine and training—one of the lessons learned was that the light divisions established as a sop to the cavalry lacked adequate staying power and should therefore be converted to panzer divisions[32]—the French High Command took the lofty attitude that "we are not Poles, it could not happen here." From France, the lesson of the Polish campaign was "that in future operations the primary role of the tank will be the same as in the past; to assist the infantry in reaching successive objectives."[33]

Throughout World War II, most armies continually reevaluated their experiences for lessons to be learned in waging war effectively. Although it had not been prescribed in army regulations,[34] U.S. commanders and their staffs early fell into the habit of concluding after-action reports with a commentary or summary of lessons drawn from recent experiences. Army Ground Forces observers scanned military operations in every theater, and their reports from the far-flung battlefields were digested and then fed to the army schools and training camps to improve doctrine, tactics, weapons, and equipment. They agreed, for example, that by the late summer of 1943:

> Combined training had been unsatisfactory. Antiaircraft artillery shot down friendly planes; airborne operations were confused; infantry and armored officers told AGF observers that their training in each other's operations had been wholly inadequate. Higher commanders and staff showed inexperience in the planning and coordinating of operations, sometimes unnecessarily employing tanks, tank destroyers, or airborne troops in inappropriate missions, or using them in such driblets that their effectiveness was lost.[35]

In Italy, Headquarters 15th Army Group compiled *A Military Encyclopedia*, some 600 pages, to illustrate "the practical application of the doctrines and methods contained in our manuals and texts under the conditions met in Italy," where the rugged terrain had often required the development of new techniques and revisions in standard tactical doctrine. Similarly, 12th Army Group in France issued a series of ninety brief papers, entitled "Battle Experiences" to help units still in training to profit from the latest combat experiences in fighting Germans.

Significantly, neither army group commander assumed that lessons learned from the specific experience of his command would necessarily apply elsewhere. Lieutenant General Omar N. Bradley cautioned that the experiences of his troops would not necessarily apply to all units in all situations, while Lieutenant General Mark W. Clark stressed that "some of the procedures and methods developed would have been impracticable or unsuitable in other theatres."[36] In other words, a lesson once removed from its original context does not necessarily teach us very much. The troops in New Guinea must have managed a wry smile when they received, as part of the regular distribution, an Eighth Army circular from Field Marshal Montgomery's headquarters in North Africa, detailing how to take out a German tank in the desert! Even von Steuben would have smiled.

From all theaters, lists of lessons reflecting the latest experience poured in. Some merely confirmed principles learned in earlier campaigns; others pointed to such commonplace lessons as the need to "stress water discipline" or to train 100 percent replacements. A special series, entitled "Combat Lessons" conveyed the details from recent operational reports to aid officers everywhere in elaborating tactical doctrine. There were official lessons, and there were also unofficial lessons—that is, the opinions of individual officers and formations that did not necessarily reflect accepted doctrine. A lesson could range all the way in scope or importance from the need to designate men to watch for snipers to a thoughtful appreciation by an English officer in the Far East of that fundamental flaw in the national character that makes the British army "blind to facts until their existence is proved by the text of war"—an observation that would have received hearty endorsement from Major General J.F.C. Fuller and Captain B.H. Liddell Hart, partners in the effort to convince the army and the nation that mechanization held the key to success in future wars. "Without a discovery of the fundamental cause of our fantastically false appreciations," this English philosopher in uniform concluded, "the study of the lessons of Malaya is just a study of symptoms and will not prevent their recurrence."[37]

During the Korean War, Special Regulations (525-85-5) were issued prescribing the procedures for ensuring the rapid collection, evaluation, and application of specific lessons learned in combat operations. The vehicle for disseminating these particular lessons learned was *Combat Information,* a series of training bulletins issued by the Office of the Chief of Army Field Forces at Fort Monroe, Virginia. "Actually, the fighting in Korea has provided few items" that could be described as lessons learned, declared an early issue, although much obviously remained that would have to be relearned:

> The mass of material from Korea . . . reaffirms the soundness of US doctrine, tactics, techniques, organization and equipment. The one great lesson that can be learned . . . is that these must be applied with vigor, imagination, and intelligence.[38]

From all indications, this is one lesson that must be relearned in every war.

Beginning in 1966, army regulations prescribed that "the commander should describe in detail any action, activity, experience, or operation which applies to training or instruction, contributes a lesson learned, or illustrates a success or failure, or indicates a need for change in doctrine, techniques, or procedures," and should identify "any tactical or technical improvisations, innovations, expedients, or strategems which may have been successfully employed by the unit."[39] This is a tall order, and inasmuch as the command report henceforth was required to end with a catalogue of lessons learned, it would be expecting too much from human nature not to see a corresponding increase in the kinds and numbers of lessons each unit learned—and constantly relearned—from its own experiences in Vietnam. Inevitably, the lessons learned portion of the combat after-action report tended to become, as one former staff officer has described it, "a grab bag of training notes, combat tips, personal gripes against higher ups . . . another numbers game, that is a contest to see how many different lessons learned you could list, with very little thought of substance."[40] No doubt this was a useful and perhaps a necessary way to institutionalize combat experience, which was especially important in the Vietnam War because of a rotation system that ensured constant turnover in personnel in each unit. However, one inevitable consequence of this approach surely has been a steady—and perhaps a studied—inflation in more recent lists of lessons learned. The eight-volume *Analysis of Combat Data* for the 1973 Arab-Israeli war contains 162 specific recommendations based on the lessons learned by the official U.S. study group, causing General William E. DePuy to observe that in such massive analytical works, "there is a danger that the central message will become lost in the medium of its transmittal."[41]

If the problem in earlier wars was an inevitable tendency to read one's own experience or convictions into any list of lessons learned, in the age of the computer there is the obvious danger that such lessons—which in former days depended in large measure on insight—have become so abundant that they now become little more than data.

As we study the lessons of recent wars throughout the Third World, what can the experiences of the last two centuries offer by way of lessons learned? First, we should probably ask ourselves what we mean by *lesson*. Does it imply a solution? Are there contradictory lessons? Can a lesson learned in one remote corner of the world be successfully applied elsewhere? Is a lesson anything more than a firm grasp of the obvious, a synonym for any casual observation or hasty conclusion, or perhaps merely the successful application of an accepted principle?

More to the point, if indeed it is a lesson, can we assume that by identifying it, even if we understand it properly, it is always or necessarily "learned"? If so, what did we learn from the honest self-examination conducted by the French army after an intensive study of 1,400 after-action reports dealing with success and failure in the Indochina Campaign? Completed in May 1955 and available in English translation at least as early as April 1969, *Lessons from the Indo-China War*, a three-volume analysis by the French Supreme Command, Far East, embraced the lessons that, "due to their importance and their politico-military character," concerned the High Command level; everything the Armed Forces have learned during the Campaign which would still apply today "should the French be called upon to counter, outside of Europe, a rebellion fed by the same sources"; and all those lessons "of a more general character" that should influence tactical principles.[42] Any U.S. officer who had read this before the nation became enmeshed in the Vietnam War could have learned many of the hard lessons in a much easier and less costly way. One suspects that many items in the French self-examination kept cropping up in redundant lists of lessons learned in American combat after-action reports.

Those who today seem intent on setting aside the hard lessons of experience in Vietnam in order to prepare the army for possible conflict in Europe might be interested to know that the French High Command concluded that many of the lessons they had learned in the Indochina war "had already been learned by the Wehrmacht as a result of its encounters with second-class Soviet divisions when these . . . overran the German positions by force of sheer numbers and . . . advanced relentlessly with no logistic support other than rude four-wheeled wagons without springs."[43]

Why do most of the lessons learned always have to be relearned? Is there no better way to institutionalize costly experience?

We need to be careful about accepting lists of lessons learned as though they exist independently of the individuals who expound, explain, and often promote them. We must always remember that such lessons do not jump out of history, even recent history, on their own; someone has identified them, and it is necessary to know the bases for their selection.

We should understand the reasons why military men in the past have failed sometimes to heed the correct lessons. Often, it has been the result of an inability to understand local conditions or to accept another army or society on its own terms. Sometimes, the guidance to observers has been so specific that the major lessons of a war went unheeded simply because observers had not been instructed to look in different directions; the European reaction to the American Civil War was a case in point. Sometimes, doctrine has narrowed the vision or directed the search, as in the case of the French army after World War I. Often, there has been a failure to appreciate that, once removed from its unique context, a specific lesson loses much of its usefulness. Every experienced historian knows this; perhaps the historical method should have a part of the attempt to identify the fruitful lessons to be learned.

Successful armies throughout history have usually been able to institutionalize lessons learned from their own experiences and from a study of the experiences of others. The German army has been particularly successful in this regard, but our own Army Ground Forces in World War II may also have something to teach us.

In every war in recent history, there have been farsighted or imaginative individuals who discerned the instructive lessons. They were often ignored in their own army. We need to understand those forces at work in a military establishment that cause it to see what it most wants to see and to explain away the unwelcome lessons. How receptive is our army to those individuals who challenge the conventional wisdom?

What is the lifespan of a lesson learned? Are there lessons that survive technological change? In what categories do we expect or assume that they will quickly outlive their usefulness?

Although historians enjoy a distinct advantage in knowing the outcome of an event before they embark on a serious research project, they may also have something to offer even in instances when the outcome is not yet clear. By training, experience, and intuition, historians have learned to be suspicious of tidy generalizations and oversimplification. They instinctively understand that there are factors unique to every situation. They know that there can be more than one valid interpretation, that it is difficult for anyone—including any observer of a military operation—to be completely objective, that the most recent event or development over the long haul may not be the most important, and that not every event signifies a trend. Historians will automatically search their memory or the archives for some meaningful precedent.

Perhaps most important of all, historians look to the past for *understanding*, not necessarily for clinching answers.

To at least this historian, the term *lessons learned* implies, somehow, a quick fix, a list of interchangeable solutions, a one-dimensional assessment of problems requiring understanding as well as identification. Not all of these constitute lessons; many of them remain unlearned; and most are forever having to be relearned.

Insights gained would be a more appropriate concept. Frederick the Great, Napoleon, and Clausewitz would clearly have understood that. Their observations, albeit in a far simpler world, led in most instances to profound understanding, and that is precisely the dimension lacking in our current approach to many situations.

Notes

1. Robert S. Quimby, *The Background of Napoleonic Warfare* (New York: Columbia University Press, 1957), pp. 26–41; Jay Luvaas, ed. and trans., *Frederick the Great on the Art of War* (New York: Free Press, 1966), pp. 51–52.

2. Carl von Clausewitz, *On War*, ed. and trans. by Michael Howard and Peter Paret (Princeton, N.J.: Princeton University Press, 1976), p. 141; Baron de Jomini, *Summary of the Art of War*, trans. by Maj. O.F. Winship and Lieut. E.E. McLean (New York: Putnam, 1854), pp. 12–13.

3. Clausewitz, *On War*, p. 173; Friedrich von Bernhardi, *On War of Today*, 2 vols. (London: Hugh Rees, 1912), vol. I, p. 49; Walter Millis, *Arms and Men: A Study in American Military History* (New Brunswick, N.J.: Rutgers University Press, 1981), p. 7.

4. Luvaas, *Frederick the Great on the Art of War*, p. 52; Thomas Carlyle, *History of Friedrich II of Prussia*, 6 vols. (London: Chapman and Hall, 1886), vol. II, pp. 337–338.

5. Frederick, *The History of My Own Times*, 2 vols. in one (London: G.G.J. and J. Robinson, 1789), vol. I, pp. xiii, xxiv, xxvii; vol. II, p. 130; and *Instruction militaire du Roi de Prusse pour ses generaux* (Frankfort, 1761), p. 84.

6. *Correspondance de Napoleon Ier: Oeuvres de Napoleon Ier a Sainte-Helene*, 32 vols. (Paris: Henri Plon, J. Dumaine, 1858–70), vol. XXXII, p. 243.

7. Frederick, *History of My Own Times*, vol. I, pp. 121–122.

8. Joseph R. Riling, *Baron von Steuben and His Regulations, including a complete facsimile of the original Regulations for the Order and Discipline of the Troops of the United States* (Philadelphia: Ray Riling Arms Books, 1966), pp. 6–7, 128–151.

9. (Jacques A. H. de Guibert) *Observations sur la Constitution militaire et politique des Armees de S.M. Prussienne* (Berlin, 1777), pp. 134–135, 141; le Comte de Mirabeau, *Systeme militaire de la Prusse et Principes de la Tactique actuelle des Troupes les plus perfectionnees* (London, 1788), pp. 237–246.

10. Spenser Wilkinson, *The French Army before Napoleon* (Oxford: Clarendon Press, 1915), pp. 97–98.

11. *Correspondance de Napoleon, vol. XV, pp. 107–110; vol. XXI, pp. 378–379.*

12. J. Holland Rose, *The Personality of Napoleon* (New York: Putnam, 1912), p. 244.

13. See Steven Ross, *From Flintlock to Rifle: Infantry Tactics 1740–1866* (Rutherford, N.J.: Fairleigh Dickinson University Press, 1979), pp. 127–154.

14. Sir Harry Jones, *Journal of the Operations Conducted by the Corps of Royal Engineers* (London: Her Majesty's Stationery Office, 1859), vol. II, pp. 577–578; Major Edmund M. Reilly, *An Account of the Artillery Operations Conducted by the Royal Artillery and Royal Naval Brigade before Sebastopol in 1854–55* (London: Her Majesty's Stationery Office, 1859), p. 201.

15. From *Pierre* (1852), book XXV as quoted in John Bartlett, *Familiar Quotations,* 14th ed. (Boston; Little, Brown, 1968), p. 698.

16. General Viscount Wolseley, *The Soldier's Pocket-book for Field Service,* 5th ed., rev. and enlarged (London, 1886), pp. 178–180. (The first edition was published in 1869.)

17. Jay Luvaas, *The Military Legacy of the Civil War: the European Inheritance* (Chicago: University of Chicago Press, 1959), p. 96.

18. See Gen. W.T. Sherman, *Memoirs of Gen. W.T. Sherman,* 2 vols. (New York: Charles L. Webster, 1891), vol. II, pp. 381–409.

19. As quoted in Timothy K. Nenninger, *The Leavenworth Schools and the Old Army: Education, Professionalism, and the Officer Corps of the United States Army, 1881–1918* (Westport, Conn.: Greenwood Press, 1978), p. 87. Several years previously, English soldiers also complained that their art of war was being made in Germany. See Luvaas, *Military Legacy of the Civil War,* p. 117.

20. C.C. Chesney and Major Stothard, *Reports written during a Continental Tour, in 1871, on subjects connected with the Late War* (London: War Office, 1872), pp. 78–79.

21. Clausewitz, *On War,* p. 173.

22. See, for example, *The Russo-Japanese War: Reports from British Officers attached to the Japanese and Russian Forces in the Field,* 3 vols. (London: His Majesty's Stationery Office, 1908), *passim.*

23. *The War in South Africa Prepared in the Historical Section of the Great General Staff, Berlin,* 2 vols., trans. by Col. W.H.H. Waters (London: John Murray, 1904), vol. I, p. 221; vol. II, pp. 324–344 *passim.*

24. Quoted in Jay Luvaas, "Cavalry Lessons of the Civil War," *Civil War Times Illustrated* 6(January 1968): 31.

25. "The British Army and Modern Conceptions of War," *Edinburgh Review* 213(1911): 338–43.

26. Lieut. General Sir Ian Hamilton, *A Staff Officer's Scrap-Book During the Russo-Japanese War,* 2 vols. (London: Edward Arnold, 1906), vol. I, p. v.

27. Timothy T. Lupfer, *The Dynamics of Doctrine: the Changes in German Tactical*

Doctrine during the First World War, Leavenworth Papers No. 4 (Fort Leavenworth, Kans.: U.S. Army Command and General Staff College, July 1881), p. 55.

28. Ibid., p. 58.

29. Pieter Geyl, *Napoleon For and Against* (New Haven: Yale University Press, 1963), p. 16.

30. "Lessons of the War Committee, *France and Belgium 1915: Somme 1916,*" typescript copy in author's possession; Capt. B.H. Liddell Hart, *The Liddell Hart Memoirs 1895–1968,* 2 vols. (New York: Putnam, 1965), vol. I, p. 212.

31. See Matthew Cooper, *The German Army 1933–1945: Its Political and Military Failure* (New York: Stein and Day, 1978), pp. 130–138; Larry H. Addington, *The Blitzkrieg Era and the German General Staff, 1865–1941* (New Brunswick, N.J.: Rutgers University Press, 1971), pp. 28–42; Col. A. Goutard, *The Battle of France 1940* (London: Frederick Muller, 1958), pp. 19–21; Alistair Horne, *To Lose a Battle: France 1940* (Boston: Little, Brown, 1969), pp. 34–36; Kenneth Macksey, *Tank Warfare: A History of Tanks in Battle* (New York: Stein and Day, 1972), pp. 97–98; B.H. Liddell Hart, *Thoughts on War* (London: Faber and Faber, 1944), p. 35. Far and away the most comprehensive study of what the French learned from World War I is Robert Allan Doughty, "The Seeds of Disaster: the Development of French Army Doctrine, 1919–1939," unpublished manuscript, ca. 1984.

32. Williamson Murray, "The German Response to Victory in Poland: A Case Study in Professionalism," *Armed Forces and Society* 7(Winter 1981): 285–98.

33. Horne, *To Lose a Battle,* p. 133.

34. AR 345-105, Changes No. 2 (January 15, 1943), specifies only that written reports by all commanders "each in what concerns his own command . . . will have annexed thereto the unit and staff journals, together with their supporting documents."

35. Kent Roberts Greenfield, Robert R. Palmer, and Bell I. Wiley, *The Army Ground Forces: The Organization of Ground Combat Troops* (Washington, D.C.: Department of the Army Historical Division, 1947), p. 412; Robert R. Palmer, Bell I. Wiley, and William R. Kenst, *The Army Ground Forces: The Procurement and Training of Ground Combat Troops* (Washington, D.C.: Department of the Army Historical Division, 1948), p. 428.

36. Allied Forces, 15th Army Group, *A Military Encyclopedia* (n.p., n.d.), pp. xxi–xxii; HQ FUSAG, "Battle Experiences," no. 1 (12 July–11 November 1944), p. 1.

37. "Lessons from Malaya," Military Attache Report, October 10, 1942, p. 2. (Copy in U.S. Army Military History Institute Archives.)

38. Office of the Chief of Army Field Forces, Fort Monroe, Virginia, *Combat Information,* Training Bulletin No. 5, 27 September 1951, p. 1. Throughout this series, the soundness of the then-current army doctrine was upheld, and increasingly the bulletins were published "to provide illustrative combat examples for the lectures and discussions of trainers" and "to explain useful 'tricks of the trade.'"

39. AR 1–19, 26 May 1966, required commanders to "describe in detail any action, activity, experience, or operation which applies to training or instruction, contributes a lesson learned, or illustrates a success or failure, or indicates a need for change in doctrine, techniques, or procedures." See also AR 525–15, *Military Operations: Operational Reports—Lessons Learned* (Washington, D.C., 25 September 1969).

40. This generalization is based on a representative sampling of the many issues of *Operational Reports—Lessons Learned* housed on the shelves of the U.S. Army Military

History Institute and on private information from officers who had been involved in the process.

41. Headquarters, U.S. Army Training and Doctrine Command, *Annual Report of Major Activities FY 1975*, pp. 1–10, 139; "General William E. DePuy to Chief of Staff, U.S. Army," 21 June 74, is a draft analysis of combat data from the 1973 Middle East war. (Copy in author's possession.)

42. The Supreme Command, Far East, *Lessons from the Indo-China War*, 3 vols. (Saigon, 1955), vol. II, pp. 1–2. (Copy of the typescript translation in U.S. Military History Institute.)

43. Ibid., vol.IIII, pp. 1–4.

4
Measuring Combat Effectiveness: Historical-Quantitative Analysis

T.N. Dupuy

The failure of the United States to perform military historical analysis of combat in the fashion pioneered by the Prussian and German Army General Staffs, and now used in the current Soviet Armed Forces General Staff, has been deplored in my own and other recent publications.[1] However, those who have not read these publications or have not been persuaded by them may ask what can be learned from military historical analysis that cannot be learned more precisely and more scientifically from modern operations research analysis. Such people may also ask if military history analysis can be useful and how it can be applied to experience of recent wars.

The answer to the first question is easy. For several years, the U.S. Army has been exhorting its officers to "fight outnumbered and win" by using "combat multipliers." However, none of our operations research centers or analysts has been able to provide any specificity to that exhortation. Yet, as will be demonstrated in this chapter, a methodology based on military history analysis—the Quantified Judgment Model (QJM)—can and does provide such specificity.

The answer to the second question is a bit less easy, because we do not have very good statistical data on these recent wars. Nevertheless, as I shall demonstrate, the same QJM methodology can be adapted to gain improved insights and understanding of these recent Third World conflicts.

First, however, a word is necessary about the methodology and its origins. Most students of military affairs will agree that about a century and a half ago, Carl von Clausewitz wrote the most profound book ever written about war, conflict, combat, and military theory: *On War*. I certainly believe that, but I do not agree with most of the scholars and military analysts who solemnly assure us that Clausewitz eschewed rigid quantitative approaches. I differ, for instance, from a widely accepted assessment of Clausewitz that states: "He distrusted set theories of war based upon mathematical computations or geometric patterns."[2]

This chapter is a synthesis of work previously published or in preparation: *Options of Command* (New York: Hippocrene, 1984) (appendix); "Let's Get Serious About Combat Multipliers," *Army* 33 (May 1983):18–25; and a book in preparation about the June 1982 war in Lebanon.

My own studies of Clausewitz and of the nature of combat have slowly led me to the conclusion that such statements reflect a profound misunderstanding of the theory of war that Clausewitz produced and presented in incomplete—but nonetheless coherent and consistent—form in *On War*. This is not an abstract issue of interest and importance only to historians. Rather, I am asserting a truth that can lead to a new, forward-looking theory of combat—and tool of analysis—essentially based on Clausewitz's deterministic, predictive, mathematically based theoretical concept.

Just as Newton's physics can be summarized by a simple formula ($F = MA$), so, too, Clausewitz's theory of combat can be summarized in an equally simple formula: $P = NVQ$, where P is combat power, N is numbers of troops, V is the operational and environmental variable factors that indicate the circumstances of a battle, and Q is the quality of the troops.

The basis for this is Clausewitz's Law of Numbers, in which he described his concept of battle outcome as a ratio, as follows:

> If we . . . strip the engagement of all the variables arising from its purpose and circumstances, and disregard [or strip out] the fighting value of the troops involved (which is a given quantity), we are left with the bare concept of the engagement . . . in which the only distinguishing factor is the number of troops on either side.
>
> These numbers, therefore, will determine victory [and are] the most important factor[s] in the outcome of an engagement. . . .
>
> This . . . would hold true for Greeks and Persians, for Englishmen and Mahrattas, for Frenchmen and Germans.[3]

This analytical concept of battle outcome can be expressed mathematically as follows:

$$\text{Outcome} = \frac{N_r \cdot V_r \cdot Q_r}{N_b \cdot V_b \cdot Q_b} = \frac{P_r}{P_b}$$

where N = numbers of troops
V = variable circumstances affecting a force in battle
Q = quality of force
r = red force identifier
b = blue force identifier
P = combat power

If that is a valid relationship—as Clausewitz asserts and I maintain fervently—then we can write the simple combat power equation for each of the opposing sides as follows:

"So what?" the reader may ask. What good does it do me—or anyone else—to know that Clausewitz had a theory for mathematical representation of the outcome of combat encounters? First, to anyone who is interested in putting real meaning into the concept of combat multipliers—so glibly referred to in current U.S. Army literature[4]—it offers a promise of mathematical specificity. In particular, it provides an independent basis for corroboration of the concept of the Quantified Judgment Model (QJM), which, until now, has given us the only serious basis for understanding and using combat multipliers.[5]

A summary of the QJM concept—virtually identical to that of Clausewitz's Law of Numbers—is as follows: The QJM provides a basis for comparing the relative combat power—and combat effectiveness—of two opposing forces in historical combat by determining the influence of environmental and operational variables on the force strengths of the two opponents. The model is applied to statistics of selected historical engagements and produces values for the combat power of each of the opposing forces under the circumstances of the engagement and a combat power ratio to ascertain—on the basis of data available in the records—which of the opposing sides should theoretically have been successful in the engagement, and by what margin.

This combat power ratio is then compared to a quantification value of the actual outcome of the battle. This outcome value represents the comparative performance of the opposing forces in terms of (1) their accomplishments of their respective missions, (2) their ability to gain or hold ground, and (3) their efficiency in terms of casualties incurred. If the combat power ratio of Force A with respect to Force B is greater than 1.0, then the result ratio for Force A should also be greater than 1.0. In the event that the combat power ratio is not consistent with the result ratio values, further exploration is necessary to explain the discrepancy. In such cases, the discrepancy is usually due to behavioral considerations, most likely the effects of surprise, or to a difference in the relative combat effectiveness of the two sides. When the effects of surprise are stripped out, the residual difference between the combat power ratio and the result ratio is a reflection of the relative combat effectiveness of the opponents.

QJM analyses have shown patterns of relative combat effectiveness values (CEV) in different forces; in World Wars I and II, the Germans had a CEV of about 1.20 with respect to the Western Allies and about 2.50 with respect to the Russians. This means that 100 Germans in combat were the equivalent of about 120 British or Americans and about 250 Russians, also in combat units. In the recent Arab-Israeli wars, the average Israeli CEV has been about 2.00; thus, 100 Israelis in combat units were the equivalent of some 200 Arabs in combat units.

This concept is expressed mathematically as a three-step process. The first step is to calculate the lethality effects of the weapons with which the opposing forces are equipped. This is done in a straightforward, consistent application of standards or procedures to the characteristics of the weapons in relationship to a standardized target array. The principal characteristics considered are rate of fire, relative incapacitating effect, number of targets affected by one weapon strike, range or muzzle velocity of a firepower weapon, reliability, and accuracy. For mobile fighting machines, such as tanks and aircraft, three additional criteria are considered: radius of action, speed, and the ability to absorb punishment. This procedure provides us with what we call the theoretical lethality index (TLI).

A final consideration is the normal tactical dispersion of real-world targets in comparison with the standardized target array used to calculate TLIs. As weapons have become more lethal over the last several centuries, troops have had to be increasingly dispersed on the battlefield to reduce the increasing deadliness of the effects. This relationship is a quantifiable factor, which, when applied to the TLI, provides us with an operational lethality index (OLI). The OLI is a measure of the lethality of the weapon against normal tactical deployments but under ideal conditions in which the degrading effects of various battlefield circumstances are not considered. The OLI can thus be considered a "proving ground" measurement of the weapon's effectiveness. In our formulas, we represent this measurement by the symbol W.

In the next step, force strength (S) is equal to the sum of OLI values for the available firepower—infantry (n), antitank (gi), artillery (g), air defense weapons (gy), armor (L), and air support (y)—after each of these components has been modified by all applicable variable factors affecting weapons effectiveness and by such variables as weather, terrain, and season. The formula for this can be expressed as follows:

$$S = (W_n \cdot V_n) + (W_{gi} \cdot V_{gi}) + (W_g \cdot V_g) + (W_{gy} \cdot V_{gy}) + (W_i \cdot V_i) + (W_y \cdot V_y)$$

In the third step, force strength is modified by a number of other operational and environmental variables—called force effect factors—to yield a value for combat power potential (P). The most important of these variable factors are surprise (*surp*, where present), mobility (m), posture (p), vulnerability (v), applicable considerations of terrain (r), weather (h), season (z), and intangible behavior factors such as leadership (le), training/experience (t), morale (o), and logistical capability (b).

Values for all of these variables—except the intangibles—were originally derived by a group of military men—infantrymen, artillerymen, tankers, and airmen with World War II combat experience—as they endeavored to quantify the effects of these variables on a set of sixty division-sized engagements that took place in Italy in 1943 and 1944. These values were tested and confirmed in analyses of another set of twenty-one battle-division engagements in Northwest Europe in 1944.

Although it proved impossible to isolate values for most of the intangibles, it soon became evident that there was a discernible value for the effect of *all* of the intangibles, in combination, on battle outcomes. This combined value of intangible effects was termed a relative combat effectiveness value (CEV).

The QJM values for the effects of surprise are postulated on the assumption that there are two principal effects: enhancement of the mobility characteristics of the side achieving surprise, and a decrease in the vulnerability of the surpriser accompanied by an increase in the vulnerability of the side that is surprised. The application of this assumption to battles in which surprise is known to have had an effect has consistently given good results in comparison with the historical outcomes.

The manner in which these force effects factors modify the previously calculated force strength (*S*) is shown as follows:

$$P = S \cdot surp \cdot m \cdot p \cdot v \cdot r \cdot h \cdot z \cdot \underbrace{le \cdot t \cdot o \cdot b}_{CEV}$$

The basic QJM formula can be further simplified by consolidating the intangible or behavioral variables as one variable, CEV, and combining all of the other operational variables as *V*. The general formula, then, can be expressed as follows:

$$P = S \cdot V \cdot CEV$$

Note the similarity of this simplified QJM formula to the formula shown earlier to represent Clausewitz's theory of combat:

$$P = N \cdot V \cdot Q$$

When Clausewitz referred to "numbers" in *On War,* particularly in his Law of Numbers, he was clearly thinking of the composite strengths of infantrymen, cavalrymen, and cannon. Thus, the symbol *N*, which appears in the formula converting that law into mathematical terms, is in reality the same kind of entity that is called force strength in the QJM. In other words, Clausewitz's *N* and the *S* of the QJM are virtually identical. It is equally clear that CEV in the QJM is conceptually identical with *Q* in the Clausewitz formula.

Now we can apply the QJM, and Clausewitz's Law of Numbers, to the quantification of combat multipliers, which are, of course, the described force effects factors.

A consolidation of rules for using the QJM—the *QJM Rule Book*—provides either tables for these factors or rules for calculating those that are not tabular. Some of the more important of these rules are as follows:

Terrain: A table of values has been developed for this variable (see table 4–1).

Weather: A table of values has been developed for this factor (see table 4–2).

Table 4–1
Combat Defense Terrain Multipliers

Terrain Characteristics	Multiplier	Terrain Characteristics	Multiplier
1. Rugged—heavily wooded	1.50	9. Rolling gentle—bare	1.20
2. Rugged—mixed (or extra rugged—bare)	1.55	10. Flat—heavily wooded	1.10
		11. Flat—mixed	1.20
3. Rugged—bare	1.45	12. Flat—bare, hard	1.05
4. Rolling foothills—heavily wooded	1.35	13. Flat desert	1.18
5. Rolling foothills—mixed	1.45	14. Rolling dunes	1.40
6. Rolling foothills—bare	1.30	15. Swamp—jungle	1.40
7. Rolling gentle—heavily wooded	1.20	16. Swamp—mixed or open	1.30
		17. Urban	1.40
8. Rolling gentle—mixed	1.30		

Table 4–2
Weather Multipliers

Weather Characteristics	Attacker Multiplier[a]
1. Dry sunshine—extreme heat	1.0
2. Dry sunshine—temperate	1.0
3. Dry sunshine—extreme cold	0.9
4. Dry overcast—extreme heat	1.0
5. Dry overcast—temperate	1.0
6. Dry overcast—extreme cold	0.9
7. Wet-light—extreme heat	0.9
8. Wet-light—temperate	0.9
9. Wet-light—extreme cold	0.9
10. Wet-heavy—extreme heat	0.6
11. Wet-heavy—temperate	0.7
12. Wet-heavy—extreme cold	0.6

[a]For defender, the value is always 1.0.

Table 4–3
Season Multipliers

Season	Attacker Multiplier[a]			
	Desert	*Temperate*	*Semitropical*	*Tropical*
Winter (January)	1.00	1.00	1.05	1.10
Spring and summer (April)	1.00	1.10	1.10	1.10
Fall (December)	1.00	1.00	1.05	1.10

[a]Defender value is always 1.00.

Table 4–4
Defense Posture Multipliers

Posture	Multiplier
1. Attack	1.00
2. Defense, hasty	1.30
3. Defense, prepared	1.50
4. Defense, fortified	1.60
5. Withdrawal	1.15
6. Delay	1.20
7. Holding (both sides)	1.20

Season: These effects relate mostly to hours of daylight and amount of foliage; values are shown in table 4–3.

Posture: The values in table 4–4 are, in effect, a quantification of Clausewitz's statement that the "defense is the stronger form of combat."

Mobility: This factor is calculated from a formula that considers the mobility characteristics of a force in relation to its manpower strength and the effects of weather and terrain on mobility.

Vulnerability: This factor is calculated from a formula that reflects the strength of a force, its posture, the nature of the terrain, and the effects of air superiority.

Surprise: This factor is calculated from a formula that reflects the effects of surprise on mobility and vulnerability, with due consideration given to other circumstances of the engagement.

Relative combat effectiveness value (CEV): This factor is calculated by dividing the outcome ratio (R/R) by the combat power ratio (P/P). It is based on the assumption that any substantial deviation of the outcome ratio from the combat power ratio is due to a difference in the quality—combat effectiveness—of the two forces. This, then, is the "given quality" for the value of the force to which Clausewitz refers. Its principal components are assumed to be leadership and training, but it also includes such other intangibles as morale, logistical capability, and the effects of chance or luck.

To see how all this works, I have selected a number of historical battles in which the successful force was outnumbered by its opponent; that is, the successful force was able to fight outnumbered and win (see table 4–5). In most instances, the victory was due essentially to the successful use of the various combat multipliers. In all instances, Clausewitz's Law of Numbers was applicable.

First, let us examine the figures in table 4–5 for the Battle of Austerlitz, where Napoleon won one of the most decisive battles of history against a more numerous army of Austrians and Russians. The principal factor in the scale of the victory was the relative combat effectiveness (CEV) of the French; at least three-fourths of this superiority, of course, was the generalship of Napoleon.

Next is the Battle of Antietam. Strategically, General McClellan was able to claim that he had stopped the Confederate invasion of the North. On the battlefield, however, his poorly coordinated efforts were repulsed by General Lee and the Army of Northern Virginia with the help of defensive posture and good use of terrain. The decisive factor was the superior combat effectiveness of Lee's army. If one assumes that the quality of troops was roughly equal on both sides— as one must after a study of Livermore's *Numbers and Losses in the Civil War*[7]— then the sole differential was generalship; if Lee was a 10.0, then it seems historically reasonable that McClellan was a 6.6.

For a World War I example, I have chosen the second phase of the German Somme offensive—the Battle of Montdidier. During the Peronne phase of the offensive (March 21–26), the Germans had overwhelmed the British Fifth Army in a surprise offensive that broke through the Allied lines. By March 27, however, the Allies had sealed the gap and, though still outnumbered and still being driven back, had at least rejoined the battle. British air power reduced the effect of German numerical superiority to some extent but of course could not offset the German qualitative superiority of 20 to 30 percent—a margin of superiority that they held over the Western Allies in much of World Wars I and II. However, the multipliers of defensive posture and terrain provided the Allied strength enhancement that finally repulsed the Germans.

As other examples, I have chosen two World War II battles, in both of which the Germans were successful though outnumbered. The first of these was the crossing of the Meuse River at Sedan by General Guderian's panzer corps. It should be noted that even though Guderian was outnumbered, he had massive air support, which gave him a substantial firepower superiority. He also had the benefit of the disruptive effects of surprise upon the French. It was essentially this multiplier, and the German combat effectiveness superiority multiplier, that more than offset the French multiplicative advantages of defensive posture and terrain.

The second World War II example is the attack of the American 34th Infantry Division against the badly battered German 3rd Panzer Grenadier Division in Operation Diadem during the Allied advance upon Rome in May 1943. Note that the Americans had virtually a three-to-one numerical advantage. Yet the Germans, despite low morale and the devastating effects of Allied air interdiction on their logistical system, were able to use the defensive strength of the C (Caesar) Line and the advantage of their residual combat effectiveness superiority to stop the Americans in a bitter four-day battle.

Next is a battle from the 1973 Middle East war—the so-called Battle of the Chinese Farm. This was the attack by General Bren Adan's division to restore communications with General Ariel Sharon's division, which had been cut off by an Egyptian counterattack after crossing the Suez Canal. Although the attacking Israelis were outnumbered about five-to-four, they had a substantial advantage in air support and so had a slight overall preponderance in firepower. That would have been insufficient to overcome the Egyptian multiplier advantages of terrain and defensive posture, however, were it not for the continuing disruptive effects of surprise on the Egyptians, plus a substantial combat effectiveness superiority.

It is perhaps instructive to note that in at least one instance in that war, the Israelis fought outnumbered and did *not* win. The Israelis had a slight terrain advantage and a substantial posture advantage, and they had an even more substantial combat effectiveness advantage. However, the Egyptians, thanks to surprise and thanks to their careful plans and rehearsals for the set-piece battle, had multipliers that—when applied to their substantially greater numerical and firepower advantages—assured a major Arab success. We must never forget that multipliers can and do work for both sides. We must also remember, as Clausewitz told us, that numbers win battles.

To show how this approach to combat multipliers could be of use to commanders who might have to fight outnumbered and who could hope to win with judicious use of multipliers, I have included in table 4–5 a hypothetical Battle of Fulda, in which a U.S. mechanized division must be prepared to face an assault by a Warsaw Pact combined arms army.

Let us assume, therefore, that you are a division commander in some unlikely place, such as Fulda, Germany, and that you must contemplate a possible attack by a Soviet combined arms army. The following portrays the possible mathematics of your potential battle. With a total manpower strength of 20,200 men, you can probably expect to be attacked by a force of 58,285, nearly a three-to-one enemy superiority. Considering the likely levels of air support for both sides, and using the OLI methodology of the QJM, you calculate the value of the firepower that you can bring to bear as 355,943 for your division and 1,740,697 for the anticipated attacker. That gives the enemy a raw firepower preponder-

Table 4–5
Battle Analyses

Forces[a]	Manpower (N)	Multiplicand (W)	Composite Environmental Variables (env)	Terrain (r)	Weather (h)	Season (z)	Posture (p)
Austerlitz (1805)							
A. *French*	75,000	161,865	0.87	1.2	1.0	1.0	1.15
D. Allies	89,000	185,580	0.88	1.2	1.0	1.0	1.15
Antietam (1862)							
A. Union	80,000	346,750	0.88	1.0	1.0	1.1	1.0
D. *Confederates*	45,000	194,940	0.88	1.3	1.0	1.0	1.3
Montdidier (Somme Phase II, 1918)							
A. Germans	600,000	10,424,000	0.98	1.0	1.0	1.0	1.0
D. *Allies*	500,000	10,157,500	0.97	1.2	1.0	1.0	1.4
Sedan (Meuse River, 1940)							
A. *Germans*	48,000	374,221*	0.56	1.0	1.0	1.1	1.0
D. French	60,000	154,339	0.75	1.45	1.0	1.0	1.3
Lanuvio (Operation Diadem, 1943)							
A. Americans	17,300	78,520	0.59	1.0	1.0	1.1	1.0
D. *Germans*	6,108	40,270	0.76	1.3	1.0	1.0	1.6
Chinese Farm (1973)							
A. *Israelis*	28,700	704,049*	0.74	1.0	1.0	1.0	1.0
D. Egyptians	36,840	690,398	0.88	1.2	1.0	1.0	1.4
Suez Canal (North, 1973)							
A. *Egyptians*	29,490	555,717	0.65	1.0	1.0	1.0	1.0
D. Israelis	4,455	187,571	0.69	1.13	1.0	1.0	1.55
Hypothetical Battle of Fulda (A)							
A. *Warsaw Pact army*	58,285	1,740,697	0.75	1.00	0.9	1.1	1.0
D. U.S. division	20,200	355,943	0.75	1.45	1.0	1.0	1.3
Hypothetical Battle of Fulda (B)							
A. Warsaw Pact army	58,285	1,740,697	0.75	1.00	0.9	1.1	1.0
D. *U.S. division*	20,200	355,943	0.75	1.45	1.0	1.0	1.5
New multiplier effects:							1.5

[a]A = attacker; D = defender. Winning side is in italics.

Table 4–5
Battle Analyses (*continued*)

Mobility (m)	Vulnerability (v)	Surprise (surp)	Combat Power (P)	Combat Power Ratio (P/P)	Relative Combat Effectiveness (CEV)	Outcome (R/R)	Remarks
1.10	1.0	1.6	342,030	1.52	2.93	3.70	Allies attacked
1.00	1.0	1.0	225,368	0.66	0.41	0.27	first; French counterattacked
1.00	1.0	1.0	335,654	1.16	0.66	0.77	
1.00	1.0	1.0	289,914	0.86	1.51	1.30	
0.94	1.0	1.0	9,602,589	0.58	1.30	0.76	
1.00	1.0	1.0	16,552,662	1.72	0.77	1.32	
1.16	0.77	1.46	300,615	1.97	1.37	2.70	*German firepower
1.00	0.70	1.00	152,738	0.51	0.73	0.37	superiority due to massive air support, somewhat degraded by environmental factors
0.84	0.73	1.0	31,248	0.55	1.20	0.65	*German CEV
1.00	0.90	1.0	57,293	1.83	0.83*	1.53	factor includes factors for morale (0.9) and logistics (0.81), suggesting actual CEV of 1.14.
1.17	0.94	2.19	1,254,852	1.27	1.66	2.10	*Israeli firepower
1.00	0.97	1.00	990,064	0.79	0.60	0.48	superiority due to air support, somewhat degraded by environmental factors
0.65	0.93	3.84*	530,602	2.42	0.58	1.41	*Includes a surprise
1.0	0.97	1.00	218,912	0.41	1.72	0.71	factor of 2.43 and a set-piece factor of 1.58
1.2	0.95	?	1,339,428	2.86	?	?	
1.0	0.93	?	467,989	0.35	?	?	
1.2	0.95	1.0	1,339,428	1.20	0.67	0.80	
1.0	0.96	2.0	114,813	0.83	1.50	1.25	
	1.03	2.0			1.50		Product: 3.55

ance of 4.89. In other words, the Soviets will enter the battle with nearly a five-to-one firepower superiority.

The raw numerical odds, therefore, are pretty grim. But you know that you have some advantages accruing from your defensive posture, which will probably outweigh some additional advantages the enemy is likely to have. For instance, according to table 4–1, you have a terrain multiplier advantage of 1.45. Table 4–2 tells you that in the likely weather conditions, the enemy strength will be degraded by a factor of 0.9, but this will be offset by a seasonal advantage in the best fighting months of the year. You can hope for plenty of warning, but you can't be sure of it, so you may not have time to carry out all of the planned defensive preparations, and you may be forced to fight in a hasty defense posture, which has a multiplier value of 1.3. A systematic calculation of the relative mobility characteristics of the forces indicates that the Warsaw Pact will have a 1.2 mobility multiplier advantage. A similar calculation of vulnerability shows that, despite your defensive posture, under the anticipated circumstances of the battle, the enemy's vulnerability will be slightly less than yours.

When you apply all of these factors to the initial opposing firepower strengths, you find that you have substantially reduced the odds, but the enemy still has a combat ratio superiority over your force of 2.86:1.00—in other words, still nearly three-to-one.

What can you do about it? The first step is to improve your defensive position. There are a number of things you can do to make it easier for your division to have the advantage of prepared defenses at the outset, even with scanty warning. For one thing, you might make a trip north to see what the British are doing in this regard. Whether or not you can get your corps commander to allow you to do what the British have done is questionable, but let's assume you can do such things and—without arousing too much antagonism among the local German farmers—perhaps even a bit more. The multiplier factor for prepared defense is 1.50, instead of 1.30. Thus, you have achieved a multiplier enhance of 1.20. This, in turn, will provide a slight enhancement to your vulnerability multiplier.

These two multiplier enhancements are not enough, however. You have only chipped at the surface of the 2.86:1.00 odds against you. You must resort to the two means that historically have been most important in enabling outnumbered commanders to defeat more powerful foes. You must figure out some way to surprise the enemy, and you must devote every possible waking thought and effort to improving the quality of your troops.

I am not about to suggest the specifics by which an outnumbered defender can achieve surprise. There is a rich historical record that can be reviewed for inspiration, however, and I hope that you and your staff and subordinate commanders can concoct a really unexpected welcome for the potential attackers. You might even be justified in estimating that your surprise will double your combat power. Doing the multiplier arithmetic, you find that this is not enough (though, of course, it may be if your surprise works better than you can dare hope).

You would be wise to assume that the enemy will still have a 1.20:1.00 advantage over your division. To have reasonable confidence in success, you will need to work on improvement of troop quality.

Improvement of the quality of troops is easy to discuss but not easy to accomplish. There is no easy road, but there is another historical example to inspire you. Through an imaginative, intensive training program and other measures within his grasp as a division commander in 1943 and 1944, Major General John Sloan was able to give his 88th Infantry Division a combat effectiveness superiority over divisions raised at about the same time. One result was that the rueful commander of the German Tenth Army called Sloan's men "Storm Troops" and shifted his reserves to counter the anticipated Allied main effort when the 88th Division was committed in the Italian battle line. It *has* been done! It *can* be done!

If you are as successful in your training and readiness program as General Sloan was, you should be able to increase your combat effectiveness (CEV) by a factor of 1.5. The result is a comfortable overall combat power margin of superiority over your potential enemy of 1.25:1.00.

Thus, it is evident that quantitative analysis of war experience, along the lines suggested by Clausewitz, can be very useful to our commanders who are exhorted to use combat multipliers to "fight outnumbered and win." However— as suggested at the beginning of this chapter—quantitative analysis of this sort can also provide insights with respect to recent wars, even though the data are sketchy for these conflicts.

To perform the QJM analyses summarized in table 4–5 required reasonably complete and accurate data. With the possible exception of the Falkland Islands campaign in 1982, no such data are available for any of the recent wars with which this book is concerned. Nevertheless, even if the data are sketchy, it is possible to adapt the QJM methodology to a somewhat less precise analysis of such wars, thereby getting a better understanding of what happened, and why, and how.

For instance, let us take the Israeli campaign in Lebanon in June 1982. We do not have sufficient data for a detailed QJM analysis. However, we do know enough about the forces engaged, the losses incurred, and the movement rates of the Israeli forces to perform a very useful analysis of the combat of Israeli and Syrian forces, using a modified QJM approach.

In brief, approximately 60,000 Israeli troops, in four divisions plus miscellaneous forces, invaded Lebanon on June 6, 1982. Of these, nearly 30,000 focused their attention on PLO forces in southwestern and western Lebanon. The remainder, after a short advance, halted when they came in contact with scattered Syrian units in southeastern Lebanon. These Israeli troops, organized into a corps-type unit of two divisions plus other units—about 32,000 men in strength—were designated the Bekaa Forces Group (BFG), commanded by Major General Avigdor Ben Gal. Except for some patrol activity and some exchanges of artillery fire with the Syrians to their front, the BFG had little activity on June 7 and 8. This was consistent with the Israeli announcement that they would not attack the Syrians if the Syrians did not become involved in the fighting against the PLO. During this time, of course, the Israelis in western Lebanon were smashing the PLO and driving the remnants back toward Beirut. Late on June 8, near Jezzine, just west of General Ben Gal's command, an Israeli brigade that would come under his command the next day had a severe fight with a Syrian brigade, defeated it, and drove it north toward the Beirut–Damascus highway (see figure 4–1).

Late on June 8, and early on June 9, the Israelis in the BFG came under heavy Syrian artillery fire. It is not clear whether or not this was because the Israelis provoked the Syrians into an artillery exchange. In any event, early on June 9, Syrian aircraft attacked elements of the BFG. The Israelis concluded, therefore, that the Syrians were not heeding their warning, and they decided to attack the Syrians in the Bekaa Valley. It is quite possible that, having virtually destroyed the PLO military organization, the Israelis were looking for an excuse for attacking the Syrians.

The Syrians had established a prepared defensive line across the southern Bekaa Valley, taking advantage of rugged Jebel Arabi, which fits like a bottle stopper in the southern valley. This position continued up the slopes of the even more rugged mountains east and west of the valley. In these positions were the bulk of a Syrian armored division and several commando battalions. The total Syrian force was about 20,000 men and 350 tanks. It was the right flank brigade of this force that had been attacked and driven back north of Jezzine late on June 8.

The two main thrusts of General Ben Gal's BFG were along the mountain roads on the slopes east and west of the Bekaa Valley. Soon after the ground troops began to smash their way through the Syrian positions, the Israeli Air Force attacked Syrian air defense missiles along the Beirut–Damascus highway and, in one of the most dramatic successes ever achieved in air-ground warfare, destroyed seventeen missile batteries without the loss of a single Israeli aircraft.

On June 9, the Israelis advanced steadily, driving through the Syrian position in the mountains on both flanks and forcing a general Syrian withdrawal. By the end of the day, Israeli spearheads had advanced more than 12 kilometers. The Syrians had already moved elements of their 3rd Tank Division into Lebanon to take up positions in another previously prepared defensive line just south of the Beirut–Damascus highway. Now they rushed the remainder of that division from the vicinity of Homs toward the front. One brigade of the division was badly damaged when it was hit on the road by the Israeli Air Force near Zahle early on June 10.

The fighting on June 10 was very little different from that on June 9. The

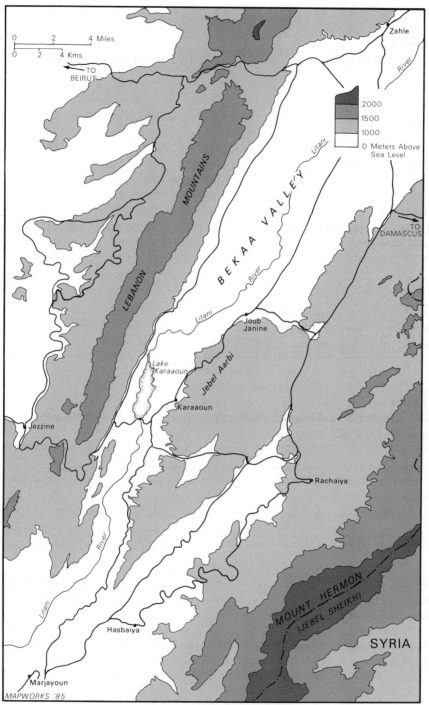

Figure 4–1. The Bekaa Valley

Table 4–6
Syrian and Israeli Force Strengths, Bekaa Valley Battle, June 8–11, 1982

	Israeli	Syrian
Troops	32,000	35,000
Tanks	750	700
Aircraft available for close support	275	225
Nonorganic air defense missiles (SAMs)	—	100

Table 4–7
Opposing Syrian and Israeli Force Strengths, Bekaa Valley Battle, Phase I, June 8–9, 1982

	Israeli	Syrian
Troops	32,000	20,000
Tanks	750	350
Aircraft available for close support	275	0
Nonorganic air defense missiles (SAMs)	—	0

Table 4–8
Opposing Syrian and Israeli Force Strengths, Bekaa Valley Battle, Phase II, June 10–11, 1982

	Israeli	Syrian
Troops	31,000	25,000
Tanks	700	400
Aircraft available for close support	225	0
Nonorganic air defense missiles (SAMs)	—	0

Syrians, despite their reinforcements, fell back to new positions south of the highway, and there they dug in. Cease-fire negotiations were begun, and a cease-fire went into effect at noon on June 11.

Now we are ready for the analysis. Table 4–6 shows the total forces deployed by Israel and Syria in the less than three days of fighting in and around the Bekaa Valley. It must be realized, however, that the Syrians added forces piecemeal during the battle. Table 4–7 shows the opposing force strengths late on June 8, when the first serious fighting broke out between Israeli and Syrian forces. Table 4–8 shows the opposing strengths early on June 10, after the Syri-

Table 4–9
Israeli and Syrian Losses, Bekaa Valley Battle, June 8–11, 1982

	Israeli	*Syrian*
Personnel		
Killed	205	800
Wounded	1,080	3,200
Missing	1	150
Total[a]	1,286	4,150
Tanks	30[b]	400
Aircraft	1	90
Nonorganic air defense missiles (SAMs)	0	76
Percentage casualties per day	1.36	5.03
Casualties by 100 per day	4.39	1.56
Inherent casualty capability per 100 per day[c]	4.39	0.74

[a]Total Israeli losses for the war (up to June 17, 1982) were 1407 (it is estimated that 90 percent of these were inflicted by the Syrians), losses against the PLO were 121.

[b]Minor damage was inflicted on perhaps 100 more Israeli tanks.

[c]Average Israeli strength, over three days: 31,500. Average Syrian strength, over three days: 27,500.

ans rushed reinforcements to the Bekaa Valley. Finally, table 4–9 is an estimate of casualties and major materiel losses of the opposing sides.

To undertake a meaningful analysis without detailed order-of-battle information, some assumptions have to be made. Principal among these assumptions are the following:

1. Relationships between force inputs and battlefield results, which have been consistent for World War II and the earlier Arab-Israeli wars, are assumed to apply to Lebanon in 1982.

2. For the circumstances of operations in and around the Bekaa Valley in June 1982, the significant QJM factors were as follows:

Israeli CEV (from 1967 and 1973 data): 2.5

Terrain (mostly rugged, with some flat): advance rate factor, .65; posture enhancement factor, 1.5

Posture (for Syrians, mixture of hasty and prepared): advance rate factor, .7; posture enhancement factor, 1.4

The advance rate factors, when applied to standard rates for types and relative strengths of opposing forces, provide a basis for estimating expected advance rates of the attacking force. The posture enhancement factors are the multipliers that, when applied to the force strength of the defender, yield a value for the defender's total combat power.

3. Modern main battle tanks, of the sort with which both Israelis and Syrians were equipped, are each the equivalent—in proving ground value—of a 100-man "slice" of the nonarmor and nonair support components of a modern army. (Such a slice would include infantry weapons, artillery, antiarmor weapons, and air defense weapons.) This assumption is based on QJM analyses of the 1973 October War and of hypothetical operations between current NATO and Warsaw Pact forces.

4. The average value of one Israeli close-support aircraft, calculated on a similar basis, is the equivalent—in proving ground value—of a 250-man slice of Israeli or Syrian troops.

5. The average value of one Syrian close-support aircraft, also calculated in the same way, is the equivalent—in proving ground value—of a 200-man troop slice.

6. The average value of one Syrian SAM air defense missile is estimated to be the same as that of one Syrian fighter aircraft.

Now, on the basis of the figures contained in table 4–6 and after application of the foregoing assumptions, we can calculate the force strengths and combat powers of Israeli and Syrian forces for the June 8–11 period as follows:

	Israeli Manpower Equivalents			Syrian Manpower Equivalents		
Troops	32,000 ×	1 =	32,000	35,000 ×	1 =	35,000
Tanks	750 × 100	=	75,000	700 × 100	=	70,000
Aircraft	275 × 250	=	68,750	225 × 200	=	45,000
Air defense missiles			—	100 × 200	=	20,000
Force strength			175,750			170,000
Terrain			—			× 1.5
Posture			—			× 1.4
Combat power (without CEV)			175,750			357,000

This permits us to make several interesting comparisons:

Force strength ratio (Israeli/Syrian): 1.03

Combat power ratio (without CEV): 0.49

Combat power ratio (with 2.5 Israeli CEV): 1.23

On the basis of this essentially static comparison, the force strength ratio tells us that there will be a standoff between the Israelis and the Syrians in Lebanon. The combat power ratio, without the CEV, is hardly more useful; it tells us that the Syrians will decisively repulse the Israeli offensive. We are able to get a meaningful comparison of the opposing forces only when we have a combat power comparison that includes consideration of the CEV. But this does not indicate an overwhelming Israeli superiority, such as was demonstrated on the battlefield.

Let us continue the analysis by looking at each of the two days of serious fighting separately. The following is a manpower-equivalent comparison of the opposing forces on June 9:

	Israeli Manpower Equivalents				Syrian Manpower Equivalents			
Troops	32,000 ×	1	=	32,000	20,000 ×	1	=	20,000
Tanks	750 ×	100	=	75,000	350 ×	100	=	35,000
Aircraft	275 ×	250	=	68,750	50 ×	200[a]	=	10,000
Air defense missiles			—			0[b]	=	0
Force strength				175,750				65,000
Terrain				—				× 1.5
Posture				—				× 1.4
Combat power (without CEV)				175,750				136,500

The resulting comparisons are as follows:

Force strength ratio (Israeli/Syrian): 2.70

Combat power ratio (without CEV): 1.29

Combat power ratio (with CEV): 3.22

This combat power ratio of 3.22 takes into consideration the previous historical combat power superiority of Israeli troops over Syrians (about 2.5 CEV) and suggests that a one-sided Israeli success was again to be expected. That is the way it was.

The Israelis advanced about 12 kilometers that day, through the extremely rugged terrain on both sides of the Bekaa Valley. Applying the advance rate factors for posture and terrain, this means that the Israelis could have expected to advance about 31 kilometers on flat terrain against the Syrian combat power opposition. In table 4–10 the (*QJM Rule Book*), taken from the standard, unmodified advance of an armored force with a combat power superiority of 3.22 is about 22 kilometers. Thus, one could suggest that the CEV was slightly more than 2.5, or about 3.2.

The following figures reflect Syrian reinforcements and force erosion due to

---

[a]An estimate of 50 Syrian close-support sorties is generous.

[b]Israeli aircraft did not begin close support until they had destroyed or neutralized the Syrian SAMs.

both combat and noncombat causes on June 10, the day that led the Syrians to request a cease-fire:

	Israeli Manpower Equivalents			Syrian Manpower Equivalents	
Troops	31,000 × 1 =	31,000	30,000 × 1 =	30,000
Tanks	700 × 100 =	70,000	400 × 100 =	40,000
Aircraft	225 × 250 =	56,250	0 =	0
Force strength		157,250		70,000
Terrain		—		1.5
Posture		—		1.4
Morale (Syrian morale had been badly shaken on June 9)				0.9
Combat power (without CEV)		157,250		132,300

The resulting comparisons are:

Force strength ratio: 2.25

Combat power ratio (without CEV): 1.19

Combat power ratio (with CEV): 2.98

Again, an overwhelming Israeli success was to be expected when the Israeli CEV was taken into consideration.

Once more, the Israelis advanced about 10 kilometers during the day. This would translate to 24 kilometers a day against the same level of combat power on flat, smooth terrain. In table 4–10 we find that the standard, unmodified advance rate for a combat power ratio of 3.0 is 18 kilometers. This suggests a CEV of about 3.3.

We have no way of assessing the daily casualties for either the Israelis or the Syrians. However, the overall casualty rates for the Israelis, compared with the estimated losses for the Syrians, provide another way of checking the validity of the comparison we have been making.

Assessment of the casualty results of World War II and the prior Arab-Israeli Wars has demonstrated that the ratio of the casualty-inflicting capabilities of two opposing forces is generally about the square of the relative combat effectiveness value (CEV). From table 4–9, we see that the total Israeli casualties against the Syrians were about 1285; the total Syrian casualties were estimated at about 4150.

The Israeli figures are close to accurate; the Syrian figures are estimates only. On the basis of these figures, we see that the Israeli casualty rate (for an average strength about 31,500) was about 1.36 percent per day; the Syrian casualty rate (for an average strength about 27,500) was about 5.53 percent per day. The cas-

Table 4–10
Standard (Unmodified) Advanced Rates (Sr) in Km/day

Resistance description	P/P	Armd Div	Mczd Div	Inf Div	Horse Cav Force
Intense[a]	1.00–1.09	4.0	4.00	4.00	3.00
Near Intense	1.10–1.19	4.5	4.25	4.25	3.25
Strong/Intense	1.20–1.29	5.0	4.50	4.50	3.50
Near Strong/Intense	1.30–1.39	5.5	4.75	4.75	3.75
Strong	1.40–1.49	6.0	5.00	5.00	4.00
Near Strong	1.50–1.59	7.5	6.25	5.75	5.00
Moderate/Strong	1.60–1.74	9.0	7.50	6.50	6.00
Near Moderate/Strong	1.75–1.89	10.5	8.75	7.25	7.00
Moderate	1.90–2.09	12.0	10.00	8.00	8.00
Near Moderate	2.10–2.39	14.0	11.50	9.00	10.00
Slight/Moderate	2.40–2.69	16.0	13.00	10.00	12.00
Near Slight/Moderate	2.70–3.09	18.0	14.50	11.00	13.50
Slight	3.10–3.59	20.0	16.00	12.00	15.00
Near Slight	3.60–4.49	25.0	25.00	14.00	20.00
Negligible/Slight	4.50–5.49	35.0	35.00	16.00	25.00
Near Negligible	5.50–6.49	45.0	45.00	20.00	31.00
Negligible[b]	6.50 plus	60.0	60.00	24.00	40.00

[a]If the P/P is less than 1.0, use advance rate of 1.0 km/day.

[b]For armored and mechanized infantry divisions, these rates can be sustained for 10 days only; for next 20 days standard rates for armored and mechanized infantry forces cannot exceed half these rates.

ualty-inflicting rate for 31,500 Israelis was 4.23 Syrian casualties inflicted per day per 100 Israeli soldiers. The casualty-inflicting rate for 27,500 Syrians was 1.56 Israeli casualties inflicted per day per 100 Syrian soldiers. However, we must remember that the Syrian capability on the defense was multiplied by a factor of 1.4 for posture and 1.5 for terrain. Thus, without those advantages (as shown in table 4–9), the normalized casualty-inflicting capability of the Syrians was about 0.74 Israelis per 100 Syrians per day.

The ratio of Israeli casualty-inflicting capability to that of the Syrians, therefore, was 4.23/0.74, or 5.96. The New Square Law tells us that the square root of this ratio should be the equivalent of the CEV for the Israelis, which is 2.44.

What does all this number-crunching tell us about the 1982 Battle of the Bekaa Valley and about the opposing Syrian and Israeli troops that fought the battle? It tells us a great deal, in fact—certainly much more than would have been possible without the analytical framework supplied by Clausewitz and embellished by the QJM.

First, of course, it shows how useless are the usual static comparisons so beloved by the denizens of the Pentagon and Langley. Static comparisons are useful only if there is some basis for assuming that the combat capabilities of the opponents are reasonably equivalent—and this means an assessment of troop quality without any consideration of the relative capabilities of the weapons. (Not that this comparison of relative weapon capability is unimportant; it is just different and *less* important than comparison of troop quality.)

Both Israeli and American authors have suggested that the Israeli performance in the Battle of the Bekaa Valley was not as brilliant as that in the 1973 War.[8] I totally disagree. The Israelis, who are apparently very capable of making their own assessments of relative combat effectiveness, had prepared for this operation with meticulous care. They have an advantage, of course, that is not shared by the U.S. armed forces: They can plan in advance for operations in a known, nearby area, against a known foe, under relatively predictable circumstances. This comment is not intended to diminish their accomplishment. The fact is that they did so plan with a brilliance at least comparable to that of the Egyptians before their Suez Canal crossing triumph of 1973.

The record is very clear that the average relative combat effectiveness superiority factor (CEV) of the Israelis with respect to the Syrians was about 2.5 in the 1967 and 1973 wars.[9] With less assurance, because of less confidence in more aggregated data, we have just demonstrated that the Israeli CEV with respect to the Syrians in 1982 was between 2.4 and 3.3. The consistency of the results from these unrelated calculations enables me to suggest with reasonable confidence that the CEV in 1982 was at least 2.5, and probably closer to 2.9. Thus, the gap in combat capability (*not* the gap in military technology) is certainly not closing, and may be still widening between the Israelis and their foes. It matters not what one's sympathies may be in the Arab-Israeli conflict—objective facts are facts. It is as important for the Arabs to understand these facts and take them into consideration in their military and political decisions relating to war as it was for the Soviet leadership to understand and take into consideration the comparable differential between their CEVs and those of the much more efficient Germans in World War II.[10]

I shall conclude with a brief, true story. In the fall of 1982, I was talking in an Arab country to a senior Arab military professional who had closely studied the Battle of the Bekaa Valley. He is one of the least emotional Arabs I know, and he is a very experienced and skilled soldier. I asked my friend: "General, does not the victory of the Israelis—who were largely equipped with American weapons— and the Syrians, who had Soviet materiel, demonstrate the superiority of American military technology over that of the USSR?"

My Arab friend responded slowly: "Soviet weapons are good. In most respects they are as good as your weapons, maybe even better in some ways. They are usually simpler and easier to maintain, and thus easier for Arab soldiers, like the Syrians, to use. No, it was not the superiority of American weapons over Soviet weapons which made the difference in the Bekaa Valley."

At almost that same time, in Jerusalem, a group of American visitors was being briefed on the Lebanon war by General Rafael Eitan, the Israeli Chief of

Staff. A retired American general (who told me this part of the tale) asked General Eitan almost exactly the same question I had asked the Arab general. General Eitan responded: "No, it was not the weapons that made the difference. If we had had their weapons, and they had had ours, the result would have been exactly the same."[11]

A few months later, I had an opportunity to repeat these anecdotes to General David Ivry, who had commanded the Israeli Air Force during the June 1982 war. I concluded: "I presume there may have been a greater differential between American and Soviet air weapons. Would you care to comment?"

General Ivry thought a few moments and then replied: "Yes, there is a greater differential between the American aircraft we had, and the Soviet aircraft the Syrians were flying. Yet," he continued, "I agree with the Chief of Staff [General Eitan]. If we had had their MiGs, and they had had our F-15s, the result would have been the same, although the loss ratio might have been a bit different. You see," concluded General Ivry, "we are able to exploit our weaponry to its maximum potential capability. This the Arabs are not yet able to do."

That is perhaps the most important lesson of the 1982 war: That superior ability of the Israelis exists. Such a superior ability *can* be offset, however—as Clausewitz assured us and the Russians demonstrated to us in World War II—by superior numbers. Someday—probably not very soon—that superior Israeli ability will erode or be matched by the Arabs. In the meantime, it must be the major consideration in any military assessment of the Middle East.

Notes

1. A recent article is "In Pursuit of the Essence of War," *Army* (January 1984). Typical of what I have written is "History and Modern Battle," *Army* 32 (November 1982); and an unpublished essay prepared for (1984) the Department of Defense, "Why We Do Not Learn from Military History."

2. *Jomini, Clausewitz and Schlieffen* (West Point, N.Y.: U.S. Military Academy, 1951), p. 37.

3. Carl von Clausewitz, *On War*, Book Three, chapter 8.

4. In "Let's Get Serious About Combat Multipliers," *Army* 33 (May 1983): 18–25, I referred to this literature as follows:

> It would perhaps be unfair to ask what is being multiplied. There is nothing in the literature that gives us either the nature or the value of the multiplicand to which the multiplier is to be applied to give us a product. Nor does the literature even hint at specific values for the multipliers. In fact, there is nothing to suggest either the size or the nature of the product, other than that it is something greater than that of the enemy (who is, of course, denied the advantage of multipliers by our unique ingenuity). . . . This is mathematics without numbers. It is also nonsense.

5. Ibid.

6. T.N. Dupuy, *Elusive Victory: The Arab-Israeli Wars, 1947–1974* (Fairfax, Va.; 1984), appendixes A and B.

7. T.L. Livermore, *Numbers and Losses in the Civil War* (Boston, 1901).

8. Martin van Creveld, "The War: A Questioning Look," *Jerusalem Post, International Edition,* December 12–18, 1982, pp. 12–13; Richard A. Gabriel, *Operation Peace for Galilee; The Israeli-PLO War in Lebanon* (New York, 1984), pp. 193, 194, *passim.*

9. T.N. Dupuy, *Elusive Victory.*

10. T.N. Dupuy, *A Genius for War: The German Army and General Staff, 1807–1945* (Fairfax, Va., 1984), appendixes C and E.

11. Personal communication with Gen. George S. Blanchard, USA, Ret.

Part II
Case Studies of Wars in the Third World

5
Ethiopia-Somalia (1977–1978)

William H. Lewis

The attack launched by regular military units of the Somali Democratic Republic in mid-1977 to seize control of the Ogaden province in neighboring Ethiopia was well conceived and had all of the early earmarks of success. Within a period of two months, all main communications points had been seized, approximately three-quarters of the Ogaden was under Somali control, and only two major towns remained in the hands of beleaguered Ethiopian forces. The Somali irredentist dream of national reunification was about to be realized. Within a brief span of a few months, however, the Somali dream would evaporate, with the Republic's regular military formations shattered and forced into flight across the Ethiopia-Somalia frontier.

The failure of Somalia to achieve its ultimate objectives is attributable less to the performance of its military commanders than to factors and forces over which it had little control. The strategies and tactics adopted by local Somali commanders were reasonable and followed doctrines imbibed from Russian military advisers. Until the outbreak of hostilities, the Soviet Union had been the primary provider of arms to Somalia, as well as its source of training and indoctrination. If anything, Russian instructors would have been impressed with the planning and execution of their protégés. They would not be permitted pride of parental supervision, however. As a result of the Somali invasion, Moscow was to engage in a dramatic about-face and to align itself with the military directorate that ruled Ethiopia. The outcome of the war would be dictated by geostrategic and ideological considerations, rather than by the prowess and capabilities of Ethiopian and Somali forces—the former initially trained and equipped by the United States, the latter by Moscow—for by 1978, the Horn of Africa had become a cockpit of East–West rivalry.

There was little reason to anticipate the sharp alteration in the alignment of political forces and the resulting shift in the balance of regional power as the decade of the 1970s unfolded. Early in 1970, Emperor Haile Selassie appeared to be firmly enthroned, troubled only by separatist movements in the northern province of Eritrea and in the Ogaden to the south—nagging problems that Selassie's American-trained and -equipped divisions were containing, albeit all too slowly. In the Somali Republic, a 1969 military coup had brought Siad Barré to the presidency, but for the moment he was concerned with the dynamics associated with consolidation of power. Within four years, the equilibrium of the region was to be irretrievably upset. Drought conditions in Ethiopia's northern provinces—ignored by the emperor, with the loss of several hundred thousand lives—together with mounting grievances and disaffection within the Ethiopian military led to the overthrow of the aged ruler in 1974. There followed in rapid succession the implantation of a military committee (the *Dergue*) to direct the affairs of the nation, the outbreak of tribal and ethnic dissidence in much of the countryside, the adoption of Marxist-Leninist ideology by the *Dergue,* and the concomitant launching of a "red terror" campaign against students and intellectuals in Ethiopia's main urban centers. The Ethiopian "empire" appeared to be completely caught up in anarchy by early 1977 and on the threshold of disintegration. For the Somali Republic, the period was propitious for armed intervention and the seizure of the Ogaden, which constituted one-fourth of Ethiopian territory (and embraced 1.5 million Somalis, the preponderant ethnic group in the province).

The war between Somalia and Ethiopia that was about to unfold presented painful policy dilemmas for their two main supporters. In both Washington and Moscow, Somali aspirations and increasingly unstable conditions in Ethiopia posed a series of policy decisions that would prove both challenging and unsettling. Since the decisions taken by the two external actors would determine the outcome of the Ethiopian-Somali war of 1977–1978, an appreciation of the perspectives and approaches of Moscow and Washington is essential.

Geostrategic Factors

Geographically, the Horn region (see map) is a hinge between the Middle East and Africa (see figure 5–1). Through its reaches, marauding tribes and conquering armies have marched for centuries, using the region as a way station to other areas. In and of itself, the Horn has little intrinsic strategic-military value in the modern age. But when linked with the adjoining Red Sea-Persian Gulf and East African-Indian Ocean zones, the combination of Ethiopia and Somalia assumes heightened importance for U.S. interests. An American congressional fact-finding mission in December 1977 underscored these factors in a special report:

> What is happening in the Horn of Africa today is much more than a conflict between two African countries; it involves the potential use of coastal areas and ports for military operations in and around the Red Sea and the Indian Ocean, and the control of naval and international commercial traffic through this vital area.
>
> Soviet strategists have recognized the importance of the Horn of Africa and

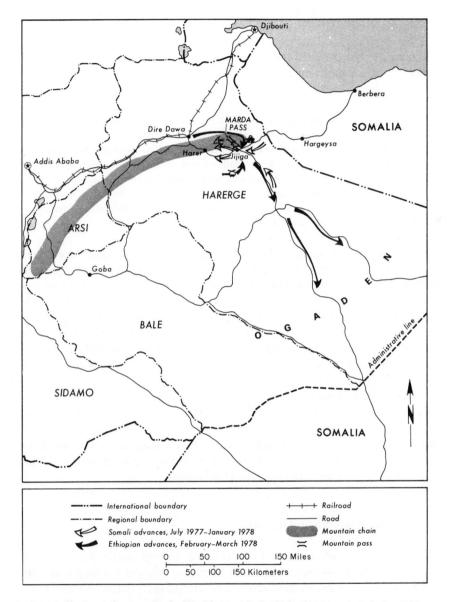

Source: *Ethiopia: A Country Study* (Washington, D.C.: U.S. Government Printing Office, 1981), p. 270.

Figure 5–1. The Ogaden Campaign, 1977–78

have shown their willingness to make substantial investments to secure Russia's interests, first in Somalia, and now Ethiopia. By undermining the fragile governments which exist in the Horn, Soviet influence could rapidly spread throughout the region and along the entire east coast of Africa.[1]

Although the congressional staff, in a moment of hyperbolic anxiety, exaggerated the extent of Soviet influence, it was on the mark in assessing the strategic factors to be considered:

Its strategic importance touches on the larger international system at many sensitive points. Geographic considerations make the northeast edge of the African Continent part of the geopolitics of the Middle East. The Horn also constitutes an important part of the northeast quadrant of the Indian Ocean, including the Persian Gulf. It is obvious that Israel's vital oil imports from Iran, plus other Suez-bound commerce from the Gulf, East Africa and Asia, must pass near the Somalia coast, and into the Red Sea parallel to Ethiopia's coast, and ultimately to the Strait of Tiran and the Gulf of Aqaba.[2]

The shifting balance in the Horn has been linked by some observers with the overthrow of the Shah of Iran in 1979, the Iran-Iraq war that erupted in 1980, and the Ethiopian-Libyan-PDRY defensive alliance fashioned in 1981—to underscore the inherent instability of the geostrategic zone that forms a so-called arc of crisis. From their perspective, recent events in this broader region have served to weaken the foundations of Western influence and, consequently, to tip the regional balance in favor of the Soviet Union.[3] It is the view of these observers that the United States, in concert with interested Western European governments, has yet to fashion an effective counterstrategy.

Whether one agrees with this assessment or is disposed to adopt a more restrained view, it is clear that events in the Horn must be examined against the background of forces operating in adjacent regions. In particular, any well-grounded evaluation must take into full account the interplay of U.S. and Soviet strategies, for the superpowers have the potential to shape the existing and future configuration of forces throughout the Horn region.

The Failure of American Diplomacy

As one of the few independent African countries throughout the European colonial period, and as an ancient Christian kingdom, Ethiopia has long held a special fascination for Americans, which was strengthened during the 1930s as a result of its victimization by fascist occupation. During the early post–World War II period, U.S. interests in Ethiopia were dictated largely by geostrategic considerations. Successive U.S. administrations looked to Emperor Haile Selassie to play a moderating role with the formation of the Organization of African Unity

(OAU) and the establishment of its headquarters at Addis Ababa. At the same time, we valued the access provided the U.S. military to Ethiopian ports and airfields, as well as the right accorded us to maintain a highly prized communications and intelligence collection station, Kagnew, located outside Asmara in the province of Eritrea.

For all these reasons, the U.S. government took particular care to demonstrate the constancy of its bilateral relationship after the overthrow of Emperor Haile Selassie. In concrete terms, the United States continued to provide grant economic and military assistance as antigovernment groups formed in Addis Ababa and in the countryside and as separatist movements organized to break away from the domination of the new ruling oligarchy. From 1974 until late 1976, successive U.S. administrations sought to demonstrate that traditional ties between the two countries could be sustained despite the basic change that had taken place in Ethiopia's form of government. Testifying before the Senate Subcommittee on African Affairs on August 6, 1976, Assistant Secretary of State William E. Schauffele, Jr., declaimed:

> We believe that our present policy toward Ethiopia will not only contribute to the stability of this second most populous country in black Africa but also assist black African states in maintaining the principle of territorial integrity, a cardinal principle of the Organization of African Unity. We believe that we would incur much criticism from our friends in Africa and elsewhere were we to withdraw support from the Ethiopian government during this time of difficulty— such a move would also be attributed to distaste for Ethiopia's brand of socialism.[4]

With respect to human rights considerations, Schauffele went on to observe:

> We are well aware that our military aid is a two-edged sword that is a major support of the present government, with whose actions we do not always agree, particularly in the field of human rights. However, for the reasons given above, although we have conscientiously refrained from advisory effort in . . . Ethiopian counter-insurgency operations, we have continued to supply Ethiopia with arms in accordance with our military assistance agreement with Ethiopia, which dates from May 1953.[5]

What security requirements and normal diplomatic circumspection compelled Schauffele to pass over were two policy decisions that had been taken prior to his appearance before the Senate subcommittee: (1) to quietly phase out the U.S. military presence at Kagnew Station, which had become redundant with the establishment of a sister facility at Diego Garcia; and (2) to reduce the level of grant military assistance to Ethiopia, requiring it to meet its needs through the Foreign Military Sales (FMS) program, on either a cash or credit basis. By 1976, the annual grant component of military assistance was well below $4 million, and discussions were underway at working levels to terminate the grant program in 1977. On the recommendation of the foreign policy experts, the outgoing Ford administration endorsed this plan late in November.

As 1976 came to a close, the *Dergue* leadership was confronting severe difficulties at home. Having toppled the monarchy and eliminated most of the emperor's supporting aristocracy, the *Dergue* proclaimed that it intended to embark on a program of social and economic reform that would end the domination and privileges of the Amhara ethnic minority that had presided over Ethiopian affairs for three-quarters of a century. Egalitarian reforms and a redistribution of political power to the peasantry and the urban working class were to be the engines of the revolution. To the dismay of the *Dergue*, its newly found ideology simply added to the fissures and instabilities of Ethiopia. Insurgency in the province of Eritrea, which had erupted in 1962, gathered fresh momentum, rather than abating; local insurgency already existed in the Somali-populated province of Ogaden and was now spreading among the Oromo peoples, the Afars, and the Tigreans. The overwhelming majority of Ethiopia's fourteen provinces were seized by dissidence, and the contagion was spreading to the cities, particularly Addis Ababa, where student groups, "Maoist intellectuals," and labor leaders were organizing clandestine cells and urging the military either to step aside or to share power with these groups.

The *Dergue*, confronted with the total collapse of governmental authority (as well as the fragmentation of the country because of separatism), determined that draconian measures were mandatory. Under the leadership of Colonel Mengistou, the military was enlarged through the establishment of a militia recruitment program, and massive attacks were launched against insurgent groups operating in rural areas. By late 1975, these offensives had yielded few victories for government forces. In the urban areas, on the other hand, a so-called "red terror" campaign produced more concrete results. Attacks were launched against university students, intellectuals, and others in an effort to eradicate potential rival power centers. Ruthlessly conducted, the campaign systematically liquidated thousands of young Ethiopians; it is estimated that 5,000 youths lost their lives in Addis Ababa alone, to the shock of a press corps and diplomatic community that reported the strife and cruelties of the contending factions. For the *Dergue*, a need for sources of external support was evident. Representatives were dispatched to the Soviet Union to elicit backing in the form of military equipment, the *Dergue* reportedly protesting its intention to declare the Ethiopian revolution in progress Marxist-Leninist in inspiration and orientation. The Brezhnev leadership reacted cautiously, far from convinced that the conversion was sincere or that a convergence of interest yet existed between Moscow and the *Dergue*. No military assistance pledges emanated from the Soviet Union as a result of *Dergue* representations, much to the dismay of Colonel Mengistou.

Within several months, the balance of forces in the Horn region began to change dramatically. The primary recipient of change was a new administration in Washington, installed in January 1977 with an avowed dedication to broad moral and ethical precepts and policies that would eschew the *realpolitik* approach of the predecessor Nixon and Ford administrations.

In February 1977, searching for candidates to chastise publicly for "gross and consistent" abuses of human rights, the president's staff pressed the State Department to prepare a list of nominees. Each geographic bureau was under pressure to respond affirmatively, outlining the abuses and recommending appropriate action to be taken by the U.S. government. The heads of the policy-planning staff and the human rights organization installed in the department were to "vet" the lists and make their own recommendations to the Secretary and to the White House. A rich and variegated constellation of candidates emerged, including several in Africa and a comparable number in Latin America. Ethiopia, because of the bloodshed associated with the "red terror," headed the African list for public excoriation. It was subsequently observed in the White House that grant military assistance was scheduled for termination in 1977—a fact not yet communicated to the *Dergue*—and that announcement of such termination might serve as a suitable "stick" for redressing the situation in Ethiopia.

The foundations for such a hopeful assessment were not obvious to area specialists. In the throes of civil war, the *Dergue* was not likely to welcome injunctions from Washington against excesses in its struggle for survival. Moreover, Ethiopia, a conquest empire brought together the previous 100 years through military means, had little experience with democratic institutions or political pluralism. The regime of Emperor Haile Selassie had been harsh and repressive, despite the outward trappings of constitutional rule, and little inclined to accept notions of a loyal opposition. Almost certainly, Washington, especially its area specialists, could not reasonably anticipate that a country undergoing traumatic changes would observe rules of conduct more acceptable among industrialized Western democracies. On the other hand, denunciation of the *Dergue* by the Carter administration would have significant impact in Moscow, where the credentials of the Mengistou regime were receiving ongoing scrutiny. Paradoxically, the Soviet Union, utilizing its own criteria, found the *Dergue* more acceptable as it declined in the estimation of President Carter. Subsequent events were to add to the legitimacy of the Ethiopian revolution in the eyes of President Brezhnev and his colleagues.

The announcement by President Carter that, because of ongoing human rights violations, grant military assistance to Ethiopia was to be terminated was greeted with outrage by the *Dergue*. A diplomatic crisis crystallized, with Ethiopian spokesmen noting that the United States, which had staunchly supported the repressive Selassie oligarchy, was now opposed to the revolutionary reforms that were being introduced by the *Dergue*. Accusing the United States of intervention in Ethiopia's domestic affairs, the *Dergue* called for the immediate closure of Kagnew Station and of U.S. information offices; in addition, U.S. medical assistance activities were brought to an end, and the size of diplomatic and economic aid staffs was reduced at the request of the Ethiopian government. (Foreign Military Sales contracts were not terminated, however, and U.S. military supplies continued to reach Ethiopia well after the eruption of the Somali-Ethiopian war in July 1977.) The reaction of other governments subject to official reproof by the United States was equally emotional, with President Idi Amin of Uganda leading the way in vituperation. Indeed, Amin actually brought relations to the point of crisis by threatening retaliatory action against American missionaries resident in Uganda.

Of greater moment was the impact of the American approach to the balance of forces in the Horn region. The perspectives of other potential actors in the Ethiopian drama were also influenced by the estrangement apparently in progress. The government of President Siad Barré in the neighboring Somali Republic saw in the event a favorable omen for Somali aspirations—that is, the annexation of the province of Ogaden as the situation in Ethiopia deteriorated. If the United States, hitherto Ethiopia's primary source for military supplies, was moving away from the special relationship that had existed for more than two decades, the risks of armed intervention would be diminished appreciably. Egypt's President Sadat, the Shah of Iran, the Saudis, and the Sudanese—all deeply disturbed by the growth of radical forces in the Red Sea area—perceived in the estrangement a signal that the Carter administration was opposed to the Ethiopian revolution. They were prepared to support Washington's endeavors and welcomed in the weeks that followed such additional signals as the dispatch of a military survey team to Sudan to examine that country's defense needs in the wake of the expulsion of Soviet arms specialists from Khartoum. In May, President Carter indicated a desire to reduce Soviet influence in the Somali Republic, and in June he communicated to President Siad Barré the willingness of the United States to provide "defensive" weapons to Somalia should that nation terminate its dependence on the Soviet Union for military equipment.

These occurrences, together with the threat of a Somali invasion of Ogaden province in violation of the principles embodied in the OAU charter, led the Soviet Union to caution Siad Barré. By the spring of 1977, Soviet cautionary demarches turned into admonitions, followed by indications that the military pipeline would be closed in the event of Somali aggression against Ethiopia. The special relationship was ending, and, with the actual invasion by Somali forces in July, it was summarily terminated.

The Somali Invasion

The causes of the conflict were relatively simple to identify. The leaders of the Somali Republic, since its independence under the auspices of the United Nations in 1960, had dedicated themselves to the reunification of all Somali peoples inhabiting northeast Africa. An essentially nomadic population that had migrated from the Arabian peninsula centuries earlier, the Somalis were deeply divided along clan and tribal lines. However, the elements of unity clearly overshadowed the cleavages: (1) all were Muslims in their confessional loyalty; (2) all shared a common sense of community—based on language, culture, and historical impulses; and (3) all wished to be united within the ambit of a greater Somali authority centered at the Somali Republic capital of Mogadishu. This aspiration was reflected in the five stars imbedded in the Somali Republic flag, symbolizing the fragmentation of Somali populations—a diaspora—to be overcome through struggle to achieve a truly unified Somali nation.

Unfortunately, the exigencies of European colonialism in the nineteenth and twentieth centuries had served to divide the Somalis. When the tide of nationalist independence consumed Africa in the 1960s, the Somalis found themselves citizens of several newly emergent nation-states. Nomadic pursuits and habits had confined the Somalis to the lowland desert region of the northeastern quadrant of Africa—a region bisected by the national boundaries of Ethiopia, Djibouti, Kenya, British Somaliland, and the Somali Republic. In fact, the Somali people predominated numerically in the dessicated areas encompassed by the low desert, where temperatures rise to 110° Fahrenheit. The terrain itself is moonscape in shape and topography, with few paved roads, virtually no fixed agricultural centers, and only a few, widely scattered town agglomerations. The frontier of a vast wasteland, the lowland region belongs to the nomads and seminomads, who are largely Somalis. Theoretically, there should be little reason to dispute the right of the Somalis to unite within this stark, forbidding landscape.

The perspective of the newly emergent nation-states must be taken into consideration, however. Ethiopia had a lengthy history of independence prior to the Italian invasions of the 1930s, but it was and remains a conquest empire brought together within its present territorial confines as a result of the military proficiencies of the dominant Coptic Christian minority. Similarly, Kenya—where the Somalis predominate in the northeast area—is an amalgam of diverse tribal communities. Even in the microstate of Djibouti, Afars compete with Issas for political hegemony. The realization of Somali irredentist aspirations threatened Balkanization of the entire northeast African quadrant, where community loyalty to central government was uncertain at best. Within the framework of the regional organization—the Organization of African Unity (OAU), formed in 1963—boundaries were to be respected, and the sovereignty and territorial integrity of member states were not to be challenged directly or indirectly. Where disputes arise, the OAU charter enjoins settlement through peaceful negotiation. Occasional military forays and local conflicts after Somali independence in 1960 were repulsed by Kenya and Ethiopia in due course. Somali pressures were only successful in British Somaliland, where London determined that financial stringencies and other priorities warranted a realignment of imperial authority.

On paper, Somali ambitions should have been neutralized by the superior military weight of Ethiopia. According to all of the conventional static indicators of national power, the balance clearly favored Ethiopia (see table 5–1). The Ethiopian military establishment had been the beneficiary of more than a quarter-century of U.S. training, arms, and indoctrination. Its senior commanders had attended various military centers, including the Command and General Staff College at Fort Leavenworth, Kansas; it had combat arms experience in dealing with local insurgencies and by virtue of United Nations service in the former Belgian Congo (Zaire). In addition, it disposed of relatively sophisticated weaponry and was fully oriented in combined arms tactics. By comparison, the Somali military suffered serious deficiencies in training, logistics, and maintenance capabilities. Although some of the Soviet-supplied military hardware was of good quality, the necessary spares and replacements were in short supply. Depot maintenance capacities were also pitifully inadequate.

Other factors served to offset the apparent advantages of the Ethiopian military establishment, however. It had suffered through fifteen years of insurgency with lack of success; in the Ogaden, its unimpressive performance in coping with a local insurgent force, the Western Somali Liberation Front (WSLF), had proved worrisome to senior headquarters commanders. Moreover, the system was under severe strain as a result of other factors:

Troop morale had diminished markedly as a result of lengthy field service and family separation.

Within the ranks, pay and emoluments were outpaced by severe domestic inflationary pressures, making enlistment and service unattractive.

After the 1974 coup, the *Dergue* leadership fell to internal quarreling, thus adding to uncertainty and doubt in the lower ranks.

The U.S. advisory services had diminished and ultimately collapsed with the near rupture in relations between Washington and Addis Ababa during the spring of 1977.

The Somali military enjoyed several advantages by comparison:

The commanders were familiar with the combat terrain and did not feel as constrained by such factors as heat, absence of good road systems, and unreliable transport.

Troop morale was relatively high, since the primary military objective—control over Ogaden—enjoyed general patriotic support.

The Somalis would be operating among a local population that overwhelmingly supported their political and military objectives.

The Somalis appeared to have the tacit backing of the United States, which had signaled its intention to provide weaponry if the Soviet Union demurred.

Table 5–1
Conventional Power Indicators: Ethiopia versus Somalia

Indicator	Ethiopia	Somalia
Geographic size	1,221,900 sq. km	637,540 sq. km
Population	35,000,000	3,000,000
Estimated GNP	$3 billion	$425 million
Defense expenditure	$165 million	$25 million
Armed forces		
Army	47,000	22,000
Navy	1,500	300
Air force	2,300	2,700
Reserves	28,000	20,000
Combat aircraft	36	66
Tanks	78	250
Artillery pieces	310	330
Paramilitary	22,400	6,000

Source: Military Balance: 1976–77 (London: International Institute for Strategic Studies, 1977).

Not to be ignored either, was that the main Ethiopian defensive force in the Ogaden was the Third Division, most of whose troops were depressed by lengthy service in an unfamiliar, inhospitable territory of vast geographic dimension. Short of aerial reconnaissance capacities, with much of its armor sidelined and almost half of its truck transport out of commission, the division was confined to occasional surveillance forays from heavily armed towns and urban centers. The division's intelligence capacity for monitoring the bulk of the Somali population was minimal, and its early-warning capability was virtually nonexistent.[6]

The Initial Phase

The tempting target presented by a deeply divided, strife-ridden Ethiopia proved too great for Siad Barré to resist. However, the Somali president needed to assure himself that the hard-pressed Ethiopians would not receive massive external assistance. The OAU member states might condemn the Somalis, but they did not command the necessary resources; Israel might proffer sympathy, but it was not a likely candidate for effective counterpressure; and even the Soviet Union was expected to proceed cautiously rather than risk Arab League opprobrium (the Somali Republic was a league member). Moreover, the United States had apparently determined that the *Dergue* was embarked on a revolutionary course that it could not endorse.

A second consideration for Siad Barré was avoidance of a war of attrition. The Somali Republic lacked the human, economic, and military resources to sustain lengthy hostilities, but he had every reason to expect that the Somali Republic would not have to undergo such an experience. The *Dergue* was already embattled, and successful occupation of the Ogaden might well produce its demise; indeed, the Balkanization of the entire conquest empire that was Ethiopia might also be a reasonable expectation.

The combat readiness of the Somali military had been buttressed by over fifteen years of Soviet equipping, training, and modernization. Of even greater significance, a number of regular Somali units had gained invaluable experience through service in WSLF formations in Ogaden. Fighting in a guerrilla war prior to the outbreak of hostilities in July 1977 provided the high command with useful knowledge of terrain conditions, Ethiopian order of battle, and soft spots in the Ethiopian defensive alignment. This actually constituted the initial phase in the Ethiopian-Somali war, beginning late in 1976 and extending into June 1977. The accomplishments of the first phase were prepossessing:

> Ethiopian troop units in the southern Ogaden were isolated and diminished in size as a result of limited Third Division reinforcement capabilities.

> Vast reaches of the central Ogaden also fell outside Ethiopian military control as the WSLF interdicted convoys and logistics centers.

> The WSLF effectively distracted the Ethiopian military and partially masked the intentions of regular Somali forces.

When the regular Somali units crossed the frontier, Ethiopia appeared ripe for divestiture of its largest province.[7]

Invasion: Second Phase

The isolation of Ethiopian units in much of the central and southern portions of the Ogaden afforded the Somali military an opportunity to plan its invasion strategy without concern for flank protection. Armored and motorized infantry could operate along classical pincer lines, utilizing the former British Somaliland protectorate and the adjacent border region as launching points for their lines of attack. The principal targets in the first thirty days were the traditional urban strongpoint cities of Harar and Diredawa. Their occupation would effectively seal the fate of Ethiopian control. It would also interdict the main line of communication between Addis Ababa and Djibouti, an important 500-mile commercial artery for Ethiopia.

The strategic approach devised by the Somali military was sound both in conception and in execution. WSLF forces consolidated their control over the southern Ogaden within the first month and extended their control—aided by regular Somali forces—into the center by the end of September. By November, Jijiga was in Somali hands, as were the key northern towns of Fiambiro and Harrawa. Only Harar and Diredawa remained as obstacles to overall military success. Both were duly surrounded by regular Somali and WSLF forces, and a period of intermittent bombardment began.

These two key centers, though heavily invested, nevertheless remained under Ethiopian control. The desperate garrisons established effective defensive perimeters and managed to hold the Somalis at bay through a combination of heavy fortifications and artillery counterfire directed at main lines of Somali advance. In the intervening period, the Somali lines were experiencing mounting difficulties:

Soviet-supplied military equipment—particularly ground transport—did not hold up well under difficult terrain conditions.

Logistical support for artillery and armored units was marginal at best, thus impairing efforts to seize Harar and Diredawa.

Air superiority was denied as a result of Soviet refusal to supply essential spare parts and because of limited Somali maintenance capabilities. Nevertheless, by November 20, 1977, the 20,000 Somali regulars, supported by an additional 10,000 WSLF irregulars, had met most of their military objectives and felt reasonably confident that the two remaining Ethiopian strongholds would soon capitulate.[8]

Invasion: Third Phase

The optimism of the Somali military leadership was shortly to collapse. It had assumed that the actual military campaign would be of short duration—a practical necessity given the uncertainty of future Soviet supply—and that it would succeed because of the political disarray that was besetting Ethiopia. The *Dergue*, in brief, was presumed to possess little if any retaliatory capabilities. Moreover, although Ethiopia had strategic depth—spatially—the high mountains and deep gorges to be traversed would severely impede Ethiopian efforts to resupply isolated forces in the Ogaden, whereas Somali forces would enjoy greater ease of movement in a more narrowly defined geographic area.

Somali estimates began to go awry in October 1977, when the Soviet Union denounced the Republic's "blatant act" of aggression and, in response to a *Dergue* appeal, announced that it was terminating arms supplies to Mogadishu. Concomitantly, Moscow announced all necessary diplomatic and material support would be extended to Addis Ababa. There rapidly developed an emergency airlift of approximately $1 billion in arms and other war materiel. Giant Antonov aircraft began to ferry materiel from the Soviet Union to Addis Ababa, frequently crossing international frontiers without advance diplomatic clearance.

Transferred to hard-pressed Ethiopian forces were entire inventories of light arms, artillery, armor, and MiG-17 through MiG-23 fighter aircraft. At the same time, two Soviet generals and 1,000 advisers were dispatched to Ethiopia to familiarize Ethiopian troops with Soviet equipment and to assist in directing the *Dergue* war effort. In due course, Soviet Army General Vasily I. Petrov was reportedly placed in charge of the overall campaign.

Soviet military strategy followed classic lines. Emergency supply was the first order of business—with 400 tanks and 50 jet aircraft provided by December 1977. This was to be accompanied by formation of an Ethiopian popular militia to mobilize available manpower. The second stage involved resupply by air of isolated garrisons in the Ogaden, while Ethiopian forces were to be indoctrinated in equipment use, tactics, and combined arms techniques. The third stage involved insertion of sufficient cadres to assist in training and to provide a cutting edge against the Somalis. For these purposes, Cuban troops were mobilized, and 12,000 arrived from the Caribbean by February 1978. Those Cubans who were not used for training, intelligence collection, and military planning were organized into three brigades; two were motorized infantry, and the third was an armored force with considerable mobility and firepower capability.

By late January 1978, the Soviet-Cuban-Ethiopian counterstrategy was codified. The initial goal would be to relieve the garrisons at Diredawa and Harar and then to push eastward to open the vital Djibouti–Addis Ababa rail link, which would permit the Soviet Union to continue its military resupply program by sea. For this purpose, the Cubans would serve as the advance force, backed by 60,000 newly recruited Ethiopian "volunteers." Somali opposition was to be "softened" through repeated MiG-21 and MiG-23 sorties, as well as by mobilized artillery units. The attack was launched in early February and within ten days was clearly successful in relieving Somali pressure against Diredawa and Harar.[9]

The intention of the attacking force was to clear the northern Ogaden, reserving for later consideration the development of a strategy to cope with WSLF irregulars in the central and southern Ogaden. If successful, the drive would destroy Somali armor and artillery, which was in short supply, and threaten retaliation in the form of seizure of the northern Somali towns of Hargeisa and Berbera. (Berbera had been a main Soviet resupply base for its Indian Ocean naval force until the rupture with Mogadishu in late 1977.) Occupation of these towns was likely to produce the overthrow of the Siad Barré regime at Mogadishu.

Within seven weeks, the Somali effort in the northern Ogaden was in a state of disrepair, with the majority of regular units retreating back across the frontier. The tactics employed by the Cubans and Ethiopians were instructive, consisting of a combination of direct assault and vertical envelopment. For example, when Somali forces retreated to the strategic hills located at the Babile Gap and established a line of fortifications, the tactics adopted by the Cubans and Ethiopians included movement of armor and light artillery pieces over the Gap with heavy-duty Soviet helicopters and encirclement of the defense positions. Rapid tactical maneuver, together with the professionalism of the Cuban forces, led to demoralization of the Somali regulars.

The collapse of the Somalis in the north afforded the Cubans and Ethiopians the luxury of time to eliminate WSLF forces elsewhere. Over a period of two years, draconian measures were applied against Somali civilian populations in the central and southern Ogaden, including "free fire zones," burning of villages, and summary executions of young males suspected of being WSLF sympathizers or recruits. By mid-1980, almost one million Somalis fled the Ogaden to eke out a marginal existence in refugee camps. At the same time, a pro-Ethiopian guerrilla force was organized to raid across the border into the neighboring Somali Republic.

The American Response

American diplomacy was ill-placed to play a significant role as the Ethiopian-Somali war unfolded. The Somali Republic was clearly guilty of violating the provisions of the United Nations Charter and the guiding principles of the OAU. Indeed, the overwhelming majority of OAU member states would condemn the Somali Republic for its blatant act of aggression. In the circumstances, the Carter administration was compelled to renege on its pledge to provide "defensive weapons" when Mogadishu turned away from Moscow as its main arms supplier. This decision surprised and sorely tried the patience of Mogadishu's allies in the region, notably Presidents Sadat and Nimeiri, the Saudi government, and the Shah of Iran.

The Carter administration was deeply concerned over the emergency arms-supply program that the Soviet Union launched in favor of Ethiopia, criticizing foreign intervention in the war and urging peaceful resolution of the conflict under the auspices of the OAU. However, Washington's complaints failed to dissuade the Soviet Union, merely reinforced Ethiopian suspicions that the United States supported the Somali invasion, and was greeted throughout much of Africa as either piously utopian or intended to undercut the right of Ethiopia to adopt all reasonable measures for self-defense.

With the entry of Cuban forces into the conflict, the tone of statements emanating from Washington became even more strident. In a March 1978 news conference, President Carter warned the Soviet Union that its military involvement in Africa was jeopardizing chances for congressional approval of any future U.S.–Soviet arms limitation agreement. This linkage of arms control and the Horn crisis produced outcries in the Soviet press, which claimed that the climate of détente might be threatened by such U.S. actions. Finally, in mid-March, senior U.S. officials cautioned Addis Ababa against movement of its forces into the Somali Republic. Addis Ababa responded that it contemplated no such action, barring further Somali provocations. With respect to Mogadishu, the Carter administration bent its considerable energies to elicit a public declaration from Siad Barré foreswearing recourse to military means to readjust the Ethiopian-Somali frontier. Such assurance was not forthcoming in 1978.

On the whole, the United States found itself without effective policies and strategies as the Ethiopian-Somali war unfolded. In part, the Carter administration was unprepared for the series of events that materialized. The actual invasion startled Washington, and the president had few constructive options at his disposal. With Soviet-Cuban intervention, the opportunities narrowed further. When the crisis had passed, by the spring of 1978, the president was addressing other issues, and the U.S. State Department was engaged in a holding action in the region. Suffice it to conclude that the war did not represent a stirring chapter in the annals of modern-day U.S. diplomacy.

The Military: After-Action Assessment

The Soviet Union became the major actor in the Horn as a result of its arms transfer policies. Initially, Moscow concentrated its efforts in the Somali Republic, creating a fairly respectable establishment after that nation acquired independence in 1960. However, the Soviet Union confronted a number of obstacles in its efforts to create an effective military system. Among the most difficult to overcome were (1) the limited technical competence of the average Somali soldier; (2) the absence of an infrastructure-logistical base from which to build a modern military system; (3) the clan and tribal rivalries that divided the senior echelons of the Somali armed forces and impaired command-and-control capabilities; and (4) the impoverished state of the Somali economy, which constrained considerations relating to the size and combat weight of Somali forces. As a result of these deficiencies, the Somali military establishment had an exceedingly limited absorptive capacity in regard to Soviet arms, ancillary material, and doctrine. At best, the Somali soldier could be expected to perform best in mobile, small-unit actions appropriate to a desert environment.

The Soviet Union, for pragmatic and ideological reasons, provided obsolescent military equipment to the Somalis. Ill-adapted to desert conditions, the material tended to break down under combat conditions with disturbing regularity, much to the chagrin of Somali commanders. Further cramping the Somalis during their 1977–1978 Ogaden campaign were a series of shortages in the logistical system—once again a product of traditional Soviet arms supply policy. What cannot be ignored was the inferior quality of the Soviet equipment provided to the Somali Republic, which was representative of the Soviet military production system of the 1950s. By comparison with U.S. and other Western weapons systems of the same vintage, the Soviet military production system must be evaluated as shabby at best.

In contrast, the Soviet arms program for Ethiopia was more impressive by most standards of measurement. Approximately $1 billion in military materiel arrived within ninety days after the decision by Moscow to reverse its field of official support. The equipment included late-1960s vintage MiG aircraft, armor, and artillery. The insertion of Cuban troops met several goals simultaneously:

The Cubans would serve as a morale booster for the hard-pressed Ethiopian military establishment.

They could provide a defensive screen for beseiged garrisons in the Ogaden.

They would assist in training and indoctrination of regular and militia forces.

They would serve as advisers and as the cutting edge of forces dedicated to the recovery of lost territory in the Ogaden.

In the years since the end of the Ogaden war, the Soviet arms program has expanded to encompass all of Ethiopia's security needs, including the creation of large militia formations. According to most Western estimates, these efforts now exceed $3 billion. However, much as in the case of its Somali program, the Soviet effort has yielded only marginal dividends for the Ethiopian military establishment, which continues to experience severe difficulties in containing insurgent movements in the northern reaches of the country. Moreover, the quality of equipment, though appreciably better than what was made available to the Somali Republic, remains substandard and ineffective for use in the mountainous terrain of Ethiopia.

This failure of the Soviet Union to provide appropriate equipment, doctrine, and guidance in Ethiopia today is all the more startling given the Soviet military involvement in Afghanistan, where climatic and environmental conditions are not entirely dissimilar. The failure to adjust may be attributable to several factors—notably, the incompetence of Ethiopian planners and commanders, the lag time between lessons learned in Afghanistan and their application in Ethiopia, and a singular lack of willingness by Soviet advisers to relate their misadventures in South Asia to the Horn of Africa.

For Somali commanders, a most painful lesson was absorbed as a result of the 1977–1978 debacle. They have neither the strategic depth, the manpower, nor the material base upon which to challenge Ethiopia directly. Barring successful secession by other ethnic or regional groups in Ethiopia—leading to fragmentation—Somali irredentist aspirations are not likely to be realized in the immediate future. The Somalis, however, are a patient desert people who believe that the sands of history favor their destiny.

Notes

1. "War in the Horn of Africa: A firsthand report on the challenges for United States Policy," Committee on International Relations, U.S. House of Representatives, Washington, D.C., February 3, 1978, p. 1.

2. Ibid., pp. 2–3.

3. Rowland Evans and Robert Novak column, *Washington Post,* December 20, 1978, p. 28.

4. See "Report of the Committee on Foreign Relations," U.S. House of Representatives, August 1976, p. 201.

5. Ibid.

6. Harold Nelson and Irving Kaplan (ed.), *Ethiopia—A Country Study.* U.S. Government, Washington, D.C., 1980.

7. "Situation in Horn Fluid," *New York Times,* July 25, 1977, p. 3.

8. "Ethiopian Offensive Begins," *New York Times,* October 4, 1977, p. 8.

9. "Ogaden Battle Widens," *New York Times,* February 3, 1978, p. 4.

6

War in the Western Sahara

William H. Lewis

Now entering its eleventh year (as of 1985), the war in the Western Sahara has become something more than a chronological oddity. That the territory in dispute, and the issues involved, should attract far-reaching international attention could be considered anomalous at first glance. The Western Sahara is a dessicated land, endowed by nature with unimpressive resources; geographically, it abuts on strategic landmarks of only marginal military significance, and its original inhabitants comprise tribal and town societies of unprepossessing importance. Nevertheless, the war that engulfs the Western Sahara has led to the overthrow of one regime in northwest Africa and has placed at risk one of the few remaining Arab monarchies; it has also jeopardized the future of the Organization of African Unity (OAU), which was organized in 1963 to foster peaceful resolution of disputes within the region.[1]

For the United States, the Western Sahara conflict impinges on important regional and global interests. American support is regarded by King Hassan of Morocco as a test of U.S. will and determination in the face of adversaries, supported by the Soviet Union, that wish to wrest control of the territory from Morocco. For the Reagan administration, the conflict represents more than a test of the American reputation as a reliable ally; at stake is the geostrategic grand design the administration has fashioned to meet threats to U.S. interests in the Middle East in general and the Persian Gulf in particular. This design assumed concrete form in May 1982, when a special security agreement was concluded between the United States and Morocco that permitted the Rapid Deployment Force of the United States to use Moroccan facilities for transporting men and materiel to meet crises in the Arab lands to the east. In exchange, the Reagan administration agreed to increase its supply of arms transfers to Morocco, to establish a special joint intelligence committee, and otherwise to support the defense of territory under Moroccan control in the Sahara. By mid-1982, in brief, Morocco had become an American "client."[2]

This chapter was prepared through a grant provided by the Sino-Soviet Institute of The George Washington University. The author, though wishing to express appreciation for this support, is solely responsible for the views and findings presented.

The principal adversary contesting Moroccan control of the Sahara has been the *Polisario*—an acronym for Popular (Front) for the Liberation of Sakiet al-Hamra (or Saguia el-Hamra) and Rio de Oro—which was formed in May 1973 for the express purpose of ending Spanish colonial rule and creating a separate and independent state. It is one of the anomalies of history that Morocco initially lent material and diplomatic support to the *Polisario*. However, in the Tripartite Agreement signed by Spain, Morocco, and Mauritania at Madrid on November 14, 1975, Spain agreed to relinquish its control over the territory in favor of Morocco and Mauritania. The treaty also stipulated that the views of the local population, as represented by a territorial council (the *Jemaa*) would be "respected." The *Polisario* has contended that no effective expression of popular sentiment has taken place and that, in essence, the treaty represented a betrayal of Sahraoui desires for independence. In brief, annexation had been substituted for a process of decolonization that had been underway during the previous half-decade. As a result, the standard of rebellion was raised by the *Polisario* against Mauritania and Morocco. Supported by Algeria and Libya, the *Polisario* proved successful in compelling Mauritania to relinquish its control over the southern portion of the Western Sahara in August 1979 (see figure 6–1); however, Morocco occupies a significant segment of the territory.[3]

Morocco's Historical Claims

The Western Sahara is only one segment in a mosaic of territories to which Morocco has laid claim. The basis of this claim lies in the loyalty of tribes that long inhabited the desert as far south as the Senegal River and that, before the imposition of European colonial rule, recognized the religious authority of the Moroccan "Commander of the Faithful." This appelation was bestowed on the Moroccan ruler, or sultan, as a result of his putative descent from the Prophet Mohammed. This spiritual and secular lineage bestowed upon the sultan the role of head of an empire designated *sherifien* (descendant of Mohammed). Nomadic tribes and oasis dwellers in Saharan regions owed fealty to the ruler, occasionally paying taxes and offering levies for *sherifien* armed forces, in the manner of *guich* tribes (a form of militia). On the other hand, the Moroccan view of a historic role is not predicated on a modern concept of territoriality, which is at the core of the notion of the nation-state. The actual boundaries of loyalty to the *sherifien* ruler tended to expand and contract before the arrival of the European colonial rulers, depending largely on the force of arms and spiritual leadership of each sultan. Prior to the establishment of French protectorate authority in 1912, the Moroccan sultan had lost control over all of the Saharan tribes; the area of his sovereign domain was confined essentially to the imperial capital of Fez and surrounding coastal lands.

There is little point in reviewing the history of the nationalist effort to termi-

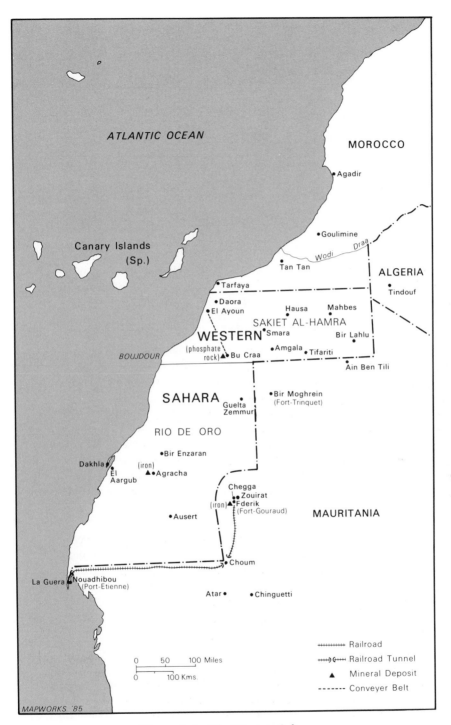

Figure 6–1. The Western Sahara

nate European protectorate authority in the Moroccan heartland. The struggle, which began in the wake of World War II, was brought to successful conclusion in 1956. At that time, the *Istiqlal* (Independence) party, which had been in the forefront of the independence struggle, began to propagate the idea of reunification of all formerly "loyal" subjects, including those in the Sahara, in a "Greater Morocco." The chief proponent of the idea was Allal el-Fasi, a charismatic co-founder of *Istiqlal*, who was greatly revered as a religious teacher and scholar. Early in 1957, el-Fasi founded a weekly Arabic newspaper, *Sahara al-Maghrib* (*The Moroccan Sahara*), to popularize the cause of Moroccan irredentism.[4]

Moroccan claims were not without merit, particularly where its borders with Algeria were concerned. The southwestern region of Algeria, especially the area around Tindouf, had long been regarded as Moroccan territory by France. Indeed, after the conclusion of the Protectorate Treaty of Fez in 1912, French authorities administered Tindouf from the Moroccan coastal city of Agadir. Only in 1952 was administrative authority transferred to French officials located in Algiers, and Moroccan troops deployed in Tindouf were subsequently withdrawn. The government of Morocco has claimed, not without foundation, that France readjusted the boundary allocating Tindouf to Algeria—which was officially an integral part of metropolitan France—only when it became apparent that the Moroccan drive for independence was gathering momentum. The discovery of rich iron-ore deposits in the Tindouf region has added an economic rationale or dimension to Morocco's claim to historic rights in the disputed zone.

The Moroccan effort to secure international recognition for "Greater Morocco" was to meet with only limited support. Independence for Mauritania and Mali in 1960 produced an outcry from Morocco, and a campaign was organized by Sultan Sidi Mohammed ben Youssef and his son, Hassan, who was to ascend the throne after his father's death in 1961, to gain support for the Moroccan position in the Arab League. The effort ultimately failed, but not without generating severe internal strains within the league—including a rupture in relations with Tunisia.

Having failed to secure international support for denial of sovereignty to Mauritania and Mali, Morocco concentrated its efforts on the continuing Spanish presence in Saguia el-Hamra and Rio de Oro. From the Moroccan perspective, the Spanish Sahara was Moroccan territory waiting to be liberated. The government of Spain, under Generalissimo Franco, was subjected to mounting pressure to retreat from the Sahara, beginning in the early 1960s. Other events and forces conspired to erode Spanish resistance:

> The situation changed . . . with the discovery of the world's fourth largest phosphate deposit at Bu Craa in 1963. Subsequently, as a result of the combined impacts of Spanish efforts to develop the local economy and the Sahelian drought of 1968–73, most of the population had become settled in small cities and towns by the end of the 1960s.[5]

In addition, the United Nations was beginning to focus its considerable energies on the Western Sahara:

> Inspired by the worldwide anticolonial movement, the new urban elite began to form modern nationalist political movements. After 1966, the U.N. General Assembly passed several resolutions calling for a U.N.-supervised referendum in the Western Sahara to enable the indigenous population "To exercise freely its right to self-determination and independence." At the same time, Morocco and Mauritania asserted historical claims to the area and argued that the results of any true consultation with the people of the territory would be favorable to their respective causes and countries.[6]

In May 1975, a UN Visiting Mission toured the Western Sahara and, after eight days of consultation with the local population, concluded that the majority of inhabitants supported both the *Polisario* and the goal of national independence for their territory.

Morocco's attention to the Western Sahara was dictated, in part at least, by its frustrating experience in extending claims to the Tindouf region of southwestern Algeria. Independence had been granted to Algeria in the Evian Accords of March 1962; in establishing a national regime under Ahmed Ben Bella later that year, the new government made clear that it had no wish to cede the disputed area to Morocco. Moroccans, who had universally supported their Algerian brethren in the traumatizing war for independence, felt betrayed by the obduracy of the Ben Bella regime. Almost inevitably, a collision of military forces arose, and in the fall of 1963, a three-week war of the oases erupted. Moroccan military contingents easily outclassed their Algerian counterparts, an outcome assured by the fact that Algerian contingents were essentially wilayist (guerilla) forces recently integrated into the newly formed national army and therefore lacked training in combined arms, tactics, logistics, and fixed-position defense. Tindouf was threatened by the Moroccan advances and, to counter the pressure, the then defense minister, Houari Boumedienne, determined to invest the urban Moroccan center of Figuig, located northeast of Bechar. The war ended as a result of the intercession of the Organization of African Unity (OAU), which led King Hassan to command the withdrawal of Moroccan forces from the Tindouf region—an action that sorely distressed some of his senior military advisers.[7]

Of somewhat paradoxical interest, the rush for the territorial heart of the Sahara also claimed the leadership of Mauritania. Partly to offset the claims of Morocco against its own right to sovereignty, Mauritania presented a competing concept—"Greater Mauritania." It was first outlined in a speech by then vice-president of the government council (later president), Mokhtar Ould Daddah. Speaking from the northern town of Atar in 1957, he declared that the people of Spanish Sahara were brethren. His claim was based not on the spiritual-secular authority of the Sultan of Morocco, but on the bloodlines of kinship. Shared ethnicity was now to vie with shared religious values. The importance of the

Ould Daddah approach should not be overlooked—since it was predicated on the concept of *ard al-bidan* ("the land of the whites"), which would embrace the populations of southern Morocco (the Dra Valley), Spanish Sahara, and parts of northern Mali and western Algeria. The Mauritanian claim was based on the eternal verities of nationhood—a common religion (Islam), a common language (Hassaniya Arabic), and common ties of culture, race, economy (Arab-Berber nomadism), and history. Mauritania, in short, was declaring its sovereignty by establishing historic and cultural claims that would rival those of Morocco. King Hassan accepted Mauritania's right to coexist in 1969 when *sherifien* claims to the territory were quietly dropped. Ould Daddah, who had become president of the Republic, succeeded in legitimizing his claims to "Greater Mauritania" and thereby gained acceptance by King Hassan II, who had succeeded his father, of the right of Mauritania to exist as a separate and sovereign nation-state. The litmus test that he devised was to create a buffer in the Spanish territory of Western Sahara.[8]

Initially—that is, from the mid-1960s until 1974—Ould Daddah supported the principle of self-determination for the population of the Spanish territory—to take the form of a plebiscite—believing that, afforded unfettered choice, the majority of Sahraouis would opt for close ties with Mauritanian kinsmen. John Damis, in his comprehensive study, defined the Mauritanian leader's views and objectives in the following terms:

> This belief was based on the close ethnic ties between Sahrawis and Moors—the two peoples share much in common, from their physical appearance to their Hassaniya Arabic language to their social customs. Moreover, many Sahrawi nomads migrated to Mauritania, and many Moors have family roots or ties in the Sahara. Mauritania's current prime minister, for example, Mohamed Khouna Ould Haidalla, comes from a small Reguibat tribe that was originally from Bir Enzaran in Central Rio de Oro. If the Sahrawi population expressed a preference for an independent state, at least Mauritania's national security would be served by a buffer between Mauritania and a potentially expansionist Morocco.[9]

Despite their diametrically opposed objectives, Morocco and Mauritania requested an advisory opinion from the International Court of Justice regarding the legitimacy of their claims to the Spanish Sahara. In a ruling rendered in October 1975, the Court rejected the Moroccan and Mauritanian claims to sovereignty over the disputed territory. The Court did acknowledge that "indications" existed at the time of Spanish colonization that "some" of the nomadic tribes of the territory had "ties of allegiance" with the Sultan of Morocco; it also observed that overlapping "ties" had existed between "almost all the nomadic tribes of Western Sahara" and the "Mauritanian entity." However, the Court found that these historic ties did not imply "effective and exclusive state activity" and therefore did not "establish any tie of territorial sovereignty between the territory of

Western Sahara and the Kingdom of Morocco or the Mauritanian entity." Hence, the Court, in its final summation, concluded that the people inhabiting the disputed territory, as a matter of equity, should be afforded an opportunity to express their preference through plebiscitary means.[10]

These means were to be denied the Sahraoui population, however. In November 1975, in a dramatic gesture intended to underscore Moroccan claims, 350,000 of its citizens, armed with the Koran, entered the northern portion of the disputed territory. The government of Spain was in disarray in the face of this challenge, with its leader of more than three decades on his deathbed and the issue of succession generating a specter of post-Franco strife. The dispirited leadership of Spain capitulated, signing the Tripartite Agreement with Morocco and Mauritania—the terms of which secured the withdrawal of Spain from the Sahara and the partition of the territory, with annexation the inevitable consequence despite the fiction of consultation with the peoples' representative assembly, the *Jemaa*. With the signing of the Tripartite Agreement, European colonial rule in the Sahara came to final conclusion. A new phase of conflict was about to begin, and with it the traumatizing effect of population upheaval, increasing economic strains, and the collapse of civilian rule in Mauritania.[11]

The Fragile Balance of Forces

The *Polisario* front was the first to act after the signing of the Madrid Tripartite Agreement. It convoked the *Jemaa,* which, in reality, was little more than a consultative body of Sahraouis appointed by Spanish colonial officials. At the behest of the *Polisario,* the *Jemaa* voted to dissolve itself and to transfer its legal responsibilities, however slender, to the *Polisario.* The *Jemaa,* which was truncated, was reconvened several weeks later, and this time at the behest of two of the parties to the Tripartite Agreement, endorsed the partition of their territory between Morocco and Mauritania. The third party, Spain, refused to permit its officials to attend the *Jemaa* confabulation on the grounds that the Secretary-General of the United Nations had declined an invitation to dispatch an emissary to witness the proceedings. Even to the present, Spain refuses to accept that the final meeting of the *Jemaa,* prior to annexation by the two northwest African claimants to the Western Sahara, constituted a free and genuine expression of the will of the Saharan people. Nevertheless, in April 1976, Morocco and Mauritania declared that the *Jemaa* action constituted confirmation of the will of the Sahraouis and proceeded to incorporate the area into their national borders.

Confronted by the prepossessing power of the combined Moroccan and Mauritanian military, which began to occupy the territory late in 1975, the *Polisario* initially retaliated by urging and subsequently organizing the movement of the majority of Sahraouis out of the contested territory. Although the precise number of "rejectionists" will never be fully known, it was obvious that the majority was "voting with its feet." They ultimately settled in refugee camps located outside Tindouf, in southwestern Algeria, where several hundred thousand victims of several years of drought in the Sahelian regions of the Sahara were already ensconced. From these refugee camps came the main recruits for the ranks of the *Polisario*—trained by Algerian specialists in insurgent warfare, armed by Libya and the Soviet Union, and increasingly supported by nations in Africa that contested the Moroccan and Mauritanian view that the principle of self-determination had been honored as the process of decolonization came to conclusion in mid-1975.[12]

As the military contest began to unfold in northwest Africa—for the war, eventually, would come to Mauritania proper and the Draa Valley region of southern Morocco—the odds appeared to weigh heavily in favor of the annexationists. Morocco and Mauritania both claimed military establishments of considerable capability when evaluated against *Polisario* forces. The combined numerical weight of the former exceeded 75,000, whereas the *Polisario* probably commanded no more than 1,500 recruits as the war began. Moreover, the Moroccan army had reasonably extensive experience in the desert, having acquitted itself well in the 1963 clashes with inexperienced Algerian troops. Moroccan units had also served in the former Belgian Congo in 1960–1961 as part of a UN contingent (they were later to be injected as a rescue force in Shaba Province in the same nation—now Zaire—in 1977 and 1978). In addition, Moroccan troops had served creditably with Arab forces against Israel in 1973. Mauritanian forces, much smaller in number, were comparable neither in experience nor in fighting qualities. Their primary duties had been a combination of ceremonial light infantry and mobile patrol for relatively remote towns and villages—in essence, an internal security service.[13]

Upon close examination, some of the disadvantages of the *Polisario* in 1975 were more apparent than real. The Moroccan military, for example, had experienced an internal crisis several years previously, when on two occasions some of its members had attempted to assassinate King Hassan II. The first incident occurred in 1971, when cadets from the NCO military academy of Ahermoumou stormed one of His Royal Majesty's palaces outside Casablanca, where he was celebrating his forty-second birthday, killed a number of the monarch's guests, and almost visited the same fate on the royal personage. In 1972, King Hassan miraculously escaped assassination when members of his air force attacked his personal aircraft when he was returning from vacation in France. The monarch subsequently eliminated all senior commanders of the army and undertook a loyalty examination of all middle-rank officers. Those of dubious loyalty were either summarily dismissed, retired, or rotated to units in more remote parts of the *sherifien* empire. An entire generation of military leadership was thereby set aside, and, thereafter, the army was incorporated into the royal household, becoming a personal instrument of King Hassan. The king exercised direct control over the officer corps—selecting candidates for promotion, frequently rotating field assignments, and otherwise seeking to ensure its future loyalty.

Concomitantly, King Hassan set in motion other processes and procedures that had the effect of maintaining rigid royal command and control over all elements of the army. For example, no senior officer was permitted overall command authority; few officers were permitted to remain in command of battalion-size forces for extended periods—to ensure against the crystallization of special loyalties or attachments; the air force command was frequently rotated; and all units were subject to regular inspection and, where deemed essential, continuous security surveillance.

The concerns of the palace were reflected in other actions taken to diminish chances of military insurgency. The number of personnel assigned abroad for advanced training declined dramatically; at the same time, the sources of modern military equipment became more diverse, with the result that the military system of logistics became complex and difficult to maintain. The army also was kept on short budgetary rations, which meant diminished training exercises, only marginal familiarity with advanced field tactics, and a severe reduction in combined arms experience. Although individual units were in reasonable fighting trim in 1975, the officer corps was low in morale, modern military equipment was in short supply, technical competence in several specialized fields was dubious at best, and the command-and-control structure under direction of the palace was rigid and left little initiative to field-grade officers who would be expected to direct battalion-size forces in the Western Sahara.[14]

The Mauritanian military establishment, which was expected to take over direct control of the southern third of the Spanish Sahara, already found its resources strained in 1975. The military claimed only a handful of senior officers with advanced staff training; logistics and communications capabilities were at exceedingly low levels; and troop discipline and morale, though seemingly sound, would not be able to sustain a lengthy war of attrition. In addition, the mobility of Mauritanian forces was exceedingly limited because of severe shortages of ground transport. Given the distances to be traversed to the Spanish Sahara, the difficulties of logistical support, and the uncertainties attending resupply, the Mauritanian military, by force of circumstances, would establish only static defensive lines around main towns such as Dakhla. The fact that a number of officers and noncommissioned ranks had family ties and some familiarity with the landfalls of the Western Sahara had little military value for the outcome of the war for Mauritania; if anything, it probably hastened the demise of the regime of President Mokhtar Ould Daddah in 1978 and the withdrawal of Mauritania from hostilities the following year.

The *Polisario* possessed a number of assets to offset its seeming military infirmities as the conflict began to unfold in 1976. Among the most salient were the following:

It had the luxury of a large reservoir of potential recruits—young men who were unemployed, fixated on grievances associated with annexation, and determined to redress these grievances.

It had an ancillary pool of manpower, constantly replenished by tribesmen who had affinities with their Western Saharan cousins and who were displaced by widening drought in the Sahel and chaffed by inactivity. Often, they also shared the sense of grievance of their Western Saharan cousins.

It had a sanctuary in which to organize, recruit, and train. Algeria, anxious to retain its "radical" credentials and suspicious of Moroccan designs in the west, was prepared to provide safe haven for the *Polisario* as well as other support services.

It had an in-depth familiarity with the prospective field of battle. The *Polisario* organization gained personnel who had a depth of experience with the terrain, places of concealment, and seasonal fluctuations that would prove of inestimable value in a lengthy campaign of maneuver.

It had the advantage in selecting targets of opportunity and the timing of assaults. The targets to be selected ranged from the Western Sahara to Mauritania to southern Morocco, which held the advantage of widening the field of maneuver, conducting assaults by stealth, and utilizing terrain features for retreat routes—all the while assuring economy of force and a high degree of surprise by attacking forces.

Added to these considerable "assets" was a physical and psychological conditioning provided by centuries of immersion in the harsh Sahara environment, which permitted *Polisario* units to operate under hardships that would demoralize military forces that lacked such experience. Given a cause and proper combat conditions, the *Polisario* entered the war with the odds against it more substantially narrowed than most military experts and area specialists realized.

The War Develops: Four Phases[15]

As the war in the Western Sahara began to evolve, several factors were likely to prove of overriding importance in prefiguring its ultimate outcome. Aside from purely military considerations, four significant factors were the morale of the populations most directly involved; the extent of their ideological commitment to the war; the internal political cohesion of the societies; and the impact of the war on their economies (as well as the resilience of the economies). At the onset of the conflict, King Hassan enjoyed far-reaching popular support for the recovery of lost Saharan territories, and he has been able to use this support as important political capital in securing endorsement of his strategies. However, with the passage of time and the worsening of the Moroccan economic situation because of the emergence of a number of untoward problems, the lengthy war has become as much an economic liability as it was once considered a political asset.

For the *Polisario* and its supporters, the conflict was treated as a matter of high ideological significance, one that assured firm morale and limited economic stress. The erosion that has occurred in *Polisario* ranks has been less apparent than in the case of Morocco; however, evidence of diminished support by Algeria and Libya, beginning in early 1983, has produced some erosion of will and determination.

Mauritania proved the weakest link in the triangle of adversaries. Already suffering from the economic effects of several years of drought, its national economy was experiencing severe stagnation in 1975. The overwhelming majority of the national population of less than two million had been uprooted and forced to relocate to new centers, where employment opportunities were minimal at best. The level of literacy and technical competence of the population was exceedingly low, and national morale might have been evaluated as less than promising in the face of a lengthy war in which slender resources might have to be diverted to an embryonic military establishment. Moreover, there had been no national outpouring of sentiment in favor of recovery of lost territories. Indeed, the prospect of war would only further enfeeble morale and, as would be demonstrated in due course, would strain both popular support for Mokhtar Ould Daddah and the cohesion of the Mauritanian ruling elite.

In terms of military factors, the *Polisario* possessed a number of advantages over its rivals, which would serve it well during the initial phases of the war. Its forces, though limited in numbers, could adapt their tactics to terrain with which they were familiar. Hence, throughout the region, they could exhibit greater capabilities than either the Moroccan or the Mauritanian forces in terms of mobility and maneuver, stealth and surprise, dispersion and concentration of forces, selection of targets, independence and initiative by local commands, and timing of attacks. In short, the *Polisario* could conduct its attacks in areas of its own choosing from the sanctuary of Algeria, and it could determine which resources it would employ and the objectives to be achieved.

By comparison, Moroccan and Mauritanian commanders were compelled to devise strategies for dealing with a low-intensity war, to be conducted over great distances, without clearly defined targets. The choices they confronted were painful—dispersion of forces or concentration, attrition or maneuver, flexibility of command and control or centralization, long-distance patrol or perimeter defense, lengthy retention of forces in the Sahara or frequent rotation of units and/or their commanders. As will be seen, the Mauritanian military never resolved these questions, and only in the past three years has Morocco fashioned an effective strategy for neutralizing *Polisario* tactics and advantages.

Phase One

The initial period of combat proved a time for testing battlefield tactics, improving troop performance, and developing reserves in depth to meet assigned missions and roles. During this period, beginning in late 1975, the *Polisario* intensified its recruitment program, organized mobile strike forces, provided them with light infantry materiel, and selected commanders capable of tactical improvisation and effective field leadership. Moroccan forces entered the northern two-thirds of the Western Sahara and, in conjunction with a program established by King Hassan to encourage Moroccan civilians to settle in the larger towns of the annexed territory, established a strategy of fixed-perimeter defense to safeguard these communities. Only sporadically did Moroccan forces conduct extensive reconnaissances in depth, and then with indifferent success because they lacked familiarity with the terrain. This approach was relatively congenial to the palace, which insisted on strict command and control from the royal throne. It also offered the prospect of retaining a low level of casualties while waiting out the *Polisario* in a war of attrition.

The first casualty of the conflict was the regime of Mokhtar Ould Daddah, which was overthrown by dissatisfied army officers in 1978. The war had been a wasting asset, and *Polisario* attacks deep into Mauritania had produced a virtual standstill in the national economy. Continuation of the war could only end in chaos for Mauritania. In August 1979, Mauritania withdrew from the war and, in a secret annex to a treaty with the *Polisario,* not only renounced all territorial claims in the Western Sahara but promised to turn over its section to the *Polisario.* Morocco frustrated the agreement by forcibly annexing the southern third of the Western Sahara and proclaimed the area as its thirty-seventh province.

Phase Two

The Moroccan military response to the expansion of its responsibilities in the Western Sahara came in three areas. First, the numerical size of local garrisons was expanded dramatically; by 1979, the overall figure grew to more than 60,000 men. Second, the palace determined that the capacity of the military to further expand its mobility and firepower required significant support. Sustained efforts were launched in the United States and in France to secure approval for the purchase of essential materiel and, in the case of the United States, to elicit a lifting of an official ban on the use of American military equipment in the Western Sahara. Finally, the palace determined that local military commanders should be afforded greater flexibility in terms of search-and-destroy operations against the *Polisario.* At the same time, a system to provide special emoluments for officers (and, presumably, enlisted personnel) who volunteered for extended service in the Western Sahara was established to compensate for family separations and to buttress morale.

The *Polisario,* fresh from its victory against Mauritania, found its own ranks swelling with volunteers. Concomitantly, new weapons were being supplied both to enhance its long-range attack capabilities and to provide its forces with needed air defense against Moroccan military aircraft. In 1979 and 1980, new opportunities unfolded for the *Polisario*. Moroccan supply lines had become extended, and the bulk of Moroccan forces were deployed to protect both these lines and widely separated towns and military installations. Taking advantage of access to Mauritanian territory and its capability for long-range operations, the *Polisario* launched a series of assaults that ranged from northern Mauritania into southern Morocco proper, including a well-publicized raid against the major administrative center at Tan Tan. The most serious setback suffered by Moroccan forces came in October 1981 at Guelta Zemmour in the Western Sahara, where a local garrison was completely overrun and several aircraft (including two aircraft supplied by the United States) were downed by surface-to-air missiles. The debacle at Guelta Zemmour proved a serious blow to Moroccan forces and compelled a reexamination of strategy.

Phase Three

In reality, King Hassan, increasingly concerned by the lack of success of his forces, had already launched a review of strategy in 1979. At that time, he consulted with several retired foreign officers. They pointed to a basic deficiency in the overall strategy that had been adopted—the failure to ensure a concentration of forces, which, as a result, had increased the vulnerability of the Moroccan military. The Moroccans had ignored the famous dictum of Frederick the Great: "He who attempts to defend too much defends nothing." In brief, dispersion of forces had produced logistical nightmares and glaring tactical weaknesses; it was better to defend a few selected centers well than to seek to protect too many potential targets. The conclusion reached was (1) that a strategy of vertical escalation would be preferable to one of horizontal escalation; (2) that concentration of forces would afford Morocco significant advantages in terms of interior lines of defense and communication, together with the preponderance of forces (sheer numerical weight) at Morocco's disposal; and (3) that a strategy of consolidation would permit Morocco to husband its resources and to benefit from recent developments in sensing technology and battlefield communications systems.

The result of this intensive review of strategy was a decision taken by King Hassan to consolidate his forces in a strategically defensible triangle called the "zone utile." This zone would encompass the capital of el-Aiun, the phosphate mines at BuCraa, and the ancient religious center of Smara. The Moroccan army—the Forces Armées Royals (FAR)—was withdrawn from six posts in the southern area that was formerly the responsibility of Mauritania and from other positions in the north-central areas. In the "zone utile," a great wall of sand was constructed, extending 400 miles along the outer perimeters of the triangle, with ground sensing devices implanted at regular intervals to detect *Polisario* efforts to breach the wall. In addition, minefields were implanted, artillery units were deployed at critical locations, small forts were interspersed, and mobile columns were stationed at main centers to reinforce units located at or near the wall. The zone embraced 90 percent of the Western Saharan population, its main mineral deposits, and key towns. The area outside was to be considered a "free fire" zone.

The strategy was well conceived and efficiently implemented. From the Moroccan perspective, it suggested a willingness to accept a lengthy war of attrition, which, at worst, meant a military stalemate. In the interim, casualties would be diminished and population centers would continue to grow under the protective umbrella of the FAR. The *Polisario* confronted the prospect of having to deal with a strongly entrenched adversary, amply protected by electronic detection and warning devices. Attacks on Moroccan positions with lightly armed *Polisario* forces threatened the decimation of attacking units. Little offsetting advantage appeared to accrue from the opportunity to roam freely through two-thirds of the Western Sahara, where access to population centers was not possible. For approximately two years, the main area of competition, given the military stalemate, would focus on the diplomatic front (particularly the Organization of African Unity). This nonmilitary phase of the conflict will be addressed in the following sections.

Phase Four

From mid-1981 until June 1983, the *Polisario* responded to the newly devised Moroccan strategy in three ways. First, it continued its recruitment and training of forces; mainline combat forces today are estimated at 8,000 men, with reserve components exceeding 2,000 volunteers. Second, a lengthy logistical system was created, beginning with the oases east of Amghalla. In these small centers, communications were established, crops were grown and stocked, and artillery was stored. Finally, with the apparent assistance of Libya, heavy artillery (ASU-57 and ASU-85 tracked artillery) and T-55 tanks were acquired and deployed forward. In addition, units reportedly were supplied with SAM-6s, heavy machine guns, and recoilless antitank guns. Over the two-year period, an entire supply network—designated the "Qadaffi Trail" in some circles—was laboriously fashioned with artillery shells and ammunition stored in caves and other well-concealed centers.

During the summer months of 1983, the *Polisario* launched its major offensive to the surprise of Moroccan commanders. Rather than continuing its past practice of sporadic, small-unit attacks, the *Polisario* launched artillery barrages from medium and long range against Moroccan positions. Of particular concern to the FAR were the intensity and lengthy duration of the barrages. For a period, Moroccan forces found themselves at considerable disadvantage because of shortages in counterfire capabilities, such as long-range artillery and shells. The air force was not inclined to launch vigorous reconnaissance or air strikes by fixed-wing units because of the rumored presence of SAM-6s, SAM-7s, and other surface-to-air systems. Ground forces, accustomed to the tactics of static defense and unfamiliar with the terrain, were less than audacious in conducting search-and-destroy missions.

By September 1983, the *Polisario* assault by artillery had diminished, and the FAR began to devise and implement its own counterstrategy. This was a two-pronged effort. The first prong consisted of slow advance of the sand wall outside the initial perimeter, extending eastward toward outlying oases in the direction of Tindouf. In December 1983 and January 1984, the second prong emerged in the form of large-formation advances to the south and east into the "inutile zone" to confront *Polisario* formations. According to initial reports, the two-pronged FAR strategy caught the *Polisario* off-balance, with substantial losses of men and equipment registered. At present, it is not clear whether the FAR approach will be sustained over a lengthy period of time or will prove to be ephemeral. If the move from static defense to offensive operations is conducted on a sustained basis, the final result could be a termination of the military stalemate in the Western Sahara. The ultimate determinant, however, is likely to lie in the regional political arena, rather than in the Western Sahara itself.

The Shifting Regional Balance

As both FAR and *Polisario* forces underwent frequent oscillations in tactics and strategy, King Hassan had to meditate upon the growing international recognition that was being accorded the political arm of his adversary, the Saharan Democratic Arab Republic (SDAR). Before the Guelta Zemmour debacle, the majority of OAU member states had extended diplomatic recognition to the SDAR. Earlier, at a 1979 summit meeting convened at Monrovia, Liberia, the OAU adopted a resolution calling for a cease-fire and an internationally supervised referendum to determine the political future of the Western Sahara. The Non-aligned Movement and the United Nations have since endorsed both recommendations on several occasions.

These were not the only pressures to induce King Hassan to embark on major diplomatic initiatives to protect the external interests of Morocco. President Carter, in the declining months of 1979, was also reviewing and revising U.S. foreign policy in the region. The injection of Cuban forces into the Ethiopian-Somali war in 1977–1978, the overthrow of the Shah of Iran in 1979, and the adventures of Colonel Qadaffi in Chad and elsewhere all served to produce a decision to sell U.S. military equipment for use in the Western Sahara to "restore the military balance." With considerable candor, the Carter administration felt constrained to admit that it was not prepared to lose another favored friend in the region. Assistant Secretary of State Harold H. Saunders admitted as much in prepared testimony before the Senate Foreign Relations Committee on January 30, 1980:

> Our interests and our values have been challenged by events . . . in the Near Eastern and South Asian area. Terrorism in Iran and invasion in Afghanistan have increased the importance to us of countries which broadly support our objectives in the world. Morocco is such a country.
>
> —We have a long history of close relations.
> —Morocco has supported us on many East-West issues.
> —It permitted U.S. military bases on its soil until 1978. . . .
> —It has historically taken a moderate position on Arab-Israel relations. . . .
> —In Africa, Morocco has consistently supported moderate forces, twice sending troops to Zaire to maintain stability in that country's Shaba province.
> —Morocco has publicly called for the release of our hostages in Tehran, and voted in the UN General Assembly for condemnation of the Soviet invasion of Afghanistan.[16]

Avowedly, according to Saunders, the U.S. government is not prepared to recognize the claim of Morocco to the Western Sahara in the absence of a referendum on the part of the population of the territory. The proposed sale of U.S. arms was intended to "strengthen Morocco while encouraging a negotiated solution to the dispute." Saunders took the position that the increase in U.S. arms flows would not afford Morocco an opportunity to achieve military victory; indeed, the best American assessment was that a stalemate was the only likely outcome of a war of attrition. Given that analysis of the situation, Saunders contended that the Carter decision on arms sales would nurture and encourage "a psychological climate in the region conducive to negotiations."[17] In short, the United States would encourage both sides to come to the negotiating table.

If by the words "both sides" Saunders meant to imply direct negotiations between the Moroccan government and the *Polisario,* he was certain to incur the wrath of King Hassan. Hassan has frequently characterized the *Polisario* as a group of "terrorists," vowing that he will never deal directly with that organization. As of the time this chapter was prepared, he continues to hold to this position.

Nevertheless, in 1981, the Moroccan government was under mounting pressure to alter its policy on the Western Sahara. In a remarkable about-face during the June 1981 OAU summit meeting in Nairobi, Kenya, King Hassan withdrew his opposition to a plebiscite among the inhabitants of the former Spanish Sahara territory. The plebiscite would afford the inhabitants a choice between independence or unification with Morocco. Proposing a cease-fire and an internationally monitored referendum, the Moroccan monarch associated his country with several UN and OAU resolutions calling for such action. By this action, Hassan temporarily disarmed his critics, many of whom contended that he was an autocratic ruler who regarded the principle of self-determination as anathema to his country. In part, the criticism being leveled against Hassan was the product of an abortive coup attempt that had been launched in March 1981 by two former members of Mauritania's Military Committee for National Salvation against the regime of Lt. Colonel Mohammed Khouna Ould Haidalla. The coup leaders were avowedly opposed to Mauritanian "neutrality" in the Western Saharan war, and their declared purpose was to align their country with Morocco in the wake of the coup. Not surprisingly, the overwhelming majority of informed observers speculated that King Hassan had encouraged—if not lent material support—to the coup plotters.

In the post-OAU summit meeting conducted at Nairobi, the Moroccan initiative was welcomed by the United States and a number of OAU member states. Almost immediately, however, the initiative began to come apart on the hard rock of incompatible positions. Hassan, as already indicated, refused to negotiate directly with the *Polisario*, declaring instead his intention to deal only with the Algerian government of Chedli ben Djedid—a position that the Algerian president declined to accommodate on the grounds that the issue was not bilateral in nature. For its part, the *Polisario* insisted on face-to-face negotiations; in addition, it levied demands that were completely unacceptable to Hassan. Among the most egregious demands were the following: withdrawal of all Moroccan forces from the Western Sahara; establishment of UN and OAU teams to monitor the cease-fire and to administer the area vacated by the Moroccans; and effective admission of several hundreds of thousands of Sahraouis to voter rolls in preparation for execution of the proposed plebiscite. It is not surprising that Hassan found these demands unacceptable.

As the diplomatic maneuvering proceeded in 1982, a decision taken by the OAU Secretary-General to seat an SDAR delegation at a meeting convened at Addis Ababa brought the regional organization to the brink of collapse. Morocco and its supporters departed the conference in protest and refused to attend any future OAU meetings at which the SDAR might be accorded official recognition in the form of delegation seating and participation in official discussions. (Morocco and its supporters commanded a "blocking" third—which precluded a quorum of attendees at OAU meetings.) The crisis appeared to have been resolved during the OAU summit meeting of mid-1983 at Addis Ababa, when the decision was taken not to seat an SDAR representative group. Morocco suffered a painful setback, however, when the majority of participants voted in favor of a resolution calling for direct negotiations between Morocco and the *Polisario*. Despite repeated appeals by various delegations from sub-Saharan nations to honor the resolution, Hassan remained obdurate. By the end of 1983, the OAU peace initiative had collapsed, and the war returned to its dreary round of attack and reconnaissance by fire—but with military stalemate the outcome most predicted by regional experts.

Final Observations

The war that has been waged in the Western Sahara has followed an all-too-familiar pattern. *Tactics* adopted by the two adversaries have shifted periodically—generally within a 18- to 24-month time frame—influenced largely by the vulnerabilities revealed by the respective sides. *Equipment* acquisitions have tended to become more complex and, hence, more costly as each adversary has maneuvered to acquire tactical advantage. *Manpower* has increased as the scale of combat has mounted. (Moroccan forces assigned to the Western Sahara have exceeded 75,000 in recent years.) *Losses* have tended to be minimal on both sides, given the sporadic nature of firefights, and therefore are well within the "acceptable" range. *Morale* has tended to fluctuate in both camps. A key factor for Moroccan forces, particularly the officer corps, has been the special emoluments accorded for Saharan service. Even enlisted personnel find duty in the Western Sahara advantageous, given the high level of unemployment in the civilian economic sector of Morocco. For the *Polisario,* no shortage of recruits is likely to confront its leadership if drought conditions persist in the Sahel and Sahara regions.

The outcome of the conflict, therefore, is likely to turn on a number of intangible, nonmilitary factors. Of critical importance is the Saudi subsidy, which, until recently, underwrote more than 80 percent of the Moroccan venture in the Sahara. Falling oil revenues has led Riyadh to curtail these subventions substantially, apparently pending the implementation of austerity measures by King Hassan that have been recommended by the International Monetary Fund (IMF). The monarch is presented with a troublesome dilemma, however. Efforts to implement the measures have engendered a firestorm of protest in Casablanca and other urban agglomerations, where levels of unemployment are relatively high. If the Moroccan economy remains in a depressed state over the next several years, alienation in these urban centers will mount, presenting the throne with local security problems that could strain the resources of its local forces and tax their loyalties if they are called upon to enforce a regime of suppression. On the other hand, a decision to dispense with austerity measures would lead to curtailment of IMF support and likely refusal by Saudi Arabia to reinstitute financial support for Western Sahara military operations at previous dollar levels.

Morocco also confronts other imponderables. For example, because of Hassan's refusal to negotiate with the *Polisario,* he risks diplomatic isolation in a number of quarters, particularly if the OAU fails to resolve the crisis. (One threat confronting Hassan is an OAU decision to seat SDAR delegations at future meetings and risk a Moroccan decision to boycott these conferences.) Hassan also cannot assume that U.S. material support will be forthcoming over the long term. The Reagan administration has sought to intensify its politico-military ties with Morocco—partly because of mutual esteem, but largely because of shared geostrategic interests. However, these efforts have attracted congressional criticism on several grounds: the Reagan administration is perceived as projecting East–West rivalries into the North African region; it is frequently criticized for having failed to induce Hassan to accept the inevitability of negotiations with the *Polisario;* and members of Congress contend that the administration has abandoned traditional American support for the principle of self-determination, thereby sacrificing any future role as peace broker. In opposition to existing U.S. policy, Congress has reduced the level of military assistance proposed by the Reagan administration, with some members enjoining the president to loosen existing politicomilitary ties with Morocco.

A major influence in the course of the conflict will be Algeria. During 1983, President Chedli ben Djedid signaled the desire of his government to have the Saharan war settled through peaceful means. Consonant with this view, he met with King Hassan in February and encouraged the initiation of measures intended to normalize relations between Morocco and Algeria. However, ben Djedid is not prepared to serve as a bridge between Hassan and the *Polisario* in negotiations; he perceives Algeria as a nonparty in the negotiating process, since the war is between Morocco and the *Polisario*. Thus, barring a shift in the formal Moroccan position, the outlook for a constructive Algerian role leading to conclusion of the war is far from promising. Under such circumstances, the influence of Algeria will remain, tilted heavily in favor of the *Polisario*—a factor that ensures that neither party will prove victorious through force of arms.

The military lessons derived from the Saharan war must be considered tentative for the very obvious reason that neither adversary has fashioned a strategy that assures ultimate victory. At the present stage in the conflict's evolution, certain paradoxes are also apparent. The classical view, in which recent "wars of liberation" have reached successful conclusion for the "liberators," is that military stalemate actually redounds to their advantage. During the period of decolonization after World War II, for example, most liberation struggles were won within the metropolises, on battlefields that were essentially political and psychological. Morocco is not a metropolis, however, and the overwhelming majority of Moroccans support the struggle because the Western Sahara is viewed as part of that nation's historical patrimony. Thus, whatever erosion of support for the war there has been has come from a minority and is not shared by the overwhelming majority of Moroccan political parties.

A second noteworthy paradox is the fact that the defense strategy adopted by King Hassan flies in the face of doctrines encountered in Western and Soviet military establishments, both of which tend to emphasize mobility, firepower, and surprise initiatives, rather than strategies based on the notion of attrition. Hassan's approach, combined with allocation of financial resources for the Sahraoui population under Moroccan control, has proved relatively successful to date. This strategy would appear to present the *Polisario* with an almost insuperable challenge—nothing less than a series of severe defeats of the Moroccan military in full-scale engagements.

Third, in the contemporary equilibrium, both adversaries appear to have achieved full integration of their objectives, policies, and strategies—at the political and military levels. As a result, the war has become a zero-sum game in which conflict termination is not likely to occur without the collapse of effort by one of the parties to the war. The ultimate paradox in the Western Sahara is that we are witnessing a limited war for unlimited objectives.

At the operational level, there have been several phases in the struggle in which offensive and defensive interactions have occurred. The paradox encountered here is that the defensive posture ultimately adopted by King Hassan is combined with an offensive character in its present stage of evolution. Moroccan forces no longer surrender the initiative to the *Polisario;* they now conduct offensive sweeps from their defense lines. The *Polisario* has yet to devise an effective counterstrategy, but considering the experiences of both adversaries, we can not rule out the likelihood of a new *Polisario* riposte. However, to the extent that Morocco will continue to garner battlefield superiority through tactical airpower—essentially in the form of helicopter gunships—it will enjoy long-term military preponderance.

Notes

1. Robert Rezette, *The Western Sahara and the Frontiers of Morocco,* trans. Mary Ewalt (Paris: Nouvelles Editions Latines, 1975).

2. William H. Lewis, "Why Algeria Matters," *African Index* 5 (March 1, 1982).

3. Almed-Baba Miske, *Front Polisario: L'Ame d'un Peuple* (Paris: Editions Rapture, 1978).

4. John Damis, *Conflict in Northwest Africa—The Western Sahara Dispute* (Stanford, Calif.: Hoover Institution Press, 1983).

5. Stephen J. Solarz, "Arms for Morocco?" *Foreign Affairs* 58(1979–80):282.

6. Ibid., pp. 282–283.

7. An interesting consequence of the 1963 war, for Algeria, is portrayed by John Damis:

> The Moroccan-Algerian frontier question remained a contentious issue between the two countries throughout the 1960s. One of the reasons the Algerian Army overthrew Ahmed Ben Bella in June 1965 was that he had considered giving up Algerian territory in his agreement with King Hassan at Saidia a month earlier. Efforts to resolve the frontier issue through bilateral negotiations produced the Treaty of Solidarity and Cooperation signed at Ifrane on January 15, 1969. A joint Moroccan-Algerian boundary commission recommended the acceptance of the frontier line adopted by the French during their final years in Algeria, and agreement was reached on the demarcation of this border at Tlemcen on May 27, 1970. King Hassan accepted the de facto border as the legal boundary in the Rabat agreements of June 15, 1972, signed at the time of the OAU summit meeting.

Algeria subsequently ratified the accord, as well as an ancillary agreement; Morocco failed to do so on the grounds, according to King Hassan, that Morocco had no parliament in existence from 1972 through 1977. See Damis, *Conflict in Northwest Africa*, pp. 18–19. Reprinted by kind permission of the Hoover Institution Press.

8. Mokhtar Ould Daddah, "Sahara: La Genese d'un Affrontement," *Jeune Afrique*, no. 79, February 27, 1976, pp. 26–7.

9. Damis, *Conflict in Northwest Africa*, p. 37.

10. See "Western Sahara: Advisory Opinion of the International Court of Justice," United Nations Document A/10300, October 17, 1975.

11. Virginia Thompson and Richard Adloff, *The Western Saharans: Background to Conflict* (London: Croom, Helm, 1980).

12. David Lynn Price, *The Western Sahara* (Beverly Hills, Calif.: Sage, 1979).

13. Tony Hodges, "Western Sahara: The Escalating Confrontation," *Africa Report.* 23 (March-April 1978).

14. See Damis, *Conflict in Northwest Africa.*

15. The analysis in this section is based on a series of interviews conducted by the author in Washington, D.C., in Paris, and during an extended visit to North Africa in mid-1983.

16. Statement by the Honorable Harold H. Saunders before the Senate Foreign Relations Committee, U.S. Congress, January 30, 1980. pp. 1–2.

17. Ibid., p. 6.

7

Lessons of a "Lesson": China-Vietnam, 1979

Harlan W. Jencks

On February 17, 1979, the People's Republic of China (PRC) launched a "self-defense counterattack to teach the Socialist Republic of Vietnam (SRV) a lesson." This was the first invasion of a communist country by another without any pretense of an ideological justification or any "invitation" by that country's people. On the surface, it was merely a fight over a disputed border. In fact, the official Chinese news media treated the "counterattack" as a virtually undifferentiated continuation of the escalating armed clashes that had disrupted the Sino-Vietnamese border since 1977. The primary stated objective of the counterattack was to pacify the border region and to permit its Chinese inhabitants to resume normal lives. During the first week of fighting, although actual war news was almost totally lacking, the PRC media carried dozens of stories about the return of peaceful normalcy that the "counterattack" had brought to the Yunnan-Guangxi border.[1]

Beyond that single stated aim were issues and goals that reached far beyond Southeast Asia. The military action could be seen as the logical continuation of a de facto choosing up of sides in East Asia throughout 1978. This process included the Brzezinski visit to China (May), the Sino-Japanese Peace and Friendship Treaty (August), the Soviet-Vietnamese Friendship and Cooperation Treaty (November), United States–PRC diplomatic recognition (December), the Vietnamese conquest of Kampuchea (December-January 1979), and Deng Xiaoping's visit to the United States (January-February 1979). The PRC-SRV border dispute thus was entangled with global power politics from the outset. The hardening of quasi-alliances was facilitated by the continuing hostility of the Soviet and U.S. governments toward China and Vietnam, respectively.

The Chinese "pacification" of the border was intended to "punish" the Vietnamese and "teach them a lesson." Exactly what this entailed was only gradually spelled out after the first week of the invasion. The initial lack of announced Chinese objectives helped keep the Vietnamese (and the rest of the world) off balance, since no one knew just how far, or for how long, or in what manner, the attack would proceed. It gradually emerged that the specific task of the Chinese People's Liberation Army (PLA) was to destroy Vietnamese gun emplacements and installations that "threatened" China, and to bloody the People's Army of

Vietnam (PAVN) sufficiently to dissuade it from further "provocations." In the latter regard, it was implied that PAVN regular divisions (as opposed to militia or border-defense units) were to be drawn into battle and "punished."[2] Chinese troops were also under orders to loot or destroy anything of economic value that fell into their hands. Factories, bridges, buildings, roads, mines, and so forth, were all demolished in a systematically punitive manner.

There were additional objectives. Although the Chinese were fairly consistent in saying that the only issue was the border dispute itself, it was evident that they hoped to relieve pressure on the Khmer Rouge by drawing PAVN forces out of Kampuchea for the defense of Vietnam.[3] A further unstated goal was to demonstrate China's regional military power and, implicitly, to reassert the traditional prerogative of "chastizing the barbarians" within the traditional areas of Chinese hegemony. Needless to say, this goal has been hotly denied, particularly in view of Beijing's ongoing campaign to paint the USSR and the SRV as "big and little hegemons."[4] Also unstated was a desire to test the PLA, which had not conducted extensive combat operations since 1962.

At the outset of the "counterattack," Chinese leaders were at pains to announce that the "self-defense counterattack" was "limited in time and space" and that China did "not want one inch of Vietnamese territory."[5] Despite the bluster of statements by both sides throughout the subsequent fighting, their conduct indicated just how strongly both wanted to keep hostilities confined to the mountains of northern Vietnam.

Although the attack was to be limited, the Chinese initially did not define just what the limits were. About a week after the invasion began, as it became clear that the PLA would not win the anticipated lightning victory, Vice-Premier Wang Zhen disclosed that Chinese forces would not go into the Red River delta.[6] The Chinese thus gave up the advantage of keeping their opponent uncertain about their military objectives. The battle would be confined to the mountains, which substantially reduced the danger of Soviet interaction (clearly the reason for Wang's statement) but also permitted Hanoi to prevent a decisive Chinese victory by simply refusing to send regular divisions into the mountains. That would not be necessary, since the economic and political heart of northern Vietnam was not in danger. From February 24 on, the PAVN had only to fight hard enough to make a face-saving show. The PLA would have to withdraw before the rainy season. The only place the PAVN made a stand thereafter was at Lang Son—and that was mainly for psychological reasons.

Conduct of the Operation

Timing

A combination of good luck and deliberate timing permitted the Chinese to strike at an extremely advantageous time with respect to both the global situation and tactical considerations. The Soviet-Vietnamese treaty threatened a considerable increase of Soviet military aid to the SRV, but the Soviet military presence in Vietnam was still fairly small in mid-February 1979. Chinese leaders probably saw time working against them in this respect and therefore wanted to strike sooner rather than later.[7] Furthermore, the Vietnamese were becoming heavily engaged in a guerrilla war against China's quasi-ally in Kampuchea. Although this was a continuing affront to Chinese prestige, it also presented them an opportunity by weakening the defenses of northern Vietnam.

Beijing had just "played the American card"; Deng had just returned from a triumphal tour of the United States, where he had loudly proclaimed his intention to "teach a lesson" to Hanoi. By launching the invasion only a week after his return, he made it appear that the "counterattack" had U.S. backing or at least acquiescence.[8] The Carter administration inexplicably reinforced this impression by allowing Treasury Secretary Blumenthal to proceed with his visit to China on February 24.

In retaliation for the Kampuchean invasion, the Chinese had cut off oil exports to Vietnam in late 1978. Since this had constituted over half of the SRV's supply, China's "counterattack" was nicely timed to catch Vietnam with very low reserves, before the Russians could make up the difference.[9]

Tactical surprise was achieved by attacking during the visit to Beijing of Indian Foreign Minister Vajpayee.[10] This was the first visit of an Indian cabinet officer to China since 1962, and it held the promise of breaking the ice between the two countries. Vietnamese leaders reasonably would have expected that the impending invasion would not begin until Vajpayee's scheduled return to Delhi on February 20.[11]

The rainy season begins in northern Vietnam in April. The PLA therefore had to move quickly if a campaign was to be conducted before the rains began. This required a trade-off against another weather/trafficability consideration far away to the north, where the spring thaw along the Amur and Ussuri rivers also begins in April or May. A Soviet ground attack into northeastern China would be facilitated by frozen ground and rivers, but it would be badly hindered by the thaw. Thus, the "counterattack" had to be timed to give the PLA a maximum of favorable weather in the south while leaving only a minimum of good weather to the Soviet army in the north. Mid-February seemed to be an optimum time.

Direct Soviet intervention was a constant threat, but the Chinese minimized it in several ways. In early 1979, the Soviets were known to be in the delicate final stages of the SALT II negotiations, and they were judged less likely to disrupt that process by reacting violently against China. Chinese spokesmen stated on several occasions that Soviet reaction had been "carefully and soberly calculated,"[12] would not be "too big,"[13] and could be dealt with if necessary. There was a certain bravado in these statements, which indicated considerable Chinese confidence that the Soviets would not, in fact, intervene. It turned out that Beijing was correct; Moscow reacted publicly only on February 18—to the effect that the USSR would "honor its commitments."[14] This proved to involve a considerable increase in Soviet supply shipments, airlift assistance, and aerial reconnaissance, all of which supported the SRV defense without risking direct involvement. It was evident to all, however, that the longer the fighting dragged on, the deeper Soviet involvement almost certainly would become.

For all these reasons, it was absolutely essential that the PLA go into Vietnam, administer the "punishment," and then get back out quickly.

Forces Committed

The Chinese press persistently referred to all PLA troops in the "counterattack" as "border guards" or "frontier guards" (just as was done in 1962). That was simply not true. Ten of China's eleven Military Regions (MRs) reportedly contributed forces to the Southern Front,[15] although the majority were drawn from the Chengdu, Kunming, Guangzhou, Fuzhou, and Wuhan MRs (see figure 7–1). Official Chinese news media depicted such equipment as 130mm and 122mm artillery pieces, 130mm multiple rocket launchers, pontoon bridges, and Type-62 light tanks—none of which was then assigned to regional or border units.[16] The combat engineer units that opened the way for the advance were virtually all main-force units, as were virtually all tank regiments.[17]

The size of the Chinese task force has been estimated variously, but the general consensus is that eight army corps (about twenty divisions) plus support units were concentrated near the border. Total PLA forces available probably numbered more than 300,000 soldiers, 700 to 1,000 aircraft, about 1,000 tanks, and at least 1,500 pieces of heavy artillery. Most of the maneuver forces and all of the aircraft were held in reserve and were never committed.[18] The initial attack was made by six or seven divisions, which later were joined by perhaps four more. At the climax of the fighting in early March, there were roughly 80,000 Chinese soldiers inside Vietnam, with up to 70,000 of them committed to the battle for Lang Son.

To meet the assault, the Vietnamese initially had about 200,000 construction troops. These proved to be much better trained, better equipped, and better led than anyone had expected. They put up a stubborn defense, which allowed reinforcements to arrive from Laos and the south—some flown in by Soviet transports.[19]

Naval and air forces were conspicuous by their absence from the battle, perhaps the most evident measure taken by both sides to limit the scope of the war. On February 24, both sides denied rumors that Haiphong had been bombed, and the Chinese spokesman added: "The Chinese air force has not been involved in the war and fighting has occurred only in border areas."[20] The conduct of both sides was shaped by their determination to limit hostilities in both time and space. For this reason, both enjoyed safe rear areas, and the war was a land battle only. Because they were restricted to jumbled and overgrown terrain, neither side had much incentive to test the other's air defenses. Effective tactical air support

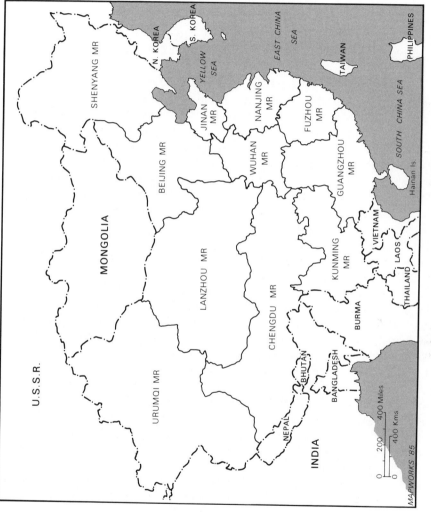

Figure 7–1. The Military Regions (MRs) of the PRC

would be difficult in such terrain, even for forces that were well trained and equipped for it (which neither the PLA nor the PAVN forces is). An air defense standoff existed in the mountains, where the PAVN was protected by its excellent Soviet-made mobile air defense systems. The PLA has only one operational surface-to-air missile (SAM), the CSA-1, which is a variant of the Soviet SA-2. It is transportable but not tactically mobile. The Chinese deployed a screen of CSA-1 along the Vietnam border on the eve of the "counterattack." It is probably no coincidence that the slant range of the CSA-1 is about 50 km and that Chinese forces reportedly were under orders not to advance more than 50 km into Vietnam.[21]

The fighting was extremely fluid. The PLA did not, and could not, occupy and pacify a solid zone of control behind its leading elements. Though initially crossing the border in some twenty-six places, the Chinese attack was aimed at about five principal objectives: the provincial capitals of Lai Chau, Lao Cai, Ha Giang, Cao Bang, and Lang Son (see figure 7–2). The PLA proceeded down principal roads, capturing population and communications centers as it went. Most of the fighting was for control of the flanking high ground that controlled these "lines and dots on the map." That the Chinese did not establish control in the entire no-man's land between their main lines of advance is seen in Chinese reports of Vietnamese troops attacking *inside China* throughout the "counterattack." In one case, scores of Vietnamese soldiers intruded into Napo country, Guangxi, on February 27—the day the battle for Lang Son was beginning far to the south.[22]

Both opponents employed the light infantry tactics of stealth and surprise for which they are justly renowned. When the Chinese attack kicked off at 5:00 A.M. on February 17, thousands of PLA infantrymen and engineers already had infiltrated into Vietnam to cut communications links, destroy selected installations, and secure crossing sites. Most of the combat actions described in the Chinese press were small-scale infantry engagements in the mountains.

The PLA added a new twist to an old tactic by "infiltrating" its light Type-62 tanks across the border through seemingly impassable terrain on February 17. There were several set-piece battles as well, and in these the PLA did not come off well. The Vietnamese defenders of Lao Cai, Dong Dang, and Cao Bang held up the initial Chinese thrust despite the attackers' massive artillery advantage.

The climactic battle was the siege of Lang Son, which early on assumed a significance far beyond its military importance. Located about twenty kilometers from Friendship Pass and 130 km from Hanoi, Lang Son controls entry into the Red River delta along the historic invasion route from the north. The Vietnamese, who slowly had been falling back on their own supply lines, easily could reinforce the town, which had long since been fortified against just this eventuality. Indeed, SRV planners allegedly intended to make Lang Son a "second Verdun."[23]

The Chinese investment of Lang Son began on February 27 with a tank-

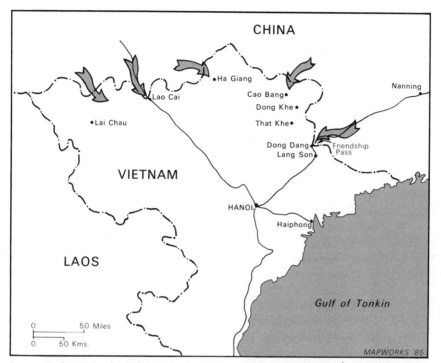

Source: Harlan W. Jencks, "China's 'Punitive' War on Vietnam," *Asian Survey* 9(August 1979): 810; adapted from *Far Eastern Economic Review,* March 2, 1979, p. 11.

Figure 7–2. The Chinese "Counterattack" of February 17, 1979

infantry assault, preceded by a massive bombardment, on the key high ground of Khau Ma Son, north of the city. In the days that followed, PLA units of up to regimental size advanced around the flanks of Lang Son, frequently fighting at night and at close quarters. The attack into Lang Son proper began on March 2, as the battle for some of the surrounding high ground was still in progress. The next three days saw the most brutal sort of combat, as the defenders were dislodged from houses, bunkers, and tunnels. The "fall of Lang Son" was reported as early as February 27 and almost daily thereafter. *Xinhua* (the New China News Agency) released a photograph "confirming" the capture on March 3, but the fighting continued for two more days.

With the capture of Hill 413, southwest of the city, at 2:40 P.M. on March 5, the PLA finally established control of Lang Son and opened the way into the delta.[24] Less than four hours later, the Chinese government announced: "The Chinese frontier troops have attained the goals set for them. . . . [and] starting from 5 March 1979, all Chinese frontier troops are withdrawing to Chinese territory."[25]

It took ten days to complete the withdrawal.[26] The PAVN followed just closely enough, and fired just enough artillery at the Chinese rear guard, to make a good show of it.[27] They clearly were not anxious to slow the withdrawal or to provoke a counterattack, any more than the Chinese were anxious to be caught inside Vietnam by the rains.

Lessons

Lessons for China

As can be deduced from the foregoing account, the 1979 Sino-Vietnamese war was underreported at the time, with most of the coverage provided by the official news/propaganda organs of the belligerents. Drawing the lessons from such an underreported war is risky business—for participants as well as for outside observers. The belligerents themselves write histories mainly for domestic consumption and to serve as justification for what happened. As John Amos notes:

> Partially, too, these histories are designed to influence the opponent. As [Anwar] al-Sadat once remarked, one of the functions of historiography, of the "lessons" drawn from events, is not to tell the opponent what one actually learned, but to lead him to believe precisely what one did not learn. Another is to provide him a cautionary tale so that he will not repeat the original behavior. But these historiographies, whatever their original purpose, have ultimately taken on credibility. Versions of events that started out as pure propaganda have come to be believed by the propagandists themselves.[28]

Sadat's observations certainly apply to the lessons learned or reputedly learned by the Chinese and the Vietnamese. It is ironic, of course, that the Chinese billed their invasion as a "lesson" for Vietnam. In fact, it appears that the Chinese learned more lessons—mostly unpleasant ones—than their opponents did. Many of the lessons China learned in this war are now being used to justify far-reaching changes inside China, particularly in the defense establishment. The lessons of 1979 also seem to validate many reforms that were already under way, or at least on the horizon, before the war began.

Political Lessons

For both belligerents, the war confirmed the usefulness of great-power backing. The United States was a useful counterbalance against the Soviet Union. This was made possible principally through the ineptitude of the Carter administration, which appeared to be supporting, if not indeed egging on, the Chinese.[29] The Chinese found that they were correct in predicting that the Soviet Union was unwilling to go to war on behalf of Vietnam, or at least unwilling to go to war unless the very existence of the Hanoi government was threatened. However, the

Chinese also noted the importance of Soviet aid to Vietnam, and they were probably somewhat surprised at the effectiveness of "nonlethal" Soviet assistance, which included military airlift within Indochina (notably, the transportation of troops from Kampuchea and southern Vietnam to the northern battlefront); air- and sealift of arms, ammunition, and petroleum products to Vietnam; and Soviet assistance with maritime reconnaissance and electronic intelligence. The Chinese also have seen, as has the world, that the war effectively cemented the Vietnamese-Soviet relationship and opened the way for permanent Soviet military bases in Indochina. It can be no coincidence that the Chinese sought to open talks with the Soviets in May 1979, very shortly after the close of the war.[30] Although they had talked very aggressively and defiantly about the Soviet Union being a "paper tiger" during the war and its aftermath, in diplomatic fact they made every effort to reopen channels of communication with Moscow. Sino-Soviet relations, though they are still bad, have been improving gradually since the end of China's invasion into Vietnam.

There were clearly some results that the Chinese had not anticipated and that caused the postwar situation to be, if anything, worse than it had been to begin with. First, the conflict along the southern border was extended to Laos, from which the Chinese were forced to remove the construction troops they had stationed there for over a decade. Vietnamese reinforcements in Laos, and a heightening of tensions, in effect spread the border war considerably farther toward the west.[31] The boundary troubles with Vietnam certainly were not settled, nor was the border pacified, and the latter was China's declared primary goal. Furthermore, there was little or no success in achieving China's main undeclared goal—assistance for the Khmer Rouge in Kampuchea. On the contrary, the Vietnamese have dug in their heels and have strongly asserted their contention that their occupation of Kampuchea is justified by the "Chinese threat."

The Chinese officially have denied or ignored the foregoing lessons. However, there have been a number of lessons that the Chinese have more or less openly acknowledged. The first of these was the incredible economic cost of the war. Although they have not released official figures on costs or on military casualties, they have given some indications. In his report to the Third Session of the Fifth National People's Congress, Finance Minister Wang Bingqian stated that the war had added RMB (*renminbi*) 2.04 billion (US$1.31 billion) to the 1979 military budget.[32] There undoubtedly were additional costs involved with replacing equipment in 1979 and 1980, which were hidden away in the budgets of various industrial ministries. A conservative guess would be that the total cost to China was RMB 5–10 billion (US$3.2–6.4 billion), which surely had a substantial impact on China's "four modernizations" effort.

Something else that the Chinese learned was that the Socialist Republic of Vietnam is a nation in arms. Quite clearly, the Chinese were shocked by the competence and intensity of the Vietnamese resistance. It now ought to be clear to the Chinese that their long-range strategy of "bleeding Vietnam white" is just not going to work. Although good evidence is lacking, it appears that the Chinese have provoked most of the artillery duels and infantry skirmishes along the Sino-Vietnamese border since 1979, usually in response to Vietnamese actions in Kampuchea. This military pressure has been combined with a comprehensive Chinese effort to isolate Vietnam internationally, especially with respect to its Southeast Asian neighbors. Although Vietnam's isolation has deepened, this has served mainly to strengthen the hand of the Soviets and to harden Vietnamese resolve.

The Vietnamese capacity for sacrifice and endurance in the face of foreign threat seems to be practically limitless, and the Vietnamese are simply not going to revolt and overthrow their government if things get tough. Unfortunately, the Chinese still appear to be committed to the "bleeding white" strategy and to the belief that they can force a change in the Hanoi regime. Thus, one vital lesson evidently was *not* learned.

The Chinese suffered a great deal of international opprobrium for their act of aggression. They antagonized not only the United States and Japan but also a substantial portion of the Third World. China's relations with all of the Association of Southeast Asian Nations (ASEAN) members were badly strained as well. For all these reasons, in the aftermath of the war, China has shifted back to more of a Third World stance in its international affairs, in contrast to acting almost like an associate member of NATO during 1978–1979. One thing the Chinese do believe—and to which they have pointed very proudly—is that they have maintained their own credibility as an ally, in that they stood up for their friends in Kampuchea. Furthermore, they believe (or claim to believe) that they have proved the Soviets to be unreliable allies, because the Soviets did not go to war to assist their clients in Vietnam.[33]

Military Lessons

On March 11, 1979, Deng Xiaoping reportedly told the Thai ambassador that the PLA "could have gone all the way to Hanoi if they wanted. . . . We have managed to face their crack divisions, and their crack divisions were not so much different from militia staying on the border."[34] The capture of Lang Son did, in fact, open the way into the Red River delta, and it was an important psychological victory. The PLA probably could not have advanced to Hanoi, however, for a number of reasons. First, of course, was the danger of Soviet intervention. That factor alone would have stayed the Chinese advance. For military reasons alone, however, it is unlikely that the PLA could have reached Hanoi unless it had been willing to commit its entire strength and absorb prohibitive losses. We have already noted that the air defense umbrella provided by Chinese SAMs reached only about 50 km from the border. Beyond that umbrella, the PLA would have been dependent on obsolescent antiaircraft artillery and short-range fighter planes based in Guangxi. Every meter of advance would have brought the invaders farther in under the modern and formidable Hanoi-Haiphong air defense system.

Out in the open delta, Vietnamese fighter-bombers, longer-range tank guns, and SAGGER antitank guided missiles could have been used to full advantage against the PLA and its lengthening lines of communications. Moreover, notwithstanding Deng's claim, few regular PAVN divisions were committed. At least five of them remained in reserve for the defense of Hanoi.[35]

In sum, the PLA had the opportunity to "conduct a modern war" after the fall of Lang Son but wisely declined it. There is no reason to believe that the PRC can project conventional military power any farther beyond its borders today than it could in 1950.

Many of the military lessons the Chinese learned have been rather explicitly publicized, and in most cases they were hard lessons. Some very bad mistakes were made, which, for the most part, have been admitted openly. There is at least the suspicion that some in the PRC government wanted to use a war with Vietnam to test the military readiness of the PLA and to determine just how prepared it was to fight a modern war. It is suggested by some observers that Deng Xiaoping and his group of civilian leaders were the main advocates of the invasion. Many senior PLA leaders are believed to have opposed the invasion because they opposed (and continue to oppose) changing the PLA, which is not prepared either materially or doctrinally for war beyond China's borders. The Chinese attempted to engage in combined arms operations, which are still rather new for the PLA. Such operations involve mutual support and coordination among artillery, infantry, tanks, antitank weapons, and so forth. One of the severe shortcomings in the Chinese conduct of the war was in command, control, communications, and intelligence (C^3I), especially at the front and corps levels. At lower levels of command, it appears that coordination, particularly between maneuver elements and fire-support elements, was very poor.

At the lowest tactical levels, a number of tactics that the Chinese have used, and that have been Chinese trademarks for many years, appear to have been called into question. For example, the Chinese quickly were able to devise tactics to dislodge the Vietnamese from the holes, bunkers, caves, and tunnels they had dug into the mountainous landscape of northern Vietnam, and Chinese publications boasted of the fact that the PLA dealt with this tactical problem so successfully.[36] The trouble with this Chinese success was that it seriously called into question China's own commitment to "dig tunnels deep and store grain everywhere," in accordance with the last military slogan left by Chairman Mao. The entire defense of northeastern China against a hypothetical Soviet invasion is predicated on defending heroically and effectively from caves, tunnels, bunkers, and holes. If the Chinese had an easy time against the Vietnamese, how much easier might it be for the Soviets, with their vastly better weapons and equipment, to deal with the Chinese doing the same thing?

Another tactical lesson that the Chinese learned was that, in the restricted mountainous terrain of southern China and northern Vietnam, their huge numerical advantage over the Vietnamese was largely nullified. They simply did not have the avenues of approach available to take advantage of their superior numbers, particularly since they had decided to undertake combined arms operations and had brought with them relatively large numbers of tanks, trucks, heavy guns, and so forth. This effectively limited them to roads, thus canalizing and restricting their attack.

Both of these tactical lessons—success against the caves and tunnels and the irrelevance of superior numbers in restricted terrain—have direct implications for the continuing development of the Chinese doctrine of "people's war under modern conditions," which is supposed to define the way China will defend itself against Soviet attack.[37] One of the few military advantages the Chinese have over the Soviets is the sheer size of the PLA, which, at least until 1979, was talking about relying heavily upon tunnels and caves. It would appear that neither tunnels nor superior numbers are necessarily a major advantage.

Beyond that, the Chinese have learned that their junior leaders are simply not very good tacticians. In the war with Vietnam, there was too much spirit and not nearly enough good tactics. The PLA reportedly incurred very heavy casualties in a number of engagements where highly motivated but poorly trained troops went charging into withering Vietnamese fire because their junior leaders simply lacked any better idea of what to do. According to some Hong Kong sources, Chinese tactics at lower and middle levels were so bad that some fairly senior PLA commanders were relieved during the conduct of the fighting. Though it lasted only a month, there were significant changes in Chinese tactics midway through the war.[38] For example, light tanks actually led some of the initial attacks, but they were relegated to a mobile fire-support role after sustaining heavy losses.

Apparently, the Chinese did maintain reasonably good communications security. They used land lines and low power on their radios, and they changed their call signs, frequencies, and procedures frequently during the course of the battle. This probably helped counteract the Soviet signal intelligence assistance that was being provided to the Vietnamese.[39] As indicated earlier, the Chinese were bogged down, as much as assisted, by their heavy weapons. Tanks and heavy artillery, and the logistical tail necessary to support them, effectively restricted the PLA to roads. It was therefore possible for the Vietnamese to ambush supply columns and reinforcements in the manner that, ironically, had originally been pioneered by the PLA.

The Chinese also learned that PLA officers did not know very much about how the Vietnamese army was organized and armed or about how it operated. They were therefore unable to take advantage of Vietnamese weaknesses. As a direct result, PLA officers are now being educated about both the Soviet and the Vietnamese armed forces. Ironically, although there was an overall lack of technical competence on the part of Chinese officers, it appears that, in a few cases, junior officers trained in the 1977–1978 period were overly oriented toward technical matters. Their training had so overemphasized machinery and technical aspects that they fell down in basic tactics and troop-leading procedures.[40]

Logistics was also an area in which the Chinese learned some very important lessons the hard way. The sustainability of a modern army in combat is a major problem. At various times and places during the course of the battle, the PLA ran short (or even ran out) of ammunition, fuel, and rations.[41] They had a severe problem with truck transportation—first because they didn't have enough trucks, and second because there were not enough roads in southern China even to get supplies up to the border. One immediate result was a major road-building program, which, in 1979–1982, produced a much-improved road net in southern China, leading right up to the border.[42] The Chinese learned that in the face of modern weapons, the old Maoist tactics of infantry charges and light infantry close combat led to very high consumption rates of both people and equipment. It was necessary for the PLA to turn to the Chinese militia for human porters to carry supplies in their time-honored way. In addition, the numbers of wounded were so high that the PLA medical system was simply unable to evacuate and care for them properly in a timely manner.

In general, senior Chinese officers were too old and set in their ways. Shortly after the war began, it became obvious that many of those in the revolutionary generation of commanders were simply not physically able to keep up with combat operations. There were cases of men in their late sixties (and reportedly even their seventies!) commanding regiments. This had an immediate impact on the cadre reform campaign within the PLA.[43] The campaign is now characterized by three slogans: "revolutionization, rejuvenation, and intellectualization." "Rejuvenation" means, first, the recruiting of younger, better-educated people into the armed forces and, second (and probably more important), the forced retirement of very large numbers of older military cadres. "Intellectualization" means not only the recruiting of better-educated people but a tremendous proliferation in military schools and academies for the formal training of military men, both officers and soldiers. By 1983, there was a systematic series of schools that an officer was expected to complete at various points in his career. The PLA had something similar in the 1950s under Russian tutelage, but the whole system was discarded during the Cultural Revolution as being "revisionist." It is all now being reinstituted and heavily emphasized.

The PLA structure was already being altered by 1978, but the lessons of the war reinforced the effort. The overall size of the PLA has been reduced considerably since 1979, and, more important, there has been a far-reaching reorganization. The engineer, artillery, and armor branches all have been reduced to the status of subdepartments of the general staff. This has considerably enhanced the general staff's ability to coordinate combined arms training by removing the obstacle of an entrenched bureaucracy atop each of the formerly separate arms. The extensive reorganization of the command structure and of C³I systems is very explicitly being attributed to the combat experience of 1979.

The Railroad Engineer Corps has been much reduced in size, and transferred to the civilian Railroad Ministry. The Capital Construction Engineer Corps appears to have been completely abolished. Border units of the PLA also have been reorganized considerably. Many former local force regiments have been converted to People's Armed Forces Border Police. This has taken place not only along the southern border but also in coastal areas, and these forces are now under the control of the Ministry of Public Security.[44]

The net result of all of these changes has been to reduce the size of the army, to relieve it of many of its nonmilitary roles and missions (for example, capital construction), and to get it largely removed from the domestic police duties it has had since the early 1960s. All of this should enhance PLA professionalism and make it a much better-trained and more purely military force. There has been a steadily increasing emphasis on conventional professional systems of rank, discipline, and status within the army. New, fairly conventional dress uniforms appeared on Army Day 1983 in Beijing. On May 22, 1984, it was announced at the National People's Congress that officer ranks would be reintroduced in the PLA. This was partly in response to widely reported problems encountered in 1979, when it was difficult to identify the officer in charge when units became intermixed and to rapidly identify replacements for officer casualties.[45]

The militia system also appears to be undergoing major changes. Again, the trend seems to be, first, toward a smaller, higher-quality force in terms of the selectivity of the people recruited. Second, some militia units are beginning to resemble conventional reserve forces. In 1983, for example, there was the first report of a militia tank unit. The personnel of this unit are all former members of the PLA tank forces who now meet occasionally to train with tanks. Although it is still called a militia unit, it appears to be part of an evolution toward a formal reserve structure.

The Chinese found that almost every item of hardware currently in PLA service is inadequate or worse. This not only has led to some improvements in military equipment but also has reinforced the effort, which was already well under way in 1978, for a major reorganization in military industry. To cite only two good examples, it was found that many of the Type-63 rifles in the hands of Chinese infantrymen were developing cracks in the receivers after firing as few as a thousand rounds.[46] This was evidently the result of poor quality control and manufacture, rather than anything wrong with the Chinese design itself. Reportedly, poor-quality steel contributed to a high breakdown rate among PLA tanks.[47] A very few Chinese designs appear to have worked out well. One of the notable successes was the laser rangefinder on PLA tanks. However, the PLA discovered—the hard way—the effectiveness of modern precision-guided antitank munitions when the Vietnamese used their Soviet SAGGER antitank missiles to destroy large numbers of Chinese tanks, particularly in the initial battles along the border. They further came to realize, in the aftermath, that modern warfare is an extremely expensive proposition, not only because of the inherent cost of modern weapons but because of the very high attrition rates in combat. The PLA not only needs modern weapons, but it needs many of them to replace the ones lost, damaged, or destroyed in battle. Another result of the war itself was that, although the Chinese had hoped for Western arms sources, Western misgivings about Chinese aggressiveness made it all the more difficult for the Chinese to get the technology. It was reported in 1979, for example, that the Harrier deal with Great Britain was delayed and finally canceled as a result of Labour back-benchers refusing to allow the sale of weapons to an aggressor.

Lessons for Vietnam

The Vietnamese have been a good deal less vocal about what they learned in the fighting with China, but some lessons obviously were learned. First, in the realm of national security strategy, the Vietnamese, too, drew some lessons with respect to the great powers. The war appeared to prove once and for all that the United States is utterly hostile to the Socialist Republic of Vietnam. It appeared to the Vietnamese, as indeed it did to the whole world, that the United States was collaborating with the Chinese in the effort to attack and damage the SRV. For the Vietnamese, the Soviet alliance was confirmed as a necessary evil. True, the Soviet connection did not deter the Chinese from attack and might not deter them from attacking again sometime. However, Soviet resupply activities, airlift, and signal intelligence, as indicated earlier, were crucial to the Vietnamese during the actual fighting. More important than that, however, was simply the Soviet role in forcing the Chinese to limit their attack. Very early in the war, the Chinese were forced to announce publicly that they would not enter the Red River delta, or attempt to overrun Hanoi, or try to destroy the Vietnamese government. This effectively nullified the huge Chinese population advantage as well as the Vietnamese disadvantage in geographical depth. Hanoi is located dangerously close to the Chinese border, but the Soviet alliance served to nullify that vulnerability.

Another lesson the Vietnamese learned was that the Chinese are not, and will not be, good neighbors. All of the ancient hostilities between the Chinese and the Vietnamese have been reopened. In this century, Vietnamese and Chinese revolutionaries have cooperated very closely, and the ingredients certainly existed for a close and friendly relationship.[48] Events since 1975, however, have returned things to the status quo ante. Chinese troops were under orders to inflict maximum damage inside Vietnam. It was organized, conscious, intentional vandalism that was clearly punitive in intent—that is, the behavior of a traditional hegemon attempting to discipline an obstreperous subordinate.

Initially, the Vietnamese were taken quite by surprise, for they had mistaken Chinese bluster for bluff. They have now learned to take PRC threats seriously, even if they do not regard another invasion as imminent, and they have prepared considerably better defenses. They have depopulated and militarized a zone along the entire length of the border, a measure they did not consider taking until 1979.[49]

Militarily, the Vietnamese found that their tactics worked well. They used fairly traditional, Maoist-style "people's war" tactics, allowing the Chinese to advance down the roads. The PAVN fought delaying actions and engaged in large-scale ambushes and raids deep in the Chinese rear. These delaying tactics were considerably enhanced by the superior long-range weapons (tank guns, antitank missiles, and the like) provided by the USSR. The Vietnamese had command, control, and communications problems of their own. In contrast to their excellent radio security during the anti-American war, they used radio a great deal and were not very secure about it. This made it possible for American and Australian intelligence services to gather a great deal of signal intelligence on the Vietnamese. Presumably, to the extent that their technology allowed them to do so, the Chinese also were able to gather signal intelligence.[50] There is no unclassified evidence, however, that signal intelligence (if any was actually collected) influenced PLA actions.

The major redeployments of Vietnamese forces from the south to the battlefront would surely have been impossible without Soviet help. This redeployment was, on the one hand, a problem in C^{3}I and, on the other hand, a problem of airlift and organization. One result of this "lesson" was the "theater of operations" concept, which the Vietnamese have adopted since 1979. As mentioned earlier, the Chinese attack in February caught the Vietnamese general staff somewhat off guard. They really hadn't believed the Chinese would do such a thing, "hence their strategic response was only an improvisation and the war was over before a true test of PAVN could come."[51] The initial brunt of the attack was met entirely by PAVN Economic Construction Divisions. Other units had to be rushed in by the Soviet airlift. The Military Theater of Operations concept was introduced in mid-1979 and was superimposed on the preexisting geographic command structure. It is intended to facilitate the defense of all communist Indochina against outside attack from any direction and particularly to facilitate defense against one or more outside attacks by defensive theaters operating more or less independently of each other. Theoretically, it should be less necessary in the future to transfer troops from, say, Kampuchea to the northern border, than it was in 1979.

There are four Military Theaters of Operations. The first, Theater A, which is the most important, constitutes the tier of provinces along the Chinese border. Here there are approximately 110,000 military construction troops (an increase of about 10,000 over 1979) and about 110,000 regular force troops (an increase of about 20,000 since 1979).[52] Theater B is a much smaller force, constituting the defenses of Vietnam along its coast from the Chinese border as far south as approximately Danang. Theater L is the northern arc from Lai Cai in Vietnam to

Phong Saly in Laos, established to block Hmong guerrillas infiltrating from China. Finally, Theater K covers the western border areas of Kampuchea. Theater K is concerned with the defense of the border against Thailand, not the internal fight against Khmer guerrillas. The Military Theater of Operations concept effectively welds together the three Indochinese armies of Vietnam, Laos, and the Heng Samrin regime in Kampuchea under the Vietnamese combined commander of each of the respective Military Theaters of Operations.

One of the major miscalculations made by the Chinese was their underestimate of what they presumed to be local-force divisions in the border areas facing China. In fact, what they encountered were what the Vietnamese call Economic Construction Divisions. Although they number only about 3,500 troops each, and therefore are approximately brigade equivalents in terms of manpower, they have very high percentages of older soldiers who are veterans of the anti-American fighting in the south. As Douglas Pike notes:

> The Chinese apparently made the mistake of regarding these troops as mere militia. . . . But because most were veterans of the long war in the South, these soldiers proved to be cool under fire, battlewise and skilled in guerrilla warfare techniques. They were, in fact, exactly the kind of military force to throw against a tank-led enemy army slowly advancing down confining mountain passes. Probably these troops were more effective against the Chinese than would have been the so-called crack divisions from Hanoi made up of younger unblooded soldiers.[53]

In terms of hardware, the Vietnamese were able to field-test many items of Soviet equipment that had theretofore not been used in combat. Most prominent among these were various types of laser devices (probably rangefinders) and, possibly, chemical agents.[54] However, in the aftermath of the 1979 fighting, there was a distinct shift in the nature of Soviet aid to the PAVN, from "guerilla-bashing" hardware (such as helicopters) to the more costly sort needed to fight a conventional limited war.[55]

In the area of electronic warfare, it is uncertain just what lessons the Vietnamese learned. As noted earlier, the PAVN had a good deal of Soviet help with signal intelligence, but it used radio rather heavily and insecurely itself. It appears, however, that the Chinese failed to exploit this to any significant degree. This may be because the Chinese are unable to do so for technical reasons, because the Vietnamese were engaged in deception, or possibly both.

Lessons for the World

Chinese behavior throughout the incident closely fits with Allen Whiting's theoretical construct of Chinese deterrence behavior.[56] The entire episode provided convincing proof, if any more were needed, that Marxism-Leninism is no guarantee against either modern nationalism or ancestral hatred. The bad blood between China and Vietnam was not significantly reduced because of a shared ideology that claims to be internationalist.

The big winners in the war clearly were the Soviets. China attacked a Soviet proxy, which, with Soviet assistance, was able to defend itself very effectively. The USSR gained the advantage of being seen as a loyal and helpful ally, while also being seen as a responsible great power. Soviet assistance to Vietnam was neither belligerent nor aggressive. There was no Soviet attack on northern China, nor were any Soviet personnel known to be directly involved in combat. Furthermore, the Soviets gained permanent bases in Indochina. They began building new installations and basing ships and planes at Cam Ranh Bay and Da Nang in the spring of 1979, just as their aid to the PAVN shifted toward more tanks, trucks, and fighter-bombers. Today, the Soviets permanently station submarine tenders and long-range reconnaissance aircraft in the SRV, and Soviet naval forces routinely use Vietnamese ports while operating in Southeast Asian waters. The increased Soviet naval presence in the area, with its implied threat to sea lines of communications, is greatly facilitated by these Vietnamese bases.[57]

Thus, many nations were ultimately affected by the war, and in almost all cases the results were detrimental to China. India, which had been extending feelers toward China, was grossly insulted when the attack took place while Foreign Minister Vajpayee was visiting China.[58] Sino-Indian relations went back into the deep-freeze, and the Indians moved closer to the Soviet Union and Vietnam. It is clearly no coincidence that shortly after the war, India became the first of a handful of nonaligned states to recognize Heng Samrin's regime in Kampuchea.

The world reaffirmed a lesson, reiterated by other authors in this volume, that modern war is incredibly lethal and costly. The initial casualty estimates made by all observers, including myself, were much too low. It appears that the Chinese had approximately 28,000 men killed in action and perhaps 43,000 wounded. Vietnamese losses are thought to have been about the same or even slightly higher. By means of comparison, that means the Chinese lost, in one month, more than 10 percent of the casualties that the United States incurred in over eleven years in Indochina.

The world noted that the sudden, aggressive onslaught strategy of the Chinese was ineffective for a number of reasons. First, the threat of Soviet intervention forced the Chinese to announce early on the limits of their advance. Second, the effectiveness of the Chinese attack was limited in time by the impending monsoon season. The Chinese were further limited by their inability to support a deep or long-lasting invasion, not only for political reasons but also because of logistical and technical factors. They were not able to advance any closer to Hanoi because of the inadequacy of PLA weapons, logistics, and tactics out in the open Red River delta. Chinese advantages in population, depth, and military manpower were nullified by the fact that it was a short war, confirming Robert Harkavy's comments in chapter 1.

In this particular war, it may be generalized that Vietnamese quality beat

Chinese quantity almost across the board. It did so (1) because of limiting terrain; (2) because of the limited time imposed for both political and climatic reasons; and (3) because of China's inability to employ effectively the forces it did have as a result of shortcomings in C³I and in personnel qualification and training and because of various organizational problems. Finally, Vietnam emerged from the conflict being perceived worldwide as a very strong middleweight regional military power. The Vietnamese have been rendered even more dangerous by the Soviet alliance and by the continued infusion of Soviet equipment since 1979. Douglas Pike believes the Vietnamese are now committed to some sort of coordinated military planning with the Soviet Union,[59] which bodes very badly for the future security and peace of Southeast Asia.

For their part, the Chinese appear to have done one thing that, in retrospect, appears more and more intelligent. According to Pike: "China's generals have indicated privately that they consider their incursion to have been a political (or psychological) victory but a military failure."[60] The Beijing leadership did what was once recommended to President Johnson: having made an advance into Vietnam, having inflicted some damage, and recognizing that they were, in fact, limited and about to become bogged down, they simply declared that they had won and pulled out. They thereby cut their losses and made it possible for those who wished to believe in a Chinese victory to do so with a certain amount of evidence to point to.

Notes

The following abbreviations are used for publications cited frequently in these notes.

AFP: Agence France Press

AS: Asian Survey

BR: Beijing Review

CQ: China Quarterly

FBIS: Foreign Broadcast Information Service (Washington, D.C.): "Daily Report—China"

FEER: Far Eastern Economic Review (Hong Kong)

GJJ: Guang Jiao Jing [Wide Angle] (Hong Kong)

JFJB: Jiefang Jun Bao [Liberation Army News] (Beijing)

MB: Ming Bao [Bright News] (Hong Kong)

PDR: Pacific Defense Reporter

XDJS: Xiandai Junshi [CONMILIT] (Hong Kong)

XH: Xinhua [*New China News Agency*]

XWB: Xin Wan Bao [*New Evening News*] (Hong Kong)

1. *JFJB*, quoted by Beijing Domestic Service, February 20, 1979, trans. in *FBIS*, no. 37, pp. E1–E2; and *Renmin Ri Bao* [*People's Daily*], February 22, 1979, p. 2. The following discussion draws heavily on Harlan W. Jencks, "China's 'Punitive' War on Vietnam: A Military Assessment," *AS* 19 (August 1979): 801–815.

2. *KYODO*, February 23, 1979, trans. in *FBIS*, no. 38, pp. A13 ff., cited an unnamed PRC source as saying: "The important thing . . . was to impress upon the Vietnamese that they have been 'hurt.'"

3. *Christian Science Monitor*, February 6, 1979, p. 4.

4. *XH*, April 13, 1979, in *FBIS*, no. 73, p. E2.

5. *XH*, February 17, 1979.

6. Nayan Chanda, in *FEER*, March 9, 1979, p. 14.

7. Soviet arms aid commitments under the treaty are discussed in *XDJS*, no. 28, February 1979, p. 38.

8. Banning Garrett, "China Policy and the Strategic Triangle," in Banning Garrett, ed., *Eagle Entangled: American Foreign Policy in a Complex World* (New York: Longman, 1979), pp. 229–250.

9. D. Rancic, in *Politika* (Belgrade), March 8, 1979, p. 1, in *FBIS*, no. 51, pp. A17–A18.

10. *AFP* and *XH*, February 15, 1979, in *FBIS*, no. 34, pp. A10–A11.

11. Russell Spurr, in *FEER*, March 2, 1979, p. 10.

12. Deng Xiaoping reportedly said this to EEC Chairman Roy Jenkins on February 23; *AFP*, February 23, 1979, in *FBIS*, No. 39, p. A1.

13. *AFP*, February 27, 1979, in *FBIS*, no. 40; also see Deng's alleged analysis in *MB*, March 4, 1979, p. 1; and *AFP*, February 21, 1979, which reports a Central Committee document to this effect, in *FBIS*, no. 37, pp. E2–E3.

14. Quoted by Mike Hanley, in *FEER*, March 2, 1979, p. 12.

15. *AFP*, February 25, 1979, in *FBIS*, no. 39. The same report cites an internal party document concerning a regiment from the Fuzhou MR that came to a bad end in a Vietnamese minefield.

16. See photographs in *BR*, no. 10, March 1979, p. 15; *Da Gong Bao* (Hong Kong), March 3, 4, and 7, 1979; and *MB*, March 9, 1979, p. 1.

17. *XH*, March 27, 1979, in *FBIS*, no. 62, pp. E4–E5; *XH*, March 1, 1979, in *FBIS*, no. 43, p. A13; *XH*, March 1, 1979, in *FBIS*, no. 44, p. A11; and *XH*, March 3, 1979, in *FBIS*, no. 44, p. A15.

18. *AFP*, February 27, 1979, in *FBIS*, no. 40. Deng confirmed to American reporters that U.S. intelligence estimates of the Chinese force's size were accurate. For statistics, see *AFP*, March 6, 1979, in *FBIS*, no. 46, p. A4; *XDJS*, no. 28, February 1979, pp. 38–39; *XH*, February 26, 1979, in *FBIS*, no. 40; Spurr, in *FEER*, March 2, 1979, p. 10; *AFP*, March 5, 1979, in *FBIS*, no. 45, p. A8; *New York Times*, February 24, 1979, pp. 1, 4; *MB*, March 8, 1979, p. 1; *KYODO*, February 20, 1979, in *FBIS*, no. 37, p. A6 (this

report mistranslates *Jun,* an army corps generally made up of three divisions, as "division"); and *GJJ,* no. 78, March 16, 1979, pp. 5–6. With more hindsight and Vietnamese sources, Michael Richardson gives somewhat higher figures in "Eyewitness at the Dragon's Mouth," *PDR* 9, no. 12, 9(June 1983): 41.

19. Spurr, in *FEER,* March 9, 1979, pp. 14–15; and J. Henri, in *AFP,* March 6, 1979, in *FBIS,* no. 46, p. A4.

20. Quoted by *KYODO,* February 24, 1979, in *FBIS,* no. 39, p. A9.

21. *GJJ,* no. 78, March 16, 1979, p. 8.

22. *XH,* March 2, 1979, in *FBIS,* no. 44, p. A12.

23. *GJJ,* no. 78, March 16, 1979, p. 7. The following account of the Lang Son battle draws on this account, supplemented by *XWB,* March 4, 1979, in *FBIS,* no. 48, pp. N3–N4; *BR,* no. 10, March 9, 1979, p. 15; *AFP,* March 4, 1979, in *FBIS,* no. 44, p. A16; *XH,* March 6, 1979, in *FBIS,* no. 45, pp. A10–A11; and *Tong Xiang* (Hong Kong), no. 6, March 16, 1979, pp. 4–7, in *FBIS,* no. 56, pp. L11–L12.

24. *XH,* March 17, 1979, in *FBIS,* no. 56, p. E5.

25. *BR,* no. 10, March 9, 1979, p. 12.

26. Premier Hua Guofeng told the visiting governor of Tokyo that the withdrawal was completed on March 15; *KYODO,* March 16, 1979, in *FBIS,* no. 53, p. A6.

27. *XH,* March 14, 1979, in *FBIS,* no. 52, p. A7.

28. John Amos, "Deception and the 1973 Middle East War," in Donald C. Daniel and Katherine L. Herbig, eds., *Strategic Military Deception* (New York: Pergamon, 1982), p. 329.

29. I disagree with Daniel Tretiak, who claims that the Chinese were disappointed by the American reaction in "China's Vietnam War and its Consequences," *CQ,* no. 80, December 1979, pp. 754–755. See my own views in Jencks, "China's 'Punitive' War on Vietnam," p. 804.

30. *Christian Science Monitor,* May 16, 1979, p. 1.

31. *MB,* November 5, 1979, p. 1.

32. Wang Bingqian, "Report on Financial Work," *BR,* no. 39, September 29, 1980, p. 13 (conversion to March 1979 U.S. dollars).

33. *XWB,* March 7, 1979. In an interview with the president of Japan's *KYODO* news service on February 26, 1979, Deng Xiaoping said that the PRC attack was intended to demonstrate that China was not afraid of the USSR; *FBIS,* no. 39, pp. A5–A6.

34. *AFP,* March 11, 1979, in *FBIS,* no. 49, p. A4.

35. Spurr, in *FEER,* March 2, 1979, p. 10. Several PAVN regular divisions were badly mauled, including the 3rd at Dong Dang, the 345th and 316A at Lau Cai, and possibly the 346th at Lang Son; *KYODO,* March 29, 1979, in *FBIS,* no. 62, p. E7.

36. *Cheng Ming* (Hong Kong), April 1, 1979, p. 6.

37. For details, see Harlan W. Jencks, "People's War Under Modern Conditions . . . ," *CQ,* no. 98, June 1984, pp. 305–319.

38. Li Man Kin, *The Sino-Vietnamese War* (Hong Kong: Kingsway International, 1982), pp. 58–59.

39. *National Times* (Australia), May 6–12, 1983, p. 7. A 1983 scandal involving the Australian Security Intelligence Organization resulted in the disclosure of fascinating details about U.S. and Australian electronic intelligence collection in 1979. I am grateful to Dr. C.A. Thayer of the University of New South Wales for providing me with relevant newspaper clippings.

40. For further details, see Harlan W. Jencks, "Regularization of PLA Ground Forces," in Gerald Segal and William Tow, eds., *Chinese Defence Policy* (London: Macmillan, 1984), pp. 53–70.

41. Li Man Kin, *The Sino-Vietnamese War,* p. 59.

42. Richardson, "Eyewitness at the Dragon's Mouth," p. 42.

43. The terms *officer* and *cadre* are used here interchangeably, although the PLA still uses only the latter term officially. Reintroduction of a formal officer rank system is imminent. The following discussion is drawn from Jencks, "Regularization of PLA Ground Forces."

44. Ibid. See also *Jiefang Jun Hua Bao* [*Liberation Army Pictoral*], no. 9, 1983, pp. 20–21.

45. *FEER*, May 31, 1984, p. 10; and *FEER*, June 7, 1984, p. 14.

46. *XDJS*, no. 63, February 1982, pp. 16, 18.

47. Li Man Kin, *The Sino-Vietnamese War,* p. 59.

48. For an excellent discussion of this point, see Bruce Burton, "Contending Explanations of the 1979 Sino-Vietnamese War," *International Journal* (Canada) 34(Autumn 1979): 702–704.

49. Douglas Pike, "Vietnam, a Modern Sparta," *PDR* 9(April 1983): 33; and *MB*, October 28, 1979, p. 1.

50. *National Times* (Australia), May 6–12, 1983, pp. 6–7.

51. This discussion is based mainly on Pike, pp. 34, 37, and 39. The quotation is from page 39.

52. Richardson, "Eyewitness at the Dragon's Mouth," p. 42.

53. Pike, "Vietnam, a Modern Sparta," p. 34.

54. Although there have been persistent rumors that the PAVN used chemical weapons, solid evidence is still lacking.

55. Pike, "Vietnam, a Modern Sparta," p. 38.

56. Allen S. Whiting, *The Chinese Calculus of Deterrence* (Ann Arbor: University of Michigan Press, 1975), pp. 202–205.

57. On the Soviet military buildup in Southeast Asia and its relationship to Vietnamese dependence resulting from the 1979 war, see Paul Kelemen, "Soviet Strategy in Southeast Asia: The Vietnam Factor," *AS* 24 (March 1984), *passim,* especially pp. 340–345.

58. Jencks, "China's 'Punitive' War on Vietnam," p. 805.

59. Pike, "Vietnam, a Modern Sparta," p. 38.

60. Ibid., p. 39.

8

Lessons from Central America's Revolutionary Wars, 1972–1984

Caesar D. Sereseres

Introduction

Since the end of World War II, internal war has become a dominant form of conflict throughout the world. In the past four decades, there have been approximately 125 to 150 conflicts (depending on which conflicts are counted and how often each is counted). Over 90 percent have taken place in the so-called developing regions of Latin America, Africa, the Middle East, and Asia, and about half of these "wars" have been, and continue to be, purely internal matters. Some have been wars for national independence from colonial rulers, and they have resulted in the creation of new states. Other internal conflicts have arisen from regional, cultural, linguistic, and religious divisions within a country. These sectarian wars (mainly defensive in purpose) have resulted in prolonged periods of civil war or, in some cases, the partition of existing states. Still other internal wars are conducted for the purpose of gaining political power by way of armed conflict. In these wars, "ideological" guerrillas explicitly seek to gain control of the state. This type of internal war, best described as "revolutionary warfare," is now taking place in Central America.[1]

The outcomes of post–World War II internal wars have been mixed: four out of five have failed (though some continue to survive), but three-fourths of the successful conflicts established new states. Only a small percentage of the revolutionary wars has resulted in the strategic expansion of the Soviet Union—the notable examples being Vietnam and Cuba. In neither case, however, was the Soviet Union a significant factor in the coming to power of either Ho Chi Minh (against the French in the early 1950s) or Fidel Castro (against Batista in the late 1950s). With the exception of the Angolan case, the Soviet role in assisting Marxist revolutionaries in Nicaragua, Ethiopia, and South Yemen began primarily after power had been taken and a regime established. Although the Soviets have intensified their political and military activities with regimes that have come to power by way of revolutionary warfare, those regimes are, for the most part,

---

A map of Central America appears on page 187.

institutionally weak, debilitated by their own internal conflicts. The only exceptions remain Vietnam and Cuba.

In 1984, some thirty major internal wars were taking place throughout the world, several of the most visible and intense being in Central America. All of these insurgencies had roots in the first wave of revolutionary warfare that took place in the 1960s, in the aftermath of the 1959 *fidelista* guerrilla success in Cuba. This chapter focuses on the revolutionary wars of Central America: the successful efforts of the *Frente Sandinista de Liberación Nacional* (FSLN) in Nicaragua in 1979, the failure of the *Ejercito Guerrillero de los Pobres* (EGP) in Guatemala in 1982, and the military stalemate between the *Farabundo Marti* (FMLN) guerrillas and the armed forces in El Salvador in 1984.[2] The conclusion of the chapter will discuss several questions: Can indigenous revolutionary movements adopt, or adapt their strategies to, the successful experiences of others? Did the FMLN and the EGP learn the right recipe for revolution from the Sandinistas? What are the unique circumstances of each internal war that determine failure or success in a guerrilla struggle?

Revolutionary Warfare as Internal War

The term *internal war* describes a situation in which there is a resort to violence within a political system for the purpose of changing the regime or its policies. Internal wars have common features regardless of the roots of the conflict, the ideology of the insurgents, or the nature of the regime in power. Harry Eckstein identifies these similar characteristics:

> All involve the use of violence to achieve purposes which can also be achieved without violence. All indicate a breakdown of some dimension in legitimate political order as well as the existence of collective frustration and aggression in a population. All presuppose certain capabilities for violence by those who make the internal war and a certain incapacity for preventing violence among those on whom it is made. All tend to scar societies deeply and to prevent the formation of consensus indefinitely.[3]

Theoretical and policy debates continue regarding the nature of internal war—its preconditions, the ways in which to carry it out effectively (or defeat it), the directions it tends to take, the consequences it has for society. The debates generally add to already long lists of explanations, supported by factual information but nevertheless inconclusive about internal war dynamics. Hypotheses about the determinants of revolutionary war abound, including Soviet and Cuban conspiracies, complex and dynamic social forces, newly emerging urban middle classes, weakened traditional social structures, the population explosion, government corruption and repression, and economic exploitation by domestic elites and foreign capitalism. The issue that is most often debated is external support for both the regime and the insurgents; in the case of a successful revolutionary war, the discussion often focuses on insufficient and untimely external assistance to the regime and significant, continual flows of external support to the guerrillas. This issue is at the center of the policy debate regarding revolutionary conflict in Central America.[4]

United States Foreign Policy and Revolutionary War

The issue of internal war and revolutionary conflicts holds a particular policy interest for the United States, especially because of the U.S. armed forces' concern with doctrinal and operational responsibilities in low-intensity conflict. Since Vietnam, the United States has done a considerable amount of soul searching about involvement in guerrilla wars. The U.S. response to the Salvadoran insurgency between 1980 and 1984 clearly exposes the loose ends of managing a security assistance program to a government involved in a revolutionary war.

To assess the adequacy of its doctrine, policies, and resources for low-intensity conflict, the U.S. government requires a systemic understanding of the nature of guerrilla insurgency and counterinsurgency, the world view of the participants, and the conditions that lead to success or failure in an internal war. More important, the U.S. government needs to assess objectively its potential for influencing allies that are fighting an insurgency, its capacity to manage military assistance under conditions of internal war, and its ability to avoid militarizing problems that are basically political. The current U.S. involvement in Central America can serve as a catalyst for a more serious and systematic look at the phenomenon called internal war.

As will be noted later in this chapter, there continue to be gaps in the understanding of *how* and *why* insurgents win or lose. The literature, academic as well as governmental, contains a substantial amount of mythology concerning success and failure in an internal war. However, despite the frequency of insurgency and direct or indirect U.S. involvement in these conflicts (usually in support of the regime in power), the U.S. government allocates few resources to exploring the subject itself or the regions of the world that are affected by such warfare. Research conducted on the lessons of Vietnam focus primarily on two themes: guerrilla warfare as a Communist political technique and the utility of U.S. military tactics and equipment in a counterinsurgency environment. The existing literature seeks to discover the Communist techniques of subversion in order to "fine-tune" U.S. counterinsurgency strategy. Little effort has been made to provide sociopsychological assessments (based on empirical studies) of why ordinary citizens become guerrillas and why insurgencies succeed or fail.

Despite the prevalence of revolutionary guerrilla warfare in the Third World, low-intensity conflict is still considered peripheral to the mission of the U.S. military. Attention now paid to low-intensity warfare is more in the area of "special operations" than the dynamics of internal war.[5] In the early 1980s, the U.S. response to existing insurgencies was to reorganize, not to rethink, the approach to internal warfare.[6]

Revolutionary Warfare in Central America

An unprecedented level of revolutionary warfare activity has taken place in Central America since 1978. The political strategy of the guerrillas is larger in scope and more complex than that which had previously existed in the Western Hemisphere. Several features characterize the region's conflicts:

Guerrilla organizations have developed broader domestic and international bases of support.

The war-fighting tactics have gone beyond the *foquista*[7] theory of the 1960s and now reflects a modified *guerra prolongada* strategy;

Guerrilla organizations have developed an elaborate and sophisticated "foreign policy" that extends to other Latin American nations, Europe, and the United States;

Governments, political parties, churches, labor unions, lobbying groups, and other external actors provide resources and are often directly involved.

These new features of revolutionary warfare in Central America have meant that internal war has been internationalized to such an extent that the outcome of a conflict can now be determined beyond the national boundaries of the country at war. The next section discusses the various factors that contributed to this new environment.

The Changing Central American Environment

The revolutionary wars currently being fought in Central America involve a second generation of guerrillas.[8] In Guatemala, Marxist-led insurgents and government armed forces have been in combat since 1962. During this two-decade period, the region has changed significantly. Throughout the 1960s, the United States was the dominant external actor—providing (without conditions) essential amounts of military, economic, and financial assistance. The governments from Panama to Guatemala were headed by conservative strongmen, closely linked (with the exception of Costa Rica) to national military institutions. Membership in guerrilla movements numbered in the hundreds, not thousands as in the 1980s.

By the early 1980s, the United States had become but one actor in the region. A Marxist regime had come to power in Managua by way of a protracted fifteen-year guerrilla war against Anastacio Somoza. Cuba, and to a lesser extent the Soviet Union, had established a political and military presence in Nicaragua. In El Salvador, 10,000 guerrillas were fighting 50,000 government troops and security forces. And the Guatemalan armed forces continued to fight the remnants of a 3,000-man guerrilla army in the Indian highlands.

United States "Disengagement" from Central America

The role of the United States in Central America has varied since the early nineteenth century. More than 150 years ago, the United States was unable to influence events in the area; by the turn of the century, however, it had become the hegemonic power. The first major challenge to U.S. hegemony in the twentieth century began when Fidel Castro succeeded in his revolutionary struggle against Batista in 1959. Castro's accession to power was soon followed by the Soviet Union's acquisition of a military outpost in Cuba. After the Cuban missile crisis of 1962, the United States came to tolerate Castro's Marxist regime (although a U.S.-financed and -directed campaign of economic sabotage and commando raids by Cuban exiles continued until 1964). Washington also came to accept the Soviet military presence, because the threat seemed marginal at the time. Despite these changes, the Caribbean Basin was still considered an "American Lake" until the mid-1970s.

During the early 1970s, the United States began to curtail its presence and capabilities in the region. The hegemonic position of the United States slowly disappeared, resulting in subtle changes in the geopolitical dynamics of the region. The U.S. "withdrawal" motivated Central American elites and revolutionaries alike to seek new allies. The fall of the Saigon government in 1975 and U.S. passivity (or paralysis, as some critics charge) to events in Angola in 1976 drew attention to America's "Vietnam syndrome," which was quickly interpreted as U.S. indifference to political events in Central America.

Such regional actors as Mexico, Cuba, and Venezuela responded with more active roles in Central America, and European political rivalries were extended into the region. The Socialist International party and the Social Democracy and Christian Democracy parties became part of the political scene as a result of newly established links with Europe. Meanwhile, the Soviet Union strengthened its military ties to Cuba as it explored traditional diplomatic links with countries in the region.

The decline in the U.S. presence and the subsequent change in the geopolitics of Central America went largely unnoticed until 1977, when a public debate on the region emerged in response to a series of events: the Panama Canal Treaty negotiations, the Nicaraguan revolution, the El Salvadoran civil war, the Guatemalan insurgency, renewed Cuban activism in revolutionary struggles, and the arrival of Central American refugees in the United States. Thus, by early 1982, it was evident that the decline in the U.S. presence in the region, the emergence of guerrilla conflicts and Cuban and Soviet willingness and ability to exploit these "targets of opportunity" had combined to seriously challenge the traditional political order of Central America.[9]

Cuba's Role in the Revolutionary Wars of Central America

How and why has Cuba come to play a role in the guerrilla conflicts of Central America? Fidel Castro's commitment to revolution and Cuba's national security interests provided the impetus for involvement in the political conflicts of Central America, and there now exists a new collaborative relationship between the Soviet Union and Cuba. In the aftermath of the 1979 Sandinista victory, the Soviet Union for the first time appears to be supportive of the Cuban strategy to assist armed struggle in the Western Hemisphere—or at least in the Caribbean Basin. The Soviets had long preferred following a more traditional approach to Latin America. Now, the USSR has to balance this "revolutionary" tint in its Caribbean Basin diplomacy with the more traditional diplomatic, trade, and arms sales efforts it had long pursued in South America.

Operationally, the Cubans, drawing on the experience of the Nicaraguan revolution, encourage a more sophisticated approach to revolutionary warfare. The current doctrine calls for the establishment of united fronts and the internationalization of internal wars. This war-fighting strategy requires that guerrilla groups form alliances and networks—domestically and internationally—with "progressive," "democratic," and "moderate" forces. Although this new war-fighting strategy was one lesson drawn from the Vietnam experience, the model did not take form in Nicaragua until 1978. Thus, although guerrilla groups in Latin America were quite aware of the lessons of Vietnam, the necessary conditions within each country and among the revolutionary groups and their non-Marxist opposition had to evolve to a point that allowed for implementation of such a strategy. In most countries of the region, internal conditions never permitted the lessons of Vietnam to be replicated. This is another indication that a successful revolutionary war needs more than just the "correct recipe."

Revolutionary war has been made viable in Central America because of long-standing socioeconomic inequities, injustice, abusive and ineffective government, and weak political institutions. These social conditions, together with Cuba's increased ability to export the technology of revolutionary warfare (not revolution itself) that is essential to sustaining guerrilla organizations and with Soviet collaboration and opportunistic strategy, doom the prospects for defusing the armed conflicts of Central America in the near future.[10]

The revolutionary war in Nicaragua was one of the first conflicts to take place within the new geopolitical and policy setting of the 1970s.[11] The next section discusses the main characteristics of the Sandinista revolutionary war against Anastacio Somoza, the politico-military strategy implemented by the

FSLN, and the model that is said to have emerged from the successful guerrilla campaign—the first in the Western Hemisphere since the 1959 *fidelista* victory in Cuba.

A Revolutionary Warfare Model: Nicaragua, 1978–1979

The fall of Somoza was not just the demise of a dictator. It also reflected upon the nature of U.S. power and purpose in Central America. To the very end, both the political right and left in the region anticipated a last-moment rescue of Somoza by the U.S. government. When this did not take place, a political disorientation took hold among many Central Americans for the greater part of 1979. In addition to the psychological implications of the Sandinista victory, the war itself had acted as a catalyst to internationalize the Central American region by establishing a global network for the funneling of financial, political, materiel, and propaganda resources. These international links continued as part of the region's conflicts in 1984. Finally, not only was the FSLN victory a vindication of the guerrilla war road to political power, it also resulted in bringing Cuba to the Latin American mainland. The victory meant that Cuba finally had a revolutionary ally in the Caribbean Basin. Thus, not only has Cuba become a visible element of revolutionary warfare in Central America, but issues of development and security raised in the aftermath of the Cuban Revolution reemerged in 1979— twenty years later.

The Internationalization of Internal War

Though in existence since 1961, the *Frente Sandinista de Liberación Nacional* (FSLN) did not gain serious prominence until August 1977, when the *tercerista* faction attacked the Nicaraguan Congress. Several costly offensives during the 1977–1978 period, and the January 1978 death of Pedro Joaquin Chamorro, editor of *La Prensa*, helped establish a more favorable climate for the FSLN's revolutionary war. By early 1978, the revised war strategy, involving three prominent guerrilla factions (representing the prolonged popular war, proletarian, and insurrectionist perspectives) required considerable assistance from the international community. According to one analyst,[12] assistance from the outside would be based on the following:

> The revolutionary conflict against Somoza required resources that could be obtained only from the international community.
>
> The FSLN revolution had to be protected from a premature identification

with Cuba—hence the requirement for diversified sources of weapons, equipment and financing.

The key to victory called for limiting all forms of assistance to Somoza from the United States.

By mid-1978, the FSLN strategy was mainly influenced by the *terceristas*—led by the Ortega brothers. One of the primary contributions made by *tercerista* strategists to the practice of revolutionary warfare in the Western Hemisphere was the establishment of independent political and military fronts and the establishment of alliances with non-Communists in both the domestic and international arenas.[13]

Thus, what emerges as the Nicaraguan model for revolutionary war took a far more sophisticated approach than any other guerrilla movement to date. The strategy was to internationalize every aspect of the struggle against Somoza and the National Guard. To accomplish this objective, the FSLN decided on the following: the creation of separate military and political fronts (the latter involving popular non-Marxist Nicaraguans); the creation of political alliances with "moderates," while the military side of the struggle remained firmly in the hands of FSLN commanders; the creation of a moderately oriented, social-democratic image that was projected domestically as well as internationally; and the creation of a bond with external actors that otherwise might not have involved themselves in the Nicaraguan war. All this meant that every effort was made to subdue Marxist language and to focus attention on the removal of a dictator, while maintaining organizational control of the military apparatus and monopolizing the resources drawn from the international community.

The Uniqueness of the Nicaraguan Model

Two elements make the Nicaraguan model unique—thus limiting its applicability elsewhere in the region. First, the figure of Somoza allowed the media, the governments and interested groups to focus attention on "the dictator" rather than on the insurgents. Little was known about the FSLN leaders *during* the struggle, and little effort was made to determine the consequences of a Sandinista victory. The war seemed to be against one man—little more. This has not been the case in either El Salvador or Guatemala.

A second element was the critical role played by international actors. Although they supplied needed material resources, external actors contributed even more significantly in three areas: they were essential in the international isolation of the Somoza regime; they were essential in imposing constraints on U.S. responses to the point that, in the end, all that could be done was to "push" Somoza out of the country; and they were essential in providing legitimacy to the

FSLN—making them appear as "just a bunch of democrats in fatigues carrying M-16s," as one U.S. foreign service officer observed.

Although the political character and disposition of the Carter administration (preference for inaction rather than reaction, priority to human rights, and a central concern for improving the worldwide image of the United States—all part of the "Vietnam syndrome") facilitated the internationalization of the conflict, events *within* Nicaragua had turned all social sectors against Somoza. Saving the National Guard would have been difficult enough; saving Somoza would have required a major U.S. military intervention. Although the Carter Administration had been accused of helping to push Somoza out, it was the only strategy that remained to save the National Guard and prevent a total military victory for the Sandinistas.

In El Salvador, a virtual mirror image of the Nicaraguan example of separate military and political fronts, worldwide diplomacy, alliances with non-Marxists, and international networks of support, the FMLN guerrillas have remained unsuccessful despite the nearby sanctuary of Nicaragua. To what extent U.S. military and economic assistance was a determining factor in the failure of the El Salvadoran guerrillas to succeed during the 1981–1982 period is open to discussion. Finally, the "no option" dilemma that existed in Nicaragua during the 1977–1979 period has not surfaced either in El Salvador (where three elections eventually brought Christian Democrat Napoleon Duarte to the presidency) or in Guatemala (where a military coup dismantled a political order that had been in power for fourteen years, implemented a devastating counterinsurgency operation, and is in the process of holding constituent assembly and presidential elections).

Before we discuss the case of El Salvador, the next section assesses the Guatemalan revolutionary war experience. The Guatemalan case focuses on a failed insurgency that had attempted to adopt many of the successful elements of the Nicaraguan model.

Revolutionary Warfare in Guatemala, 1972–1982

Second-Generation Guerrillas

The Guatemalan insurgents of the 1980s trace their roots to the 1944–1954 "decade of revolution." Today's guerrilla leadership claims a special tie with the "unfinished revolution" of President Arbenz. Even though the 1954 "liberation" did not return Guatemala to the pre-1944 era—or even undo most of the major legislation of the Arevalo-Arbenz regimes—it created a sense of "history denied" that has shaped the radical consciousness for twenty-five years. Idealized and romanticized by intellectuals, the "decade of revolution" and the radical leaders involved in it have provided today's guerrillas with a mythology and a sense of identity.[14]

While Guatemalan military officers and civilians were learning conflicting lessons from the successful counterinsurgency campaign of the 1960s, surviving Fuerzas Armadas Rebeldes (FAR) and Partido Guatemalteco del Trabajo (PGT) guerrilla leadership underwent searching self-criticism concerning the intellectual, political, and military assumptions that contributed to their failure.

After several years of travel in Cuba, Vietnam, and other Third World nations that had experienced revolutionary war, several of the survivors, joined by a cadre of new revolutionaries, formed the nucleus of the Ejercito Guerrillero de Los Pobres (EGP) in the remote Indian region of Ixcan. Beginning with a cadre of twelve members in 1972, the EGP grew strong enough to operate as a military and political force in six highland departments by 1980. The leadership of the EGP began the highland-based insurgency with a revolutionary strategy distinct from that of the 1960s. This second-generation guerrilla leadership became more sophisticated than its predecessors about opponents, opportunities, and capabilities,[15] and it rejected the *foquista*-insurrectionist strategy of revolutionary warfare. Although this model had proved successful for Cuba's *fidelistas* in 1959, the strategy resulted in guerrilla failures in Venezuela, Peru, Bolivia, Colombia, and Argentina during the 1960s. Such a strategy had left the previous Guatemalan insurgents politically and militarily isolated. With no secure geographical and population bases from which to recruit, the insurgents could use only one form of action—military. Because the guerrillas had little outside assistance and no international support network, it was easier for government forces to destroy the insurgents as a military force.

Therefore, the EGP leadership carefully analyzed the failures of the past and developed a new strategy with the following principles:

Reject *foquismo* and plan for a *guerra prolongada.*

Establish a guerrilla base and political infrastructure in a remote but populated area.

Involve the Indian population (previously ignored by the radical left and orthodox communists) in the armed revolutionary struggle.

Pursue a second, equally important front in the international community.

Three years elapsed between the arrival of the small political cadre in Ixcan in 1972 and the first major political act against the armed forces. By 1975, the EGP had established itself as the leading edge of the renewed guerrilla struggle. By late 1980, the EGP was joined in the armed struggle by three other groups: the Organización del Pueblo en Armas (ORPA), the Fuerzas Armadas Rebeldes (FAR),[16] and a dissident faction of the Partido Guatemalteco del Trabajo (PGT).

In November 1980, these four guerrilla groups signed an agreement to form the Unidad Revolucionaria Nacional Guatemalteca (URNG).

With this agreement, the guerrilla struggle assumed a unified front—if only on paper. The *appearance* of unity was important, because it was the price of assistance from abroad, especially from Cuba. The leaders of the respective guerrilla organizations also formed the Comandancia General Revolucionaria (CGR) to coordinate internal and external activities, plan military strategies, and formalize links to front organizations and international solidarity networks in Mexico, Central America, the United States, and Europe.

During the formative years of the EGP, there were few prospects for Cuban support. Although many of the leaders of the EGP had been trained in or had traveled to Cuba and other socialist countries during the 1960s, there is little evidence of a concrete Cuban interest in the revolutionary struggle in Guatemala. The death of Che Guevara in Bolivia in 1967, closer relations with the Soviets after the invasion of Czechoslovakia in 1968, the courting of military "progressives" in Peru and Panama in the early 1970s, support for the "peaceful road to socialism" (as exemplified by Chile), and the desire to improve diplomatic relations in Latin America all contributed to a lessening of Castro's commitment to revolutionary armed struggle. After the period of accommodation, Cuba focused attention on Africa beginning in 1975. Thus, the EGP developed and evolved virtually independent of Cuba, the Soviet Union, and the Communist support network. The EGP and the other guerrilla organizations had few prospects of significant and sustained Cuban assistance until the success of the Sandinistas in 1979. Today, the relationship between the EGP and other Guatemalan guerrilla organizations and Cuba is significantly influenced by the Cuban experience in the Nicaraguan civil war.[17]

In the mid-1960s FAR, MR-13 (Marimiento Revolucionario 13 Noviembre), and FAR-PGT guerrillas operated effectively only in the capital and fewer than five departments, mostly in the Oriente province. Never numbering more than 300 to 500 armed guerrillas, never operating in a column of more than thirty, and never taking a department capital, their most destructive attack against the military was the 1966 ambush and killing of twelve soldiers in Zacapa. In contrast, the EGP began with a cadre of twelve in 1972, but by late 1980, guerrilla efforts and counterproductive government counterinsurgency tactics had combined to increase guerrilla manpower to more than 3,000 fighters.[18]

By early 1982, guerrilla units operated in at least half of the republic's twenty-two departments; maintained a deeply rooted infrastructure in a six-department region of the northwestern highlands; sometimes operated in columns of as many as 200; and systematically attacked and often occupied and destroyed government municipalities, police stations, military outposts, and other symbols of public authority. Between 1978 and 1982, guerrillas had killed more than 1,000 national policemen and military and paramilitary personnel. During the

Zacapa insurgency, casualties among antiguerrilla forces accounted for only a small fraction of the total deaths. Thus, by 1982, the guerrillas had become a formidable political and military force in Guatemala and, just as important, had diplomatically extended their reach to the international community.

Military Politics and Counterinsurgency

Although allegations of electoral fraud in the March 1982 election were the immediate cause, the coup of March 23 was a response to high officer casualties, a growing insurgency, the loss of institutional and national prestige, and the absence of prospects for change. The young officers made the following statement in their first radio communique after troops surrounded the National Palace:

> [Given] the situation to which the country has been taken by means of the practice of fraudulent elections, accompanied by the deterioration of moral values, the splintering of democratic forces, as well as the disorder and corruption in public administration, it has become impossible to resolve these problems within a constitutional framework. All of which makes it imperative that the Army assume the government of the Republic.[19]

General Rios-Montt, in one of his first public statements, noted that the coup was a political act that would lay the basis for *political* solutions for the nation. Later, in a major address to the nation, Rios-Montt provided an assessment of Guatemalan national security and the nature of the subversive threat that, despite his removal on August 8, 1983, still influences military strategy:

> If we close our eyes, increase the number of soldiers and policemen, and we attack the subversives, we can do it [defeat the guerrillas]. And in three months the guerrillas will return. . . .
> Security does not consist of arms, tanks, and airplanes. This is not even five percent of the requirement for a national security policy. Security lies in the relationship between the state and the people. . . . Security lies in the sense of trust between state and people—that both will meet their respective obligations. . . . We have given the communists a flag. If we were, in fact, a democracy, Guatemala would be well today. But we have been corrupt. . . . We [the military] are here to complete a mission: institutionalize the state and channel resources and benefits to those in need[20]

The counterinsurgency campaign waged under Rios-Montt began on July 1, 1982, under the name Victoria '82. The strategy had three essential elements, the first of which was to increase the number of men under arms and deploy and maintain larger numbers of smaller units throughout the "zones of conflict" in the highlands. The key to the operational aspects of the government's counterinsurgency strategy was to substitute manpower for mobility. Operationally, the counterinsurgency strategy depended on *agrupamientos tácticos*—tactical combat groups—operating in the departments of Chimaltenango, Quiché, and Huehuetanango.

From the field headquarters of the tactical groups, small patrols were sent out to saturate areas under guerrilla influence. The terrain required the use of small-unit operations and saturation tactics. Short on manpower, the Guatemalan army mobilized some 5,000 reservists and former soldiers to assist in the initial buildup and new tactics. The zones of conflict covered all or portions of the nine highland departments. Some two million people inhabited the area—residing in more than 3,000 small towns and villages. Most of the villages were isolated by rugged mountains and by the absence of major roads and communication networks. The only way to gain government control of the area was to increase the number of soldiers on the ground and to establish a military presence in the isolated but populated villages of the highlands.

The chief of staff also improved command and control in the planning, implementing, and monitoring of military operations. Along with this, a military code of conduct was issued in July 1982 to improve relations between the army and noncombatants.

The second element of the counterinsurgency strategy was to expand and intensify efforts to establish civilian defense forces (CDFs) in the highlands. The military made special efforts to mobilize thousands of Indians into village CDFs in the "Ixil triangle," a region in northern Quiché department located in the geopolitical heart of the EGP. The civilian defense units were not just paramilitary organizations; they became a political entity at the local level—the only organization that could counter the guerrillas' local cadre, the *fuerzas irregulares locales* (FIL).

The third element of the counterinsurgency strategy was to initiate a socioeconomic assistance plan in the zones of conflict, a tactic reminiscent of the military's successful civic action programs against the guerrillas in the 1960s. The National Reconstruction Committee (CRN) provided food and services and coordinated small development projects in rural communities affected by the violence. Formed after the 1976 earthquake to coordinate international assistance, the CRN became a coordinating agency for civic action and social assistance to encourage the establishment of civil defense forces. The ultimate purpose of the strategy was to establish trust between the armed forces and the rural population.

The Victoria '82 campaign lasted for less than six months. It was during this time—with a mobilized, expanded army fighting in smaller units throughout the highlands, with the support of several hundred thousand CDF *patrulleros* (civil patrolmen) and the CRN, which assisted some 300,000 rural inhabitants directly affected by the violence—that deaths rose sharply and that several thousand refugees arrived in Mexico.[21]

Despite having broken the guerrillas—especially the EGP—*militarily* by late

1982, a *political* struggle has continued between the insurgents and the government over the allegiance of thousands of inhabitants not only in the rural highlands but now along the Mexican border from San Marcos to Peten, along the South Coast—areas that guerrillas were pushed into by Victoria '82. In mid-1984, both sides continued to mobilize the population, both realizing that the loyalty of the rural inhabitants will ultimately determine the outcome of the Guatemalan internal war. It is worth noting that although the potential pool of human resources for an insurgency in Guatemala is staggering—given socioeconomic conditions, poor government performance, and violence at the hands of government and nongovernment forces—the population has yet to be converted into a mass revolutionary movement.

On the diplomatic front, under Chief of State Gen. Oscar Mejia .Victores, Guatemala's foreign policy was changed to include a more active and constructive participation in the Contadora process.[22] Though still dubious of its potential effectiveness, the Guatemalans see the Contadora negotiations as one means to prevent the Central American conflicts to their south from spilling over into their own nation. One side benefit of more active participation in Contadora is an opportunity to discuss bilateral issues with Mexican government officials, especially the foreign minister. Using the regional Contadora process to enhance the bilateral relationship has improved the climate of cooperation and dialogue regarding border and refugee issues. The Guatemalan leadership seeks a secure border with Mexico, but it also desires to preserve a cooperative, bilateral relationship. The Guatemalans have come to realize that military pressure alone will not achieve this; serious diplomacy is also essential.[23]

Although the more sophisticated warfare strategy of the FSLN proved successful in Nicaragua, it has for the moment proved less successful, if not a failure, in Guatemala. The results in each case can be traced to several differences between the countries. Somoza was a prominent figure who provided a specific, clear focus to define the internal war. The Nicaraguan civil war was a struggle against a family dynasty. History was on the side of the insurgents, and enough individuals and institutions inside and outside Nicaragua wanted to be part of that history. Both Somoza and the National Guard made tactical mistakes that helped swell the ranks of the Sandinistas and contributed to the further isolation of the regime. Partial paralysis took hold in the U.S. government as efforts were explored to respond to what was seen as the inevitable fall of a dictator. The end came in the wake of an infusion of supplies from diverse sources (including the Cubans) and the institutional collapse of the National Guard. That collapse came about not as a result of a military defeat at the hands of the FSLN but as a result of Somoza's own spiteful intrigues as he departed Nicaragua for exile.

In Guatemala, the armed forces have been fighting insurgents since 1962. The military institution has maintained no alliances with individuals (as in Nicaragua) or with private economic interest groups (as in El Salvador). The Guatemalan armed forces have learned to change their tactics in the face of military and institutional crises. The military institution remains the most independent in the region as a result of three decades of U.S. intervention, Marxist-led insurgencies, and subtle conflict with the rightist sectors (economic and political) of Guatemalan society. Most important, at the necessary moment, it has been prepared to arm the civilian population in the battle against guerrillas.

These differences (there are many others) suggest why revolutionary warfare has been less successful in Guatemala than in other countries in the region. The next section examines the case of El Salvador, where the ongoing conflict remains unresolved despite more than $1 billion in U.S. military, economic, and financial assistance since 1980.

Revolutionary Conflict in El Salvador, 1978–1984

On October 15, 1979, a military coup led by progressive elements of the El Salvadoran armed forces ended thirty years of institutionalized military rule. The coup was in response to a political crisis that had begun with the election of General Carlos Humberto Romero in 1977. During the Romero presidency, guerrilla and popular organizations entered a new stage of armed and political activities. The coup brought about an end to a system of military rule and oligarchic economic domination in which neither was able to accept, or tolerate, political opposition, worker organizations, or discussion of land reform. Wealth and power in pre-1979 El Salvador centered on land ownership and little else.[24]

Much like the experience of Nicaragua, the revolutionary movement consists of diverse personalities, organizations, and war-fighting strategies. As will be noted, the first step toward armed struggle was taken by Cayetano Carpio when he formed the Fuerzas Populares de Liberación-Farabundo Marti (FPL-FM) in 1970 after a break with the El Salvador Communist Party. Carpio proposed a *guerra popular prolongada* strategy for revolutionary struggle. In 1971, the Ejercito Revolucionario Popular (ERP) was formed, headed by Joaquin Villalobos; it reflected an insurrectionist approach as the means to guerrilla victory. Later, in 1975, the Fuerzas Armadas de Resistencia Nacional (FARN) was established by Ferman Cienfuegos. This organization had split from the ERP.[25]

Each guerrilla organization was able to create a political front: the FPL had the Popular Revolutionary Block (BPR), numbering more than 50,000; the ERP had the Popular Leagues-28 February (LP-28), numbering 5,000; and the FARN had the Front of United Popular Action (FAPU), numbering 10,000 to 15,000. In April 1980, the Democratic Revolutionary Front (FDR) was established to act as an umbrella political front organization for all the guerrilla front and opposition political parties and associations. Later in 1980, a military political alliance was formed between the FMLN and the FDR.

Although those interested in the mythology of revolution point to the *Matanza* of 1932 as the root of the current conflict, Salvador Cayetano Carpio's break from the orthodox Communist party in 1970 is a more significant benchmark in the evolution of armed struggle in El Salvador.[26] Deciding that armed conflict was the most efficacious road to political power and social transformation, given the El Salvador political and economic order, Carpio formed the Fuerzas Populares de Liberación (FPL). With only several hundred hardcore members in the early 1970s, the FPL began its revolutionary war in the rural countryside of Chalatenango in northern El Salvador.

Since this modest beginning in 1970, the revolutionary war has evolved from small, fragmented armed groups, working independently within El Salvador and in the international community, to what is now labelled an "alliance" among the five guerrilla organizations. The Frente Farabundo Marti de Liberación National (FMLN) umbrella organization represents all five guerrilla groups: the People's Revolutionary Army (ERP), the Popular Liberation Forces (FPL), the Armed Forces of National Resistance (FARN), the Armed Forces of Liberation (FAL), and the Central American Revolutionary Worker's Party (PRTC). In mid-1984, the number of armed insurgents (including armed militia) was estimated to range from 8,000 to 12,000. It is believed that an additional 40,000 to 50,000 *masas*—mainly family members—provide direct and indirect support to the armed cadre of the FMLN.

Guerrilla zones of influence have expanded significantly since the late 1970s. From northern Chalatenango, FMLN activities spread to the departments of Cabañas, San Miguel, Morazán, portions of Cuscatlan, San Vicente, and Usulután. Usulután is believed to be the major access point for material support arriving from Nicaragua. One indicator of the growth in guerrilla strength during the 1980s can be seen in the number of municipalities that could not vote in March 1982 and March 1984. In 1982, voting could not take place in twenty-eight municipalities because of security problems. In the 1984 elections, twice that many did not vote. Although some of these municipalities were abandoned by the population between the two elections, the numbers do indicate the geographical expansion of the war between late 1980 (just prior to the FMLN's failed "general offensive") and mid-1984 (shortly after the May election of President Duarte).

Building Revolutionary Organizations and Alliances

Much like the FSLN's experience in Nicaragua—and critical to the sustaining of the revolutionary war—was the need to build alliances and organizations linked to the international community. In 1980, a strategic alliance was formed between the FMLN and the Democratic Revolutionary Front (FDR). In the early stages of its development, the FDR represented popular mass organizations (including labor and peasant movements) that on several occasions during 1979–1980 were able to put several hundred thousand people into the streets of San Salvador. During 1980, both the leadership and the rank-and-file of FDR member organizations were decimated by government and right-wing paramilitary activities. By the time of the "general offensive" in January 1981, the mass organizations had become mere paper entities—virtual empty shells. The failed guerrilla offensive marked the beginning of the militarization phase of the revolutionary conflict in El Salvador.

The FDR's function today is mainly to represent the FMLN in the international community. On paper, the FDR represents diverse "democratic" groups, such as the party of FDR President Guillermo Ungo, the National Revolutionary Movement (MNR) and the Popular Social Christian Movement (MPSC), made up of those who left the Christian Democratic Party in 1980. The FDR is also composed of representatives from various professional associations. It serves as the FMLN's foreign ministry, providing the guerrilla leadership with extensive ties to the non-Communist international community.

Thus, three characteristics that proved essential to the success of the FSLN in Nicaragua also appear in the case of El Salvador:

The creation of a military and political front, including the involvement of well-known, non-Marxist Salvadorans in the political front;

The enhancement of FMLN access to external sources of support by the "strategic alliance" with moderate groups represented by the FDR;

The promotion of a "social democratic" image to the international community by way of such moderate spokesmen as Ungo, while the power of the revolutionary movement remained totally in the hands of Marxist guerrilla commanders.

It may have been coincidence, a mimicking of the successful example of Nicaragua, or, as some argue, softly induced pressure from the Cubans that during 1980—less than one year after the Sandinista victory—caused the insurgency in El Salvador to begin to take on a structural appearance similar to that of the FSLN. Despite earlier military and political gains, however, the FMLN has not been able to match the revolutionary dynamics that catapulted the Sandinistas to political power in Nicaragua.

In the mid-1970s, the Nicaraguan guerrillas were seen as "losers" after more than fifteen years of struggle against Somoza. After the failed offensives of late 1977 and 1978, they were pronounced seriously, if not terminally ill by observers of the conflict. The offensives reduced the FSLN guerrilla cadre to less than 500 armed personnel; by early 1979, the guerrilla force had been built back up to 5,000, and by June 1979, a 1:1 ratio (15,000 each) existed between the National Guard and the FSLN guerrilla force.

In El Salvador, the guerrillas have grown from several hundred in the early 1970s to a few thousand in 1980, to more than 10,000 in 1984. The military, however, grew from less than 15,000 in 1980 to more than 40,000 in 1984. There are an additional 10,000 armed personnel in the security forces—the National Guard, the National Police, and the Treasury Police. The growth and development of those responsible for combating the guerrillas are mainly the result of some $400 million in U.S. military assistance. However, external assistance from the United States may be secondary in explaining the failure of the FMLN (rather than the success of the counterinsurgent forces).

The Limits of the FSLN Model

Though not pronouncing the FMLN dead as a revolutionary movement, certain critical elements in the Nicaraguan case either have not been present in El Salvador or, if present, have not been properly exploited by the revolutionary leadership. The general offensive in El Salvador, unlike that in Nicaragua, did not turn the world against the regime. The guerrillas failed to take a major urban area—unlike the FSLN in Nicaragua. Had the FMLN succeeded in capturing an urban center, the El Salvadoran air force possessed few aircraft to retake the city. The Nicaraguan air force inflicted serious damage and numerous casualties among the civilian population in the cities taken during the 1978 FSLN offensive. These air attacks against the northern urban centers provided the FSLN with a youthful manpower pool to expand at a critical period in the revolutionary struggle. Such a situation never materialized in El Salvador in the 1982 guerrilla offensive.

Second, the death of Archbishop Romero in 1980, unlike the death of Pedro Chamorro, did not galvanize "moderate" opposition to the existing regime. Furthermore, the guerrillas could never focus attention on one individual as *the* problem; that is, after the October 1979 military coup and the reforms of 1980–1981 under a series of "governments" that included Christian Democrats, the armed opposition had to talk in more abstract terms, not in terms of the removal of a single individual.

Despite the conditions for revolution in El Salvador in terms of socioeconomic inequalities, repression and brutal violence directed at those involved in political dissent, political corruption, and economic exploitation of the rural peasantry, the FMLN has been able to survive militarily in El Salvador while consistently losing political ground in the international community since the 1982 elections. Several factors explain FMLN shortcomings in El Salvador in light of the FSLN experience:

An independent moderate opposition has survived and provides leadership as well as rank-and-file members.

Elections appear to make a difference for a significant majority of the population—especially those living in the areas of conflict.

Government intransigence is not prevalent (as in the case of Somoza); individuals and parties have been and appear to be willing to relinquish power via the electoral process (and considerable pressure from outside—namely, the United States).

International actors, while carrying on dialogues with the FDR and pressuring for negotiations in El Salvador, have provided little direct military assistance to the FMLN.

In summary, actors external to El Salvador—the vital element in the internationalization of the internal war—though active, have not played the same role as they did in Nicaragua. The Cubans have not been able to come in on the coattails of such external actors as Costa Rica, Venezuela, Panama, and Europe. Nicaragua has had to play the role once played by those international actors in providing material assistance to the Sandinistas. Although the logistical supplies coming from Nicaragua are important to the FMLN, the "legitimizing" function played by external actors providing assistance is less significant and less visible. Thus, there is a political cost to the FMLN-FDR for having as its principal external supplier (however minimal, or whatever the assistance) Marxist and Cuban-allied Nicaragua. No country, with the exception of Cuba, that materially (especially militarily) assisted the Sandinistas in 1979 is assisting the FMLN today. The FSLN guerrilla success may well be a major reason for the eventual failure of the FMLN guerrillas in El Salvador.

Conclusion

The Central American experience seems only to add to the academic and policy debate regarding what makes for successful guerrilla warfare. Analysts do not seem to have advanced much further than the revolutionaries, if Central America is to be a gauge in our knowledge about such political phenomena. In light of the military failures of all but one guerrilla insurgency since the 1959 Cuban revolution in Latin America, and the mixed results in Central America, one is left with the impression that there is no correct revolutionary war "recipe."

Comparing the Cases of El Salvador and Guatemala

The internal wars of Guatemala and El Salvador raise several questions: Is U.S. assistance (and the conditions for such assistance) a help or a hindrance to a government fighting an insurgency? Would the Guatemalans have been as successful *with* U.S. military assistance? Would the El Salvadoran military be more successful today *without* U.S. assistance? Or is it necessary to go beyond the factor of external military assistance to understand the differences in the two countries?

Between 1980 and 1983, the armed forces of El Salvador were alone in the countryside combating guerrillas. Government programs and services were not effectively coordinated with a national military strategy, nor was a concerted effort made to mobilize the citizenry into local civil defense forces until early 1984. In Guatemala, the Victoria '82 campaign linked government programs, local development efforts, civil defense, and counterinsurgency operations. Thus, the Guatemalan military was not alone in its fight against the guerrillas.

Guatemalan military officers were forced to rethink their counterinsurgency approach. Not only was the size of the guerrilla force increasing, but the Guatemalan army faced the serious dilemma of diminishing resources. The force multiplier became people (the CDFs), not helicopters, attack aircraft, or artillery. The army reorganized itself in the field. All this took place without much tutelage or pressure from outside Guatemala.

Why were there such differences between the Guatemalan and El Salvadoran counterinsurgency experiences? It is necessary to look at the institutions themselves. The key to success in counterinsurgency is not outside assistance but the ability to move beyond a one-dimensional strategy dominated by military considerations, resources, and objectives to one that complements the comprehensive politico-military-diplomatic strategy of the guerrillas of the 1980s.[27] Would the Guatemalans have been as successful with Victoria '82 if Nicaragua had been a close neighbor able to support Guatemalan guerrillas directly? The answer is yes; for external assistance to be effective in an insurgency, it requires an infrastructure, communication links, secure areas, and a sympathetic population in the areas of conflict. Beginning in June 1982, the Guatemalan military strategy was directed at all the critical structures required to maintain an active insurgency. At that moment, short of direct outside intervention, no amount of external assistance would have made a difference to the Guatemalan guerrillas.

Who Are the Guerrillas?

Good organization, the correct revolutionary ideology, external supply of weapons, socioeconomic inequities, government terror, and repression do not guarantee success for the guerrilla. The success or failure of guerrillas appears to depend more on whether enough of the population is prepared to become part of a guerrilla apparatus, whether people are willing to give their lives to the revolutionary movement. The critical question then becomes what can transform an elitist-led and oriented revolutionary war into a mass-based movement. The more heterogeneous the population pool of the guerrilla leadership, the more likely the ability to *sustain* the conflict. How much does this recruitment depend on guerrilla leadership qualities and tactics, and how much does it depend on the counterinsurgency tactics of the government?

Since the 1979 fall of Somoza at the hands of a largely self-trained guerrilla army of youths, revolutionary war has emerged in El Salvador and Guatemala. Although a considerable amount of discussion has taken place regarding the "leadership" and the "organization," little is known about the individual guerrilla. What motivates a 15-year-old youth to take up arms against a professional army? What are the decision-making processes through which an individual passes before making a decision to join? Who joins the guerrillas, and who leaves them?

Even more important, what kind of individual decides *not* to join the guerrillas? Mythologies and stereotypes are generally relied on to explain why individuals join the rank-and-file guerrilla base. Knowing who joins and why—as well as who does not join—and what keeps someone in a guerrilla movement (despite the hardships) while others become defectors would help in determining the following factors:

The potential available pool of combatants for the guerrilla organization;

The length of a war and the ability of *individuals* to withstand the personal rigors of such a conflict;

The effectiveness and efficacy of counterinsurgency tactics, including psychological operations and civic action, on guerrilla combatants, on those who have not decided whether to join or not, and on a family that could affect the decision of a youth to join or not join.

Guerrillas, especially the rank-and-file, are not aliens from another planet; they are not extraterrestrial beings who have been "beamed" into Central America to fight in a revolutionary war. Guerrillas, as individuals, are deeply rooted in their respective societies. Despite the fact that guerrillas become products of their own propaganda—that the government is about to fall or that all that is necessary is "one more offensive" for final victory—analysts (and policymakers) fail to describe and understand the conflict in the terms of those who are fighting. Without sufficient knowledge of the types of individuals engaged in guerrilla warfare and the factors that motivate the individuals' actions, the dynamics leading to success or failure will continue to evade the analyst. The Central American wars have yet to shed light on this aspect of inquiry.

Under what circumstances does a "limited" guerrilla insurgency become a mass-based revolutionary movement that can sustain itself over time, with or without external support—with or without popular support?[28] The examples of Nicaragua, Guatemala, and El Salvador suggest different answers to this basic question. All three cases suggest that external support for guerrillas does not guarantee victory, that "popular support" is a nebulous and uncertain factor, and that a militarized, repressive counterinsurgency strategy does not guarantee victory for the government.

Several concluding observations deserve recognition. The revolutionary conflicts of Central America provide additional insights into the global phenomenon of internal war. Are geography, terrain, and size factors in who wins? The case of

El Salvador demonstrates that smallness is not protection against the establishment of a guerrilla war. Until 1984, short lines of communication, short response time, and small areas to control did not provide the military with a decided advantage over the guerrilla. The FSLN in Nicaragua languished for fifteen years in the uninhabited rural areas of the north. It was not until a dramatic shift to a war-fighting strategy in the cities that the Sandinistas began their successful campaign to topple Somoza. Isolated Indian villages in the Guatemalan highlands provided protection for the EGP until the military devised a strategy to turn the villages into hundreds of quasi-military outposts by establishing the civilian self-defense forces.

In the long run, geography and terrain were of less consequence to the outcome of the internal war as the relationship between population and military evolved—either in a more antagonistic direction (as in Nicaragua) or in a more cooperative direction (as in Guatemala). The evolution of the relationship between population and military was in the hands of the military—not the guerrilla. Thus, military leadership capable of developing a counterinsurgency strategy appropriate to the unique circumstances of each respective country was an essential factor in the outcome. A war-fighting strategy that involves the local population has proved to be more successful than one that does not—especially if the army is willing to arm a selective portion of civilians for joint operations with military forces.

Socioeconomic factors affecting the insurgency varied in each case. In Nicaragua, all sectors (including the middle class and the business community) simply tired of Somoza. In Guatemala, the Indian population—a very conservative, traditional, and somewhat geographically isolated segment of society—was penetrated and mobilized by the guerrillas. Although only a fraction of a percent of the total Indian population actively participated in or supported the insurgency, the revolutionary conflict was depicted as an Indian rebellion against the landed oligarchy and a repressive army bent on genocide. In El Salvador, political paralysis and corruption helped open the door to a national crisis of civil war proportions. In each country, poverty, concentrated wealth, and an uncaring and ineffective government were evident. These conditions helped to create a revolutionary cadre and a viable political opposition.

However, poverty was not a determining factor in transforming small, isolated guerrilla factions into large insurgent movements. The army's strategy, especially tactics that affected noncombatants, was far more responsible for the growth of revolutionary movements than the efforts of the guerrilla organizations. Nicaragua is a clear case of this. A military coup in Guatemala prevented a similar situation from coming to fruition. A coup, U.S. military and economic assistance, and major institutional changes in the military in El Salvador have contributed, for the moment, to a situation favoring the government.

Finally, Central America has not escaped the Vietnam analogy debate. What comparisons might be made between these two revolutionary war experiences of the United States? For the most part, historical comparisons are only marginally relevant for the purpose of drawing out "lessons." The problem is that different lessons were said to have been learned for the next time the United States enters into a similar situation. Yet several significant parallels between Vietnam and Central America deserve recognition. First, the United States, as a superpower with a global perspective and a large bureaucracy, finds it difficult to focus on a small country that is caught up in a small internal war. The United States, because of size, bureaucratic structures, and military doctrine does not easily engage in "splendid little wars." Second, the United States must show considerable restraint when assisting a small ally fighting an insurgency to avoid the "Americanization" of the conflict or becoming captive to an unpopular, ineffective regime.

The Vietnam analogy tends to shed more light on the United States than on an understanding of the dynamics of internal war. Nevertheless, the unique qualities of each of the wars in Central America are a continual reminder of how much we did not understand about Vietnam and how much we still have to learn about why individuals join in armed struggle and why some insurgencies succeed while others fail.

Notes

1. These figures can change according to how one categorizes the nature of the conflict and the consequences. Basic data sources include Melvin Small and J. David Singer, eds., *Resort to Arms* (Beverly Hills, Calif.: Sage, 1982); Brian Crozier, ed. *Annual of Power and Conflict, 1971* (London: Institute for the Study of Conflict, 1972); *Annual of Power and Conflict, 1980–81* (London: Institute for the Study of Conflict, 1981); "List of Wars and Armed Conflicts, 1898–1967," in David Wood, *Conflict in the Twentieth Century,* Adelphi Papers No. 48, June 1968; Marvine Leibstone, "Surveying the Small-War Syndrome," *Washington Times,* October 6, 1983; Istvan Kende, "Wars of Ten Years (1967–1976)," *Journal of Peace Research* 15 (1978).

2. For an overview of the revolutionary climate of Central America see Robert S. Leiken, ed., *Central America: Anatomy of Conflict* (New York: Pergamon, 1984); and Richard Alan White, *The Morass: United States Intervention in Central America* (New York: Harper & Row, 1984).

3. See Harry Eckstein, "On the Etiology of Internal Wars," *History and Theory* 4(1965): 133–163.

4. The U.S. Civil War, also an internal war, did not escape this debate. For a general treatment of the determinants of this conflict, see Lee Benson and Cushing Strout, "Causation and the American Civil War—Two Appraisals," *History and Theory* 1(1961).

5. For a discussion of U.S. preparedness for and thinking about low-intensity conflict, see Richard Shultz, "Low Intensity Conflict and American Strategy in the 1980s," *Conflict Quarterly,* Winter 1982. On the problems of learning from the Vietnam experience and innovating U.S. counterinsurgency doctrine, see Cincinnatus, *Self Destruction:*

The Disintegration and Decay of the United States Army During the Vietnam Era (New York: Norton, 1981).

6. See Richard Halloran, "Army Plans New Command to Curb Leftist Insurgencies," *New York Times,* September 17, 1982, p. B6.

7. The doctrine of the guerrilla *foco* was postulated in its purest form in Ernesto Guevara, *Che Guevara on Guerrilla Warfare* (New York: Praeger, 1961). The foremost chronologer of *foco* warfare is Regis Debray, *Revolution in the Revolution: Armed Struggle and Political Struggle in Latin America* (New York: Monthly Review Press, 1967). A challenge to orthodox Marxist theory, the *foquista* approach to revolution emphasized the military dimension of conflict, arguing that a small, armed group could create the conditions for revolution without the necessary urban, mass base. All the guerrilla movements following the *foco* strategy succumbed to military defeat during the 1960s.

8. For a discussion of the first wave of guerrilla warfare in Latin America during the decade of the 1960s, see Richard Gott, *Guerrilla Movements in Latin America* (Garden City, N.Y.: Anchor Books, 1972).

9. U.S. Department of State, *Cuba's Renewed Support for Violence in Latin America*, Special Report No. 90 (Washington, D.C.: Bureau of Public Affairs, 1981).

10. For a list of existing guerrilla organizations in the region, see Peter Janke, *Guerrilla and Terrorist Organizations: A World Directory and Bibliography* (New York: Macmillan, 1983).

11. Although the U.S. responses to Vietnam (1973–1975), Angola (1975–1976), and Iran (1978–1979) were also affected by these changes, Nicaragua provides an example of an internal war situation with few loose ends in terms of ascertaining the time frame, the actors, and the choices facing the insurgents and in terms of the incumbent government, the U.S. government, and other external actors involved. One perspective that seeks to draw lessons from these changes is found in Jean J. Kirkpatrick, "Dictatorships and Double Standards," *Commentary,* November 1979.

12. See Adriana Bosch-Lemus, *Nicaragua: The Internationalization of Conflict and Politics in Central America* (Santa Monica, Calif.: Rand Corporation, forthcoming).

13. For a discussion of the evolution and unique dimensions of the FSLN revolutionary warfare strategy, see George Black, *Triumph of the People: The Sandinista Revolution in Nicaragua* (London: Zed Press, 1981); and Humberto Ortega, *50 Años de Lucha Sandinista* (Havana: Editorial Sciencias Sociales, 1980).

14. As the years go by, mythology replaces fact for the October Revolution and the Liberation of 1954. A close look at both is provided in Marta Cehelsky, "Guatemala's Frustrated Revolution: The Liberation of 1954," Unpublished master's thesis, Columbia University, 1967. The "successes" and "failures" of revolution and counterrevolution and the myths that arose, noted by Cehelsky, are helpful in understanding the insurgency of the 1980s.

15. Labeling the guerrilla strategy of the 1960s as nothing more than *acción improvisada* (improvised action), the founders of the EGP set out to learn the lessons of the past before reentering politico-military warfare. A personal account of the origins of the guerrilla force in Ixcan and its growth from 1972 to 1976 is found in Mario Payeras, *Los Días de la Selva* (Mexico City: Editorial Nuestro Tiempo, 1981).

16. A rejuvenated FAR, after several years of dormancy, rejoined the armed struggle after serious defeats in the metropolitan region of Guatemala City during 1970–1972. The plight of the FAR under the leadership of Pablo Monsanto is described in a series of

articles published in the Mexico City daily, *Uno Mas Uno*. See Victor Aviles, "Tres Semanas con las FAR guatemaltecas," *Uno Mas Uno,* August 29–September 1, 1982.

17. Materials that help develop this point include Edward Gonzalez, "Institutionalization, Political Elites, and Foreign Policies," in Cole Blasier and Carmelo Mesa-Lago, eds., *Cuba in the World* (Pittsburgh: University of Pittsburgh Press, 1979); William M. Leogrande, "Foreign Policy: The Limits of Success," in Jorge I. Dominguez, ed., *Cuba: Internal and International Affairs* (Beverly Hills, Calif.: Sage, 1982); Edward Gonzalez, *Cuba Under Castro: The Limits of Charisma* (Boston: Houghton Mifflin, 1974), pp. 113–145; *Cuba's Renewed Support for Violence in Latin America,* Special Report No. 90 (Washington, D.C.: Bureau of Public Affairs, 1981); and John Maclean, "Cuba and Panama Giving Aid to Somoza's Foes," *Chicago Tribune,* June 17, 1979.

18. In testimony, Deputy Assistant Secretary of State for Inter-American Affairs Steven Bosworth stated that the guerrillas constituted a formidable threat to the Guatemalan government. He indicated that "full time, trained, armed guerrillas may number as many as 3,500 . . . supplemented by approximately 10,000 irregular 'local defense' guerrillas . . . and a support infrastructure of some 30,000–60,000 sympathizers." This information was provided to the House Banking Subcommittee on August 5, 1982. By comparison, one estimate by Guatemalan military intelligence placed the number of armed guerrillas in 1981 at 5,000 to 6,000, with at least five times that number in the *fuerzas irregulares locales* (FIL) and support infrastructure. The four guerrilla groups operated in a dozen distinct military fronts throughout Guatemala by 1981.

19. Translated by the author from Military Communique #1, issued in the late morning of March 23, 1982.

20. Translated by the author from a transcript of a broadcast to the nation by Rios-Montt on April 5, 1982.

21. Human rights, church, and academic organizations, as well as solidarity committees and guerrilla-linked front groups, continued to claim into late 1983 that the level of violence and government involvement in abuses remained largely unchanged. The debate over a break with past practices may well depend on the time frame used to assess the data. Military operations during the Victoria '82 campaign resulted in some 300 deaths per month between July and November 1982. By early 1983, military operations were reduced as civilian patrols assumed a more extensive security role and as guerrillas fled into new areas along the Mexico-Guatemala border. From a high of more than 500 deaths in July 1982, reported deaths (guerrillas, government forces, civilian patrolmen, and noncombatants) averaged less than 100 a month, and reported kidnappings averaged 15 to 20 per month in 1983. Current reporting on human rights abuses by international organizations seems to rely heavily on refugee camp inhabitants in Mexico. Most of these refugees arrived in Mexico during September–December 1982. A combination of factors may have produced the flow of refugees to Mexico, including military attacks against villages, fear of a pending military attack, and a guerrilla decision to send supporters that they could no longer protect into Mexico for propaganda purposes. Whatever the case, refugees provide a two-year-old picture of Guatemalan military operations and life in the small highland villages. For a discussion of human rights abuses and the changes that may or may not have come about since the March 23, 1982, coup, see *United States Policy Toward Guatemala,* Hearings before the Subcommittee on Western Hemisphere Affairs, House of Representatives, U.S. Congress, 98th Cong., 1st sess., March 1983; *Guatemala: Massive Extrajudicial Executions in Rural Areas Under the Government of Rios Montt*

(London: Amnesty International, July 1982); and "Death and Disorder in Guatemala," *Cultural Survival Quarterly* (Spring 1983).

22. Within the Reagan administration, there are serious misgivings and suspicions that Guatemala and Mexico formed a tacit alliance within the Contadora process. For the past several years, Guatemala has remained uncooperative as the United States has sought a regional alliance against Nicaragua. Since 1979, Guatemala has maintained a nonhostile, public dialogue with Nicaragua on economic, financial, and regional affairs.

23. For a further discussion of Guatemala–Mexico relations, see Caesar D. Sereseres, "The Mexican Military Looks South," in David F. Ronfeldt, ed., *The Modern Mexican Military: A Reassessment*, Center for U.S.–Mexico Studies, Monograph Series 15 (San Diego: University of San Diego, 1984).

24. A concise overview of El Salvadoran politics, socioeconomic conditions, the evolution of the revolutionary struggle, and U.S. policy response to the current civil war can be found in Enrique Baloyra, *El Salvador in Transition* (Chapel Hill: University of North Carolina Press, 1982).

25. One intriguing analysis presented by a Mexican scholar depicts the guerrilla and political opposition leadership as prone to internecine warfare. Such internal conflicts have been responsible for the creation of a variety of revolutionary organizations, as leaders have been literally killed off by ideological colleagues pursuing personal gain. See Gabriel Zaid, "Enemy Colleagues," *Dissent*, Winter 1982.

26. For an assessment of the peasant uprising in 1932, see the definitive study by Thomas P. Anderson, *Matanza: El Salvador's Communist Revolt of 1932* (Lincoln: University of Nebraska Press, 1971).

27. Bernard Fall, the noted observer of revolutionary conflict in Vietnam, concluded that guerrilla warfare (and I believe the same would apply to counterinsurgency warfare) is a tactical appendage of a larger political contest. Fall suggested that no matter how expertly fought by competent and dedicated individuals, such conditions cannot make up for the absence of a political rationale. See Fall's classic study of insurgency and counterinsurgency, *Street Without Joy: Insurgency in Indochina, 1946–63*, rev. ed. (Harrisburg, Pa.: Stackpole, 1963).

28. One school of thought suggests that revolutionary insurgencies are dependent not on popular support but rather on securing resources, both domestically and internationally, that are needed to maintain and expand guerrilla operations. See Nathan Leites and Charles Wolf, Jr., *Rebellion and Authority* (Chicago: Markham, 1970).

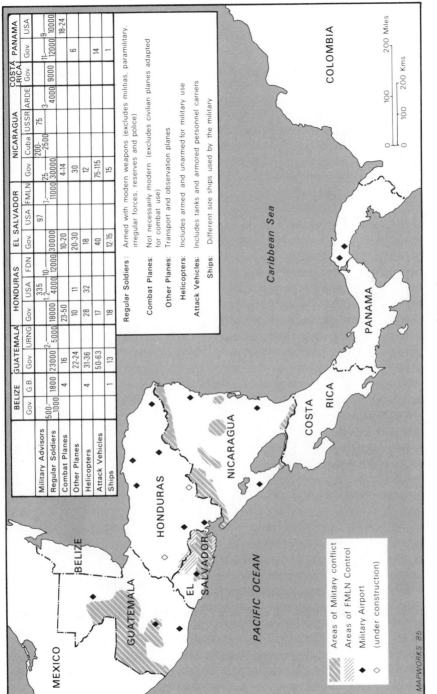

	BELIZE		GUATEMALA		HONDURAS			EL SALVADOR			NICARAGUA				COSTA RICA	PANAMA	
	Gov	G.B.	Gov	URNG	Gov	USA	FDN	Gov	USA	FMLN	Gov	Cuba	USSR	ARDE	Gov	Gov	USA
Military Advisors				2	1.2	335	10-		97	7-	25-	200-	75	3-		11-	9-
Regular Soldiers	500-1000	1800	23000	2-5000	18000	4000	12000	30000		11000	30000	2500		4000	9000	12000	10000
Combat Planes		4	16		23-50			10-20			4-14						18-24
Other Planes			22-24		10	11		20-30			30						
Helicopters		4	31-36		28	32		18		12						6	
Attack Vehicles			50-63		17			40			75-115					14	
Ships		1	13		18			12-15			15					1	

Regular Soldiers: Armed with modern weapons (excludes militias, paramilitary, irregular forces, reserves and police)

Combat Planes: Not necessarily modern (excludes civilian planes adapted for combat use)

Other Planes: Transport and observation planes

Helicopters: Includes armed and unarmed for military use

Attack Vehicles: Includes tanks and armored personnel carriers

Ships: Different size ships used by the military

Areas of Military conflict
Areas of FMLN Control
Military Airport
(under construction)

MAPWORKS '85

Figure 8–1. Central America

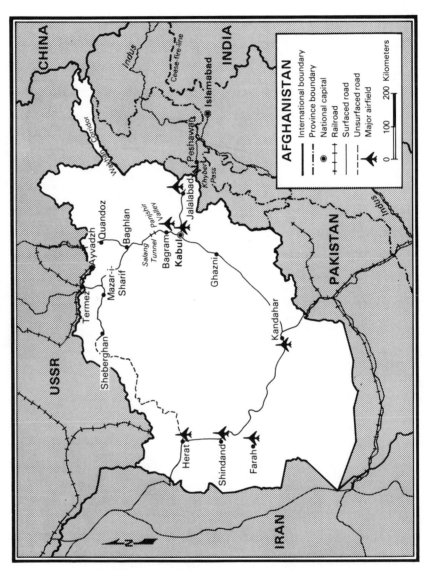

Figure 9–1. Afghanistan

9
The Soviet-Afghan War

Joseph J. Collins

The Soviet-Afghan war has now lasted longer than World War II did for the Soviet Union. At its initiation in 1979, the invasion appeared to be yet another dramatic extension of Soviet influence, with the same promise of success already achieved by proxy in Angola and Ethiopia. Now, nearly five years later, despite the presence of 4 percent of their ground forces, the Soviets are no closer to securing Afghanistan than they were in 1980. Moreover, although they are learning valuable military lessons, the war has become a persistent, though not crushing, problem for the Soviet military. Having built an army for World War III on the plains of Europe, the Soviets are finding that it is not performing well in the mountains of South Asia.

Assessing the performance of any army in combat is a difficult task. Factors such as morale, esprit de corps, discipline, and tactical proficiency are difficult to weigh, even when the data are readily available. This type of assessment is doubly difficult when one is dealing with a subject like Soviet military operations in Afghanistan. Both the Soviets and the freedom fighters "manage" the flow of information from the war zone, and the decentralized nature of the conflict poses significant obstacles to any analyst. In spite of these facts, with the passage of nearly five years since the invasion in December 1979, it is possible to develop a preliminary assessment of the effectiveness of Soviet forces in Afghanistan and tentatively to glean some general lessons from their conduct of the war.

Preinvasion Activities

The April Revolution of 1978 was, like many Communist revolutions, an urban coup d'etat. The prime movers behind the coup were the People's Democratic Party of Afghanistan (PDPA), led by Nur M. Taraki and Hafizullah Amin, and the Soviet-trained Afghan armed forces. Soviet involvement in the actual coup

The views expressed herein are those of the author and do not purport to reflect the position of the Department of the Army or the Department of Defense.

cannot be definitely established.[1] On the other hand, no one can accuse the So-viets of having neglected to build a superstructure for the coup; from 1956 to 1977, the USSR and its allies trained more than 4,000 Afghan officers and deliv-ered more than $600 million worth of military supplies to Afghanistan. By 1977, the Soviet military advisory group numbered some 350 men. In the same period, Soviet economic aid (mostly loans) totaled more than $1.3 billion, a sum that was exceeded in the Middle East and South Asia only by the amount given to Egypt, Syria, and India.[2]

Taraki's government very quickly came under pressure from three directions. First, rural tribesmen revolted because of the regime's internal repression, its di-sastrous land reform program, and its poorly concealed pro-Soviet sympathies. Second, Taraki's own party split, and many of the *Parcham* (banner) faction were jailed or exiled. This rupture has prevented Taraki and his two successors from forming a strong, united government, especially since there were only a few thou-sand PDPA members in 1978.[3] Third, having noted these facts and having been horrified at the regime's abortive attempt to rescue kidnapped U.S. Ambassador Adolph Dubs, Western nations suspended nearly all aid after February 1979, further limiting Taraki's freedom of action.

In March 1979, the rebellion of Afghanistan took an ominous turn. An army mutiny, coupled with a rebel attack on the western city of Herat, turned into a crisis for the Soviet Union. In a single day in the Herat incident, it is quite possible that the USSR suffered more casualties than it did in all of its post-1955 activities in the Third World put together. An American analyst summed up the tragedy as follows:

> Soviet advisors were hunted down by specially assigned insurgent assassination squads conducting house-to-house searches. Westerners reportedly saw Russian women and children running for their lives from the area of the Soviet-built Herat Hotel. Those Russians that were caught were killed; some were flayed alive, others were beheaded and cut into pieces which were then paraded around the city impaled on pikes.[4]

As might be expected, the Afghan government and the Soviets reacted strongly to the deaths of as many as 100 Soviet civilians and military personnel. On the Afghan side, domestic repression increased, with one estimate of the final total of slain political prisoners (April 1978–January 1980) as high as 20,000.[5] In April 1979, an Afghan army unit (with Soviet advisors in attendance) sacked the town of Kerala and massacred 640 of its male inhabitants.[6] On the Soviet side, an authoritative *Pravda* article of March 19, signed by the pseudonymous I. Aleksandrov, for the first time accused "some Western countries"—China, Iran, and Pakistan—of instigating unrest in Afghanistan. In a more substantive vein, General Alexei Yepishev, chief of the Main Political Administration of the armed forces, was dispatched to Afghanistan and apparently recommended an increase in military aid and advisors, then estimated at 1,000 personnel. Among the weapons subsequently provided were 100 T-62 tanks and 12 MiG-24 helicopter gunships.[7]

Despite increased pressure, the resistance movement, disorganized as it was, began to grow, and further escalatory measures were taken by the Soviets. From August to October, General Ivan Pavlovskiy, Commander-in-Chief of the Soviet Ground Forces, visited Afghanistan along with twelve other generals and fifty other officers. At the same time, the role of Soviet advisors was broadened to include advising at the company level and routine flying of active combat missions.

In September 1979, after attending a nonaligned conference in Havana, Taraki visited Moscow. In retrospect, it appears likely that, in Moscow, Taraki was urged to oust his deputy, the radical Hafizullah Amin, who had by then become the repressive power behind the throne.[8] Upon Taraki's return, a gun battle broke out in the Arg Palace, and, when the smoke cleared, Amin was in control. Taraki was apparently executed shortly thereafter.[9]

Relations between Amin and the USSR remained officially cordial, but under the surface they were deteriorating. No doubt, Brezhnev was embarrassed by Taraki's demise less than a week after their "fraternal" meeting. Were this not enough, the war continued to go badly for Amin. In August, army forces mutinied in Kabul. In September, rebels temporarily captured the Salang Pass, the key choke point on the road from Kabul to the USSR. Desertion by whole army units had become commonplace, and Amin was having difficulty staffing a government without *Parcham* or Taraki supporters. Despite pressure, Amin, acting like an "Afghan Tito," refused to broaden the base of the ruling party or to adopt more moderate policies. He apparently rejected offers of Soviet troops, and a member of his government openly criticized the Soviets for interfering in the internal affairs of Afghanistan. Shortly thereafter, Amin demanded the recall of Soviet Ambassador A. Puzanov, who was implicated in the original attempt to assassinate Amin in September.[10]

It is not difficult at this point to reconstruct the Soviet estimate of the situation in Afghanistan in the fall of 1979.[11] Internally, as Generals Yepishev and Pavlovskiy had witnessed firsthand, Amin's regime was crumbling. His army would not fight, and he had no political base, having by this time begun to staff some key government positions with his relatives. The economy was in ruins and, even by Soviet estimates, government control over eighteen of twenty-six provinces was in doubt.[12] Soviet inaction certainly would have resulted in Amin's ouster. This, in turn, would have been a blow to Soviet prestige, a violation of the spirit of the Soviet-Afghan friendship treaty, and, in ideological terms, a Chilean-type thermidor on the Soviet Union's border. Moreover, the Soviets might have believed that a radical, Islamic-oriented regime, allied with Iran and friendly to China, would take over in Kabul. Thus, Afghanistan could have been seen as a threat to stability in Soviet Central Asia.

In summary, Soviet activities before the invasion set the stage for what has become a major counterinsurgency operation. Blinded by "success" in Angola, Ethiopia, South Yemen, and so forth, the Soviets became increasingly entangled with a hopelessly ineffective regime. Furthermore, the USSR myopically viewed the regime's problems as military in nature. In one sense, we cannot blame the Soviet leadership for turning to its military. The instrument had performed well in the previous decade, and reliance on Soviet military support had become an important part of the its Third World policy. Ironically, having watched the United States very closely in Vietnam, the Soviets drew some inappropriate lessons of their own. Two insightful American analysts concluded—on the basis of a content analysis of more than 850 Soviet articles:

> Americans drew conclusions from Vietnam that would, for example, warn them about the dangers of a significant military intervention in Afghanistan. The lessons the Soviets drew, however, did not warn them of the dangers of such an intervention by Soviet forces. On the contrary, the frequent assertion that aid from the Soviet Union and other socialist countries had been important in Vietnam may have increased their propensity to intervene in Afghanistan. Similarly, the frequently expressed views that only communists could have accomplished such a victory as Vietnam, and that the political and military doctrine of the Vietnamese communists had been correct, may have added to the sense that a communist leadership headed by someone with "correct" views could reverse a deteriorating situation in Afghanistan.[13]

The Invasion

On December 8, 1979, lead elements of a 1,000-man airborne unit landed at the Soviet-controlled air base at Bagram, north of Kabul. On December 20, this unit moved north and cleared the Salang Tunnel area of rebel activity, thus securing the highway from Termez in the Soviet Union to Kabul.[14] This action was complemented by the call-up of Soviet reservists in late October and November to man the five Category 3 divisions then near the Afghan border. Bridge equipment was brought up to the Amu Darya (Oxus River), and a command post for the invasion, headed by Marshal Sokolov, a first deputy defense minister, was established at Termez, near the Soviet-Afghan border.[15]

On Christmas Eve, despite prior American warnings and the presence of an Afghan armored division nearby, the Soviets began landing commandoes and an airborne division at Kabul Airport. On December 27, following a three-day airlift that averaged 75 to 120 flights per day, *spetznaz* troops deployed to the Darulaman Palace outside Kabul destroyed Amin's guard and its eight tanks and killed President Amin.[16] The account of a KGB major now in the West is eloquent testimony to the speed and efficiency with which this task was accomplished:

Along the road the column was stopped at an Afghan checkpoint. Afghan troops gathered round to find out what was happening. Suddenly the flaps of the front vehicle went up and the Afghans were machine-gunned to the ground. The column rolled on. When it reached the palace, the special troops attacked from three sides, while Colonel Bayerenov (the head of the KGB's terrorist-training school) led the assault on the palace. The attack got off to a good start. It would have been even better had the leading armored vehicle not got caught up in the palace gates. Moscow wanted no Afghans left to tell the tale of what had happened in the palace. No prisoners were to be taken. Anybody leaving the building was to be shot on sight. Amin was found drinking in a bar on the top floor of the palace. He was shot without question.[17]

Beginning on December 27, two motorized rifle divisions—one destined for Kabul and the other for Kandahar in southern Afghanistan—led the procession of Soviet troops across the border. By the first week in February 1980, elements of seven Soviet divisions had been identified in Afghanistan. With the exception of the 105th Guards Airborne Division and other airborne elements, these units were composed of at least 50 percent reserve fillers on a 90-day call-up. Interestingly, a large number of the Soviet reservists (perhaps as many as 90 percent) were Central Asian.[18] Throughout the initial stages of their invasion, Soviet advisors played a key role in neutralizing Afghan army units whose loyalty was questionable. This was accomplished by Soviet control over fuel and by deceptions, such as having the questionable units turn over their ammunition for inventory or having them turn in vehicle batteries for winterizing.[19]

Any assessment of the invasion must be mixed. On the positive side of the ledger, the Soviet military and security *apparat* proved (1) that it is capable of rapid (though detectable) mobilization; (2) that it can perform major operations without severe logistical breakdown; (3) that it has sufficient ground forces to mount major, conventional operations in low-intensity environments outside the Warsaw Pact or Chinese border area; and (4) that it is reliable in "political" operations, such as assassination and the disarming of unreliable "friendly" forces. On the other hand there were some glaring judgmental errors. The massive use of Central Asian reservists—evidently designed to facilitate movement and communication with the populace—was a mistake. Many of these reservists had spent their active duty in noncombat units and were poorly trained for fighting. Many were also guilty of fraternization, and a few even defected.[20] More will be said on this point later in the chapter.

Also on the negative side, mention again must be made of the Soviet estimate of the situation in Afghanistan. Only someone with a pathetic ignorance of Afghan culture and history could have believed that the Afghans would not fight a foreign invasion force or that their quisling, Babrak Karmal, could ever hope to gain popular support or even acceptance in the countryside. To view Afghanistan as a replay of events in Czechoslovakia was a key error and a disastrous attempt at trying to apply historical lessons as maxims. In summary, the Soviet leadership made the most fundamental military mistake: they failed to identify the nature of the conflict and accurately to gauge the relationship between means and ends in Afghanistan. They entered the country prepared for an occupation, fundamentally underestimating their opponent's will and overestimating the power and proficiency of their invading units. No tactical error could have damaged the Soviet cause as much as this strategic misjudgment. As Clausewitz said:

> The first, the grandest, and most decisive act of judgement which the Statesman and General exercises is rightly to understand in this respect the War in which he engages, not to take it for something, or to wish to make of it something, which by the nature of its relations it is impossible for it to be. This is, therefore, the first, the most comprehensive, of all strategical questions.[21]

Current Operations

On the domestic scene, the Soviets apparently believed that a decisive show of armed might, coupled with a change in rulers, would reunite the ruling party, restore order to Afghanistan, and prevent a potential "encirclement" of the Soviet Union. At the same time, all of this would preserve the neosocialist "revolution" on their southern border. Delivered in the combat trains of the Soviet invasion force, Babrak Karmal, the Soviet-picked replacement for Hafizullah Amin, was to have restored domestic political order, while the Soviet forces were to have frightened the guerrillas back to their villages. To put it mildly, the Soviets have not accomplished their objectives. Babrak Karmal has failed in his efforts to reunite the Khalq (masses) and Parcham (banner) factions of the People's Democratic Party of Afghanistan. Khalq-Parcham infighting continues and is still a major problem for the Afghan army, a traditional Khalqi stronghold. In September 1982, the Khalqi general commanding the Central Army Corps was found shot to death in his office under circumstances apparently not connected to the fighting. In May 1983, the Khalqi defense minister physically assaulted the defense minister after having been passed over for promotion! Military defections are frequent, and seven Afghan communists have been reported fighting alongside the *mujahiddin*. In all, the rate of military accessions barely equals the rate of desertions. The Army is still only a third the size it was in 1978 and—with rare exceptions—is close to useless as a military force.[22]

Nearly 25 percent of the prewar population have become refugees. As a result of Soviet military operations, the population of the cities has swelled, with the population of Kabul now three times its prewar size. In the spring of 1983, Babrak Karmal still claimed that, without Soviet support, "it is unknown what the destiny of the Afghan Revolution would be. . . . We are realists and clearly realize that in store for us yet lie trials and deprivations, losses and difficulties."[23] Just two weeks before, Prime Minister Keshtmand had admitted that half of the country's schools and three-quarters of its communication lines had been destroyed since 1979.[24] Based on his own observations during a 2,000-kilometer trip through Afghanistan, Olivier Roy, a French soldier wrote:

> One thing stands out: neither the Soviets or the Afghan army, weak and drained, venture beyond a restricted perimeter around the large cities and three paved roads. . . . Forty percent of the districts do not even have a symbolic government presence. In most of the others, the government's authority extends to the administrative post's machine gun range.[25]

The military situation in Afghanistan as of the summer of 1984 pitted roughly 120,000 Soviet and 30,000 Afghan troops against 85,000 to 100,000 freedom fighters. Soviet forces (the 40th Army), according to unclassified sources, are composed of seven motorized rifle divisions and five Air Assault Brigades (about 2,000 men each), backed up by an undisclosed number of *spetznaz* (airborne ranger) units, about 240 gunships, 400 other helicopters, several squadrons of MiG-21s and MiG-23s, and at least one squadron of SU-25 attack aircraft. The deployment of the SU-25 aircraft is significant in that the Soviets have chosen Afghanistan as the location for its first operational deployment.[26] Recent reports indicate that MiG-25s configured for reconnaissance may also be in the country. Persistent reports also indicate an unknown number of Cuban, Vietnamese, and East European advisors and troops in Afghanistan.[27]

Soviet forces include more than 80,000 ground forces, 30,000 general support troops, and 10,000 air force personnel. These forces are supported by about 30,000 support and air force personnel in the southern part of the USSR. Divisional deployments are geographically balanced, with about one-third of the total ground force in the Kabul area and other major deployments at Mazar-i-Sharif and Qonduz in the north, Herat and Farah in the west, Kandahar in the south, and Jalalabad in the east. Major airbases are located in Herat, Shindand, Farah, Kandahar, Kabul, Bagram, and Jalalabad.

The freedom fighters come from ten major resistance groups and fight in anything from platoon to regimental strength. Armaments vary, with some units having one Kalashnikov (AK) automatic rifle per platoon, while others have nearly all of their fighters equipped with AKs.[28] Fire support is limited, in the main, to rocket-propelled grenades, machine guns, and mortars. Although some analysts put foreign aid to the freedom fighters (reportedly funded by the United States and Saudi Arabia) at the $100 million per year level, relatively little materiel has found its way to fighting units. Some observers noted that the open market price of an AK in Pakistan—about $2,800—did not decline appreciably from 1979 to 1982. Air defense weapons and mortar ammunition are in especially short supply. The best source of arms is still the Soviet and Afghan forces. One active, local commander estimated that 80 percent of his weapons came from the Soviet or Afghan forces.[29]

Overall, since mid-1980, the Soviet position in Afghanistan has deteriorated, though not yet to the point where it might jeopardize the entire operation. Although territorially based estimates are necessarily suspect, experts have increased their estimate of rebel-controlled territory from 75 percent of the country to as much as 90 percent.[30] It would be more accurate to say that perhaps as much as 90 percent of Afghan territory is controlled neither by the Soviets nor by the freedom fighters on a permanent basis. Soviet forces are free to move in strength into almost any area, but neither they nor their Afghan allies possess the numerical strength to occupy and pacify major areas of the country. In most cases, the freedom fighters depend too much on mobility and concealment for their survival to establish effective control. In any case, the major cities and base areas are only safe for the Soviets during daylight hours. In the countryside, only the narrow strip joining the People's Republic of China (PRC) to Afghanistan— the Wakhan Corridor (which has been occupied by the Soviets)—and the thinly populated areas in the extreme northwest and southwest of the country are relatively free of rebel activity.

To date, Soviet strategy appears to have been to hold the major centers of communications, limit infiltration, and destroy local strongholds at minimum cost to their own forces. In essence, the Soviet strategy is one wherein high technology and superior tactical mobility are used as a force multiplier and as a means to hold Soviet casualties to a minimum. In effect, Soviet policy has been a combination of "scorched earth" and, in anthropologist Louis Dupree's words, "migratory genocide."[31] Numerous reports have suggested that Soviet forces, particularly their helicopter gunships, have been deliberately used to burn crops and destroy villages to force the population—the main source of resistance logistical support—to flee to Pakistan or Iran. Other reports imply that the Soviets have used a "free-fire zone" approach in areas with strong resistance forces.

Soviet terror tactics have increased in their ferocity since mid-1980, and the Soviet monopoly on high technology has magnified the destructive aspects of their behavior. As one expert testified:

> The International Red Cross and other humanitarian organizations are denied access to Afghanistan. Between last October 26 and November 2 [1981], three hospitals, operated by a French humanitarian medical organization, in three separate provinces, were demolished by helicopters that singled them out for bombing and rocketing. Helicopters set the crops aflame just before the harvest; village granaries are emptied and destroyed—all in an effort to starve the people into submission. The planes often bear Afghan markings, but the pilots are Soviet, as they have been since mid-1979—although they reportedly sometimes wear Afghan uniforms.[32]

The use of plastic, caseless mines, usually dropped from helicopters, has greatly affected the resistance's morale and ability to maneuver. One resistance leader noted in 1982:

> The Soviets also drop small antipersonnel mines by helicopter. These mines are in the form of watches, ballpoint pens or even books. They have caused enormous damage among the civilian population and livestock and many women and children have lost feet or hands.[33]

Responsible analysts have noted that the war in Afghanistan cost the Soviets more than $12 billion up to the end of 1983.[34] Total Soviet casualties (killed and wounded) have been estimated at 20,000, and the Kremlin may have suffered again as many casualties from sickness and disease. Exact figures on the number of Soviets killed in action are impossible to obtain, but responsible analysts have cited estimates from 5,000 to 10,000.[35] Up to the end of 1984, the freedom fighters may have suffered ten times the total number of Soviet casualties, with undoubtedly a higher percentage of deaths. In all, despite the costs, the Soviets are preparing for a prolonged stay. Permanent logistics facilities and barracks are being constructed. Airfields are being upgraded, and the construction of a permanent bridge across the Amu Darya has been completed. The tour of duty for Soviet soldiers has also been set at two years, with rotations of one-quarter of the force taking place on a semiannual basis.[36]

Operationally, new or untried Soviet equipment (for example, the improved BMP, the AK-74 rifle, the Hind helicopter, scatterable mines, the AGS-17 automatic grenade launcher) has been tested, and some technical innovations have been made. For example, the Soviets have experimented with a new main armament on their standard BMP infantry-fighting vehicle. Based on their Afghan experience, they have moved to replace the slow-firing 73mm cannon on some BMPs with an automatic 30mm cannon.[37] This change will enable Soviet ground forces to achieve an even larger volume of suppressive fire. The use of helicopters is also an important facet of operations in Afghanistan. Helicopters are used for resupply, reconnaissance, troop transport, fire support, and command and control. Pilot training in Afghanistan is superb. As one Soviet officer described it:

> Flying in the mountains and above the desert, plus the real possibility of coming under fire by anti-aircraft weapons which are making their way from Pakistan to the bandits operating on DRA territory—this is a real training school. . . . No wonder they say that after a month in Afghanistan helicopter pilots can be awarded the top proficiency rating without testing their piloting ability.[38]

This pilot training is also costly, however. The rebels have shot down as many as 300 Soviet helicopters, mostly of the troop-carrying variety, with small arms and antitank weapons.

Chemical weapons have also been tested in Afghanistan. According to two highly detailed U.S. State Department reports, Soviet forces have used chemical weapons in at least fifteen provinces of Afghanistan. Witnesses have made a total of fifty-nine separate incident reports, and the State Department noted that at least thirty-six of the reports were corroborated by additional evidence. The Soviet use of chemical weapons—incapacitants, lethal chemicals, and perhaps even mycotoxin biological weapons—continued after the first detailed U.S. report appeared in March 1982 but appeared to diminish in 1983. The reports conservatively estimate that the attacks have resulted in 3,000 deaths. One other ominous detail did not go unnoticed: detailed survey and monitoring operations following some of the strikes showed that the Soviets were obviously "interested in studying after-effects, lethality, or some other quasi-experimental aspect of a new chemical weapon."[39]

Why the Soviet Union would use chemical agents is not difficult to understand. These weapons generate tremendous fear and encourage panic. They can also be used to guard exposed flanks and to clear built-up areas or caves of deadly snipers or ambushes. In other words, while inflicting damage and panic on the enemy, they enable the user to conserve troop strength and minimize casualties.

There is very little reliable information on the performance of Soviet troops in Afghanistan. A distillation of the scant information that is available reveals the following:

1. The initial invading divisions—except the airborne units—were Category 3 units, manned primarily by Central Asian reservists. These units were poorly trained and unreliable, and collusion with the freedom fighters was commonplace. Ghafoor Yussofzai, a former lawyer and now a resistance leader, gave this eyewitness testimony of collusion between Central Asian soldiers and their coreligionists:

> In the very beginning, when the Soviets first entered our country in 1979 . . . most of the soldiers were Soviet-Central Asians. . . . When these people realized that the only people they were fighting in Afghanistan were Afghans . . . then these Soviet Central-Asians began helping us. They began leaving us packages with ammunition and weapons and caches. They left it in the ground and covered it with earth and just left a little of it emerging. In the beginning we were very suspicious and cautious and poked at this with sticks afraid that they would prove to be mines. And when we finally uncovered these things, we found out that they were parcels of weapons and ammunition that these Soviet-Central Asians were leaving for us. The Soviets finally became aware that this was going on and [have] since withdrawn Soviet-Central Asian troops from Afghanistan and now they have just brought their own red-faced troops.[40]

2. The initial complement of regular forces were not trained in counterinsurgency or mountain warfare techniques. In December 1981, one Soviet source even reported that "it took a while for [an Afghan] soldier to believe that the majority of Soviet servicemen had first seen mountains here—in Afghanistan." This training problem has apparently been solved, but even the Soviets are not yet pleased with their training for "mountain warfare." Not finding the Chinese or American "agents" whom they were told were causing the trouble has also been bad for morale. Recent interviews with Soviet POWs indicate widespread discontent among Soviet forces concerning their role in the war.[42]

3. The pace of operations ranges from frantic "offensives" or "damage-limiting" operations to long periods of boredom. Soviet soldiers apparently are not coping very well with this, and reports of the use of hashish have surfaced. Numerous separate sources have confirmed the widespread use of hashish and the fact that Soviet soldiers have traded truck parts, uniforms, ammunition, and even rifles for hashish or other local drugs. When asked about drugs in the 40th Army, an enlisted defector in 1984 said:

> Drugs? Nobody can deal with them because a great deal of drugs are being used. . . . For the most part they smoke hashish and cocaine. There are also those who shoot. There are some. The soldiers get hold of drugs by means of sale and exchange. They sell literally everything possible . . . [including] arms and ammunition.[43]

4. Soviet tactics still tend toward an overreliance on motorized rifle and tank troops employed in sweep or "hammer and anvil" operations. Air assault operations—usually of company or battalion strength—are becoming more important, although they are usually conducted in conjunction with movements by motorized rifle units. Tanks are apparently being used mostly in a fire support role. Much of the Soviet operational experience apparently has been in convoying supplies and road-clearing operations, designed to keep open the ground lines of communication. On the whole, airborne and air assault troops seem to be held in higher esteem by the freedom fighters than troops from the motorized divisions.

An Afghan army colonel, who later defected to the resistance, observed the Soviet forces as both ally and adversary. He characterized them as "oversupervised," "lacking initiative," and addicted to "cookbook warfare," wherein proved "battle recipes" are mechanically applied to new situations. S.B. Majrooh, another close observer, said that Soviet soldiers were "generally undisciplined, isolated, and not motivated."[44]

Given their knowledge of the terrain and their excellent intelligence network, guerrilla ambushes of various sizes have proved to be very effective. An

Afghan army major described their tactics in a conversation with a Soviet reporter:

> Usually they operate in groups of 30–40 men. They used to assemble in larger gangs. They prefer to use ambushes by bridges, or in defiles. They destroy the bridge or block the road and then open fire from the commanding heights. If a strong army subunit is moving, they allow the reconnaissance and the combat security detachment to go by. All of a sudden, they open up with volleys of well-aimed fire and then rapidly withdraw. They mine the roads, then cover the mined areas with small arms fire. The hand of professional foreign instructors can be felt at work.[45]

On the whole, Soviet forces deal very poorly with ambushes. Apparently, Soviet forces have no counterambush drills, as are held in Western armies. Soviet forces prefer to let the resistance take the vehicles they have disabled and move the rest of the convoy to safety. A few eyewitnesses have reported that after having moved from the ambush site, Soviet tanks will turn and shell the disabled vehicles. Also, villages close to the ambush site will normally be bombed after an ambush.[46]

Soviet efforts to date have not produced the desired results. Contrary to Soviet propaganda, the bulk of the fighting has been done by Soviet troops, sometimes opposed by mutinous Afghan Army forces. After nearly five years, Soviet forces are still fighting to maintain their hold on the cities and their lines of communication. Costs continue to increase. For example, based on an actual count of destroyed vehicles in seven provinces, a French doctor estimated Soviet vehicle losses throughout Afghanistan at 3,000 to 4,000.[47]

The number of major battles involving multiple, battalion-sized units apparently increased from 1981 to 1984. Although there were periodic reports of intraresistance fighting, three major groups formed the Islamic Unity of Afghan Mujahiddin coalition early in 1981 and a year later fought a coordinated battle in Paktia Province in which they defeated two Soviet regiments, destroying twenty-five vehicles and killing sixty Soviet soldiers in the process. Other reports of coordinated operations appeared early in 1983, but they are still far more the exception than the rule, and they are usually the result of local coordination rather than intergroup agreements.[48]

There are few accurate accounts of entire battles by which we can judge the state of Soviet military art in Afghanistan. One month-long operation was witnessed by *Christian Science Monitor* correspondent Edward Giradet.[49] The battle apparently was designed to eliminate the 3,000 fighters of Ahmed Shah Massoud who had been implicated in numerous raids, including at least one successful penetration of the Bagram air base. Four previous Soviet forays into the Panjsher Valley had failed to eliminate this unit of freedom fighters. Although the operation was significant because of its size, it was also important because it appeared to represent a typical Soviet "battle recipe" that has been used time and again in Afghanistan.

After an entire week of aerial bombardment, Soviet and Afghan forces were inserted by helicopter into the narrow east–west Panjsher corridor on May 17, 1982. The freedom fighters, having been warned of the Soviet battle plan, had escaped down the side valleys or onto the top of the ridge lines. As a *Pravda* military correspondent noted, the first waves of attackers encountered a "multi-level system of fire prepared in advance."[50] Three days later, a tank and motorized rifle force entered the valley, bringing the total of Soviet and Afghan forces to 12,000 to 15,000. A series of sharp engagements followed, and within the first ten days, fifty Soviet vehicles and thirty-five helicopters were destroyed in the fighting (at least by resistance reports). The freedom fighters kept control of the valley and may have netted 100 Soviet rifles. The Soviets destroyed up to 80 percent of the dwellings in some areas and killed nearly 200 freedom fighters and close to 1,200 civilians, more than 1 percent of the Panjsher's population, but they were forced to begin withdrawing on June 13.[51]

After a subsequent offensive also failed, the Soviets entered into a truce with Massoud that lasted from January 1983 until April 1984. During that time, Massoud took the opportunity to repair his logistical base in the valley, recruit more soldiers, and increase his operations outside the valley proper.

By April, the Soviets had had enough of the charismatic Massoud and decided to put an end to him and the Jamiat Islami forces in the valley. Supported by more than fifty TU-16 long-range bombers based in the Soviet Union, more than 20,000 Soviet troops entered the valley. Massoud's forces, for the most part, beat a hasty retreat. Despite claims of victory and "final solution" in the Panjsher, however, the battle continues. Although Afghan units have garrisoned parts of the valley, they have not captured Massoud, nor have they destroyed his forces. Panjsher VII, along with the many other operations in the Soviet spring offensive, may have represented a new level of commitment on the part of the Chernenko regime, but it remains to be seen whether the reinforcements (approximately 20,000 since January 1982), and the bombers will destroy the freedom fighters' will to resist.[52]

It must be noted at this point that the end of this war is not in sight. Although it is clear that the Soviets do not have sufficient forces in Afghanistan to pacify a country the size of Texas, it is likewise clear that they have not moved significantly toward a withdrawal, nor have they made a decision to attempt to conclude the war wholly on a military level. Although they are not on the verge of being ejected from Afghanistan, their poor performance would seem to suggest that options preferable to the present policy of "muddling through" exist.

Overall, Soviet efforts to gain a diplomatic solution to the war in Afghanistan also have not progressed very far. At the end of 1983, Afghanistan and Pakistan—speaking indirectly through UN intermediaries—were still far apart on a number of issues, including the fate of the Karmal regime, the scope and speed of the Soviet withdrawal, and the nature of international guarantees of the solution. The Soviets have not put all their effort into making peace. The rigidity of their proposals, coupled with their military measures inside Afghanistan, suggests that, even though they are pessimistic about the present situation in Afghanistan, they do not perceive the costs of continued operations in Afghanistan to be over- whelmingly excessive. As an American diplomat in Moscow noted, it is quite possible that they believe they have absorbed the worst of the costs (the grain embargo, the Olympic boycott, and so forth) and that now it is simply a matter of endurance and fortitude, virtues that their historical experience and highly authoritarian political system have given them in great quantities.[53] The Soviets are prepared either for peace on their terms or for the continuation of warfare at the present level for the foreseeable future.

In light of the earlier examination of Soviet motives, it is not difficult to un- derstand why there has been such little change in Soviet peace proposals. The potential for PDPA disintegration is still present, and the threat to the Soviets' own security, in their eyes, is still there as well. Indeed, there is even less likeli- hood that a new, non-PDPA regime—given cultural constraints—could ever be- have in a "good neighbor" fashion toward the Soviet Union. It is one thing to desert an ally, but it is even more damaging to your prestige if you try very hard to save him and then fail.

Conclusions

The Soviet experience in Afghanistan supports a number of conclusions, some of which have only slight claim to novelty and all of which could have been arrived at without mounting an invasion. First, Afghanistan is proof positive that great power does not insulate its holder from great mistakes. Indeed, having great power tempts the possessor to regard itself as invincible, especially under low- risk circumstances. Afghanistan vividly demonstrates that even superpowers are at the mercy of religious, ethnic, and other such forces in their dealings with Third World countries. Armored divisions and unusable ICBMs have rarely overcome the indigenous forces of nationalism and religious faith. Great powers must take this into account in their dealings with Third World countries. Partic- ularly in Third World insurgency conditions, military planners should exercise— in Robert Harkavy's term—"humility in defense planning." Short-war strategies may be appropriate for conventional limited wars, but in the case of insurgencies or conflicts that could degenerate into an insurgency, the short war is a pipedream.

Second, in organizational framework, Afghanistan suggests that armies will do well only those things for which they habitually prepare and practice. Soviet forces performed well in the movement into Afghanistan, but they have done poorly in dealings with the insurgency itself. To date, the Soviets are only beginning to adjust to the conditions present in Afghanistan. Short of genocide, the methods in use at present will continue to be ineffective.

Third, in the area of doctrine, Afghanistan appears as a unique case. Although the Soviets have in the past shown a strategic appreciation for limited war,[54] they were put in the awkward position of having a force structure and tactics that did not match the military situation. Moreover, it was a situation that required an independent, decentralized style of command that is somewhat alien to the Soviet experience.[55]

In analyzing the Soviet-Afghan War, one finds a great deal of data that support the image of the dogged, inflexible Russian who time and again attempts to make circumstance adapt to practiced technique. The observation of German generals at the close of World War II appear to have retained a measure of their validity:

> The commanders of Russian combined arms units were often well trained along tactical lines, but to some extent they had not grasped the essence of tactical doctrines and therefore often acted according to set patterns, not according to circumstances. Also, there was the pronounced spirit of blind obedience which had perhaps carried over from their regimented civilian life into the military field. . . .
>
> The inflexibility of Russian methods of warfare was evidenced repeatedly. Only the top Russian command during the last years of the war was an exception. This inflexibility manifested itself as high as army level; in divisions, regiments, and companies it was unquestionably the retarding factor in the way the Russians fought.[56]

Although Soviet performance has been dominated more by style than by doctrine, tactical adaptations, as noted earlier, have taken place and are in evidence even in Soviet accounts of battles in Afghanistan. The Soviet military press is alive with articles discussing "mountain training" and exhorting leaders to pay more attention to developing the illusive "initiative" and physical fitness among their subordinates. The clearest example of this appears in the training guidance given by General V.I. Petrov, Commander-in-Chief of the Soviet Ground Forces, after the 26th Party Congress in 1981. After praising a guards major for his conduct of a night training exercise over mountainous terrain, Petrov directed his subordinate commanders and inspectors to emphasize, *inter alia,* physical training, mountain and desert operations, inclement weather training, continuous day-night operations, and operations while "separated from the main forces, on an independent axis, and in the advance guard or flanking detachment."[57] *Voennyy Vestnick (Military Herald)* showed a steady increase in articles on mountain warfare, from none in 1978, to three in 1979, to fifteen in 1981.[58] Time and experience will undoubtedly enable the Soviets to turn this evolving body of information into working doctrine, but if we assume that the lessons of recent history dominate the minds of decision makers, it will probably be some time before the Soviets take another turn at counterinsurgency.

A note of caution on this point is in order. Soviet behavior toward Afghanistan has demonstrated conclusively that the Soviets are capable of misreading situations and drawing lessons that are inappropriate or inaccurate. United States decision makers must not glibly assume that the lessons we perceive are the ones that the Soviets have deduced. For many analysts, the difference between success in Angola and quagmire in Afghanistan can be found in the strength of situational variables. This conclusion, however, may be alien to the Soviet mindset. It may well be true that, in the near term, there will be a "no more Afghanistans" consensus in the Soviet leadership, but it is certainly too early to tell how the Soviets will read the lessons and what effect they will have on the general thrust of Soviet policy.

Even given this caution, however, the Soviet experience in Afghanistan would seem to make a Soviet move into Iran only a remote possibility in the near term. The conditions that led to the Soviet move—a pro-Soviet government, a long history of direct involvement, the Friendship Treaty, a low probability of a direct American response—are all, at least for the present, absent from Iran. The Soviets looked favorably on their experience in Czechoslovakia in 1968 and attempted to use the Czech "recipe" in Afghanistan. It is unlikely that they will attempt to apply the Afghan "recipe" to Iran. Finally, as both Keith Dunn and Joshua Epstein have pointed out, Iran is a tough nut to crack. The Soviets know this, and their Afghan bases would be of only limited assistance in invading Iran.[59] Although it is clear that the Soviets will benefit, at least marginally, from being able to move their air assets closer to the Indian Ocean, it is not similarly clear that this or any other "asset" secured in Afghanistan would help them in an invasion of Iran.[60]

The difficulty of invading Iran and the limited utility of Afghanistan for that purpose are facts long known to the Soviets. In a World War II study, a Soviet intelligence officer accurately described the terrain, transport, and climatological difficulties present in Iran and concluded that an invasion of Iran was possible but that these difficulties "ought not be underestimated."[61] Comparing approaches to Iran and the Persian Gulf from the north and east, a Soviet political analyst noted in 1982:

> If one speaks about Soviet action in Afghanistan, was it a prelude or preliminary action towards action against Western oil interests in the Gulf, then I say that it is patent nonsense, because every strategist knows that there are quicker approaches than the approaches via Afghanistan—the gateway to the Persian Gulf from Soviet Transcaucasus is much more obtainable.[62]

One ought not believe, however, that the Afghan experience has been totally negative for the Soviet armed forces. The Soviet experience in Afghanistan has given them valuable experience in mobilization, although unfortunately, from their point of view, many of the lessons learned were painful. The performance of Central Asian troops in the initial invasion was poor, which could lead to greater emphasis on reserve training and changes in active duty manning policies. Marshal Ogarkov, then the Soviet chief of staff, highlighted the role of the reserves in a 1981 article in *Kommunist:*

> If an aggressor unleashes a war, the prepared reserves of personnel and equipment assigned to formations and units must reach them in extremely short periods of time. Hence, the task of constant readiness for immediate mobilization deployment of troops and naval forces is of great state significance.

Later, he added that "supplying the troops with prepared reserves of personnel and equipment predetermines the need for efficiently planned measures even in peacetime."[63] All in all, the Soviet reserve forces and mobilization procedures bear further watching. Changes based on their experience in Afghanistan may already be taking place.

In the area of weapons and personnel, Afghanistan has been a prize (though a very expensive one) for the Soviet military. Training deficiencies will be detected, and combat experience, though it tends to be fleeting, will ensure a more seasoned Soviet army. Particularly significant has been the performance of Soviet pilots; we can be assured that the Soviets will hone their fire support skills to a fine edge in Afghanistan. If nothing else, Soviet command cadres in future conflicts will be better able to control their air and ground firepower.

One Soviet "adaptation" that should alarm the West is the use of chemical weapons. The use of these weapons in Afghanistan and Southeast Asia again confirms that—not surprisingly—the Soviets find them put to their best use against unprotected subjects that are incapable of retaliation. Afghanistan is proof positive that the Soviets do not consider these devices "special weapons." Considerations of utility, not morality, will govern their use of such weapons in future conflicts.

The Soviet use of chemical weapons in Afghanistan also suggests that the validity of future arms control agreements rests heavily on whether the West can retaliate in kind if those agreements are violated. It is clear from the experiences in both Southeast Asia and Afghanistan that the various treaties the Soviets have signed on chemical and biological weapons are of questionable value in curbing either the manufacture or use of such weapons by the Soviet Union.

Finally, we should pause at this point and reflect on the concept of learning lessons from recent history. First, we must be aware that the contest is far from over. Years from now, the record of events in Afghanistan may appear to be far different than that which has been described in the concluding section of this chapter. The Soviets believe that time is on their side and that they do not need a quick victory. The Soviet ability to "hang tough" and "muddle through" far surpasses our own. As a French doctor, himself a veteran of the Soviet-Afghan war, sadly noted:

> The Russians do not need smashing victories to announce to their citizenry, as Soviet public opinion does not influence Soviet policy. Catastrophes, such as that in the Salang tunnel where several hundred Soviet and communist-regime troops (and civilians) were killed, do not incite an outcry in Moscow for Soviet "boys" to come home. The Soviet army can wait it out as long as it did for the Basmachi revolt to end—and it waited for that for 20 years. It can wait even longer if necessary.[64]

Notes

1. For a contrary assessment that points toward Soviet complicity, see Alvin Rubinstein, "The Last Years of Peaceful Coexistence: Soviet-Afghan Relations, 1963–78," *Middle East Journal*, Spring 1982, pp. 174–83.

2. Data on Soviet aid to Afghanistan can be found in CIA, *Communist Aid to Less Developed Countries of the Free World, 1977,* ER 78-10478U (November 1978), pp. i–ii, 1–2, 4–11, 35–36; and Andreas Tenson, "The Soviet View of Soviet-Afghan Economic Relations," *Radio Liberty Research Bulletin*, RL 84/80, February 25, 1980, pp. 1–4.

3. Louis Dupree, "Afghanistan Under the Khalq," *Problems of Communism*, July-August 1979, p. 40.

4. Patrick Garrity, "The Soviet Military Stake in Afghanistan: 1956–79," *RUSI: Journal of the Royal United Services Institute for Defense Studies*, September 1980, p. 34. Also, see Henry S. Bradsher, *Afghanistan and the Soviet Union* (Durham, N.C.: Duke University Press, 1983), pp. 100–03.

5. *New York Times*, February 18, 1980, p. 4.

6. *New York Times*, February 17, 1980, p. 10.

7. Garrity, "The Soviet Military Stake in Afghanistan." The public aspects of Ypishev's visit were reported in *Kabul Times*, April 5, 7, 8, 9, 11, and 12, 1979.

8. The emergence of Amin is neatly described in Dupree, "Afghanistan Under the Khalq," pp. 34–43.

9. The Soviet press originally reported the Amin succession as a routine leadership changeover; see *Pravda*, September 17, 1979, p. 5. On Taraki's death, see the Karmal regime's account in *Kabul New Times*, January 23, 1980, p. 3.

10. Selig Harrison is the major proponent of the idea that the Soviet inability to control Amin was a major factor in the Soviet decision to invade; see *New York Times*, January 13, 1980, p. 23. A full account of the dispute over Soviet interference and the subsequent confrontation between the Afghan foreign minister and a high-ranking Soviet diplomat can be found in Cable 07444, U.S. Embassy, Kabul, "Signs Continue of Strained Relations Between President Hafizullah Amin and the Soviets," October 11, 1979, p. 2.

11. For a more detailed examination of Soviet motives, see Joseph Collins, "The Soviet Invasion of Afghanistan: Methods, Motives and Ramifications," *Naval War College Review*, November 1980, pp. 56–58; Jerry Hough, "Why the Russians Invaded,"

Nation, March 1, 1980, p. 232; and the Brezhnev interview in *New Times* (Moscow—English language edition), January 1980, p. 6.

12. R.A. Ulyanovskiy, "The Afghan Revolution at the Current Stage," *Voprosy Istorii KPSS*, April 1982, p. 13, translated in JPRS, *USSR Report: Political and Sociological Affairs—Current Political Issues*, no. 1279, July 20, 1982.

13. William Zimmerman and Robert Axelrod, "The 'Lessons' of Vietnam and Soviet Foreign Policy," *World Politics* 34, no. 1 (October 1981): 19–20. Copyright © 1981 by Princeton University Press. Excerpt reprinted with permission of Princeton University Press.

14. *New York Times*, January 1, 1980, pp. 1, 4.

15. Garrity, "The Soviet Military Stake in Afghanistan," p. 35. U.S. Congress, House Committee on Foreign Affairs, *East-West Relations in the Aftermath of Soviet Invasion of Afghanistan*, 96th Cong., 2d sess., January 24 and 30, 1980, pp. 39–40.

16. The low estimate of seventy-five is cited in Jiri Valenta, "From Prague to Kabul: The Soviet Style of Invasion," *International Security*, Fall 1980, pp. 124–127; and IISS, *Strategic Review* (London: International Institute for Strategic Studies, 1979). The high estimate comes from David Charters, "Coup and Consolidation," *Conflict Quarterly*, Spring 1981.

17. *Time*, November 22, 1982, pp. 33–34. Copyright 1982 Time Inc. All rights reserved. Reprinted with permission from TIME.

18. *East-West Relations in the Aftermath*, p. 39. See also Peter Kruzhin, "The Ethnic Composition of Soviet Forces in Afghanistan, *Radio Liberty Research Bulletin*, RL 20/80, January 11, 1980, pp. 1–2. Kruzhin is skeptical about the 90 percent figure.

19. Valenta, "From Prague to Kabul," p. 134. See also Edward Luttwak, "After Afghanistan, What?" *Commentary*, April 1980, pp. 46–47. The most detailed description of Soviet deception techniques can be found in Anthony Arnold, *Afghanistan: The Soviet Invasion in Perspective* (Stanford, Calif.: Hoover Institute Press, 1981), pp. 94–96.

20. On the experience of Central Asians during their active service, see Enders Wimbush and Alex Alexiev, *The Ethnic Factor in the Soviet Armed Forces*, R278771 (Santa Monica, Calif.: Rand Corporation, 1982), pp. 24–34. On their performance in Afghanistan, see Alexandre Bennigsen, "Soviet Muslims and the World of Islam," *Problems of Communism*, March-April 1980, pp. 46–49; and *Time*, November 22, 1982, pp. 33–34. Evidence of unrest or dissatisfaction in Soviet Central Asia concerning Afghanistan is mixed. See *New York Times*, April 11, 1980, p. 1; and *Newsweek*, August 9, 1982, p. 36.

21. Carl von Clausewitz, *On War*, ed. Anatol Rapoport (Baltimore, Md.: Penguin, 1968), p. 121.

22. On factional feuding, see U.S. Department of State, "Soviet Dilemmas in Afghanistan," Special Report No. 72, June 1980, pp. 1–3; U.S. Department of State, "Afghanistan: Three Years of Occupation," Special Report No. 106, December 1982, pp. 1, 6–7; K. Wafadar, "Afghanistan in 1981: The Struggle Intensifies," *Asian Survey*, no. 2, February 1982, pp. 148–50; and U.S. Department of State, "Afghanistan: Four Years of Occupation," Special Report No. 112, December 1983, pp. 4–6.

23. TASS (in English), April 28, 1983 in FBIS—Soviet Union-III-89-4/6/83-p. 2.

24. *New York Times*, April 12, 1983, p. 6.

25. *Le Monde* (Paris), November 15, 1983, pp. 1, 7.

26. The deployment of the SU-25 was confirmed in an unofficial 1982 State Department document, "Glossary of Soviet Military Terms," and in *New York Times*, September

26, 1982, p. 7. For order-of-battle information, see David Isby, "Afghanistan 1982: The War Continues," *International Defense Review,* no. 11, November 1982, pp. 1523–1526; and U.S. Department of State, Special Report No. 112, pp. 1, 3.

27. *New York Times,* December 26, 1980, p. 3; and December 20, 1982, p. 10; see also, Agence France Press dispatch (Spanish), November 28, 1980 in FBIS—South Asia-VII-232-2/1/80-p. C8.

28. See *New York Times,* January 12, 1982, p. 2; and *Christian Science Monitor,* June 22, 28, July 2, 7, 9, 1982.

29. On foreign assistance to the freedom fighters, see *New York Times,* January 22, 1981, p. 3; *New York Times,* April 14, 1981, p. 3; *New York Times,* September 23, 1981, p. 15; and Carl Bernstein, "Arms for Afghanistan," *New Republic,* July 18, 1981, pp. 8–10. On arms, see *New York Times,* January 12, 1982, p. 2; and Francis Fukuyama, *The Future of the Soviet Role in Afghanistan,* Rand Research Note N 1579-RC (Santa Monica, Calif.: Rand Corporation, September 1980), p. 12. For the local commander's estimate, see *Washington Post,* October 18, 1983, p. 1, 12, *passim.* For a more recent description of the ineffectiveness of foreign aid, see *Washington Times,* March 21, 1984, p. 1C.

30. *New York Times,* December 26, 1980, p. 7; and U.S. Department of State, "Afghanistan: Two Years of Occupation," Special Report No. 91, December 1981.

31. Nicholas Wade, "Afghanistan: The Politics of Tragicomedy," *Science,* May 1981, pp. 521–523. On starvation in Afghanistan, see *New York Times,* June 6, 1984, p. 11.

32. See Rosanne Klass' statement in U.S. Congress, Senate Committee on Foreign Relations, *Hearings on the Situation in Afghanistan,* 97th Cong., 2d sess., March 8, 1982, pp. 71–5.

33. *Les Nouvelles d'Afghanistan* (Paris) 10(July-December 1982), pp. 4–16 in JPRS 81812, September 21, 1982, p. 21.

34. Remarks by a State Department official during a background briefing at the National Forum on Afghanistan, sponsored by the University of Nebraska and the U.S. Department of State, Washington, D.C., December 13, 1983.

35. In 1983, some U.S. government officials began to use 10,000 as the high-range estimate of Soviets killed in action. This was noted by Ambassador Charles Dunbar—former U.S. charge d'affaires in Kabul—at the Harvard–State Department Conference on Afghanistan, Cambridge, Mass., October 1983.

36. U.S. Department of State, Special Report No. 72, p. 3.

37. Mining operations are described in *Washington Post,* July 8, 1980, p. 1. Photographs of the new scatterable mines can be found in *Soldier of Fortune,* April 1981, pp. 23–24. Also see, Defense Intelligence Agency (DIA), *Review of Soviet Ground Forces,* May 1980, February 1981, June 1981, for details on AK-74, and AGS 17. On the improved BMP (BMP-2) see DIA, *Review of Soviet Ground Forces,* April 1982, and also *New York Times,* November 8, 1982, p. 1.

38. Col. V. Stulovskiy, "Stationed in Afghanistan," *Voyennyye znaniya,* March 1981, as cited in Douglas Hart, "Low Intensity Conflict in Afghanistan: The Soviet View," *Survival,* March 1982, pp. 66–67. For a description of helicopters in resupply and medevac roles, see *Komsomolskaya Pravda,* February 4, 1983, p. 4.

39. U.S. Department of State, "Chemical Warfare in South Asia and Afghanistan," Special Report No. 98, March 1982, and Special Report No. 104, November 1982. The

quotation is from the former publication, p. 25. See also Special Report No. 106, p. 5, and the unpublished U.S. State Department collection of media reports, "Reports of the Use of Chemical Weapons in Afghanistan, Laos and Kampuchea, Summer 1980," pp. 4–30. On nonuse of chemical weapons in 1983, see *New York Times,* February 22, 1984, p. 7.

40. *Soviet Human Rights Violations in Afghanistan,* the unedited transcript of a presentation by five Afghans on the massacre at Padkahwab-e-Shana, Georgetown CSIS, Washington, D.C., February 1, 1983, p. 21–22.

41. For a stinging indictment of deficiencies in Soviet mountain training, see the unsigned lead editorial, "Gornaya Podgotovka Voysk" ("Mountain Training of Troops"), *Voyennyy vestnik (Military Herald),* no. 5, May 1985, pp. 2–5. The quotation can be found in *Krasnaya zvezda,* December 31, 1981, p. 2, in FBIS, *Daily Report—Soviet Union,* January 6, 1982, p. D4. An interview with a Soviet officer POW can be found in an Agence France Presse dispatch of April 29, 1982, from Hong Kong. An interview with Soviet enlisted defectors can be found in *Die Welt,* October 29, 1982, p. 8, translated in FBIS, *Daily Report—Soviet Union,* November 2, 1982, pp. D1-D3; and in *U.S. News and World Report,* December 19, 1983, p. 13.

42. *Die Welt,* October 29, 1982, p. 8; *Washington Post,* September 28, 1981, p. 15; *Washington Post,* December 27, 1981, p. 1; *New York Times,* January 12, 1982, p. 2; and Agence France Presse dispatch of December 3, 1980, in *Daily Report-South Asia 8,* no. 235, December 4, 1980, pp. C2-C3. The quotation is from *Radio Liberty Research Bulletin,* RL 121/84, March 19, 1984, pp. 1–16.

44. On road-clearing and convoy operations, see, for example, *Komsomolskaya pravda,* August 7, 1981, p. 2, in FBIS, *Daily Report—Soviet Union,* August 13, 1981, pp. D5-D9, and *Krasnaya zvezda,* January 7, 1984, p. 3. The quotation on performance is from an interview with Colonel A.A. Jalali, Washington, D.C., April 6, 1983. S.B. Majrooh, now director of the Afghan Information Service in Pakistan, made his remarks at the Harvard–State Department Conference on Afghanistan, Cambridge, Mass., October 1983.

45. *Pravda,* June 5, 1980, in USAF, *Soviet Press: Selected Translations,* September 1981, p. 273.

46. Interviews in Paris, April 1984, with Bernard Dupaigne and Tim Cooper, a freelance journalist, both of whom had witnessed Soviet behavior in ambush situations.

47. Speech given by Claude Malhuret, M.D., at the Harvard–State Department Conference on Afghanistan, Cambridge, Mass., October 1983.

48. Interview with Colonel A.A. Jalali, former Assistant Chief of the Military Committee of the Islamic Unity of Afghan Mujahiddin, in Washington, D.C., April 6, 1983. See also *New York Times,* April 21, 1983, p. A11.

49. *Christian Science Monitor,* June 22, 28, July 2, 7, 9, 1982. Also see the description in U.S. Department of State, Special Report No. 106, pp. 2–4.

50. *Pravda,* August 3, 1982, p. 6. Both the *Pravda* military correspondent, a rear admiral, and Giradet reported that the *mujahiddin* had at least portions of the Soviet battle plan before the start of the battle.

51. The scale of destruction in the Panjsher was reported by an eyewitness, Dr. Lauren Lemonnier, at the Columbia University Center for the Study of Human Rights conference on Afghanistan, New York, February, 1984.

52. For early reports of the fighting in the Panjsher VII operation, see *Afghan Information Centre Monthly Bulletin* (Peshawar, Pakistan), April 1984, pp. 4–6; *Les Nouvelles d'Afghanistan* (Paris), pp. 4–8; and *Newsweek*, June 11, 1984, pp. 54–56.

53. Interview with Foreign Service Officer Robert Clark in Moscow, January 3, 1983.

54. For examples of Soviet thought on limited war, see V.M. Kulish, *Military Force and International Relations*, May 1973, JPRS 5847, pp. 101–105, 167–176; I. Shavrov (General of the Army), "Local Wars and Their Place in the Global Strategy of Imperialism," *Military Historical Journal*, March 1975, as translated in USAF, *Soviet Press: Selected Translations*, 75–78, 79, August and September 1975; and V. Matsulenko (Major General) "Lessons of Imperialist Local Wars," *Soviet Military Review* (Moscow—English), January 1982, pp. 44–46.

55. On the general subject of military style, see Chris Donnelly, "The Soviet Soldier: Behavior, Performance, Effectiveness," in John Erickson and Eric Feuchtwanger, eds., *Soviet Military Power and Performance* (London: Macmillan, 1979), pp. 114–120.

56. Department of the Army, *Historical Study: Russian Combat Methods in World War II*, Pamphlet No. 20–230, November 1950 (reprinted 1983), pp. 12, 25.

57. Petrov's article, "The Main Concern Is Combat Training," appeared as the lead article in *Voyennyy vestnik* (*Military Herald*), no. 3, March 1981.

58. Defense Intelligence Agency, *Review of Soviet Ground Forces*, July 1982, pp. 13–16.

59. Joshua Epstein, "Soviet Vulnerabilities in Iran and the RDF Deterrent," *International Security*, Fall 1981, pp. 126–158; and Keith Dunn, "Soviet Strategy, Opportunities and Constraints in Southwest Asia," Paper presented to the 23d International Studies Association Convention, March 24–26, 1982 Cincinnati, Ohio.

60. The Soviet advantage yielded by their occupation of Afghan bases is described in Dunn, "Soviet Strategy," and in the testimony of Zalmay Khalilzad before the Senate Foreign Relations Committee, March 8, 1982.

61. *Soviet Intelligence Estimate—Iran*, 1941, p. 239.

62. BBC (domestic radio service), February 27, 1982, 2110 hours GMT.

63. Nikolai Ogarkov, "For Our Soviet Motherland: Guarding Peaceful Labor," *Kommunist*, no. 10, 1981, in JPRS 79074, September 25, 1981, p. 95. Ogarkov repeated the point in a recent pamphlet and added his concern about Russian language proficiency in the armed forces, a fact that could very well be related, *inter alia*, to the poor performance of Central Asian reservists in the initial invading force. See *Always in Readiness to Defend the Homeland*, January 1982, in USAF, *Soviet Press: Selected Translations*, nos. 9, 10, 11, 12, 1982; and no. 1, 1983. The appropriate passages are in no. 1, 1983, pp. 19–22.

64. Claude Malhuret, "Report from Afghanistan," *Foreign Affairs* 62(Winter 1983–84): 435.

10
Iran-Iraq (1980–   )

William O. Staudenmaier

The failure of Saddam Hussein to win a quick victory in Iraq's invasion of Iran in 1980 has led to a costly, prolonged war of attrition, the end of which is not yet in sight.[1] Neither side seems sufficiently strong militarily nor confident enough politically to take the risks needed to end the fighting. Casualties to both sides now total more than 240,000 dead and 700,000 wounded,[2] and over three years of war have left both sides' economies in shambles. The miscalculations of the high command were, as usual, paid for in blood on the battlefield and in grief at home.

Why have the generals and diplomats been unable to end this costly war? The answer to this question lies in the misperceptions that led Saddam Hussein to opt for war to settle his differences with Iran over four years ago. Two major factors influenced this decision: first, the specific event that led to war, and second, the perception of the correlation of forces that led Hussein to believe that he could win. This combination of grievance and expectation not only influenced the decision to go to war but was also an important factor in determining the policy that governed the intensity with which the war was fought and the conditions under which it might be ended.

The Decision to Go to War

The Gulf war has ancient historical roots. For over a thousand years, religious, ethnic, and territorial disputes between Arab and Persian have periodically disturbed the peace of the Middle East.[3] However, the proximate cause of the Iraqi invasion of Iran in September 1980 was Saddam Hussein's belief that the Ayatollah Khomeini was intent on exporting the Islamic revolution to Iraq and the rest of other Arab Gulf States.[4] The repeated exhortations by Khomeini to the Iraqi people to overthrow Saddam Hussein and his Baathist secular government posed

---

The views expressed in this chapter are those of the author and do not reflect the official policy or position of the Department of Defense or the U.S. government.

a clear danger to the Iraqi Sunni government in view of its large Shiite population.

This continual meddling in Iraq's political and religious affairs, despite the postrevolutionary disarray Iran was experiencing—finally provoked Hussein to act. The chaos in Iran that followed in the wake of the overthrow of the Shah was an opportunity for Iraq to settle several old scores. Not only could the military weakness that surely engulfed Iran's armed forces enable Hussein to recover certain disputed territories, but the defeat of the Iranian forces would stem the export of the Islamic revolution to the Arab Gulf States, thereby conceding the leadership of the entire region to Hussein and Iraq.[5] Consequently, Iraq renounced the 1975 Algiers Treaty with Iran, which had set the current boundary of the Shatt al-Arab in favor of Iran.

To demonstrate to the world that Iraq was now the strongest state in the Persian Gulf and fit to lead the nonaligned movement, Saddam Hussein demanded that Iraq be accorded unconditional sovereignty over the Shatt al-Arab and certain other disputed border territory promised to Iraq as part of the 1975 Algiers Treaty but never delivered. Hussein also sought the return of Abu Musa and the Greater and Lesser Tunbs to the United Arab Emirates. These three Persian Gulf islands are strategically located near the Strait of Hormuz. The perception of Iraqi military strength and Iranian military weakness that Iraq's demands apparently assumed bears closer inspection.

The Military Balance, 1980

It seems clear that the antagonism of the Iranian revolutionary regime toward the Baathist leaders in Baghdad precluded any real chance for Hussein to realize Iraq's territorial aspirations through diplomatic means. In coming to a political decision to use military force to topple Khomeini and wrest territorial concessions from Tehran, judgments relating to the correlation of forces or the military balance between the opposing forces must have been weighted heavily in favor of military intervention. The way Hussein and the ruling Revolutionary Command Council perceived the situation in Iran may be gathered from a speech delivered by Tareq Aziz, deputy prime minister of Iraq, who in May 1980, just four months before the invasion, characterized Iran as being militarily weak, economically destitute, and in the grip of internal anarchy.[6] To understand how this impression could be seriously accepted by Iraq's leadership when just a few short years before, under the Shah, Iran was considered to be the most powerful military force in the Persian Gulf region requires an analysis of the leading indicators of military power.

A review of the static indicators of the military balance in 1980 reveals that Iran and Iraq were evenly balanced, but a slight edge should be accorded to Iraq because of its larger army and tank force (see table 10–1). However, the balance tips even more in Iraq's favor when some of the key qualitative factors that affect

Table 10–1
The Iraqi-Iranian Military Balance, 1980–1983

Military Indicator	1980		1983[a]	
	Iran	Iraq	Iran	Iraq
Population	38 million	13 million	41.5 million	14.3 million
Defense expenditure	$4.2 billion	$2.7 billion	$6.9–13.3 billion	$7.7 billion
Armed forces	240,000	242,000	205,000	517,250
Army	150,000	200,000	150,000	475,000
Navy	20,000	4,250	20,000	4,250
Air force	70,000	38,000	35,000	38,000
Reserves	400,000	250,000	400,000	75,000
Combat aircraft	445	332	70	330
Tanks	1,985	2,850	1,040	2,460
Artillery pieces	1,000 +	800	1,000	800
Paramilitary forces	75,000	79,800	2,500,000	450,000
Revolutionary Guards	—	—	150,000	—

Source: International Institute for Strategic Studies (IISS), *The Military Balance, 1980–81,* and *The Military Balance, 1983–84* (London: IISS, 1981 and 1984).
[a]Losses make estimates tentative.

the balance are included, such as combat experience, training, logistics, and command and control.[7]

If either side's armed forces had had extensive combat experience in mid-intensity conflict in the years immediately preceding the outbreak of the war, it could be viewed as a positive factor. As it was, however, neither army had recently engaged in a mid-intensity combat to any significant degree. Several Iranian army units—and some air and naval elements—received some combat experience during the Dhofar Rebellion in the 1970s, but because of the purge of the military that followed the fall of the Shah, many of those veterans were not in the service in 1980. The Iraqi army had played a small but important part in the battles in Syria during the Yom Kippur War in 1973, which was fought at the mid-intensity level, and—along with the air force—had successfully completed a decade-long counterinsurgency campaign against the Kurds in 1975. Although combat in a guerrilla war at the high-command level differs greatly from mid-intensity warfare, the experience gained by the lower ranks operating in a hostile environment cannot be acquired in peacetime simulation training.[8] Thus, the edge in combat experience, however slight, must go to Iraq.

Training also posed a problem for both armed forces, because they were both involved in ambitious force expansion and modernization programs. Iran was finding it difficult to integrate the sophisticated American equipment it had purchased while the Shah was in power, and the Iraqi armed forces were still coping with the turbulence generated by an expansion program, begun in 1973, that was aimed at doubling the size of their force by 1980. To train, expand, and modernize simultaneously is a difficult task for even the most experienced army; it is a task that is beyond the capabilities of most developing nations. Since training should lead to improved combat readiness, it is clear that on the eve of the war, both nations had some reason to question the effectiveness of their combat formations.

A nation's logistic system also affects its ability to initiate and sustain military operations.[9] Neither Iran nor Iraq possessed a significant indigenous arms industry, so each had to rely on other nations to supply it with the arms, ammunition, and repair parts needed to sustain modern combat. In this respect, in 1980, Iraq seemed to be better off than Iran. Iran was isolated from its major arms supplier and from most of the international community as a result of the American hostage issue and from most of the nations of the region because of its militant advocacy of Islamic fundamentalism. Although estimates of Iran's ability to sustain combat were uniformly pessimistic in 1980, Iraq was thought by most military analysts to be capable of conducting effective modern military operations using materiel it had acquired from Soviet and Western sources.

Finally, the command-and-control factor favored Iraq because of the political disarray that persisted in Iran. The Iranian command-and-control system was flawed in two ways—both resulting from the pernicious effects of the Islamic revolution on the armed forces. First, as a consequence of the military's close identification with Western ways during the reign of the Shah, the armed forces—especially the officer corps—were decimated in a purge led by the *mullahs*. The purge, which included summary execution and imprisonment of many of the Shah's officers, began slowly but accelerated during 1980, by which time the armed forces had been figuratively beheaded. The officers who were left were held in low repute by the *mullahs* who ruled Iran.

Second, the Iranians could not achieve unity of command because the split between the *mullahs* and the armed forces has continued to affect military operations to this day. Even the establishment of the Supreme Defense Council after the war, started under the leadership of Bani-Sadr, then president and commander-in-chief of the armed forces, did not end the struggle between the armed forces and the *mullahs*, who continued to interfere in military operations. By June 1982, Bani-Sadr had lost the battle and fled Iran. The result of this bitter internecine struggle was a parallel chain of command that effectively stifled coordination on the battlefield between the secularly led regular forces and the clerically led Pasdaran, or Revolutionary Guards. Although this situation has improved marginally over the past few years, many defense analysts believe that one of the major reasons Iran is unable to sustain an offensive that could end the war is the disunity caused by this dissension.[10] Had the Iranian forces been faced with a more formidable foe in 1980, the consequences could have been catastrophic.

Ironically, the Iraqi command-and-control problems are just the opposite. Whereas the Iranian chain of command is diffused, the Iraqi command-and-control system is highly centralized. The secretive, centralized defense decision-making apparatus in Iraq is further flawed by being a small, cohesive group that is well known more for its loyalty to Saddam Hussein than for its objectivity. Despite this command-and-control system that causes delay and indecision on the battlefield, in 1980, Iraq still maintained a comparative military advantage because of the disorder within the Iranian government.

Geographic Considerations

Another key factor affecting Iraq's decision to use force is the geography of the theater of operations. The most salient factor is Iraq's lack of strategic depth.[11] Baghdad is about 100 kilometers from the Iranian frontier, while Tehran is 700 kilometers inside Iran, effectively putting it out of easy reach of the Iraqi army (see figure 10–1). Therefore, in strategic terms, Iraq had to mount a forward defense of its extremely long eastern border with Iran, while Khomeini could afford to trade space for time.

The second important geographic factor relating to the war is the effect that terrain and climate has on maneuver. Military operations in the battle area must virtually come to a halt in November with the onset of the rainy season, and they are retarded until late spring. The coastal plains around Abadan, Ahwaz, and Basra—the area in which most of the fighting has occurred—are most seriously affected by the climate. Flooding, both natural and deliberate, has been used to good advantage. The rainy season tends to favor the Iranians, who are less dependent on armor and air operations than the Iraqis, but it also tends to favor the defense over the offense. Nor is the climate very conducive to intense campaigning during the dry season because of the extreme heat and dust.

Finally, each nation has three areas of strategic significance. In Iran, the oil-rich southern coastal plain in Khuzistan (including Kharg Island), Tehran, and the Bandar Abbas area adjacent to the Strait of Hormuz are of strategic value. Similarly, there are three areas of strategic interest in Iraq—Basra, astride the Shatt al-Arab, Baghdad, and, in the north, the Kirkuk oil fields. These geographic considerations have shaped the strategy and doctrine of the war to a substantial degree.

Iraqi Strategic Planning

Considering the balance of military power as it was perceived to exist in September 1980 and the characteristics of the theater of operations, Saddam Hussein and his close advisors might have concluded that only a limited attack for limited objectives was possible. However, objective analysis was not a strong point of the Iraqi high command. At least three miscalculations were made by the architects of the plan to invade Iran and topple Khomeini. First, it was assumed by the

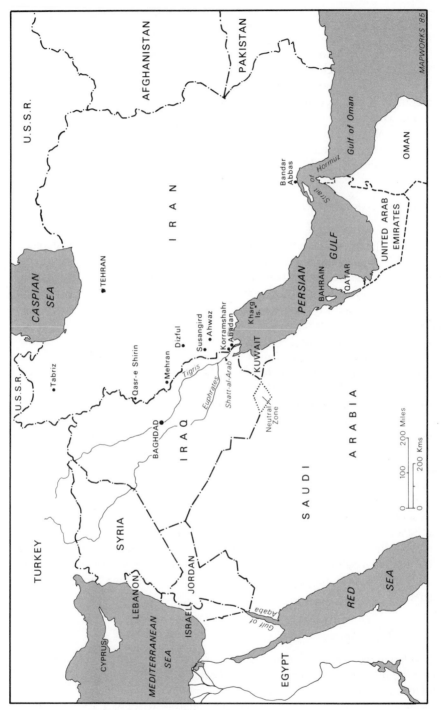

Figure 10–1. Persian Gulf Region: Iran-Iraq

war planners that the Iranian army was in such a state of disintegration that it would not effectively resist Iraqi forces. After recovering from the initial shock, the Iranian army, particularly the Pasdaran, fought fiercely and bravely, exacting a heavy toll in Iraqi lives during the early fighting for control of the Shatt al-Arab.

Second, the Revolutionary Command Council also assumed that the Iraqi invaders would be welcomed as liberators by the Arab population of Khuzistan. Instead, Iranian nationalism and Islamic revolutionary fervor proved to be a more potent force than Arab solidarity. In the event, more than one million Arabs in the war zone left their homes and possessions and fled eastward.

Third, the Iraqi strategic planners completely misread the hold that the Ayatollah had on the Islamic revolution and Iran. In fairness, Saddam Hussein and his coterie were not the only ones to underestimate the military resilience and political cohesion of Iran; most Western analysts would have agreed with them that Iran was indeed weak and vulnerable in 1980. Nevertheless, it was the Iraqis' choice of political objectives, defense policy, and strategy that was to lead to failure, not simply the decision to opt for a military solution.

War Policy

The aim of military strategy is not simply to restore peace—although that may be its most beneficial outcome—but to achieve some political objective. To accomplish this, there must be a coherence between the military strategy and the political policy that guides it in the prosecution of the war. The policy function includes the setting of political objectives or war aims.[12] This coherence is not easily obtained; in the Gulf war, the political objectives and security policy of Iraq, in particular, put demands on the military strategy that were impossible to satisfy.

The logic of the strategic process requires that the ends—political objectives—dictate the means—strategy. In this case, the Iraqi war aims were as follows:[13]

To topple Khomeini and his government;

To gain control of the entire Shatt al-Arab;

To regain certain disputed territory along the Iran-Iraq border;

To regain control of the three Persian Gulf islands;

To establish Iraq as the leader of the nonaligned movement and the strongest state in the Persian Gulf.

Given political goals, the task of the military strategist is to choose military objectives that will lead to their accomplishment. In a conventional war, the selection of military objectives is influenced by the location of the mass of the enemy armed forces and the vulnerability of the enemy's capital and its vital industrial, commercial, and communication centers to destruction.[14] At the beginning of the Gulf war, the Iranian forces were scattered around the entire perimeter of Iran and were therefore not in a suitable configuration for Iraq to target them for destruction.[15] Thus, the military objectives would have to be some vital geographic area. Of Iran's three strategic areas, Tehran was out of reach—adequately protected by the rugged Zagros Mountains and the vast distance it lay from the Iraqi border; but Khuzistan and the Kharg Island oil complex were closer at hand, and, though somewhat more distant, the Bandar Abbas area was not heavily defended.

The capture of these military objectives could have led to the realization of Iraq's political objectives. Iran could not allow these strategic areas to fall into the hands of Iraq without a decisive fight, because it would mean economic strangulation.[16] It is doubtful the Islamic revolution could have survived for long in the face of such a catastrophe. If Iran chose to fight to retake these military objectives, it would have had to attack an Iraqi army that surely would have been dug in on excellent defensive terrain. From what we have seen of Iraq fighting in prepared defensive positions, the outcome might have been the piecemeal defeat of the Iranian armed forces. Iraq could not win, however, without the decisive defeat or defection of the Iranian army, given Hussein's political objective to overthrow Khomeini.

In the event, Iraq chose a less bold strategy and set of military objectives. Apparently believing that the Iranian army would turn on Khomeini at the first sight of Iraqi troops in Khuzistan, Saddam Hussein opted for a cautious offensive aimed at securing relatively low-risk, limited objectives across the Shatt al-Arab. However, even these modest objectives were to elude him because of policy and doctrinal constraints. The type of offensive warfare that would bring the Iranian army to battle where it could be decisively defeated—that is, decentralized, mobile warfare—was denied Iraq by both policy and doctrine. Because the Iraqi government has habitually been plagued by internal instability, and the Shiite majority of the population that was the target of Khomeini's propaganda was primarily located in southeastern Iraq, the Iraqi high command could not risk heavy casualties among the enlisted ranks, which were composed principally of Shiites (approximately 75 percent of the Iraqi enlisted men were Shiites).[17] Consequently, the Iraqis entered the war with a major element of their security policy designed to keep enlisted and Shiite casualties to a minimum. This policy was at odds with the demands of destroying the Iranian armed forces in a quick war of annihilation. The doctrine that the Iraqi army developed as a result of the decade-long counterinsurgency against the Kurds also militated against the use of blitzkrieg tactics. As one Western military analyst described it:

> Further, the long campaigns against the Kurds . . . had led the Iraqi forces to adopt a very peculiar style of fighting. The Iraqi forces could not suppress the

small Kurdish guerrilla units, so they adopted tactics based on massing against Kurdish villages, towns, and strongholds. These tactics involved massing against the objective, sealing it off, and then methodically using artillery fire and strafing to disorganize the defense.[18]

Although these tactics eventually wore down the Kurds, particularly after the Algiers Treaty effectively cut off Iranian aid, they did not prove effective against the Iranians. Furthermore, being steeped in these ponderous tactics prevented the Iraqis from adopting the offensive armor tactics demanded by the political objectives and the strategic situation.

Had Saddam Hussein and his generals resolved the conflicting demands between their political policy and their military capabilities, it might have been possible to devise a set of limited objectives achievable with these military means. It is clear that the more ambitious objectives of the Iraqi Revolutionary Command Council were beyond the military capability of the Iraqi armed forces, despite the turmoil in Iran in 1980. It was perhaps possible to retrieve the disputed lands along the central border area and to seize some of Khuzistan Province, but there was little possibility that the Shatt-al-Arab could be secured or the three islands captured, because the Iranian navy could not be swept from the Persian Gulf. Nor could Khomeini be overthrown, because the Iranian Army could not be decisively defeated, particularly in view of the policy and doctrine that constrained the Iraqi military strategy.

The Nature of the Gulf War

The Gulf war may be conveniently, if somewhat arbitrarily, divided into four phases that describe the character of military operations within them:

Phase I, Iraqi offensive: September 1980–December 1980

Phase II, stalemate: January 1981–August 1981

Phase III, Iranian initiative: September 1981–February 1984

Phase IV, escalation: March 1984–present

For a chronology of the major events of the war, see appendix 10A.[19]

Phase I—Iraqi Offensive

Iran and Iraq had been fighting off and on during the summer of 1980, and conflict flared anew in early September. When Iraq annexed two Iranian villages in the disputed zone and Iran did not respond effectively, Iraq decided to launch its invasion on September 22, 1980. The attack began with a preemptive air strike on ten military airfields in Iran—an unsuccessful attempt to destroy the Iranian air force on the ground in the early hours of the war. Although the air attack achieved surprise, it failed to knock out the Iranian air force because of flawed air tactics—a factor that was to plague the Iraqi air force throughout much of the war. Iraq's failure to achieve air superiority on the first day of the war enabled Iran's air force to retaliate the next day against Basra, Baghdad, and other cities.

At sea, Iran quickly established sea control of the upper Persian Gulf—a control that it still maintains. The Iranian fleet has blockaded the upper reaches of the Persian Gulf, which has prevented the Iraqi government from exporting oil from its oil fields near Basra. The Iranian navy, however, has not been able to stop war materiel from entering Iraq from Saudi Arabia's Red Sea ports and transiting Saudi Arabia or from being transshipped from Kuwait. War materiel also entered Iraq through Jordan via the Gulf of Aqaba.

The Iraqi main ground attack, composed of five divisions, struck in Khuzistan. Although the offensive inched slowly forward, it was able to isolate Khorramshahr and Abadan from Ahvaz. However, the attacks on Ahvaz and Dizful were halted short of those important objectives. Unaccountably, the Iraqis failed to secure critical terrain objectives north of Dizful that would have prevented Iranian reinforcements coming from farther north from reaching the Khuzistan front. This tactical error was compounded when the salient thus formed threatened the Iraqi logistical network in the area. Supporting attacks were also launched that seized Mehran and Qasr-e-Shirin, which, in turn, protected the flank of the Khuzistan operation and prevented Iran from mounting a ground threat against Baghdad. A subsidiary attack in the Musian area occupied territory that was claimed by Iraq but disputed by Iran. By the end of September, Iraq proclaimed—a trifle prematurely, as it turned out—that the territorial objectives of the war had been won.

The initial Iranian response to the invasion, although uncoordinated, was able narrowly to avoid a collapse of the Khuzistan front. It was uncoordinated because the Revolutionary Guards, who bore the brunt of the Iraqi offensive, responded to the clergy, while the regular units were commanded by Bani-Sadr. Defeat was staved off only by the valor of the Iranian soldier and by the inept tactics and strategy of the Iraqi high command, which insisted on controlling the war from its headquarters in Baghdad. Consequently, opportunities that were presented on the battlefield could not be exploited by Iraqi commanders on the spot. This, of course, did not stop the high command from blaming field commanders for battlefield reverses. Usually, by the time field requests were transmitted to Baghdad and directives were forthcoming in return, the opportunities were lost.

In an effort to resolve their command-and-control problems, the Iranians created the Supreme Defense Council in the middle of October to coordinate the entire war effort, but this reorganization came too late to save Khorramshahr, which fell to Iraqi forces on October 13. By December 1980, with the capture of Panjwin in the northern sector by Iraq, operations settled into a routine that was not to be broken for a year.

Phase II—Stalemate

As winter took command of the war zone, operations came to a virtual stand-still—a *sitzkrieg* reminiscent of the Western Front in Europe in 1940. Iran launched an ill-fated offensive in the Susangerd area in January 1981 that was soundly defeated by the Iraqi army. It soon became clear that Iraq would not continue its attack and would be content to assume the strategic defensive and attempt to consolidate gains already made.

Iran, once again in the throes of internal dissension caused by the dismissal of Bani-Sadr as president in June 1981 and by an anticlerical terrorism campaign that resulted in the death of several high-ranking civilian and military leaders, was also in no position to prosecute the war effectively. Thus, the war continued throughout most of 1981 despite the best efforts of the United Nations, the Islamic Conference Organization, and the nonaligned movement to negotiate its end.

During this phase, the air war was marked by unimaginative tactics and lost opportunities on the part of Iraq and by a steady dwindling of Iran's air assets because of inability to obtain repair parts and an absence of skilled mechanics. Air strikes of both nations were aimed at countervalue targets such as oil facilities and urban centers, which both air forces could strike at will since neither nation had effective air defenses.

The ground war settled into a routine reminiscent of World War I, the attacker suffering enormous casualties for relatively insignificant gains. The war at sea continued as expected, with Iran in control of the waters of the upper Gulf. Iran's superiority at sea meant that Iraq could neither export oil nor import war materiel through the Gulf. It also neutralized Iraq's ground control of the Shatt-al-Arab. Slowly, however, Iran was growing stronger, and by August the Iranian armed forces were poised to take the initiative.

Phase III—Iranian Initiative

During 1981, Iran had shown an increasing ability to coordinate and control multidivisional formations in offensive warfare. There were even instances that spring when they were able to combine ground and air forces in offensive operations. In September 1981, the Iranians launched Operation Thamin ul-A'imma across the Karun River, thereby breaking the year-long Iraqi siege of Abadan. A second offensive in November 1981 near Bostan confirmed that the initiative had passed from Iraq to Iran, but the approach of winter once again brought active operations to a virtual halt.

When the fighting resumed in earnest in March 1982, the stage was set for a series of Iranian offensives that would drive Iraq back to the border. Two offensives achieved that and the recapture of Khorramshahr, thereby nullifying Iraq's only real tactical victory of the war. These Iranian military successes were quickly followed in April by a diplomatic coup in which Syria agreed to close down the Iraqi oil pipeline that traversed its territory en route to the Mediterranean. This resulted in a reduction of Iraqi oil exports to about 600,000 barrels per day, far below what was needed to finance the war. This diplomatic setback was somewhat mitigated by the Soviet agreement to resume arms deliveries to Iraq, which had been stopped when the war began, and by the financial aid provided by the Gulf States, which amounted to about $1 billion per month.[20]

During 1982, the Iranians launched five offensives, which were typified by night attacks spearheaded by Pasdaran infantry to avoid the effects of a slowly improving Iraqi air force. These human wave attacks were defeated by the well-supported Iraqi defensive forces. In response, Iraq resumed its strategic air attacks against Kharg Island and other oil and economic targets. The use of surface-to-surface missiles (Soviet FROG-7s) with conventional warheads against Iranian cities was also resumed. The question at the end of 1982 was whether Iran would press its attack against Iraq to end the war.

Iran's answer was another series of offensives—in 1983 and continuing into 1984—code-named Val Fajr ("behold the dawn"), with the avowed purpose of achieving a decisive victory. However, these new attacks did not fare any better than those of 1982, and they turned the war into a costly battle of attrition. In fact, the battles in 1983 seemed to be a replay of the earlier offensives, in which the Iranians suffered casualties at a 3 to 1 ratio compared to Iraq. After five inconclusive operations, the war seemed ready to take a new turn in October, when Iraq announced that the French were supplying it with aircraft capable of inflicting damage on the supertankers calling at Kharg Island. This, together with the mining of the harbor at Bander Khomeini, seemed to signal an escalation of the war.

Phase IV—Escalation

Although the Val Fajr offensives continued into 1984, interrupted only by a limited-objective attack in the far northern sector in Iraqi Kurdistan that succeeded in capturing a small border outpost, it was the escalation potential that drew the attention of Western analysts. This escalation was demonstrated in three ways: (1) Iraq's attempt to shift the war's center of gravity from the land battles in the vicinity of Basra to an air siege of the Kharg Island oil terminal, using French-supplied jet aircraft and Exocet missiles; (2) the threatened "big push" by Iran in the vicinity of Basra, where an army variously estimated at 300,000 to 500,000 men was concentrating; and (3) the use of mustard gas by Iraq in what seemed a clear threat to respond with chemical weapons if Iran launched its "final offensive."

The announcement of the blockade of Iran's key oil port—Kharg Island—and the concomitant declaration of a military exclusion area that included, in addition to Kharg Island, the port cities of Bandar Khomeini and Bushehr, followed several weeks of deliberate attacks by Iran and Iraq on one another's urban population centers. By May 1984, more than twenty commercial oil tankers had been sunk or damaged by Iraqi air attacks. Although international insurance rates had increased dramatically and Iran's oil exports had been reduced somewhat, shipping continued to call at Kharg Island.[21]

In response, Iran continued massing its huge army, now approximately a half-million men, in the Basra sector and initiated air attacks of its own on Arab shipping in the Persian Gulf outside the military exclusion area in the territorial waters of the Gulf States. The Arab League responded to these attacks diplomatically by roundly condemning Iran. Saudi Arabia responded militarily by shooting down two Iranian aircraft over the Gulf. To mitigate the effects of the increased commercial insurance rates, Iran also offered oil discount rates to entice tankers to Kharg Island.

In June 1984, the attacks on population centers had resumed. However, both Iran and Iraq reacted favorably to a UN call for a truce, halting the deliberate city attacks. After the "city truce" had been agreed to, Iran proposed a truce on attacks against Gulf shipping, but Iraq could not agree, and its attacks resumed on June 24, 1984. The war continues; but even as it continues, some operational lessons may be tentatively derived from its course thus far.

Operational Lessons

Three major operational lessons can be learned from the Gulf war: first, the defense has been the dominant form of warfare; second, air superiority has been a significant factor in favor of the defense; and third, modern states, with cash, can sustain a "high-tech" war.

The history of warfare may be traced by observing the interaction of the offense versus the defense. In this century, two dramatic shifts have occurred in the relative dominance of one form of warfare over the other. In World War I, the defense was ascendant by virtue of barbed wire, the machine gun, and artillery; however, by the beginning of World War II, the tank and close-support aircraft had restored the advantage to the offense. Many military analysts interpreted the events of the 1973 Arab-Israeli war, with its technological demonstration of missile accuracy and "smart bombs," as an indication that the defense was once again dominant. Subsequently, however, Western military thinking has restored maneuver and the offense to the place of honor on the battlefield. The Iran-Iraq war challenges that determination, for there the defense has had the upper hand. Whether this judgment is due to any intrinsic advantage of the defense or to a lack of offensive expertise on the part of Iran or offensive spirit on behalf of Iraq is, of course, a key issue.

Coming to grips with this issue will require a consideration of the offensive and defensive tactics of both parties. The initial Iraqi attack was patterned on the offensive doctrine that served them so well during the Kurdish insurgency. This doctrine was characterized by slow, deliberate offensive operations, heavily supported by tactical airpower and artillery and an extensive but ponderous logistical network. This type of offensive was incapable of dealing with the situation at the beginning of the Gulf war. When the Iranian army did not immediately collapse, the tactical logic of the Iraqi strategy fell apart. Consequently, Iraq surrendered the initiative to Iran after the first months of the war. The most pertinent model for this offensive was the limited attack initiated by Egypt in 1973 against Israel on the Sinai front. The objective of that attack was the politically limited one of merely disturbing the status quo so that the political situation could be changed in Egypt's favor.[22] Curiously, the strategic aim of the attack was not to end the war in a single stroke but simply to *start* a war. Had Iraq similarly limited its objective, its operational offensive doctrine might have contained more strategic logic.

Iran did not fare much better than Iraq on the offensive. For a brief period in 1981, it appeared as if the Iranian army might have been able to mount multidivisional attacks using combined arms techniques. That is, Iran was showing some signs of using modern arms—tanks, artillery, air defense, and close-support aircraft—in coordination to achieve a synergism that would result in the great increase in combat power and intensity in battle that is the aim of offensive doctrine. However, these operations were stillborn, because their logistical support broke down and the required organizational framework was lost amid the internal chaos in Iran at the time. Iran then introduced a style of offensive operations that has persisted to this day.

Iranian offensive tactics have had the following attributes:[23]

1. An attack would usually begin at night to avoid Iraqi air attack. The Pasdaran would attack in human waves, attempting to saturate the Iraqi forward defense and infiltrate a few miles to the rear.
2. At first light, the Iranian regular forces would use their firepower to blast away at the Iraqis trapped between the Pasdaran and the regular forces.
3. The Iranians would attempt to secure key road junctions and waterways to prevent the enemy from reinforcing the original frontline.

These tactics involved only one offensive action in a single sector of the front; Iran was never able to sustain attacks at several points in different sectors so as to stretch the Iraqi defensive forces to the breaking point. Using these tactics, Iran has never been able to effect a decisive breakthrough or to cause the Iraqi defenders to retire in disorder.

The most professional military operations conducted during the war have been the Iraqi defensive operations, which are patterned after Soviet doctrine.[24] The Iraqi defense normally consists of three dug-in defensive bands about six miles in depth.[25] Each band uses triangle-shaped strong points, varying in size from platoon to company, that provide all-around protection by making use of alternative firing positions and well-dug-in tanks in hull defilade positions.[26] Each strong point is protected by the interlocking fire of another strong point and by massed artillery. In combination with the air superiority enjoyed by Iraq, this constitutes a formidable defense that will not easily be breached, particularly by Iranian troops that are neither trained in offensive warfare nor adequately supported by armor or air. Moreover, the Iraqi defense makes extensive use of engineering support to construct minefields, field fortifications, and lateral roads usable by Iraq to reposition its units rapidly.

The second important operational conclusion concerns the continued value of tactical airpower, not only in an offensive role but also in a defensive role despite the use of poor air doctrine. The air war began with a preemptive air strike on Iran's major airfields that was botched because of poor air tactics. Because of either poor training or faulty doctrine, the Iraqi pilots concentrated on the runways rather than on the combat aircraft parked on the aprons or on the soft support facilities. In attacking targets, the Iraqi air force does not attempt to mass its aircraft in large formations; it persists in attacking from high altitude to avoid missile defenses, and it often drops its ordnance short of a defended target rather than pressing the attack.[27]

Of late, however, the Iraqi pilots have pressed their attacks with more vigor and determination and, consequently, with greater effectiveness. Iraq does make better use of its attack helicopters, which have been effective against Iranian tank forces. With all of its limitations, however, the Iraqi airpower has been a net positive factor. Iraqi air superiority has caused the Iranians to fight at night, and the Iranian soldier knows that anything flying over the battlefield belongs to the enemy. This is a potent psychological factor. With 500 operational aircraft, the Iraqis are capable of supporting ground operations as required, but the Iranians, down to a mere handful of operational combat aircraft, are capable of, at best, only 65 sorties on a surge basis.[28] The lesson to be learned is that quantity counts and that air superiority is critically important to defensive operations.

Logistics links operations and strategy. The major operational-strategic lesson to be learned from the Gulf war in logistics is that although it is possible to avoid losing when one does not control the wherewithal of war, it is nevertheless difficult to win without an adequate indigenous military industrial base. Iran is a case in point. It lost its ability to use airpower, because it could not keep its combat aircraft operational. It had to virtually ground its air force (and lost a major portion of its armor force), because it could not secure supplies from the West, where most of its tanks and aircraft were manufactured, and because its maintenance personnel did not have the requisite skills to keep the sophisticated equipment operational. The lesson seems clear: with cash, a nation can sustain a war at a given level of intensity; however, if that level is not sufficient to win, a nation without an adequate indigenous logistic system, including stockpiles of arms and ammunition, is at the mercy of its international arms suppliers.

War Termination

Concerning the "end game" of this conflict, four war termination issues seem to have been paramount.[29] First, the declared war aims of each party require the unconditional capitulation of the other. At the beginning of the war, Saddam Hussein emphasized territorial claims as the rationale for the war, but it soon became clear that what was at stake for Khomeini was the survival of the Islamic revolution. In parallel, almost from the moment Iraq launched its invasion, Iran demanded the overthrow of Saddam Hussein and his Baathist regime. When the survival of a nation—or its leaders—is at issue, the room for diplomatic maneuver is obviously severely limited.

Second, neither nation has the military capability to defeat the other decisively on the battlefield. In the current international system, the use of force often appears to be the only recourse for sovereign nations that cannot resolve some real or imagined grievance. This war system only works, however, when the use of force can be decisive. The logic of the system requires a scaling down of objectives and a negotiated settlement when a decision cannot be reached on the battlefield at a cost commensurate with the objectives sought. By 1981, Hussein had come to the conclusion that the costs of the war far outweighed any objective that he could gain. He was willing to settle for the status quo ante; but meanwhile, the Ayatollah discovered that an external enemy served to revitalize a faltering revolution. The consistent war aim of Iran has been the overthrow of Hussein. Until that changes or until a military combination can be developed that will enable operations to become decisive, the war will continue.

Third, domestic affairs in both countries have not afforded their leaders much freedom of action. Iran and Iraq each have quarreling factions that have been active throughout the war—more in Iran than in Iraq, however. In Iran, there was, first, the American hostage crisis, then the opposition headed by Bani-Sadr and the street riots, terrorism, and purges that occurred after his dismissal, and then the recent emergence of a split in the Ayatollah's own camp.[30] These factors further burdened a regime that was in the midst of consolidating and exporting a violent revolution. In Iraq, Hussein has similar problems. He is still in the process of consolidating his power base in a country that has been renowned for its internal dissension,[31] and he leads a minority party that cannot afford a catastrophic military defeat. Thus, their domestic situations severely constrain both Hussein and Khomeini in their ability to negotiate an end to the war.

Finally, the international situation has not been conducive to intervention by external actors to bring the war to a halt. The United States was embroiled in the hostage crisis with Iran when the war started, which dramatically reduced its ability to act. The Soviet Union saw opportunities to gain increased influence in Iran. Israel has been in no hurry to end a war that divides the Arab world into opposing camps, so it does what it can to keep the war from ending, largely through aid to Iran. The other states in the region also see some utility to the continuation of a war between the two strongest and most militant powers in the Gulf area. So long as their oil continues to be exported, the other Gulf States will support Iraq in its fight with Iran, but they also believe that a solution in which the warring parties fight to mutual exhaustion is not all that bad. International organizations such as the United Nations and the Islamic Conference continue to seek ways to end the war, but they have no real power to enforce their solutions. The West and Japan were initially concerned that the war would result in an interruption of the oil flow, but since this eventuality has not come to pass, the urgency to end the war from that quarter has been considerably dampened. In short, the international situation does not readily dictate superpower intervention, and the rest of the international community apparently will not be urgently motivated to intervene so long as the oil continues to flow through the Strait of Hormuz.

Generally, the best time to think about how to end a war is before it gets started. However, there is not much evidence that nations give much serious consideration to how they will end a war before they start it. A classic case in this regard was Japan in World War II. Japan had planned one of the most successful operations in military history in the Pearl Harbor surprise attack, but, incredibly, it had no plan to end the war even if that attack was successful.[32] Judging from events in the Persian Gulf, Saddam Hussein had no plan to end the war against Iran, other than some vague hope that the Iranian people would depose Khomeini when an Arab army appeared in Khuzistan.

Conclusions

Three general caveats apply to any lessons, strategic or operational, that may be derived from the events of the Gulf war. First, any lessons derived before the war ends must be considered tentative at best, since future events could invalidate some or increase the importance of others. If the "lessons" of World War II had been published before the atom bombs were dropped on Hiroshima and Nagasaki, they would have missed the events that revolutionized warfare in our time.

Second, it is entirely possible that there may not be any lessons to learn about effectiveness of·modern weapon systems, such as the lessons that were gleaned from operations during the 1973 Yom Kippur War or the 1982 Israeli invasion of Lebanon, because neither the Iraqi nor the Iranian soldiers seem to have been very skilled in the use of the sophisticated weapon systems with which they were armed. (Of course, this observation may be an important lesson in itself.)

Finally, Westerners can only view the Iran-Iraq war through a cultural prism that tends to distort their vision and skew their judgment. This is the case when interpreting any cross-cultural event, but it is magnified by the sensitivity of both war and military strategy to cultural influences. Because the foreign press and Western military observers were denied access to the battlefields by both Iran and Iraq for most of the war, this constraint takes on added significance when one attempts to uncover the lessons of the war.

Several conclusions may be drawn from this analysis of the Iran-Iraq war. First, when using force to achieve political objectives, it is crucial to consider carefully how one intends to end the war before the first bullet is fired in anger. Hussein had not thought this problem through. Second, it is a strategic matter of primary importance to translate the war aims into suitable military objectives that will lead to the desired political effect. If this cannot be accomplished, it is better to abandon the entire enterprise because there will be little chance for success. Third, the strategic plan must be flexible enough to allow for rapid change in the event that the political or strategic assumptions that drive the plan prove to be invalid, as was the case with Iraq. Fourth, the strategy must envision operations from the beginning of the war to the end. That is, the plan must be comprehensive; it must consider how the war will end as well as how it will start. Finally, war planners and policymakers must understand that war in the field is vastly different from war on paper. The danger, uncertainty, and fatigue that accompany operations in the field make it very difficult to predict where the use of force will lead.

The most important operational lesson that may be derived from this war concerns the ascendancy of the defense over the offense. This conclusion runs counter to the conventional wisdom that considers offensive operations, as epitomized by the Israeli operations against the Arabs, the dominant recent form of war. This conclusion must be considered tentative until more detailed and more expert analysis can be brought to bear.

The final—and in my judgment the most important—lesson from the Gulf war, particularly for U.S. policymakers and military strategists, is the indispensable need to coordinate war aims, policy, and strategy. Policy and strategy have never been adequately integrated on either side in the Iran-Iraq war. It is absolutely essential in the dangerous world in which we live to ensure that military strategy is the servant of political policy to provide as much rational control over war as it is within our power to provide. There are more than 200,000 dead Iranian and Iraqi soldiers to attest to the proposition that a military strategy that is at odds with the political policy is paid for in blood on the battlefield.

Notes

1. For information pertaining to the early events of the war, see Edgar O'Ballance, "The Iraqi-Iranian War: The First Round," *Parameters* 11(March 1981): 54–59; Claudia Wright, "The Iraq-Iran War," *Foreign Affairs* 59(Winter 1980–81): 286–303; William O. Staudenmaier, "A Strategic Analysis," in Shirin Tahir-Kheli and Shaheen Ayubi, eds., *The Iran-Iraq War: New Weapons, Old Conflicts* (New York: Praeger, 1983), pp. 27–50. For later stages of the war, see "Within the Persian Gulf: Impact of a War: in International Institute for Strategic Studies (IISS), *Strategic Survey, 1983–1984* (London: IISS, 1984), pp. 76–81; Anthony H. Cordesman, "An Escalating Threat to the Gulf and the West," *Armed Forces Journal International*, March 1984, pp. 22–24, 27, 30, 75; Dov Tamari and Mark Heller, "The Iran-Iraq War" in Mark Heller, ed., *The Middle East Military Balance* (Tel Aviv: Tel Aviv University, 1983), pp. 17–24; and Shahram Chubin, "The Iran-Iraq War and Persian Gulf Security," *International Defense Review*, 17(1984): 705–720.

2. Cordesman, "An Escalating Threat," p. 24. Casualty figures reported during war are notoriously inaccurate, and since independent journalists have not been able to report the Gulf war consistently, the problem is compounded in this case. For example, Chubin, in "Iran-Iraq War," reports the following casualty figures, which differ sharply with those reported by Cordesman:

	Iraq	*Iran*	*Total*
KIA	50,000	300,000	350,000
WIA	100,000	200,000	300,000
POW	70,000	20,000	90,000

3. Robert Litwak, *Security in the Persian Gulf 2: Sources of Inter-State Conflict* (Montclair, N.J.: Allanheld, Osman, 1981), pp. 1–24.

4. Tamari and Heller, "Iran-Iraq War," p. 18. See also R.K. Ramazani, "Iran-Iraq War: Underlying Conflicts," *Middle East Insight* 3(July/August 1984): 8–11.

5. Harvey Sicherman, "Iraq and Iran at War: The Search for Security," *Orbis* 24(Winter 1981): 711–717.

6. Richard Cottam, "The Iran-Iraq War," *Current History* 83(9 January 1984): 489.

7. For a discussion of the qualitative aspects of the prewar military balance between Iran and Iraq, see Richard A. Gabriel, ed., *Fighting Armies: Antagonists in the Middle East—A Combat Assessment* (Westport, Conn.: Greenwood Press, 1983); for Iraq, see John S. Wagner, "Iraq," pp. 63–84; for Iran, see Donald Vought, "Iran," pp. 86–107.

8. Ibid.; see also Anthony H. Cordesman, "Lessons of the Iran-Iraq War: Part Two—Tactics, Technology, and Training," *Armed Forces Journal International*, June 1982, pp. 68–85.

9. Wagner, "Iraq," pp. 63–84; and Vought, "Iran," pp. 86–107.

10. Mansour Farhang, "Push Iran, Burdened, For Peace with Iraq," *New York Times*, July 27, 1984, p. A25; and Sandra Feustel, "Iraq Claims New Attack in Gulf, Says it Will Continue Siege," *Washington Post*, August 10, 1984, p. A-1.

11. The military, particularly the army, is accustomed to considering the geographic factors that relate to any given strategic situation as a matter of course. Recently, however, the defense community in general and the academic community in particular seem to have discovered the importance that geography holds for the development of military strategy. See, for example, Patrick O'Sullivan and Jesse W. Miller, *The Geography of Warfare* (New York: St. Martin's Press, 1983); and Robert E. Harkavy, "Recent Wars in the Arc of Crisis: Lessons for Defense Planners" in Stephanie G. Neuman, ed., *Defense Planning in Less-Industrialized States* (Lexington, Mass.: Lexington Books, D.C. Heath, 1984), pp. 283–289. For a detailed description of the climate, terrain, and other aspects of the Persian Gulf region, see Alvin J. Cottrell, gen. ed., and C. Edmond Bosworth, R. Michael Burrell, Keith McLachlan, and Roger M. Savory, eds., *The Persian Gulf States: A General Survey* (Baltimore: John Hopkins University Press, 1980), especially the appendixes, pp. 539–666.

12. For an elaboration of the relationship between policy and strategy and the content of policy, see William O. Staudenmaier, "The Strategic Process: Considerations for Policy and Strategy in Southwest Asia," in Shirin Tahir-Kheli, ed., *U.S. Strategic Interests in Southwest Asia* (New York: Praeger, 1982), pp. 11–35.

13. Cottam, "Iran-Iraq War," pp. 9–10.

14. US Army, *Field Service Regulations—Larger Units,* FM 100-15, June 1950, p. 20. More recent editions of this manual omit the discussion on selection of objective.

15. Vought, "Iran," p. 98, table 6, "Imperial Iranian Ground Force, Major Installations and Stationings, 1979."

16. In the fall of 1980, Iran was shipping about three million barrels of oil per day, most of which was being exported out of the Persian Gulf ports. If these ports were destroyed or captured, Iran's survival would be threatened. See Bijan Mossavar-Rahmani, "Economic Implications for Iran and Iraq," in Shirin Tahir-Kheli and Shaheen Ayubi, eds., *The Iran-Iraq War: New Weapons, Old Conflicts* (New York: Praeger, 1983), pp. 51–64. Also see Anthony H. Cordesman, "Lessons of the Iran-Iraq War: The First Round," *Armed Forces Journal International,* April 1982, p. 34.

17. "Iran Seen Gaining Edge on Iraq in War," *Aviation Week and Space Technology,* January 25, 1982, pp. 24–25.

18. Cordesman, "The First Round," pp. 41–42.

19. The data presented in this section and in the chronology (appendix IIA) were compiled from International Institute for Strategic Studies (IISS), *Strategic Survey* for 1980–1981, 1981–1982, 1982–1983, and 1983–1984; and Encyclopedia Britannica, *Britannica Book of the Year* for 1981, 1982, 1983, 1984. These references supplemented various accounts in newspapers, newsmagazines and other periodicals. The cutoff for research for the chronology was June 30, 1984. Also see note 1.

20. *Facts on File* 41(December 25, 1981): 949. In fifteen months of war, the Gulf States provided loans to Iraq of about $15 billion per month; *Facts on File* 43(August 12, 1983): 600–601. By May 1983, the Iranians estimated that the war had cost about $136 billion; Chubin, "Iran-Iraq War," pp. 705–721.

21. David Butter, "Stakes Rise on the Iranian Cargo Run," *MEED* 28(May 11–17, 1984): 28–29.

22. This interpretation of Egypt's war aim in the 1973 war was advanced by two Egyptian brigadiers who participated in the war and was independently confirmed by an

Israeli officer who also fought in the war. Their statements were made in conversations with the author.

23. George C. Wilson, "Iranian Offensive Appears as Large as Push In March." *Washington Post,* May 7, 1982, p. A19.

24. "Iraqis Confident in New Positions." *Financial Times,* April 14, 1982, p. 4.

25. Ibid.

26. The term *tanks in hull defilade positions* means that the tanks are situated in such a way that only the turrets of the tanks are exposed to enemy observation and direct fire. In this way, they present the smallest target possible but are still able to use their main guns in defense.

27. O'Ballance, "Iraqi-Iranian War," pp. 56–57.

28. Cordesman, "An Escalating Threat," p. 38.

29. Julian Lider, *Military Theory* (New York: St. Martin's Press, 1983), p. 73.

30. Drew Middleton, "On 'Final' Assault: Dissension in Iran?," *New York Times,* June 12, 1984, p. A12.

31. W. Seth Carus, "Defense Planning in Iraq," in Stephanie G. Neuman, ed., *Defense Planning in Less-Industrialized States* (Lexington, Mass.: Lexington Books, D.C. Heath, 1984), pp. 29–51.

32. Fred Charles Iklé, *Every War Must End* (New York: Columbia University Press, 1971), pp. 2–8.

Appendix 10A: Chronology of the Iran-Iraq War

1980

January
25 Presidential elections held in Iran; Bani-Sadr wins.

February
19 Bani-Sadr appointed commander-in-chief of Iranian armed forces.

April
 8 Khomeini urges Iraqi armed forces to depose Saddam Hussein.
 9 Border clashes reported at Qasr-e-Shirin.

July
10 Military coup in Iran fails; 300 arrested.

August
 5 President Hussein visits Saudi Arabia; first visit of Iraqi head of state since 1958.

September
10 Border clashes in disputed area between Iran and Iraq.
17 Iraq denounces 1975 Algiers Treaty.
20 Iran mobilizes.
22 Iraq invades Iran; battles rage on land, sea, and in the air.
24 Iraqi aircraft strike Kharg Island oil terminal.
28 UN issues call for immediate cease-fire in Gulf war.
30 United States sends four Airborne Warning and Control System (AWACS) aircraft to Saudi Arabia at Saudi request.

October
 1 Iran pledges not to block Strait of Hormuz.
 2 Main theater of war continues to be battle for control of Abadan/Khorramshar.
 7 Air war is aimed at oil and economic targets of both sides.

13 Khorramshar falls to Iraqi forces.
14 Iran attacks Baghdad by air.
17 Islamic Conference calls for cease-fire.
27 Iraq and Jordan announce establishment of Joint Military Command.

November
 4 Saddam Hussein warns Iran of a wider war if his offer of a cease-fire and peace is not accepted.
30 Intensity of war abates with onset of winter.

December
25 Iraq announces invasion of Iran in Kurdistan, near Panjwin.

1981

January
 5 Iran launches unsuccessful counteroffensive near Susangerd area.
20 Iran releases U.S. hostages.

February
 4 Gulf Cooperation Council (GCC) established.
19 Olof Palme, UN mediator, fails to end Gulf war.

May
21 Heavy fighting erupts in Khuzistan after four-month lull.

June
 7 Israeli warplanes attack Iraq's Osirak nuclear reactor.
10 Bani-Sadr ousted as leader of Iran's armed forces.
22 Bani-Sadr dismissed as Iran's president.

June
28 Terrorists bomb headquarters of the Islamic Republican party in Tehran.

August
 2 Iran mounts airstrikes against Iraq's oil facilities at Tikrit.
30 Bomb detonates in Tehran, killing Bani-Sadr's successor as president—Mohammed Ali Rajai.

September
27 Iranian offensive—Thamin ul-A'imma—results in the lifting of the siege of Abadan.

October
 1 Iran mounts air raid against Kuwait's oil facilities at Um-Aish.
 4 Kuwait recalls its ambassador to Iran.
 5 Iran elects new president—Mohammed Ali Khomeini.
28 United States agrees to sell five Airborne Warning and Control System (AWACS) aircraft to Saudi Arabia.

November
29 Iran launches offensive—Tariq ul-Quds—near Bostan.

December
16 Bahrain defeats Iranian-sponsored and -supported Islamic revolution.
26 Saudi Arabia and Iraq and long-standing border dispute.

1982

January
7 Iraq's major oil pipeline into Turkey is sabotaged.

March
3 Jordan announces it has sent a volunteer force to aid Iraq.
22 Iran launches major spring offensive—Fath ul-Mubin.
27 Saddam Hussein calls for cease-fire.

May
3 Iran opens offensive operations in Khuzistan.
7 Iranian troops reach Iraqi border.
24 Operation Bait ul-Mugaddas results in Iranian recapture of Khorramshar.

June
20 Iraq announces that it will withdraw its forces from Iran; Iran asserts it will continue the war.
29 Iraqi forces withdraw from Iran.

July
13 Iran invades Iraq as part of the Operation Ramadan, aimed at Basra.
21 Iranian jets hit Baghdad.

August
18 Iraqi bombers strike Kharg Island.

September
7 Iraqi aircraft repeat attack on Kharg Island.
15 Former Iranian Foreign Minister Ghotbzadeh executed for plotting against Khomeini.
30 Near Mandali, the Iranian army launches a new offensive—Muslin Ibn Aqil.

October
2 Explosion in Tehran kills 60 and injures 700.
4 At Iraq's request, United Nations calls for Gulf war cease-fire.
6 Iran rejects UN cease-fire proposal.
24 Islamic Conference Organization declares Gulf war peace efforts are deadlocked and pulls out as mediator.

November
2 Iran opens Operation Muharram in area west of Dizful.

1983

February
8 Iran launches first Val Fajr ("Behold the Dawn") offensive, designed to end the Gulf war.

March
2 Iraq causes large oil spill in Persian Gulf by destroying a portion of an offshore oil rig.
9 At nonaligned nations summit meeting in India, Iraq proposes an end to the war, but Iran rejects the idea.

April
1 Val Fajr-1 offensive, opened in March by Iran in Khuzistan, is stalemated after two weeks of fighting.

May
4 Iran dissolves Communist Tudeh party; eighteen Soviet diplomats ordered out of the country.
26 Iran rejects another Iraqi proposal to end the war, this time under UN auspices.

July
23 Val Fajr-2 launched by Iran in vicinity of Piranshahr; stalls three days later.

August
2 Iraq defeats Val Fajr-3 in area west of Mehran.

October
9 Five French Super Etendard warplanes delivered to Iraq.
19 Iran attacks near Pajwin in Val Fajr-4 operation.

1984

February
11 Iraqi surface-to-surface missiles strike civilian targets in Dizful.
12 Iran retaliates against civilian targets in Basra.
16 Iran launches Val Fajr-5 in the Mehran area.
18 Iran and Iraq agree to a partial cease-fire against civilian targets.
23 Iran opens its second major offensive of the month—Val Fajr-6—in the Dehloran area.
27 Iraq begins its blockade of Kharg Island with a series of air attacks.
29 Iraqi oil field at Majnoon Island is captured.

March
1 Iraq claims to have sunk seven ships in the Persian Gulf.

  4 Iran accuses Iraq of using chemical weapons, killing 400 Iranian soldiers and injuring 1,100 since February 27, 1984.

15 Iraq recaptures bridgehead on Majnoon Island.

27 Iraqi Exocet missile hits Greek tanker.

April

18 Panamanian tanker struck by Iraqi naval missiles in vicinity of Kharg Island.

26 Saudi tanker suffers explosion shortly after leaving Kharg Island.

May

  7 Saudi tanker hit by Iraqi missile.

16 Saudi supertanker *Yanbu Pride* attacked by Iranian aircraft.

20 Arab League condemns Iran for attacks on Arab shipping while in their own territorial waters.

24 Iraq resumes attacks on Gulf shipping after a five-day lull.

29 United States authorizes sale of 400 Stinger missiles to Saudi Arabia.

June

  5 Iran and Iraq resume attacks on one another's civilian population centers. Saudi jets down two Iranian fighters over Gulf.

12 Iran and Iraq agree to suspend bombing of urban centers.

24 Iraq renews attack on Gulf shipping after fourteen-day hiatus.

11
Profound or Perfunctory: Observations on the South Atlantic Conflict

Harlan K. Ullman

In 1982, Argentina and Britain went to war over the Falklands (see figure 11–1).[1] Although the intensity of the conflict over relatively insignificant islands surprised many, the nature of the conflict intrigued others. It was, after all, the first extended naval campaign fought since World War II in which both sides faced a combined sea, air, and ground threat. In addition, it was a war between industrial states that were equipped, if not with the highest-technology weapons, at least with jet aircraft, cruise missiles, and diesel and nuclear submarines. Such a conflict promised to produce a gold mine of information pertaining to both broad political-strategic and specific tactical-technical issues and to provide an abundance of "lessons learned." However, most of the published analyses of the Falklands war to date have been disappointing, offering relatively mundane conclusions about lessons learned. This chapter will review the conflict with a view to determining further lessons to be learned.

The War: A Chronology

The dispute between Great Britain and Argentina over the sovereignty of the Falklands is an old one. Before the diplomatic breakdown in March 1982, there had been seventeen years of ongoing negotiations between the two nations. Complaining that Britain's unwillingness to set a time frame for negotiations was merely procrastination, Argentina declared that it was "not prepared to let things drag on indefinitely."[2]—a statement that was not taken seriously by Britain. This was only the first of many misunderstandings between the two countries before the war. In fact, Argentina's preparation for an invasion of the Falklands had already begun in late December 1981.[3]

Argentina's plan for occupying the Falklands began to unfold in mid-March 1982 when scrap metal merchants were encouraged to land on South Georgia without British permission. By the last week in March, Britain publicly announced concern over the possibility of an Argentine invasion of the islands. In response to British initiation, the United Nations passed Security Resolution 502,

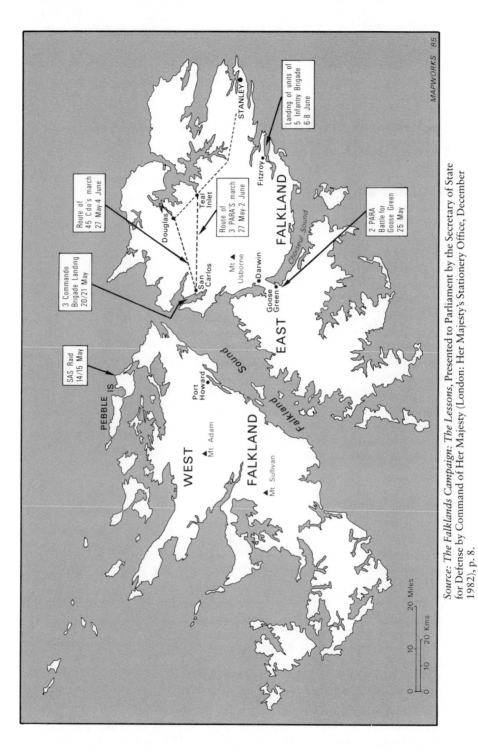

Source: The Falklands Campaign: The Lessons, Presented to Parliament by the Secretary of State for Defense by Command of Her Majesty (London: Her Majesty's Stationery Office, December 1982), p. 8.

Figure 11–1. The Falkland Islands

Route of 45 Cdo's march 27 May–4 June

Landing of units of 5 Infantry Brigade 6–8 June

Route of 3 PARA's march 27 May–2 June

3 Commando Brigade Landing 20/21 May

2 PARA Battle for Goose Green 25 May

SAS Raid 14/15 May

STANLEY

Teal Inlet

Douglas

FALKLAND

Fitzroy

Choiseul Sound

San Carlos

Mt. Usborne

Darwin

Goose Green

EAST

PEBBLE IS

Port Howard

Falkland Sound

WEST

Mt. Adam

FALKLAND

Mt. Sullivan

20 Miles

20 Kms

0   10

0   10

"calling on the governments of Argentina and the United Kingdom of Great Britain and Northern Ireland to refrain from the use of the threat of force in the region of the Falkland Islands (Islas Malvinas)."[4]

On April 2, 1982, Argentina invaded and took control of South Georgia, and the Falklands were seized the next day. Britain's response, announced to the House of Commons on April 4 by Prime Minister Margaret Thatcher, was "to see that the Islands are freed from occupation and are returned to British administration at the earliest possible moment."[5] Because attempts at further negotiations appeared to be pointless, on April 5 Britain assembled and dispatched a task force that eventually would total 114 ships. Argentina's financial assets in Great Britain were frozen, and sales of military equipment and arms to Argentina were prohibited. On April 7, Britain announced a 200-mile exclusion zone around the islands. Any Argentine ship in that area would be at risk of attack. On April 10, the European Economic Community (EEC), except Italy and Ireland, voted to support Great Britain's economic sanctions and arms embargo.

The conflict ultimately consisted of four phases. Phase I was Argentina's seizure of South Georgia and the Falklands. Argentina's military planning hardly went any further than that, on the assumption that Britain would take no action to recapture the islands and would resort, instead, to negotiations. The remaining phases were therefore the result of British initiatives to return possession of the Falklands—by force if necessary—to Her Majesty's government.

Britain's defense plan was more extensive; it was based on applying incremental political, diplomatic, economic, and propaganda pressure to Argentina to force return of the Falklands. Failing that, Britain was prepared, if necessary, to resort to direct assault on the islands to regain them. As Phase II of the conflict, Britain organized and mobilized sufficient forces to retake the Falklands should that be necessary. The British task force, Operation Corporate, was sailed at deliberate speed to allow political and diplomatic steps to be taken. Despite the worsening weather in the Falklands as winter approached, the transit time enabled complete military planning to be conducted for the amphibious assault.

Phase III was the preliminary sparring between both sides, which many pundits saw as something of a semicomedy. Britain's plan was to increase military pressure on Argentina by bombing raids using the Royal Air Force (RAF), naval gunfire, and commando raids to harass Argentine forces ashore in the Falklands. All this was meant to force Argentina to surrender without a direct assault. The initial sparring quickly escalated, however, as ships on both sides were attacked and sunk. Phase IV was Britain's direct assault on the islands, which ultimately led to Argentine surrender.[6]

The war itself unfolded as follows. In mid-April, the British task force entered the Falklands operating area and began harassing Argentine operations as a prelude to invasion, although British leaders hoped that the conflict might be resolved short of that. Operation Blackbuck (the bombing of Stanley by the Royal Air Force) was begun. On April 26, South Georgia was recaptured and, in the attack, an Argentine submarine was sunk alongside the wharf there. The sinking of the Argentine cruiser *General Belgrano* on May 2 brought the first real casualties of the conflict. Hit by straight-running torpedoes fired at close range from HMS *Conqueror,* a British nuclear submarine, the *Belgrano* took at least 300 Argentine sailors with her to the bottom. Although Britain did not realize it at the time, this sinking effectively discouraged Argentina from using its surface fleet during the war.[7]

The war intensified as Argentina began major air attacks and Britain increased its pressure on the Falklands with raids of its own. On May 4, the guided-missile destroyer HMS *Sheffield* was attacked by two Super Etendard aircraft firing AM-39 Exocet missiles. One Exocet missile hit and did not explode but started uncontrollable fires. HMS *Sheffield* had to be abandoned and taken in tow; it finally sank on May 10. The loss of HMS *Sheffield* brought what had been regarded as a semicomedy into clearer focus, as it had become a serious, costly, and dangerous war.

Attacks by both sides continued. On May 9, two British Harriers attacked and sunk *Narwal,* an Argentine intelligence collection vessel, in the British exclusion zone. Two days later, the destroyer HMS *Alacrity* attacked and sank *Islas De Los Estados,* an Argentine naval cargo ship. Argentine air raids increased. On May 12, the guided-missile destroyer HMS *Glasgow* suffered bomb damage, and on May 14, in perhaps the most publicized raid of the conflict, eleven Argentine aircraft, an ammunition dump, and a mobile land-based radar were destroyed at Pebble Island by the British Special Air Service (SAS).

On May 20, the British mounted the major amphibious landing on San Carlos that ultimately wrested control of East Falkland Island from Argentina. The timing of the attack was based on the element of surprise; it was therefore delayed until weather conditions of overcast and fog prevented early Argentine detection of the assault force as it approached San Carlos Sound. Diversionary raids were mounted on the East Falklands to distract the Argentine land command and to further obscure the intended site of the assault. Some 5,000 British troops, largely Royal Marines supported by paratroopers, directly assaulted the beachhead, using landing craft and helicopters. Local Argentine opposition, which was small, was overwhelmed. In conducting the assault, Britain lost only two helicopters and their crews.

To secure and defend the beachhead around San Carlos, Britain deployed a four-layer naval defense against Argentine air attack. The outer layer consisted of Sea Harrier aircraft from the carriers HMS *Invincible* and HMS *Hermes* used in air defense roles. The second layer was an anti–air weapons (AAW) screen formed by ships on distant picket stations northwest of the Falklands. The third layer included AAW ships with point defense missiles and frigates with guns, all in San Carlos Sound. The fourth layer consisted largely of ground-based Rapier missiles and other anti–air weapons ashore. To complement distant warning, British SSN's were deployed along the likely air routes of Argentine strike aircraft. Given the extreme range of operations over the Falklands, Argentina had to fly direct routes and could not maneuver deceptively because of limitations of aircraft endurance.

Argentina conducted an intense air offensive, and losses on both sides, as will be noted, were heavy. Up to two sorties a day were flown against the British once fighting became heavy. After May 2, a total of about 300 Argentine sorties were flown against British surface ships and the amphibious force. The Argentine air force attacked at low altitude, mostly with 500-pound and 1,000-pound "iron bombs," many of which failed to explode because the attacks were made at low altitudes and the fuses could not arm properly. Rocket and strafing attacks were common. Five Exocet missiles were launched by Super Etendard aircraft, and unguided rockets were fired by MB-339 aircraft. Canberra and Pucara aircraft were also flown by the Argentines in the attack role, but apparently without effect. Argentina lost forty-three aircraft in these attacks, and others were so badly damaged that the air force was virtually destroyed. Britain lost HMS *Ardent,* HMS *Coventry,* and HMS *Antelope,* and six other British ships were damaged.

Argentine air attacks were also directed at the British naval force, with the two carriers the highest-priority targets. Northeast of the Falklands, *Atlantic Conveyor,* a British cargo ship carrying precious helicopters, was hit by two Exocet missiles and eventually sunk. The loss of *Atlantic Conveyor* was a major one, because these helicopters were crucial in providing mobility for the ground forces. Without them, many land forces had to walk the rugged sixty or seventy miles from San Carlos to Port Stanley.

Britain's next move was to secure Camilla, Creek House, and Darwin/Goose Green. Two paratroopers batallions, backed by extensive naval gunfire support, were used in these attacks, and Harriers provided close air support for the paratroopers. On May 29, Argentina surrendered Darwin/Goose Green. This was one of two major land actions.

On May 30, while the 45th Royal Marine Commando (CDO) and Third Paratrooper Battalion secured Douglas settlement and Teal Inlet, the SAS recaptured Mount Kent and Mount Challenger. On June 4, after discovering that the Argentines had evacuated Fitzroy, the British established an advanced base there and moved quickly to take Bluff Cove and the crucial surrounding area. Then, on June 7, the Royal Marines captured Mount Low, overlooking the Stanley airfield.

On June 8, the landing ships *Sir Tristram, Sir Galahad,* and HMS *Plymouth* were attacked and seriously damaged by Argentine Skyhawks and Mirages. *Sir Galahad* was beyond repair and eventually had to be scrapped.

The final skirmish of the war began on the night of June 11 with the British attack on Port Stanley. Once again, British naval vessels successfully created a diversion so that the Third Commando Brigade's attack was launched in complete surprise. Mount Longdon, Two Sisters, and Mount Harrier were all recaptured. On June 12, the final missile attack was launched against the Royal Navy when a land-based Exocet hit HMS *Glamorgan,* causing only minor damages. On the night of June 13, Britain staged more attacks and recaptured Wireless Ridge, Tumbledown Mountain, and Mount William.

On June 15, Margaret Thatcher announced to the House of Commons:

> Early this morning in Port Stanley, 74 days after the Falkland Islands were invaded, General Moore accepted from General Menendez the surrender of all Argentina forces in East and West Falkland together with their arms and equipment.[8]

In the final reckoning, 225 British soldiers were killed and 777 British casualties were reported. Argentina reported 712 men killed in action and 1,000 injured. In addition to the human losses, both sides incurred heavy equipment losses. Six British ships were sunk and eighteen others were damaged, while thirty-seven aircraft and helicopters were destroyed either by enemy action or by operational factors, such as bad weather. Seven Argentine ships, including a cruiser and a submarine, were sunk and two others were damaged. Fifty-seven percent of Argentina's air force inventory—103 aircraft and helicopters—was destroyed, and about fourteen were damaged beyond repair.

Lessons to Be Learned

This, then, is how the war over the Falklands was fought and won. Curiously, however, despite the uniqueness of this conflict and the scope of its military action, the major conclusions and "lessons" drawn from this war, with one or two exceptions, have generally been unsurprising. Analysts have largely tended to ignore the strategic or broader issues, focusing instead on the tactical-technical level of analysis.[9] Even then, the results have not been unusual or unexpected. Given this relatively rare instance of war between an advanced industrial state and a less advanced industrial state, it is interesting that more far-reaching observations have not been forthcoming, especially when one considers the lengthy absence of this type of conflict and the alleged first-time use of relatively advanced weapons and associated technologies.

There are several possible explanations for this apparent difficulty in deriving significant lessons from the Falklands war. First, it might have been thought that no important geostrategic lessons could be drawn from that war. One side initiated hostilities; the other responded. Although the actual unfolding of events provided considerable action and perhaps some surprises, there may have been few significant changes or crucial new lessons to be noted.

Second, it is inherently difficult to transpose events, lessons, and observations from one situation to other, certainly different and perhaps more complex, circumstances. Consider the difficulty in transposing broader or profound lessons from the Falklands conflict to other potential conflict situations. In the Falklands, Britain deployed about 8,000 marines and soldiers—about the size of a U.S. brigade—a relatively small body of men transported over a very long distance. Britain's two small aircraft carriers operated some two dozen Harrier jump-jet fighter aircraft, supported by about twenty warships, against an Argentine air threat of eighty to ninety attack aircraft, largely A-4 Skyhawks built in the 1950s and 1960s, with a total inventory of six Exocet cruise missiles. In addition, Argentina's surface fleet posed virtually no threat to British forces, especially after the sinking of the Argentine cruiser *Belgrano*. Although the Royal Navy still believed that Argentina's surface-launched cruise missile threat was substantial, the Argentine submarine force numbered four, two of which were useless because of maintenance problems.

The contrast between the Falklands experience and one potentially faced by U.S. or Western forces operating against a Soviet threat or against an unconventional threat indicates how difficult it would be to transfer even profound military and naval lessons from one situation to the other. In war against the Soviets, high-threat maritime operations might require four or five U.S. carrier battle groups (CVBGs), supported by land-based tactical air and national reconnaissance means (that is, space reconnaissance), and large amphibious forces of perhaps 20,000 to 25,000 men or more to reinforce allies or seize beachheads elsewhere. Each carrier would be operating about ninety aircraft in its air wing—almost five times the number used by the entire British force in the Falklands. The Soviets could mount attacks with dozens if not hundreds of cruise missiles, fired from large numbers of modern aircraft, submarines, and ships at ranges in excess of 300 miles to close-aboard U.S. forces. These attacks would be followed up by submarines closing to within torpedo range. The actual size and shape of the threat, of course, would vary, depending upon many factors. Furthermore, the United States would employ a variety of measures and countermeasures to make life very difficult, indeed, for a would-be attacker, including the ability to use its carrier-based fighters at 500 or 600 nautical miles from the U.S. battle force and, depending on location, land-based airpower at perhaps longer ranges. However, the types of multiservice, joint operations involving allies that could be required in a war with the Soviets seem to be far more complicated than the operations Britain undertook in the Falklands. Landing an amphibious force four or five times that of the British would be no easy feat.

In unconventional situations, such as the Beirut bombing that killed 241 U.S. Marines in October 1983 or the threat to close the Persian Gulf by terrorist action, the nature of war may have changed so drastically that few or no conventional conclusions are applicable. High-threat operations against the Soviets could entail coordination and control of ten or twenty times the number of engaged units that fought in the Falklands—and at distances hundreds or thousands of miles greater (although this by no means diminishes the challenges Britain successfully overcame). Given these qualitative and quantitative differences, attempts to transpose observations, no matter how profound, from the Falklands to other situations could prove inexact and just plain wrong.

Third, there is a general tendency to become transfixed on the tactical-technical level of detail and to be fascinated with the performance of men, machines, and weapons under the stress of mortal conflict. This concentration on the tactical-technical level is very understandable. The way weapons worked or failed, the drama and excitement of war, and, most important, the courage and ability of men under fire are entirely interesting and worthy subjects for comment. They are closely related to and bear heavily on daily defense program decisions made in compiling annual military budgets. They are also easier to come to grips with than comparisons of data to postulate changes or alterations in the nature and conduct of politics and war—changes that are caused by a variety of factors. When more than occasional pressure arises to mix marketing requirements for defense budgets with objective analysis, tactical-technical details become central for both advocates and critics of specific weapons and other defense programs, who generally find sufficient grounds and data to prove their point while disproving and refuting the arguments of their opponents.

Suppose, however, that genuine strategic or profound conclusions exist and can be drawn from the South Atlantic conflict. Are these conclusions likely to be obscured by the difficulty in transposing them to other potential conflict situations and by the important but not necessarily crucial debate over such tactical-technical issues as the merits of large and small aircraft carriers, fixed and vertical-take-off aircraft, diesel and nuclear-powered submarines, and the alleged vulnerability of ships to "smart" cruise missiles? If they exist, can these strategic conclusions be identified, and can they then be applied to other, perhaps more complex potential conflict situations?

The purpose of this chapter is to address these questions by offering a means of identifying and prioritizing observations and lessons according to their strategic, theater, or tactical applications by evaluating selected key issues in terms of their broader and specific relevance to the defense plans and policies of the United States. This method illuminates what may be profound and provides a means for examining the more perfunctory lessons against a broader perspective.

The range of implications to be drawn and applied to all three levels of inspection is broad. The primary argument, which extends beyond the conflict in the Falklands, is that warfare, especially at sea, has reached a new stage of complexity and scope because of the expanded potential for long-range detection, targeting, and killing; the potential distribution of highly lethal weapons to many different land- and sea-based platforms and launchers; and the unexpectedness with which states and forces can find themselves engaged in conflict. In peacetime, this has made more difficult the tasks of anticipating and preparing for relatively short-warning, intense, joint maritime operations that may be required against expected or unexpected adversaries. This expansion in complexity and, perhaps, unexpectedness has also made mandatory the requirement that genuinely multiservice operations and command, control, and communications capabilities keep pace with these developments; if not, they will prove to be the fatal flaws in any combat operation. Debate over this larger argument is important for an improved understanding of war and its control. Other observations equally apply to broader elements of overall U.S. policy.

In categorizing and evaluating the events and observations of conflict, Carl von Clausewitz provided a useful guide. Clausewitz identified three levels of military and political analysis. The first—and the broadest—is the overall strategic level of analysis, which includes not only the context in which the war was fought but also implications of the conflict that extend beyond the belligerents and that may affect other states and the overall conduct of policy. For example, in their assessment of the crisis in the Falklands, both Argentina and Britain miscalculated. Britain did not believe that Argentina would seize the islands, and, after its occupation, Argentina did not expect the British to attempt a recapture. It is important to determine whether this type of misperception is likely to exist in other conflict situations in the future and the degree to which our strategic and contingency plans should be shaped to anticipate the very unexpected. These considerations should also incorporate cultural differences. For example, critics often observe that the United States expects that its adversaries reason like Americans or need education to bring their strategic thinking in line with U.S. values. That criticism may be unfair, but it does point out how perceptual differences can exacerbate conflict.

Several questions arise. For example, has the Falklands conflict significantly affected the long-term relations between the United States and Latin America?[10] Will the short-term British victory affect the long-term Latin American and Central American perspective for the better (such as the newly installed democratic Alfonsin government in Argentina) or for the worse—or do such considerations draw more from the conflict than really existed? What about Soviet reaction? Given British steadfastness and resoluteness, what do British actions in the Falklands suggest regarding Soviet perceptions of British will in Europe and the effectiveness of Britain's nuclear deterrent in response to any Soviet military actions against NATO?[11]

Clausewitz's second level of analysis deals with the theater of operations and how the campaign was conducted—what Liddell Hart termed "grand tactics." What can we learn from the conduct of the campaign by both sides? Are there any major implications to be drawn, especially regarding anticipation and preparation for possibly more complex and unexpected conditions of war, increased weapons and sensor capabilities, and the requirement for multiservice or joint operations?

The third level of analysis is concerned with tactical-technical details and how the battle was fought, especially the interplay in combat among men, machines, weapons, and logistics. It is generally on this level that most analysis has been conducted, such as determining the effectiveness of the Exocet cruise missile, the Harrier vertical-take-off jump-jet, the diesel submarine, the vulnerability or invulnerability of surface ships in high-threat operations, and the advantages and disadvantages of large and small aircraft carriers.

These levels of analysis are by no means separate and discrete; some overlap is useful. However, this means of analysis can separate the various sets of observations and data into an appropriate hierarchy, allowing some conclusions to be drawn.

The Strategic Level

Although most causes of conflict are beyond the scope of this chapter, any attempt to derive lessons from the Falklands war must focus, first, on the important category of strategic perceptions that proved both correct and incorrect. Argentina clearly misperceived and miscalculated British resolve and response, and Britain equally misperceived Argentina's need and intent to regain the Falklands.

During the Falklands war, perceptions on each side concerning the motivations, capabilities, qualities, and performance of the other were by no means accurate or well considered in advance. Each side was generally unaware of the other's military capabilities, level of training, and readiness to fight; they relied on *Jane's Fighting Ships* as the basic intelligence source to determine one another's naval strength. Argentina generally had high regard for British forces, whereas the British generally exaggerated the quality of the Argentine fighting man but were surprised by the exceptional courage of the Argentine air force. Accurately estimating an adversary's qualities and capabilities may seem less a function of perception than of military intelligence and information, yet if any strategic implication can be drawn, it is the requirement to perceive accurately the strengths and weaknesses not only of likely adversaries but also of adversaries who might arise suddenly from unexpected and unpredictable quarters. This conclusion is not new, but it is often forgotten.

Surprise and perception are difficult to separate in conflict situations. The historical observation that surprise is always successful in dominating the first phase of hostilities remains true, although winning the first battle, even by default, does not necessarily win the war. Despite advanced warning, Britain did not expect Argentina to invade and occupy the Falkland islands; hence, Argentina was initially successful. In turn, Argentina did not expect the British to reinvade. Surprise was also evident in Argentina's failure to anticipate the British amphibious landing at San Carlos, which was probably the only landing site capable of providing all the necessary requirements for safely disembarking the British force. But is this a great lesson? Despite increased intelligence collection, surveillance, and warning and communications capability, surprise can still be strategically manipulated to advantage—although, in this case, Argentina's short-term exploitation of surprise must be balanced against Britain's ultimate recapture of the Falklands. The broader implication, however, must focus on the importance of intelligence, warning, and response; on how well the unfolding of potential future crises is anticipated; and on whether steps can be taken in advance either to preempt crises or restrict them from enlarging. In this regard, attempts to develop a greater national capacity for crisis contingency planning are highly important and are aided by concurrent strengthening of overall national intelligence capability.

Theater Lessons

Examination of two significant, possibly profound, and related issues emerging from this conflict is particularly relevant to the theater level of analysis. The first issue concerns the peacetime preparations for and the ability to exercise successful command and employment of modern forces in a relatively modern and largely unexpected war. The second issue reinforces the explicit requirements posed by modern conflict for joint operations. Fundamental confusion in the Argentine command structure and the remarkable success of British forces in recapturing the Falklands under the most adverse conditions of environment and distance from supply bases obscured these two issues, although success or failure in future battles will largely hinge on these issues and on the requirements for genuinely multiservice or joint operations.

What distinguishes higher-technology warfare from its antecedents and increases the complexity of conflict for operational commanders is the longer reach of weapons and sensors and the potential distribution of highly lethal weapons among many diverse land- or sea-based platforms. In the past, a lucky hit or a single, stealthy unit—such as a submarine—could impose a great deal of unexpected damage. Generally, however, attacks had to be mounted in fairly large numbers to be successful. What the Falklands war highlighted was the widespread threat of highly lethal cruise weapons, coming covertly and with minimum warning, even though "iron bombs" dropped by low-flying Argentine A-4 attack aircraft imposed far more damage than Exocet cruise missiles. Yet, if Argentina had had 20, 30, or 200 of these Exocet missiles—not the half-dozen or so with which it began the war—could this have tipped the balance? If so, is this observation significant?

Furthermore, despite the existence of high-technology weapons (although Exocet is far from leading-edge technology), neither side had fully prepared for their use, nor had the two sides taken full advantage of peacetime to examine completely all the operational implications. If they had, Argentina surely would have procured more missiles, perhaps stationing them ashore, and Britain might have developed or improved its countermeasures, especially software and fire-control programs, to cope with the magnitude and complexity of the threat, since the effort and cost were small. Clearly, each side was limited by peacetime budgets and attendant constraints. In retrospect, however, perhaps this traditional line of explanation should be reexamined.

The combination of technology issues and the complexity of conflict was succinctly reflected by Rear Admiral Sir John Woodward, the senior task group commander of Britain's expeditionary force:

> We were going to war at the end of an eight thousand mile pipeline outside the NATO area, with virtually no shore-based air we normally count on, against an enemy of which we knew little, in a part of the world for which we had no concept of operations.[12]

On the Argentine side, command was not centralized anywhere; there was great competition in controlling operations between service staffs and operational headquarters in Buenos Aires.[13] Thus, the Argentine commander ashore in the Falklands was subjected to divided authority and control and apparently did not have sufficient command authority to utilize effectively the forces that should have been under his operational control. In addition, other than two well-coordinated Exocet missions, there was virtually no sense of joint operations on the Argentine side. Clearly, despite or because of the century and a half of peace Argentina had enjoyed, its operational commanders were completely unprepared for the conflict as it subsequently unfolded.

On the British side, the complete story of command and control has not fully emerged. At the highest command level for the conflict—the defense staff (consisting of the service chiefs and the chief or head of the defense staff)—the chief of the defense staff became the principal military advisor to the government, rather than just the most senior member of the defense staff. During the early stages, there was strong division of opinion and certainly some conflict among the various staffs in planning the operation, largely because the ultimate political objectives of the conflict were undergoing continuous review and because the relative suddenness of the task simply needed ample time for careful decision. The arrival at Ascension Island of Admiral Sir John Fieldhouse, the Fleet Commander-in-Chief, to review and coordinate operations with Admiral Woodward and his staff (while the task group was still in transit and in the Ascension area) was essential for matching political objectives and decisions with operational planning and for bringing a sense of unity to the divided command structure.

It is true, of course, that the excruciating pressure of conflict is impossible to simulate adequately in peacetime and that, in the early stages of war, all commanders and staffs need more seasoning. The British navy, mainly because of the size and tradition of its officer corps, generally produces very experienced operational commanders, but the Falklands conflict was a most demanding test for the Royal Navy. Although Admiral Woodward was successful in winning the battle for the Falklands (and that was a prodigious feat), coordinating, deploying, and integrating the operations of the two small aircraft carriers—HMS *Invincible* and HMS *Hermes*—with a total of about twenty or thirty Harriers and numerous helicopters was not easy, given the adversary, the weather conditions, and the urgent need to keep those two ships undamaged in battle.[14]

Comparisons of British and U.S. naval capabilities as applied to the Falklands miss the point. If the U.S. Navy, with two, three, or four carrier battle groups, could not have easily defeated and destroyed Argentine naval opposition, the U.S. taxpayer has grounds for supreme discontent. The issue, rather, is—given a high-threat situation that would require multicarrier operations—how well postured is the U.S. Navy, in terms of its command-and-control arrangements and its preparations for senior commanders, to prevail under such conditions? By most accounts—and despite the British navy's deserved reputation for professional competence—British control of its relatively small force would probably pale in comparison with the operational complexities of controlling and coordinating eighty or ninety aircraft from each of three or four aircraft carriers against a 360-degree, round-the-clock, all-weather threat.

The second critical corollary is the importance of joint operations. The involvement of land—whether for sensors, for shore-based aircraft, or for contesting physical control—has become as important for navies as the seas they operate in. Traditional navy-versus-navy battle is virtually impossible without major involvement of land-based capabilities. The Soviets, for example, are dependent on land-based maritime air forces; and in Third World situations, it is difficult to envisage involvement in which land is not central. Hence, whether because of the need to seize points ashore or the need to fight forces based ashore, future major maritime operations (other than reprisal raids) will demand ground, air, and sea components that extend beyond naval capabilities. Therefore, unless the closest operational integration of the services is accomplished in peacetime, it is unlikely that success will result in war. Conflict has become too complex and diversified for any one service to operate in isolation.

How, then, does a state prepare successfully for these contingencies? In World War II, Admiral Nimitz observed that the Naval War College had prepared U.S. naval officers for every possibility, with the exception of kamikazes. As it still took the United States several years to coordinate its operations and turn the tide of battle in that war—even with the far-sighted preparations of its military leadership—what might happen when there is neither time nor adequate preparation? The British may have muddled through brilliantly in the Falklands, but is that approach sufficient for the United States, and is there anything that can or should be done about preparing for joint operations in conditions of increasingly complex, high-intensity conflict?

The ability of the overall British command system to direct an extraordinarily prompt and effective mobilization effort has been well documented; it certainly must rank with the most impressive wartime achievements. The converting and commandeering of so many different merchant ships for wartime duties was a remarkable effort. The innovation and ability to accomplish complicated, heavy industrial tasks literally overnight are not skills that can be practiced in peacetime to ensure smooth operation in crisis. However, the organization and, more important, the manner in which the British command was able to slice through all the bureaucratic layers are useful lessons.

Tactical-Technical Lessons

As noted earlier, most of the analyses of lessons learned from the Falklands conflict have focused on the tactical-technical level.[15] In general, these lessons can be grouped into two categories: (1) readiness and training and (2) conduct of operations.

Readiness and training, including physical fitness, have been cited by the British as among the foremost reasons for their success and among the key factors contributing to Argentina's failure. Few would argue the need for highly ready, well-trained military forces. In Britain's case, its professional volunteer force performed well, in stark contrast to the Argentine conscripts, who were poorly trained and ill-suited for their mission. However, detailed translation of this lesson into a practical application of enhancing readiness and training has been missing. The issue, therefore, is the actual implementation of the lessons learned into programs, plans, and actions that will lead to improved readiness and training.

Conduct of operations has occupied the largest share of analysis. There are numerous interesting lessons to be drawn from the performance of men, materiel, weapons, and logistics support, three of which merit review here:

1. The conduct of the naval war, including the issue of alleged surface ship vulnerability;
2. The merits of large and small aircraft carriers;
3. The conduct of the land war—specifically, the issue of "light" versus relatively fixed forces.

The loss of British ships in the Falklands has rekindled a longstanding debate over surface ship vulnerability. Those who have argued that the cruise missile and submarine have rendered surface ships ineffective point to Britain's loss of four warships and two merchant ships and to the restraints imposed on Argentina's surface navy by the threat of the Royal Navy's nuclear submarines after the sinking of the *Belgrano*. Advocates of surface ships have argued, on the contrary, that neither British aircraft carrier was successfully attacked and, given the intensity of Argentine air attacks, that British losses were not "unacceptable."

There are two applicable observations here. First, war inevitably entails losses, which may be heavy under certain conditions. To some degree, *any* force engaged in combat is at risk. To be blunt, Britain "traded-off" destroyers in San

Carlos Bay to ensure putting its landing force ashore safely. That is the nature of war. Second, in comparing this conflict with the historical record of high-threat operations, British losses were not exceptionally high. During the Okinawa campaign in 1945, U.S. and British forces fought the Japanese for nearly three months. Against that invasion force, Japan flew a total of approximately 6,000 sorties, 1,900 of which were kamikazes. Of 1,750 allied ships at Okinawa, 900 were of 1,200 tons or larger, including 331 combatants. Of all these larger ships, 368 were damaged by attack and, within that total, 98 combatants and 20 auxiliaries were sunk, put out of commission, or damaged. Thus, over this intensely fought campaign, almost one-third of the larger allied combatants (98 of 331) were put out of action, despite clear allied air and sea superiority.[16]

In the Falklands, the British deployed 37 combatants, 22 Royal Fleet auxiliaries, and 45 civilian ships taken up from trade.[17] Clearly, not all were directly involved in the fighting, and some were stationed outside the reach of Argentina's air arm.[18] Even then, Britain lost six surface ships (two to cruise missiles, the rest to bombs)—about 5 percent of all ships involved, but probably no more than 15 percent of the ships actually in harm's way. It may be argued, of course, that Okinawa is not a valid comparison here and that the development of modern technology precludes any real parallel. Using other World War II examples, however—such as the resupply of Malta and the North Cape of Russia—the British losses incurred at the Falklands do not support the arguments of those who would automatically consign surface ships to oblivion.

Part of the vulnerability argument concerns the debate over large and small aircraft carriers and fixed and vertical-take-off aircraft. Proponents of large aircraft carriers argue that Argentine airpower would have been useless against modern, fixed-wing fighters and airborne early warning (AEW) radar aircraft. Proponents of small aircraft carriers argue that even with limited aviation capability, Britain still won; hence, the expense of large aircraft carriers and fixed-wing aircraft in future procurement programs may not be justified.

This debate over the utility and vulnerability of large and small aircraft carriers and fixed and vertical-take-off aircraft is not completely relevant by inference from the Falklands conflict, because both types of aircraft carriers and their respective air wings presumably would have been successful. In high-threat operations, either a strategy of attrition—which uses relatively large numbers to overwhelm the enemy—or a strategy of the "indirect approach"—to outflank and outmaneuver the enemy's strength—is possible. In both strategies, tactical airpower of some sort is crucial, and, given economies of scale, large aircraft carriers with fixed-wing aircraft are more cost-effective than smaller carriers. Indirect or maneuver methods will not necessarily work in a war of attrition, such as that in Okinawa, where large numbers of highly capable forces are important. Since the Falklands war fell well between these two extremes, conclusions about the utility of large and small aircraft carrier forces should be cautiously examined. Both large and small carrier forces would have carried the day for Britain.

The presence of a large carrier with AEW and long-range fighter aircraft would have greatly eased Admiral Woodward's task, but the smaller carriers did prevail and, if numbers count, are seen to have provided the winning edge. What the debate over large and small aircraft carriers and their air wings has overlooked, so far, however, are two very important points arising from the Falklands conflict.

First, discussion of large and small aircraft carriers has rested only on *individual* comparison of the strengths and weaknesses of each type of ship. The broader issue of the overall impact of a mix of small and large carriers on the size, shape, and capability of the navy has not yet been examined. Second, regardless of the flight-deck size, the effective operation of many aircraft carriers and airwings together is by no means automatic, and command and control remain crucial to successful operations.

The use of small aircraft carriers, whether as replacements or supplements for larger carriers, will clearly require corresponding major changes in fleet composition, employment, and tactics. Requirements for escort surface combatants, submarines, and land-based aviation may be crucially affected. Yet none of these points appears to have been a major consideration in the debate over large and small carriers associated with the Falklands lessons.

Command and control of multicarrier operations are extraordinarily complex. The general rule of thumb is that at least three or four large-deck carrier battle groups (CVBGs) or more small-deck CVBGs are required for successful and continuous operations in high-threat areas. Yet there is no formal doctrine or employment manual for ensuring effective command and control of three or four big-deck CVBGs in coordinated operations. It is also likely that increasing the number of aircraft carriers that are operating together will increase command-and-control problems. Thus, further examination of multicarrier operations in high-threat areas to determine if there is a saturation point in how many decks can, in fact, operate successfully and effectively together is essential and will also serve to sharpen debate and decision about the entire carrier issue. Those who argue for more, smaller decks often omit the central issue of how these forces will be controlled and coordinated.

Three aspects of the land campaign to recapture the Falklands are particularly relevant to the discussion here. First, the manner in which a light, highly mobile force defeated a larger, though admittedly poorly trained and unprepared entrenched force has application in conditions of warfare in which the sides are more evenly balanced.

Rarely will a good, small force defeat a larger, better one without the intervention of one or more critical external factors. Mobile, light infantry without heavy support would be no match for heavy Soviet armored divisions operating on the central plains of Europe. However, in Third World states, especially where there are extraordinary differences in terrain, including both mountains and relatively flat land where tanks can operate, the utility of mobile, fast, light infantry is potentially great. Heavy armor would have proved useless in much of the East Falklands. If the forecast of more frequent low-intensity conflict in the Third World proves correct and requires a greater Western response, then application of the type of light, mobile forces the British used in the Falklands appears to be an effective alternative to the traditionally heavy and difficult to deploy land forces required for European contingencies.[19]

Another ingredient of the British land campaign—perhaps the main ingredient of its success—was the degree to which innovation and imagination were manifest in British operations. Institutionalizing brilliance, innovation, and imagination cannot be accomplished easily or quickly, if at all. But the British, in all aspects of service life, training, and preparation were able to do just that. The Special Air Service (SAS) and Special Boat Service (SBS) performed daring and successful hit-and-run raids to confuse, harass, and weaken the Argentine troops in the Falklands. Less well known was the role of the destroyers, which provided accurate naval gunfire support, in many cases directed by naval observers ashore.[20] The sailing of the destroyer HMS *Alacrity* through San Carlos Harbor to serve as an expensive minehunter was another good example of tactical innovation. There were also reports of the use of British submarines, with SAS and SBS units ashore in Argentina, to serve as distant early-warning radar pickets.[21]

The third aspect of the British land campaign to be noted here involves the traditional British toleration of idiosyncratic behavior. A system that permits and encourages this type of behavior, though risking potential challenges to authority, can reap great rewards.[22] Two examples from the Falklands experience suffice. In the recapture of South Georgia, the advanced reconnaissance team was led by a Royal Marine commando who had expert mountain-climbing credentials. He had been allowed the time to develop this passion while in the service, and it paid off handsomely on the wind-swept glaciers. Another Royal Marine officer, part of the planning cell for the amphibious assault, had, while previously serving in the Falklands, used his solo sailing skills to navigate the Falklands and had charted literally every bay and inlet. Thus, by tolerating and encouraging these personal interests in peacetime, Britain reaped a later reward in conflict.

Conclusions

The Falklands conflict provides some highly important conclusions relevant to policy, politics, and conflict. The most profound, though not necessarily new, conclusion deals with the expansion in the scope, intensity, and unexpectedness of modern war, which may be outdistancing peacetime preparations and command capabilities to deal with such situations. Indeed, invisibly paralleling the larger conventional aspects of the Falklands conflict are emerging unconventional threats that are likely to pose even greater challenges to Western security and responses.

Regarding the broadest category of strategic judgments, the following observations and conclusions from the South Atlantic war must be emphasized. First, the capacity for any state—but particularly a democratic state—to rally around its leadership in time of crisis should not be underestimated. This implication was probably not lost on the Soviets. Although no hard evidence is available to demonstrate Soviet attitudes toward the conduct and conclusion of the conflict, the following thesis is certainly plausible. To the Soviets, it was probably surprising that Britain committed such a large measure of national treasure, credibility, and prestige to islands literally oceans away that had no real strategic, economic, military, or geopolitical value. This display of resolve is not unrelated to the entire deterrent calculus. Therefore, one can postulate that from the Soviet view, deterrence in Europe, particularly given the British commitment to acquire Trident nuclear ballistic missile submarine capability, may well have been reinforced as surely as British truculence, decisiveness, and perseverance were demonstrated. Despite the implementation of the two-track decision to deploy U.S. cruise and Pershing II missiles in five NATO states, which has produced grave concern within the alliance, one implication of the Falklands conflict, when viewed from Moscow, may have been that, in crisis—especially if that crisis is perceived as unambiguous and unacceptable external military aggression—NATO may choose not to back down and, indeed, may present much greater than expected resolve (regardless of individual members opposing implementation of the two-track decision).

Second, the longer-term perceptions in Latin America concerning outside interference and, ultimately, future U.S. choices and policies have yet to crystallize. Under these conditions, it is premature to draw conclusions on which to base action. However, the United States has not always had (as most countries do not have) long-term mechanisms and procedures with which to carry out far-sighted policy actions that might preempt or prevent potential future challenges to our interests. Indeed, our memory is often short; it is interesting, for example, that the Kissinger Commission on Central America did not consider the relevance of the Falklands experience to potential militarization or stabilization issues. Certainly, one lesson from the Falklands war must be the renewed appreciation of Latin American sensitivity to outside interference and the need for determining ways for the United States to turn those perceptions to advantage while reinforcing the goodwill of the states that remain well-disposed. Given the possible deployment of U.S. soldiers and carrier battle groups on a "routine" basis to Central America, the ultimate effectiveness of these actions is now crucial to U.S. choices and decisions. Although this show of force may work—and may be one of our only policy instruments for action—careful consideration of the aims and expectations of such a demonstration of force is essential. Lingering memories of the Falklands conflict, reinforced by U.S. actions in Central America, could influence the stabilization or militarization prospects for Latin America, create buffers or opportunities for further Soviet or Cuban exploitation and penetration, and ultimately encourage pro- or anti-American sentiment. At the minimum, our ability to discourage those negative trends will largely rest on our sensitivity to Latin American perceptions as they emerge and on making certain that U.S. actions are undertaken with full regard to the existence of those perceptions.[23]

Warfare, by virtue of expanded weapon and sensor capabilities, has become far more complex, especially as engagement and weapons standoff ranges have increased; as the distribution of more lethal firepower spreads among more platforms; and as associated command-and-control requirements for offensive and defensive operations increase. Given what appear to be increasing costs of these combat systems, including personnel to operate them, if this argument is correct, preparations in peacetime for wartime contingencies never had greater urgency in terms of ensuring that doctrine, training, and readiness are fully consonant with the rigors and requirements of future conflict conditions.

Given the difficulties that Britain faced in the Falklands—admittedly operating two carriers in ways perhaps never envisaged—it becomes absolutely essential that the United States ensure that the backbone and centerpiece of its naval strength—the multicarrier battle group—be ready in every sense to operate in mutual support, both under conditions of high threat and in less defined, probably more difficult unconventional situations. This suggests that multicarrier doctrine, training, and preparations and command-and-control procedures for operating two, three, or four carriers together may not be sufficiently mature to ensure success, given the likely rigors of future high-threat operations or unconventional situations. Furthermore, a system for ensuring continuity of turnover of operational lessons and experience between and among carrier battle group staffs must be put in place.

Second, the requirement for joint operations has been indisputably reconfirmed. The role of the navy and its place in national strategy must be viewed in the context of how the navy supports national objectives. The U.S. Navy may be able to defeat the Soviet Navy hands down, but that by no means demonstrates that the United States and its allies would be successful in winning an overall conflict. Hence, establishing the U.S. Navy's roles and integrating them, where appropriate, with the other services (and allies), both strategically and tactically, is essential. The current direction, reinforced by the memoranda of agreement between the navy and the air force emphasizing joint operations, is very positive. If any lesson from the Falklands is applicable to U.S. policy, it is the requirement for the closest service cooperation in joint operations. This must be relentlessly pursued; otherwise, the complexities of future war may prove overwhelming.

In the larger political context, the Falklands experience was useful in showing how fragile mutual perceptions can be—and in showing that surprise should come as no surprise. This reinforces the need for accurate and timely political assessment, largely derived through intelligence organizations. Corresponding contingency plans must be sufficiently prepared so that key decision makers have a range of well-conceived options from which to choose. Enough cannot be said in support of strengthening national intelligence capabilities to that end.

War is expensive. Weapon lethalities continue to increase, perhaps disproportionately to defense against them. Hence, the cost of waging future war may exceed even the most conservative current estimates. Expansion in reach and lethality of weapons has also increased the complexity of war, which will test our peacetime preparations for war. The history of war reveals how often peacetime preparations fell short of reality. Before World War I, both sides planned for a war that would be swift. Before World War II, the future allies prepared for stalemate, and Hitler had no idea that his U-boats would refight the 1914–1918 battle for the Atlantic against merchant ships. The U.S. war plans for the approaching war in the Pacific—even without the attack on Pearl Harbor, which sank the Navy's battleships—would have been useless if implemented. These lessons were reinforced by the Falklands experience. Thus, to prevent future conflict, our only choice may be to reintensify our efforts in peacetime preparations so that, through these actions, force will not have to be used.

Notes

1. The use of *Falklands* (rather than *Malvinas*) throughout this chapter does not reflect bias for or against either belligerent.

2. Paul Eddy, Magnus Linlater, and Peter Gillman, eds., *War in the Falklands: The Full Story* (New York: Harper & Row, 1982), p. 25.

3. Ibid., p. 26.

4. Ibid., p. 112.

5. *The Falklands Campaign: A Digest of Debates in the House of Commons, 2 April to 15 June 1982* (London: Her Majesty's Stationery Office, 1982), p. 4.

6. For further details, see ibid. and the Sunday Times of London Insight Team, *War in the Falklands* (New York: Harper & Row, 1982). For the Argentine side, see Juan Carlos Murguizur, "The South Atlantic Conflict—An Argentine Point of View," *International Defense Review*, February 1983, pp. 135–140. See also Max Hastings and Simon Jenkins, *Battle for the Falklands* (New York: Norton, 1983), p. 384.

7. From discussions with senior British officers.

8. *The Falklands Campaign*, p. 350.

9. A refreshing exception is Stansfield Turner, "The Unobvious Lessons of the Falklands War," *Naval Institute Proceedings*, April 1983, pp. 50–57.

10. For its own reasons, the Kissinger Commission on Central America chose not to consider the possible spillover, if any, from the Falklands in affecting the potential militarization issues, residual anti-imperialist sentiments, or positive benefits, such as having Alfonsin in power.

11. Despite British resoluteness, which could not have gone unnoticed in Moscow and perhaps was not fully understood, the current deployment of U.S. cruise and Pershing II missiles in five NATO states certainly has divided alliance loyalties and opinions. Thus,

it can be argued that any Falklands dividend has been paid off. From a Soviet view, however, the difference must be that in genuine crisis, NATO may not cave in and may respond in surprisingly resolute ways against overt and unmistakable Soviet actions.

12. Press release by Admiral Woodward in a statement before allied officers, February 21, 1983. See also Sunday Times Insight Team, *War in the Falklands,* pp. 145–148.

13. Murguizur, "The South Atlantic Conflict," p. 138.

14. From discussions with senior British officials.

15. For example, see U.S. Navy, *Lessons of the Falklands* (Washington, D.C.: U.S. Navy, 1983), p. 66.

16. The United States had nearly 1,400 fighter aircraft, of which 400 to 500 were on station on Combat Air Patrol (CAP) during a given attack. Of the 1,900 kamikazes, 855 (45 percent) were shot down by CAP, 576 (30 percent) were shot down by close-in antiaircraft fire or missed their targets, 190 (10 percent) returned to base, and 279 (15 percent) hit or made damaging near misses. No data on nonkamikaze attacks are available. Of the combatants rendered *hors d'combat,* 85 percent were destroyer types, 8 percent were carriers, 7 percent were battleships and cruisers, and none were carriers.

17. Her Majesty's Government White Paper on The Falklands Campaign (London, June 1983), pp. 37, 39.

18. Had Argentina's submarine force attacked the British supply lines, the conflict might have had a different complexion.

19. It is interesting to note that the U.S. Army is moving toward the "light" division concept for some of its forces. The lessons of the Falklands should be very applicable to these efforts.

20. This was part of the harassment operation before, during, and after establishing the San Carlos landing. In fact, many of the destroyers had only one gun. Opposed gunfire-support missions are served more compatibly with two mounts—one for counterbattery to suppress enemy fire.

21. From discussions with senior British officials.

22. Ensuring that healthy idiosyncratic behavior does not create a raft of "Colonel Blimps" is crucial. Some critics of British forces assert that this is the case. In practice, the tendency to delegate down the chain of command, which is strong within British forces, usually permits idiosyncrasies to exist.

23. This is not an argument for or against deploying U.S. forces to Central America. Rather, it is an argument to ensure that we consider in advance the range of possible reactions and responses to our initiatives so that we do not find ourselves surprised by events as they unfold.

12

Military Lessons of the 1982 Israel-Syria Conflict

W. Seth Carus

During the summer of 1982, Israel and Syria fought a short war, the
fourth between those two countries in the last thirty-five years. This
conflict was a small part of the larger Lebanon war known to the Israelis
as Operation Peace for Galilee. It was a war limited in both time and space. Most
of the fighting between the two countries took place during a forty-eight-hour
period starting on June 9 and ending on June 11 in a battlefield about 30 miles
wide and 25 miles deep that included a Lebanese valley known as the Bekaa and
the surrounding mountains and hills.

Despite the limited character of the fighting that took place, the battles
fought in the Bekaa area have justifiably fascinated military pundits, primarily
because of an interest in the activities of the Israeli military forces. Their high
quality, their effective and sophisticated use of advanced weapons systems, and
their employment of innovative tactics have put the Israelis at the cutting edge of
modern warfare. In particular, the use of Western-style equipment and tactics
against an army relying on Soviet systems makes specific aspects of the conflict
of interest to those concerned with the defense of Western Europe.

Although there is much to be learned of potential importance, caution
should be exercised in assessing the lessons of this conflict. War is a complex
phenomenon, and the interactions between factors are often less than obvious
even to the experienced analyst. The strengths and the objectives of the combatants, the size and character of the theater of operations, and even diplomatic and
political considerations can have a dramatic impact on the outcome and character of a conflict. This was clearly true during the fighting between the PLO and
Israel during 1982, but the same can also be said of the battles between Israel
and Syria.

The Air War

Israel's air operations during the summer of 1982 were extraordinarily successful. Not even the men who planned the campaign had anticipated that so much

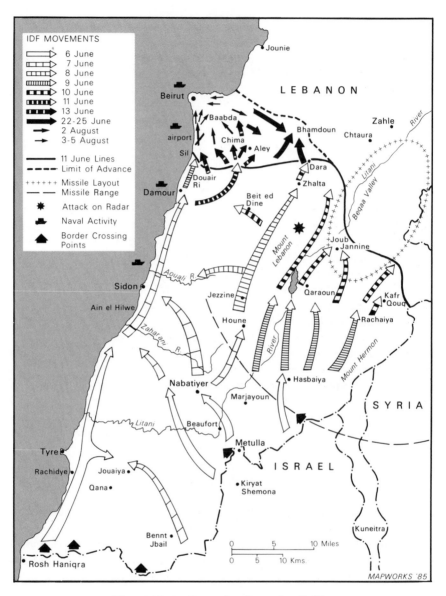

Figure 12–1. Operation Peace for Galilee

could be accomplished with such small losses. When the operation was conceived, it was expected that perhaps a dozen or more planes would be lost. In the actual event, Israel lost only two aircraft during the entire summer of 1982. Although other aircraft were also badly damaged, it appears that they were eventually put back into service.

Whereas the Israeli air force took few losses, the Syrians suffered a devastating defeat. They lost a complete air defense system, including twenty surface-to-air missile batteries and in excess of eighty-five fighter aircraft. Because of this defeat, Syrian ground forces in Lebanon had virtually no defense against Israeli air attack and as a result suffered from intense air attacks. This was a complete reversal of the 1973 Arab-Israeli war, when Egyptian and Syrian air defenses destroyed more than a hundred Israeli combat aircraft and as a result reduced the Israeli air force to comparative impotence for much of that war.

Suppressing Air Defenses

The apparent ease with which Syrian air defenses in Lebanon were obliterated was the most remarkable Israeli achievement during the 1982 war—and the one least expected by outside military analysts. Syria's antiaircraft defenses in Lebanon, concentrated in the Bekaa region, consisted of 7 SA-3 launchers (two batteries), 12 SA-2 launchers (two batteries), 60 SA-6 transporter-erector-launchers (fifteen batteries), SA-7 hand-held missiles, 200 ZSU-23-4 radar-directed 23mm antiaircraft guns, and two or three early-warning radars.[1] The Israelis destroyed seventeen of the missile batteries during their initial attacks without losing a single aircraft. At least nineteen SA-2/3/6 batteries and numerous SA-8/9 launchers were knocked out during the summer of 1982 with the loss of only one aircraft, a Phantom, to Syrian groundfire. (The second Israeli plane shot down by ground fire, an A-4 Skyhawk, was credited to Palestinian SA-7s.)[2]

The destroyed Syrian missiles had been in Lebanon for a little more than a year. A plan to attack these missiles in 1982 was delayed by bad weather that forced the Israeli Air Force to postpone the operation. Subsequent diplomatic pressure from the United States forced Israel to cancel the operation altogether.[3]

During the thirteen months that followed the entry of the missiles, the Syrians considerably strengthened their defenses. As a result, they had considerably many more missiles and guns in June 1982 than they had in April 1981. Nevertheless, the Israelis also were able to take advantage of the delay to fully investigate the capabilities of this new air defense system. Although spies on the ground undoubtedly contributed some information, sophisticated technical intelligence methods provided most of the required data.

Starting in May 1981, Israeli drones flew surveillance missions over the missile batteries, sometimes accompanied by reconnaissance planes. Northrop Chukars, normally used to simulate manned aircraft in live ammunition antiaircraft training, were used in these sorties.[4] The drones were not used for surveillance purposes; rather, they simulated manned aircraft to induce the Syrians to activate their air defenses. The Israeli air force was willing to lose some drones to Syrian missiles, and Israeli accounts indicate that at least five of these drones were shot down (the Syrians claimed at least eight).

Every time the Syrians fired at a drone, however, Israel learned more about how the Syrian air defenses would react to a real attack. RF-4E reconnaissance aircraft accompanied the drones to monitor electronic emissions, and it can be assumed that other collection systems were also employed. Thus, the Israelis discovered all they needed to know about Syrian radar characteristics, communications equipment and procedures, command-and-control structure, weapons capabilities, and air defense tactics.

The Israeli attack started at 1400 hours on June 9, 1982. This operation, the outcome of the previous year of planning, was a complex plan tailored specifically to deal with the circumstances to be faced in Lebanon, and it involved the integrated use of a variety of disparate systems.

The attack began when a large number of decoy drones of types never previously used in combat were launched against the Syrians. Two different systems were used: the Samson, an air-launched unpowered glider, and the Delilah, a ground-launched powered drone. The Samsons were particularly important; they had the radar profile of the Phantom, and they carried an electronic countermeasures package. They were released from F-4 Phantoms with the sun behind them. (Since it was early afternoon, the Phantoms were west of the Bekaa.) This meant that the Syrians could not track the drones optically, and they had to rely on their radars. To the Syrian radar operators, the Samsons appeared to be Phantoms, which made it seem as though numerous strike aircraft were about to attack the Syrian positions. The drones diverted attention from the manned aircraft following behind them; they led the Syrians to activate their radar fire control systems, making them vulnerable to antiradiation weapons; and they led the Syrians to use up their ready surface-to-air missiles against fake targets. The drones thus made the Syrians more vulnerable and made it less likely that Israeli aircraft would be shot down during the attack.[5]

When the missile batteries went into action, they were hit by a coordinated attack employing a combination of ground-launched and air-launched weapons. The air part of the operation concentrated Syrian air defenses in the central and northern part of the Bekaa, too distant to be destroyed by ground systems. A squadron of F-4E fighter-bombers (possibly twenty-four planes) fired antiradiation missiles from low altitudes against the now active Syrian fire control radars. American-built Shrike and Standard ARM missiles were used in these attacks. These missiles differed from the models in use in the United States, since both types had been modified in Israel to give them more capable seekers and other improvements. The F-4s flew near the ground at high speeds, making it difficult for the Syrians to detect them even under better conditions. At the same time, they used self-protection jammers and chaff to confuse the fire control radars used to direct the fire of Syrian air defense missile and gun systems. Since the aircraft were approaching from the west, out of the sun, they could not be attacked using optical control systems.

The Israelis also used ground-based weapons against the Syrian missiles. Three long-range artillery systems probably were involved: American-built 175mm M-107 self-propelled guns firing extended-range artillery ammunition with a range considerably in excess of 32 kilometers; Israeli-built MAR-290 multiple rocket launchers with a range of 40 kilometers; and the new Israeli LAR-160 multiple rocket launchers with a 30 kilometer range and cluster bomb warheads carrying 1,200 bomblets. Using remotely piloted vehicles, such as the Scout drone, to direct the artillery fire, highly accurate attacks were possible. In combination, these weapons devastated radars and surface-to-air missile batteries.[6]

Unconfirmed reports have asserted that Israeli forces used ground-launched antiradiation missiles, but it is impossible to confirm such reports. One account claims that these were ground-to-ground rockets (or missiles), called *Zeev* (meaning "wolf" in Hebrew), fitted with radar-homing systems with a 40-kilometer range.[7] If so, the system referred to might be Israel's largest ground-to-ground rocket, the 290mm medium attack rocket (MAR-290). Another source asserts, however, that the weapons used were modified Standard ARM missiles. Normally, the Standard ARM is an air-launched version of the Standard surface-to-air missile with a radar homing seeker, but the U.S. Navy has deployed antiradiation surface-launched versions.[8]

It has also been claimed that ground-launched rockets loaded with chaff were fired at Syrian radar sites to mask the activity of Israeli aircraft and to add to the confusion created by active electronic jamming techniques. The development of such a system should not be difficult, but it is not possible to confirm that Israel actually used it. The Israelis apparently also used harassment drones to destroy radars, especially those associated with fire control radars, such as the Gun Dish of the Soviet ZSU-23-4 antiaircraft gun.

As a result of these attacks, most Syrian radars were destroyed. Even the ones that remained intact were turned off after the attack for fear of the antiradiation weapons. Although the initial attacks often left the missile launchers intact, many were destroyed during subsequent strikes involving some sixty to eighty attack aircraft (F-4 Phantoms, A-4 Skyhawks, and Kfirs). American sources claim that the aircraft made extensive use of cluster-bomb ammunition in the attacks, but Israelis assert that most of the strikes were made using conventional "iron" bombs.[9]

Electronic warfare aircraft played an important role in these attacks. Three or four types were used by the Israelis. Hawkeye E-2C airborne early-warning aircraft, primarily used to monitor Syrian fighters, are equipped with the ALR-59 radar detection system, which can detect, track, and identify up to 300 radar signals at distances of up to 500 miles. Two of these aircraft used together could locate the radars by triangulation. Finally, the E-2Cs have a data link that permits information to be transmitted to ground command-and-control stations.[10]

Israel's RC-707 aircraft were heavily modified commercial Boeing 707 transports equipped with Israeli-built radar and communications jamming systems. Reportedly, this equipment was designed to radiate signals only against radar frequencies actually being used by Syrian radars, to ensure that Israeli radars were not jammed and to concentrate all the power of the jamming transmitters against active Syrian radars. The RC-707 aircraft were probably supplemented by Israeli-built Arava light transports and U.S.-supplied CH-53 helicopters that were converted into electronic warfare aircraft.[11]

It is also thought that many of the Israeli F-4 Phantoms were configured as electronic warfare aircraft similar in concept to the Wild Weasel types used by the U.S. Air Force. Such planes are specifically designed for defense suppression and are equipped with an array of detection and jamming systems, along with such antiradiation missiles as the Shrike and the Standard ARM.

The effectiveness of the Israeli air strikes was enhanced by several Syrian mistakes. The Syrians' tactics were clumsy, and their electronics security was poor. They often left radars in operation unnecessarily, making it easier for them to be identified and located.[12] They also did not take advantage of the mobility of the SA-6 missile launchers, leaving their missile batteries in the same spot for extended periods of time. Finally, their antiaircraft missile sites were poorly protected, making them easier to destroy when they eventually were attacked.[13]

Moreover, the Syrians failed to provide their missile batteries with enough early-warning radars. Israeli accounts indicate that there were only two early-warning radars in the Bekaa to supplement the surveillance radars attached to each battery. In comparison, Soviet surface-to-air missile units would have had eight to ten early-warning radars to support a force of nineteen missile batteries.[14] This implies that the Syrians had only about a quarter of the early warning radars required by Soviet doctrine. The terrain also worked against the Syrians. The Bekaa is surrounded on three sides by mountains, which masked the coverage of Syrian early-warning radars. It is also likely that the mountains to the west of the Bekaa shielded attacking Israeli aircraft from SA-6 missiles during their approach. As a result of the Lebanon experience, the Syrians now have twice as many radars attached to each battery as they had in 1982.[15]

Finally, the homogeneity of the Syrian air defenses made it easier for Israeli planners to organize an attack.[16] Two weapons predominated in the system: SA-6 missile batteries and ZSU-23-4 radar-guided guns. During the 1973 Arab-Israeli war it was demonstrated that the effectiveness of air defenses was enhanced by using a variety of weapons with differing capabilities to create an integrated and variegated system composed of mutually supporting weapons. Thus, a typical Soviet air defense system relies on SA-2, SA-4, SA-6, SA-8, SA-9 or SA-13, and SA-7 or SA-14 missiles, supported by ZSU-23-4 guns.

Despite the Syrian mistakes, the results of the June 1982 strikes contrasted starkly with the events of October 1973, when far less experienced Syrian air defenses had little difficulty downing many Israeli aircraft. The magnitude of the Israeli success in 1982 suggests that the ability of air forces to suppress air defenses has increased enormously over the course of the past decade. Medium- and long-range surface-to-air missiles, so lethal in 1973 and almost impossible to locate with equipment then in use, now are highly vulnerable to attack. The increased sophistication of modern surveillance equipment and the availability of real-time intelligence systems have made it easier to quickly locate and destroy surface-to-air missile batteries, especially if they are located close to battlefields, where ground-based weapons can reach them.

Yet it is not altogether certain that other Western air forces would have similar success against Soviet air defense systems. Cooperation between ground and air forces, a vital part of the Israeli air defense suppression scheme, is rare in other countries, where interservice rivalries and roles and missions disputes interfere. Israel also employed weapons and tactics that other nations do not have. For example, whereas Israel had a formidable array of electronic warfare aircraft, most European NATO countries do not. Similarly, whereas drones were used extensively in Lebanon, no other air force in the world—not even the U.S. Air Force, which pioneered the use of such systems—currently operates them in such profusion for so many different functions.

Finally, certain circumstances allowed Israel to use tactics that probably would not work elsewhere. Israel could act on the assumption that its operations would take place under clear skies, since bad weather rarely interferes with air operations in that part of the world during the summer. This eliminated the need for the all-weather attack aircraft that NATO countries require in Central Europe. Moreover, the small size of the theater eliminated the need for deep penetration strikes into heavily defended areas. Thus, Israel has limited need for such aircraft as the F-111 or the Tornado, which are configured for deep penetration missions, or for electronic warfare escort aircraft, such as the EF-111, which can accompany strike aircraft deep into enemy territory. As a result, Israel's tactics and equipment could not be applied directly by other air forces in other parts of the world.

Air-to-Air Combat

When the Israelis attacked the Syrian air defenses in Lebanon, the Syrian air force sent fighters to support the antiaircraft positions. Israeli pilots, using mainly American-built F-15 and F-16 fighters, decisively defeated their Syrian counterparts, who were flying Soviet-supplied MiG-21 and MiG-23 aircraft. During the summer of 1982, the Israeli pilots shot down some eighty-five Syrian aircraft without suffering the loss of a single plane in air-to-air combat.[17]

The air-to-air combat between Israeli and Syrian aircraft during the summer of 1982 confirmed an already well-known fact—that Israeli pilots flying the best fighters in the world, armed with the most sophisticated air-to-air missiles, will consistently defeat Syrian pilots flying mediocre aircraft with poor-quality air-to-air missiles. Israel's kill ratio of 85 to 0 was only a more extreme version of what Israel had accomplished in earlier wars.[18]

The F-15 and F-16 fighters are generally acknowledged to be the two best fighters in the world today. They are clearly more maneuverable and have superior electronics to the MiG-21 and MiG-23 fighters flown by the Syrians. For example, the F-15's APG-63 radar has a 50-kilometer range and can track targets flying at altitudes lower than the F-15, whereas the MiG-23's High Lark radar has a range of only 20 kilometers and has no look-down capability. According to the U.S. Air Force, Israeli F-15s have destroyed fifty-six Syrian aircraft without suffering a single loss since they first went into action in 1979 (this includes those destroyed in 1982). Included in the kills are twenty-three MiG-21s, three MiG-23s, three MiG-25s, one helicopter, and thirty-four MiGs of "unspecified types."[19]

In addition, Israeli aircraft were armed with considerably better weapons than the Syrian planes had. Most Syrian aircraft were shot down with new all-aspect infrared homing air-to-air missiles, either the AIM-9L Sidewinder, from the United States, or the Python-3, produced in Israel. These missiles can hit a target from almost any angle, giving them a decided advantage over aircraft armed only with older infrared homing missiles, which are limited to attacking targets from angles at which the heat of the engine can be tracked. The Israelis often fired these all-aspect missiles from directions at which Syrian pilots could not even see their Israeli opponents. This could be done because an elaborate command-and-control system vectored Israeli planes against enemy aircraft, whereas the Syrians had no information concerning the location of the Israeli planes.[20]

Other types of air-to-air weaponry were of considerably less importance. Some experienced Israeli pilots used Israeli-built Shafrir infrared homing missiles to down several aircraft when it was realized that many Syrian aircraft were being attacked from angles at which this older weapon would be effective. The AIM-7F version of the Sparrow air-to-air missile used on the F-15 was somewhat less successful: eleven were fired to obtain two confirmed kills and one possible kill. The reasons for this low success rate are unclear. The Israelis typically fire Sparrows only when no other weapon can be used, often in conditions when chances of success are limited. As a result, no firm conclusions can be drawn from this experience about the general utility of radar-guided air-to-air missiles. Finally, aircraft cannon accounted for only about 7 percent of the Syrian planes, confirming 1973 indications that the infrared missile has supplanted the gun as the primary weapon of air-to-air combat.[21]

The most important feature of the aerial battles that took place in Lebanon, however, had nothing directly to do with the aircraft or weapons employed. More significant was Israel's innovative use of highly sophisticated battle management techniques to control the operations of its fighter aircraft. In the modern electronic battlefield, success in air-to-air combat is likely to require such a system to provide extensive coordination between fighters and an integrated command-and-control net that can pass real-time information to pilots.

The focal point of the Israeli system was the Northern Command Regional Control Unit. Into this center flowed all available information about Syrian and Israeli aircraft movements being gathered by a variety of sources: surveillance and electronic warfare aircraft, ground-based surveillance radars, drones, ground-based electronic intelligence stations, and balloon-mounted sensors. The information was displayed on a real-time basis.

Crucial to the operation of the system were Israel's four Hawkeye E-2C airborne early-warning aircraft. The Hawkeye's APS-125 radar system has a range of over 400 kilometers, allowing the Israelis to detect Syrian aircraft when they left their air bases.[22] They then tracked them as they headed toward Lebanon, and when they finally entered Lebanon, the E-2Cs directed friendly interceptors, usually F-15s or F-16s, against them. Thus, even though Syrian air bases were often only two or three minutes' flying time from Lebanon, the Israelis were rarely surprised by the unexpected appearance of a Syrian fighter.[23]

The RC-707 electronic warfare aircraft were also important. They monitored and jammed radio transmissions between airfield tower and aircraft. As a result, it appears that Syrian pilots received no support from ground control stations. Unlike their Israeli counterparts, the Syrians had no advance knowledge of what to expect.[24] In addition, remotely piloted vehicles (RPVs) were routinely stationed over air bases inside Syria, giving the Israelis real-time television images of aircraft taking off.[25]

Other aspects of the Lebanon fighting also emphasized the growing importance of electronic warfare in air-to-air combat. According to one source, the Syrians sometimes sent two groups of MiG-23 fighters into Lebanon at the same time; the first flew at high altitudes and was expected to attract Israeli aircraft, and the second operated at low altitudes and was expected to use look-up radar to detect Israeli aircraft intercepting the first group. (This appears to be a standard Soviet tactic; it was apparently used by the aircraft that downed the KAL jetliner in 1983.) The Israelis reportedly defeated this tactic by using chaff and jammers to disrupt the radars of the low-flying MiG-23s.[26]

In the future, it is likely that this kind of electronic combat will become an important element in dogfights. In fact, under modern conditions, the electronic capabilities of a fighter have become as important as its aerodynamics. The best fighter aircraft will have to include countermeasures equipment against both heat-seeking and radar-guided missiles and will have sophisticated detection systems to warn pilots that they are under attack and to activate jamming devices. Most existing fighter aircraft were not designed with the requirements of electronic warfare in mind. Many now have only minimal electronic warfare suites, and even those usually depend on electronic pods that provide less than complete coverage. Using stealth technologies and an integrated electronic warfare suite, the next generation of fighters, which will not appear until the 1990s, will be the first to give electronics an emphasis equal to maneuverability.

The Ground War

Not enough information is currently available to permit a balanced view of the battles fought between Syria and Israel in the Bekaa. Although considerable controversy has been attached to Israel's conduct of the ground war against the Syrians, much of the criticism has been affected by extraneous factors, including hostility toward the purposes of the war or toward Israel. Without better data, however, it is impossible to join this debate. As a result, the following discussion focuses on a few subjects of which enough is known to allow for lessons to be drawn that can apply to other areas of the world as well.

Tank Weapons

The tank was the most effective antitank weapon used in Lebanon, and the most potent tank armament was the L7A1 105mm gun used by the Israelis. According to one estimate, it accounted for 60 percent of all the Syrian tanks destroyed.[27] That these guns penetrated even T-72s at long ranges suggests that this venerable weapon, a mainstay of Western battle tanks for twenty-five years, can remain effective through at least the end of this decade.

The success of Israel's 105mm guns was due in part to the use of new ammunitions with enhanced penetration capabilities. Most important was the M-111 Arrow armor-piercing fin-stabilized discarding sabot (APFSDS) round. One senior Israeli armor officer has asserted that this ammunition was "the main technological advantage that we had while entering the war" in 1982.[28] Reportedly, the M-111 can penetrate as much armor as the ammunition initially developed for the new 120mm gun being adopted by the U.S. and West German armies.

The M-111 was devastating against older T-55 and T-62 tanks and was also credited with some eight or nine T-72 kills. Reportedly, the T-72s were engaged at ranges of as much as 3,500 meters. This casts considerable doubt on the claims of some U.S. authorities that modern Soviet tanks are immune to ammunition fired by 105mm guns.[29] The effectiveness of the M-111 is good news for NATO, since it is widely used in Europe: Diehl of West Germany produces it under license as the DM23 for the Bundeswehr, and the Canadians use it for their small European force of Leopards. Similarly, the armies of Denmark, Switzerland, and Sweden have also purchased the M-111 round in large quantities.[30]

Improved digital fire control systems with laser rangefinders were almost as important as the new ammunition. Whereas four or five rounds might be needed by a well-trained gunner to destroy a tank at 2,000 or 3,000 meters using esti-mation techniques, a less-skilled gunner using a digital fire control system might need only one or two rounds to accomplish the same at 3,000 or 4,000 meters. This advantage is crucial, since tank battles are usually won by the side that fires the first accurate shot. Reportedly, many of the Syrian tanks were destroyed at ranges in excess of 3,000 meters using the new fire control systems.

Such equipment can be extremely expensive; a complete digital fire control system can cost $300,000. As a result, only part of the Israeli armored corps was provided with such systems in 1982.[31] Among the tanks with such equipment were new U.S.-built M-60A3 tanks with a U.S. system. Both systems are consid-ered equally effective.[32]

Israeli success with tank fire control systems suggests that, despite their ex-pense, programs in the United States and elsewhere to develop such equipment are well conceived. Although many military reformers decry "high technology" as a burden, this is one instance when practical experience appears to demon-strate that selective use of advanced technology can significantly improve combat effectiveness.

Tank Protection

Israeli armor philosophy stresses the need to minimize casualties. In part, this reflects the Israeli desire to keep losses as low as possible. It also results from an Israeli idea that momentum in armor warfare results from the willingness of tank crewmen to advance in the face of enemy defensive fire and that reducing the risk of being killed or wounded makes tank crewmen more likely to continue an attack.[33]

This concept was embodied in the Merkava, the first tank designed and built in Israel. The Merkava uses an elaborate spaced-armor system with sharply sloped frontal armor to increase the effective armor thickness, ammunition stored in protected compartments to isolate it from the crew, and a Halon fire suppressant system to prevent explosions.[34] The armor system of the Merkava was extremely successful in Lebanon, and senior officers invariably tried to spearhead their attacks with units equipped with this tank.

The Israeli armored corps also strengthened its older tanks. The most widely noticed enhancement was the add-on armor for U.S. M-60 and British Centurion tanks. This was a reactive armor system, consisting of a set of modular protective elements, weighing about one ton, that covers the upper hull and turret of the tank. The individual elements look like boxes. The operating parts of the system are the outer surfaces of the elements, which consist of an explosive charge molded between two pieces of sheet metal. The explosive charge detonates when hit by a shaped charge round, disrupting the penetrating jet. The detonating mechanism has not been revealed, but it is known that the elements do not ex-plode when hit by shrapnel or small-arms fire. The Israelis claim that the system provides complete protection against RPG-7 rocket grenades over the entire front of the hull, but only protects over 70 percent of the same area for Sagger missiles. The system does give complete protection for the sides of the turret against Saggers.[35]

Various techniques were also used to reduce the damage that results when a tank is penetrated. Many Israeli tanks were fitted with the Spectronix fire suppression system. Similar in conception to systems devised in the United States and Great Britain, the Israeli system consists of several sensors connected to Halon dispensers that inject that gas into the crew and engine compartments when a fire is detected. Since fires cannot burn in its presence, even small amounts of Halon are sufficient to suppress combustion. The Halon is evacuated after the fire is put out, well before the crew is asphyxiated. The entire process typically takes a tenth of a second. Systems of this type usually cost less than $10,000 and are certainly a good investment for protecting a tank that costs 200 times that much to build.[36] Besides the fire suppression system, Israeli armor crewmen are given special suits made of a material that includes Nomex, a fire-retardant cloth. As a result of these two efforts, it is reported that Israel suffered many fewer severe burn casualties in 1982 than in 1973.[37]

Soviet-supplied T-72 tanks used by the Syrians also have a special form of armor. The upper hull of the T-72 is reportedly protected by a special laminate armor consisting of layers of steel and plastic. Little is actually known about this armor system, but the Soviets claim that it can resist penetration from existing antitank missiles, and some sources claim that—using standard antitank missiles or RPG-7 rockets—the Israelis were unable to penetrate it. In addition, the armor provides better protection against kinetic energy rounds.[38] Despite these claims, opinion in Israel is divided on the merits of the T-72. Some argue that its overall protection is inferior, because the design of the tank makes it likely to explode when penetrated.[39] The automatic loader for the 125mm gun is considered responsible for this, although the gun itself is extremely powerful.

The success of the improved tank protection systems has made shaped-charge weapons, as used on the current generation of antitank missiles, relatively ineffective. This contrasts to the claims made by critics ten years ago—after the 1973 Arab-Israeli war—that antitank missiles and rocket launchers were so effective that the tank was obsolete.

In addition, tactical factors have also minimized the danger posed by infantry antitank weapons. Armored tactics now usually include measures to reduce the effectiveness of antitank missiles. Israeli techniques, which were used successfully in Lebanon, are similar to those used by most Western armies. Smoke grenade launchers and smoke shells fired from 81mm mortars mask tank forces from missile operators, while suppressive fire is used to attack spots thought to be occupied by missile operators.

Nonetheless, it should be recognized that countering infantry shaped-charge weapons does not mean that the battle tank in its current form will continue to be a viable weapon type. The reduced effectiveness of existing shaped-charge weapons will merely force development of new types of antitank weaponry, and these new weapons may be sufficiently effective against existing tanks to give antitank forces the edge once again. It should be expected that the development of new types of weaponry will make even the new generation of battle tanks—including the Merkava, the M-1, and the Leopard II—obsolescent during the beginning of the next decade.

Infantry Fighting Vehicles

The fighting in Lebanon demonstrated that existing infantry fighting vehicles (IFVs) cannot survive on the modern battlefield. The IFV is a specialized vehicle that carries infantry, mounts weapons allowing it to fight other armored vehicles, and is intended to accompany tanks into areas held by enemy forces. Existing IFVs include the West German Marder, the U.S. M-2 Bradley, and the Soviet BMP. In contrast, armored personnel carriers such as the U.S. M-113 are "battle taxis" that take infantry to the proximity of the battlefield, but they are not expected to operate where there are enemy forces. In recent years, the infantry fighting vehicle concept has come to be accepted by virtually all armies.

Both the Israelis and the Syrians found that their standard infantry fighting vehicles suffered heavy losses. The Israelis used modified M-113A1 armored personnel carriers as IFVs.[40] Before 1982, the Israelis thought M-113s could survive on the battlefield despite light armor protection by using proper tactics, including support from artillery and tanks. It was thought that enough firepower could suppress hostile fire, so they modified their M-113s by equipping them with several machine guns and a small 52mm mortar. Configured in this fashion, an M-113 could generate considerable firepower. In addition, vulnerability was reduced by mounting the fuel tanks outside the vehicle.

Despite these improvements, the Israelis found that their M-113s were extremely vulnerable. The enormous number of antitank weapons available to the PLO meant that a great many M-113s were lost in the coastal area. Reportedly, paratroop units abandoned their M-113s and reached Beirut by riding on the tops of their supporting tanks, since they thought that they were safer in the open than inside the M-113s.

It might be argued that the Israeli experience merely indicates that the M-113 was misused. After all, the M-113 was originally intended as a battle taxi, not as an infantry fighting vehicle. The force of this argument is undermined by the similar failure of the Soviet-supplied BMPs used by the Syrians. The BMPs were extremely easy to destroy, since they do not have enough armor to defeat even small antitank weapons. When penetrated, a BMP almost always burns and explodes, since it is almost inevitable that something combustible will be hit. As a result, the Syrians also suffered heavy losses among their mechanized infantry forces.[41]

These failures have serious implications, since most Western armies are now in the process of adopting infantry fighting vehicles. For example, the U.S. Army intends to purchase nearly 7,000 Bradley IFVs by 1990. These Bradleys will cost about $1.4 million each—more than half the cost of an M-1—for a total procurement cost of about $10 billion.[42] Unfortunately, Israeli and Syrian experiences in Lebanon suggest that the Bradley may not justify this high price.

The Israeli army has opted to develop infantry carriers with more armored protection than existing vehicles have. Efforts are apparently under way to improve the M-113, although even modified versions probably will be used only in areas that are lightly defended by antitank weapons.[43] Of more interest are attempts to develop new types of infantry carriers. By early 1984, some Centurion tanks had been transformed into IFVs by removing the tank turret and providing them with a troop compartment. Like the tanks, these vehicles are also protected by reactive armor boxes.[44]

The inadequacy of infantry fighting vehicles also extends to other kinds of lightly armored vehicles, such as armored cars and light tanks. In recent years, a great many vehicles of this type have been purchased by many armies. Even the U.S. military, long opposed to use of lightly armored vehicles, has procured such weapons, such as the LAV-25 armored car; yet it is by no means clear that they will be able to survive on the battlefield. Although these vehicles are inexpensive and easy to operate, their operational utility must be considered marginal, except in security and support roles.

Artillery

Although Syrian artillery played only a small role in the fighting in Lebanon, Israeli ground forces unveiled two significant innovations that are an indication of the revolutionary changes beginning to take place in the once staid artillery forces. These innovations were cluster-bomb ammunition (also known as improved conventional munitions) and long-range multiple rocket launchers (MRLs).

Improved conventional munitions are artillery shells loaded with large numbers of small bomblets. Except when attacking fortified positions, such ammunition is considerably more effective than conventional high-explosive rounds, especially when fired at antiaircraft missile batteries and at tanks. The Israeli artillery uses varieties of this ammunition built in both the United States and Israel.[45]

Cluster-bomb ammunition was extremely effective in Lebanon. Israeli experts believe that existing submunitions are a potentially greater threat to tanks than antitank missiles. Most antitank weapons have to penetrate tank armor where it is thickest, but artillery-delivered submunitions hit the tank on the top, where armor protection is weakest.[46] For example, whereas the frontal armor of a T-62 is equivalent to 200mm of armor, the top armor is only 30mm thick.

In recent years, the Israelis have increased their reliance on MRLs. Two different systems were used in Lebanon. The newest is the LAR-160, a 160mm rocket system with a range of about 30 kilometers. Each rocket carries some 125 bomblets. Thus, a battery of four launchers, each with twenty-five rockets, could put 12,500 bomblets on an area in a period of less than a minute. Somewhat older is the MAR-290, a 290mm system with a range of 40 kilometers, normally mounted on a Sherman tank chassis. Both systems apparently worked well in Lebanon.[47] Despite some claims to the contrary, there is no evidence that the Israeli army used any sophisticated, "smart" submunitions.[48]

Remotely Piloted Vehicles

Israel was the first country to use small remotely piloted vehicles (RPVs), commonly known as mini-RPVs, in battle. Their employment had a tremendous impact on Western military analysts, although there was nothing revolutionary about the mini-RPV systems used by Israel. The Israel Aircraft Industries Scout and the Tadiran Mastiff were simple, generally incorporating standard off-the-shelf components.[49] The mini-RPV concept did not originate in Israel. After the 1973 Arab-Israeli war, the United States became interested in developing mini-RPV concepts, but by the late 1970s, most of the projects were abandoned, and the United States never fielded such a system.[50] In contrast, Israel has fielded three generations of mini-RPVs since 1976 and is currently working on a fourth for deployment in 1986 or 1987.[51]

Mini-RPVs are small, making them hard to see, and their 20-horsepower engines generate little noise or heat. In addition, because they are largely made out of synthetic materials, they are virtually undetectable by radar. As a result, it is claimed that none were shot down by enemy ground fire. Even if the enemy should manage to shoot down a mini-RPV, however, the cost is marginal, since the typical cost of one is only $20,000 to $50,000.

Mini-RPVs provided observation capabilities that allowed intelligence officers operating safely behind the front lines to visually survey any portion of the battlefield on a real-time basis. For the first time, ground forces could routinely see "over the next hill," even in the presence of strong air defenses. Especially valuable was the use of mini-RPVs to provide forward observation for artillery. Since the appearance of aircraft during World War I, forward observers in observation planes have significantly improved the accuracy and timeliness of artillery fire. Unfortunately, modern air defenses make light spotting planes extremely vulnerable, and modern armies cannot count on such assistance. The mini-RPV is the successor to the artillery- spotting plane, providing real-time pictures to observers safely ensconced far behind the front lines.

Conclusions

What lessons can be learned from the Syria-Israel war in Lebanon during 1982? The foregoing discussion has indicated the importance of pilot quality in air-to-air combat, the importance of tank crew quality in armored warfare, and the significance of particular pieces of equipment, such as the M-111 antitank ammunition, the Samson drone, and the AIM-9L Sidewinder air-to-air missile. Fundamentally, however, the most important lesson of the war is the increasing importance of electronic warfare. The 1982 Lebanon war was by no means the first conflict in which electronic warfare featured prominently, but it certainly demonstrated the extent to which electronic systems have become integral parts of the modern battlefield.

This is reflected in part by the intense interest people in the electronic warfare community in the United States have shown in the Lebanon war. It is perhaps significant that it was the head of an American company specializing in electronic warfare who asserted: "The lessons of Lebanon will dominate military thinking for the next 10 years."[52]

It is perhaps obvious that "smart" weapons—such as wire-guided antitank missiles, laser-guided bombs, and television-guided missiles—are dependent on electronics. Less evident is the extent to which even Israel's highly accurate use of conventional iron bombs depended on computerized weapons delivery and navigation systems that make it possible for "dumb" bombs to be delivered with "smart" weapon accuracies. Similarly, the accuracy of Israel's tank and artillery fire resulted largely from the use of digital fire control systems.

This integration of electronic systems into weapons has had a profound influence on the character of modern war. In benign environments, such "smart" weapons as surface-to-air missiles can be extremely lethal, but, as the Israelis demonstrated, the effective use of electronic countermeasures can make them totally ineffective. Thus, electronic warfare gear has become as important as weaponry. Although some Western air forces treat electronic warfare gear and weaponry as competitive systems, apparently believing that there is some kind of trade-off between the two, the simple reality is that they are complementary. An aircraft sent into action without support from electronic countermeasures is all too likely to be shot down before it can inflict damage on the enemy.

Israel's development of an integrated air defense suppression capability has influenced U.S. programs. According to Edith Martin, the deputy undersecretary of defense for research and advanced technology:

> Lessons learned during the Mideast conflict have resulted in an increased emphasis on distributed electronic warfare (EW) systems, particularly for tactical engagements.
>
> Experience clearly demonstrated the advantages of combining tactics with various EW techniques, for example drones, decoys, stand-off jammers and de-

fense suppression in order to achieve a decisive victory with minimum losses. In view of this, our EW technology program is being restructured to provide more emphasis on techniques supporting a mixed force concept.[53]

Despite the evident importance of electronic warfare, with its high-technology equipment, one important lesson should not be forgotten. Electronic warfare is a "force multiplier," but without well-trained troops, there is nothing to "multiply." Ultimately, it is not the machines but the people who use the equipment who are important. The most sophisticated equipment in the world still has to be intelligently used by brave troops who are familiar with tactical requirements.

Notes

1. Col. Gordon M. Clarke et al., "The 1982 Israeli War in Lebanon: Implications for Modern Conventional Warfare," Research report submitted to the faculty of the National War College, National Defense University, April 1983, p. 16.

2. There were at least seven Israeli attacks on Syrian air defenses during the summer of 1982. See "Israel Reports Knocking Out a Syrian Missile Battery," *New York Times*, September 9, 1982, p. A8; "Israel Reports Knocking Out Another Syrian Missile Unit," *New York Times*, September 13, 1982, p. A8; David K. Shipler, "Israeli Jets Strike Lebanon Positions of Syria and P.L.O.," *New York Times*, September 14, 1982, p. A1. According to Anthony Cordesman, *Jordanian Arms and the Middle East Balance* (Washington, D.C.: Middle East Institute, 1983), p. 124, the SA-8 missiles were operated in part by Soviet crews.

3. William Claiborne, *Washington Post*, May 12, 1981, p. A1; David K. Shipler, *New York Times*, May 12, 1981, p. A1.

4. *Defense and Foreign Affairs Daily*, May 20, 1981, p. 1; and "Syrians Fire at Israelis," *Flight International*, January 30, 1982, p. 212, give accounts of these operations.

5. This account of the June 9–10 air strikes is based on Clarence A. Robinson, Jr., "Surveillance Integration Pivotal in Israeli Successes," *Aviation Week and Space Technology*, July 5, 1982, pp. 16–17; Clarke et al. "The 1982 Israeli War in Lebanon," pp. 17–18; and, Moshe Fogel, "The Syrian Missiles," *IDF Journal*, December 1982, p. 43. The description of the drones comes from Drew Middleton, *New York Times*, September 19, 1982, section 4, p. 2. The *Samson* was originally developed in the U.S. by Celesco (now known as Brunswick). See Clarence A. Robinson, *Aviation Week and Space Technology*, December 13, 1978, p. 14. According to Bill Gunston, *An Illustrated Guide to Spy Planes and Electronic Warfare Aircraft* (New York: Arco/Salamander, 1983), p. 155, the Celesco drone can be "carried in multiple by combat aircraft (for example, in F-4 missile recesses) and released to glide on flip-out wings." It "flies programmed manoevers and carries radar augmenters, jammers, or other EW payloads at Mach 0.9."

6. Paul S. Cutter, "Lt. Gen. Rafael Eitan: 'We Learned Both Tactical and Technical Lessons in Lebanon,' " *Military Electronics/Countermeasures*, February 1983, p. 96.

7. Robinson, "Surveillance Integration Pivotal," pp. 16–17.

8. Chris Heath, "EW lessons from the Falklands and Lebanon," *Pacific Defense*

Reporter, July 1983, p. 22. The range of the Standard ARM is taken from "Gallery of USAF Weapons," *Air Force Magazine*, May 1983, p. 160.

9. Robinson, "Surveillance Integration Pivotal," pp. 16–17, reports on American claims that BLU-72 cluster bombs were responsible, while Moshe Fogel, "The Syrian Missiles," *IDF Journal*, December 1982, p. 43, gives an Israeli account that disagrees with this.

10. *Aviation Week and Space Technology*, June 28, 1982, p. 19; "Lebanon Proved Effectiveness of Israeli EW Innovations," *Defense Electronics*, October 1982, p. 43; Charles Mohr, "Radar Aircraft Built in U.S. Play Role in Israel's Success," *New York Times*, June 12, 1982, p. A7.

11. John V. Cignatta, "A U.S. Pilot Looks at the Order of Battle, Bekaa Valley Operations," *Military Electronics/Countermeasures*, February 1983, pp. 107–108; Drew Middleton, *New York Times*, September 19, 1982, section 4, p. 2.

12. Cordesman, *Jordanian Arms and the Middle East Balance*, p. 121; Ray Moseley, "Soviets help rebuild Syria Military," *Chicago Tribune*, February 25, 1984, section 1, p. 5.

13. "SAM Suppression: Mid East Lessons," *Defence Update*, no. 37, 1983, p. 56.

14. Ibid.; and see David Isby, *Weapons and Tactics of the Soviet Army* (New York: Jane's, 1981), pp. 220ff, for a description of Soviet air defense equipment and tactics.

15. Ray Moseley, *Chicago Tribune*, February 25, 1984, section 1, p. 5.

16. Ibid.

17. According to the figures provided by General Wilbur Creech, then commander of the U.S. Air Force Tactical Air Command, as reported in *Defense Science and Electronics* 1(1982): 11. General Creech also claimed that the F-15 shot down forty of the planes and that most of the rest were downed by F-16s. Phantoms also are credited with a small number of kills. There are other estimates of Syrian aircraft losses. According to Robinson, "Surveillance Integration Pivotal," p. 17, the Syrians lost eighty-one fighters (equally divided between MiG-21s and MiG-23s) and four helicopters.

18. Zeev Schiff, "The Israeli Air Force," *Air Force Magazine*, August 1976, pp. 31–37.

19. Eugene Kozicharow, *Aviation Week and Space Technology*, March 5, 1984, p. 19. The breakdown comes from "Predator with a Pedigree," *Air International*, March 1984, p. 142.

20. John V. Cignatta, "A U.S. Pilot Looks at the Order of Battle," pp. 107–108.

21. "Northrop Offers Mideast F-20 Support With U.S. Support," *Aviation Week and Space Technology*, May 23, 1983, p. 94; *Defense Science and Electronics*, Vol. 1, No. 3 (1982), p. 11; Clarke et al., "The 1982 Israeli War in Lebanon," p. 19.

22. Mohr, "Radar Aircraft Built in U.S. Play Role in Israel's Success"; Robinson, "Surveillance Integration Pivotal," p. 17.

23. "Lebanon Proved Effectiveness of Israeli EW Innovations," *Defense Electronics*, October 1982, p. 43.

24. Robinson, "Surveillance Integration Pivotal," pp. 16–17.

25. "Lebanon Proved Effectiveness of Israeli EW Innovations," *Defense Electronics*, October 1982, p. 43; Paul Cutter, "ELTA Plays a Decisive Role in the EOB Scenario," *Military Electronics/Countermeasures*, January 1983, p. 137.

26. Cordesman, *Jordanian Arms and the Middle East Balance*, p. 113.

27. *Financial Times*, March 16, 1983, p. 4.

28. *Defense Update International,* no. 44, 1984, p. 34, quoting the new head of the Israeli Armored Corps, General Amos Katz.

29. Defense Minister Ariel Sharon originally claimed that nine T-72 tanks were destroyed by Israeli Merkava tanks, according to Michael Getler, "Syria's Soviet-Built Tanks Seen Vulnerable," *Washington Post,* June 6, 1982. Additional reports giving more information appear in *Newsweek,* February 28, 1983, p. 13; Edward Luttwak, *New York Times,* December 31, 1983, p. 19; and *Financial Times,* March 16, 1983, p. 4. According to Benjamin F. Schemmer, *Armed Forces Journal International,* August 1983, p. 30, U.S. Army sources assert that the Soviet-improved T-72 and T-80 tanks are invulnerable to 105mm ammunition. In contrast, the same issue contains a report by Anthony Cordesman, "Year of the Tank," p. 28, in which the French claim that existing 105mm APFSDS rounds can penetrate any existing Soviet tank. It is likely that the French are correct in this instance.

30. See Mark Urban, "Merkava," *Armor,* November-December 1981, p. 46, for German use; *Defense and Foreign Affairs Daily,* June 2, 1982, p. 2, on Swiss interest; David K. Shipler, "At School in Tyre, Guns and Rockets," *New York Times,* June 17, 1982, p. A2 on the Swiss purchase; Mark Hewish, "Improvements to Swedish Army Centurions and S-tanks," *International Defense Review,* December 1982, p. 1720, on the Swedish purchase.

31. Arie Hashavia, "Tanks Shoot on the Move with Digital Aiming System," *Defense Electronics,* October 1983, pp. 178–180.

32. Lee Ewing, *Army Times,* March 5, 1984, p. 5.

33. Short discussions of Israeli tank design philosophy appear in Dial Torgerson, *Los Angeles Times,* April 26, 1980, and David Lennon, *Defense Week,* April 6, 1981, pp. 6–8.

34. This description is taken from the ones given by Richard Gabriel and John Moriarty, "Israel's Main Battle Tank Pounds Its Message Home," *Military Electronics/Countermeasures,* January 1983, pp. 124–132; Mark Urban, "Merkava," *Armor,* November-December 1981, p. 46; "An Israeli tank ready for series production: The Merkava Mk 1," *International Defense Review Special Series—11: Armoured Vehicles* (Geneva: Interavia, 1980), pp. 35–38 (the article originally appeared in 1977).

35. "The Puzzle of Israeli Add-on Armor," *Armor,* January-February 1983, pp. 26–27; Joshua Brilliant, *Jerusalem Post,* October 17, 1983, p. 1; *Military Technology,* October 1983, p. 94. This armor is now being marketed as Blazer.

36. *International Defense Review,* no. 1, 1979, p. 75. Richard A. Gabriel, *Operation Peace for Galilee* (New York: Hill and Wang, 1984), p. 198.

37. Lee Ewing, "Crew Protection Pays Off in Israeli Merkava Tank," *Army Times,* March 5, 1984, p. 5, indicates that in the past, 25 to 30 percent of tank crewmen wounded in action suffered burns. No crewmen serving on Merkava tanks were severely burned. See also Richard A. Gabriel, *Operation Peace for Galilee,* pp. 197, 207.

38. The best discussion of the T-72 is given by Steven J. Zaloga, "Soviet T-72 tank," *Jane's Defence Review,* no. 5, 1983, pp. 423–434.

39. Lee Ewing, *Army Times,* March 5, 1984, p. 5.

40. D. Eshel, "Infantry Fighting Vehicles," *Defence Update,* no. 40, 1983, pp. 12–24. See also *Financial Times,* March 16, 1983, p. 4.

41. *Financial Times,* March 16, 1983, p. 4. "B.M.P.-1: The Soviet APC," *Defense*

Update International, no. 26, 1982, pp. 22–26, gives an Israeli assessment of the weakness of the BMP.

42. "Report of the Secretary of Defense Caspar W. Weinberger to the Congress on the FY 1985 Budget, FY 1986 Authorization Request and FY 1985–89 Defense Programs," February 1, 1984, p. 120.

43. Douglas Watson, *Baltimore Sun,* January 9, 1983, p. 2.

44. The *Jerusalem Post, International Edition,* February 12–18, 1984, p. 12, carries an interesting picture of such a Centurion conversion.

45. The first sale of improved conventional munitions to Israel was made in 1977. *Congressional Record,* September 12, 1977, p. S14716.

46. R.D.M. Furlong, "Israel Lashes Out," *International Defense Review,* no. 8, 1982, p. 1006.

47. See ibid., pp. 1003–1004, for descriptions of these two weapons.

48. Ibid., and Jonathan C. Randal, *Washington Post,* July 1, 1982, p. A22, both claim that Israel made some use of "smart" submunitions. Furlong contends that infrared homing submunitions were used, while Randal alleges that a version of the U.S. SA-DARM, a system that (according to the article cited here) uses either infrared or television homing guidance. Both accounts are wrong.

49. For descriptions of the Israeli mini-RPV systems, see David M. Russell, "Israeli RPVs: The Proven Weapon System DOD Will Not Buy," *Defense Electronics,* March 1983, pp. 86–94; Philip J. Klass, "Israel Demonstrates Mini-RPV Utility," *Aviation Week and Space Technology,* October 4, 1982, pp. 59–63; Graham Warwick, "Scout: Israel's combat-proven RPV," *Flight International,* February 6, 1982, pp. 307–308.

50. On earlier American interest in mini-RPVs, see Philip J. Klass, "Mini-RPV Program Spawns Wide Range of Vehicles," *Aviation Week and Space Technology,* July 14, 1975, pp. 49–50; Philip J. Klass, "Image Return Methods Tested for RPVs," *Aviation Week and Space Technology,* March 8, 1976, pp. 50–53; and Philip J. Klass, "Increased Use of Mini-RPVs Foreseen," *Aviation Week and Space Technology,* May 17, 1976, pp. 58–61.

51. On the new generation of systems, see Foreign Broadcast Information Service, *Near East/Africa Report,* March 1, 1983, p. I12, translating a February 25, 1983 report from *Ma'ariv;* Foreign Broadcast Information Service, *Near East/Africa Report,* March 16, 1983, p. I7, translating a March 11, 1983 report from IDF Radio; *Defense and Foreign Affairs,* February 1984, p. 2.

52. Leslie Wayne, *New York Times,* June 20, 1982, p. III-4.

53. *Defense Week,* March 26, 1984, p. 14.

13
Questions? Answers? Hypotheses? Lessons?: A Summary

Stephanie G. Neuman

T his chapter will attempt to integrate some of the issues discussed in the foregoing chapters. It was motivated by my own desire to see, first, how the conclusions and queries of the individual authors converge or differ from one another and, second, whether any recurrent themes can be extracted from the individual chapters when they are considered together. In the interests of space, only some of the issues raised will be discussed here.

Questions of Method

One of the first questions raised by several authors was, "What is a lesson?" To them, the term implies conclusions about cause-and-effect relationships in warfare, and they have therefore counseled caution in applying it. In their view, war is so complex a phenomenon that it defies generalization and prediction. Lessons derived from events that take place in one situation and applied to events under different circumstances are bound to be misleading. Consequently, some of the contributors look upon a comparative approach to the study of war with suspicion. As Jay Luvaas observes in chapter 3: "A lesson once removed from its original context does not necessarily teach us very much."

The editors, however, had a less rigorous and exacting definition of "lessons learned" in mind when we conceived this project. We are as open to the proposition that wars have unique elements as we are to one that declares they are comparable and that general truths can be derived from them. To us, such statements are hypotheses that remain to be tested and may not be antithetical. In our view, lessons can be learned from questions as well as from answers. We believe no research can answer questions that are never asked and that learning what the significant questions are is perhaps the most rewarding lesson of all.

Our choice of method is closely related to our concept of a lesson and our assessment of the field. As the chapters by Harkavy, Starr and Most, Dupuy, and Luvaas suggest, there are many ways to study wars and their outcomes. In this volume, we have chosen the historical-descriptive case study method. Given the state of the field—with information about recent wars scattered among a variety of sources of uneven quality and quantity—we believed we had no other option. The case study method is used here as a means of providing a collection of data that can then be subjected to a more comparative, functional analysis in volume II.

We view this volume as an inductive exercise. In fields where there is a dearth of material, studies such as this one—which provide basic, descriptive information in some chronological order—can be important first steps toward more rigorous analysis. By simply being gathered together in one volume, case studies describing events that appear to be relevant only to a particular war may, when compared with others, take on larger significance. Thus, hypothetical cause-and-effect relationships or propositions that distinguish between unique and general behaviors in war—which may have eluded the individual analysts—may emerge for the reader, in effect creating a whole larger than its separate parts. We agree with Starr and Most that "it is logically impossible to identify cause-and-effect relationships and to sort out genuine linkages from those that are the result of happenstance unless one adopts an explicitly comparative approach." This statement assumes, however, that there is enough information to compare, and it implies a later stage of analysis.[1]

In this volume, we have set our conceptual sights somewhat lower, concentrating on gathering descriptive data, asking questions, and searching for patterns and historical trends. However, by placing a number of detailed cases in close proximity to one another, we hope we have provided new comparative insights that will bring the investigative process to a higher level of understanding. To us, these would be important lessons learned.

Types of War

Our choice of case studies for this project was, in itself, a statement about changes in who fights wars and where they are located. Before World War II, wars were primarily European wars, fought in Europe by European countries. Since then, most wars have taken place in other regions of the world. As Sereseres reports in chapter 8, approximately 125 to 150 conflicts have occurred since 1945, over 90 percent of which have been fought in the Third World. Furthermore, although conventional (or interstate) wars were the main form of combat in earlier periods, unconventional wars (wars involving nonstate actors as combatants) have increased in number.

In planning this project, the editors self-consciously included both types of war, implicitly accepting the commonly held belief that they represent separate and distinct modes of conflict. However, the case studies presented here raise a question about the validity of our assumption. As I read through the chapters, I was struck as much by the similarities as by the differences between them. Although war in the Third World appears to vary sharply from "modern" war (that is, armed conflict between developed countries), wars fought between LDC uniformed national troops or between such troops and guerrillas seem to share many characteristics.

First, upon reading the case studies, it is clear that the mix of forces facing each other has not been very different, regardless of the type of war being fought. For example, LDC navies have been conspicuous by their absence or their modest operations and, with the exception of Israel, LDC airforces have played a secondary role. Almost without exception, wars in the Third World have been won or lost by ground troops.

Second, the type of war has not necessarily determined the tactics used; in fact, it has blurred the differences between them. For example, Vietnamese government troops used "traditional Maoist-style 'people's war'" methods in their engagement with the Chinese army—allowing the Chinese columns to advance and putting up little resistance before launching effective ambushes and small unit raids deep in the Chinese rear—whereas the *Polisario* guerrillas launched a conventional offensive against the Moroccan army during the summer of 1983.[2]

Furthermore, as the frequent oscillations in tactics and strategy suggest, both irregular and regular armies in recent wars have shared much in terms of their ability to implement offensive doctrine. With the exception of campaigns involving an industrialized power, it seems that defense has become the most effective form of warfare in the Third World. In the long term, it has held the upper hand. Making this point in connection with the Iran-Iraq war in chapter 10, Staudenmaier muses: "Whether this judgment is due to any intrinsic advantage of defense or to a lack of offensive expertise on the part of Iran or offensive spirit on Iraq's behalf is, of course, a key issue. However, neither Iran nor Iraq fared well on the offensive." One could make the same assessment for the other wars. With the exception of Israel and the war in Lebanon, none of the Third World combatants that have used an offensive doctrine has been able to effect a decisive breakthrough or cause the defenders to retire in disorder and defeat.[3]

Third, the duration of recent wars also supports our hypothesis. Wars involving unconventional forces have generally been protracted and have engaged large arrays of national and subnational forces, but most of the wars fought between regular LDC armies have not been shorter or less total.

It is not that short-war strategies have not been attempted by one side or the other in recent wars; it is just that they have met with generally poor success because neither side has possessed the capability to inflict the decisive blow. Whether planned for conventional wars or for insurgencies, short-war strategies, as Collins points out in chapter 9, have proved to be a "pipedream." Only Israel among the Third World states has been able to achieve its military objectives quickly. Although the Chinese withdrew from Vietnam after three weeks of combat, forced by the oncoming monsoon period to mount their invasion and teach their lesson swiftly, they left without completely fulfilling their goals. Furthermore, as recent incidents imply, there is little reason to think that their dispute with Vietnam is over or that hostilities have ended permanently. Similarly, Iraq and Somalia, sure of their short-war scenarios in their attacks on Iran and Ethiopia, respectively, found themselves unable to implement them. Iraq is bogged down in a stalemated contest of attrition, and for Somalia, even defeat has not been final—its contest with Ethiopia over the Ogaden continues intermittently, ready to burst again into full-scale violence.

In fact, the unresolved nature of recent conflicts has blurred the historical distinction between peace and war. Losers appear to regard defeat as only temporary and peace as a limited cease-fire during which they can prepare for the next round. Whether it involves regular or irregular armies, war in the Third World seems to be endless and its absence only a fleeting condition.

A fourth pattern observed in recent wars, irrespective of type, is the extent of external involvement. As Starr and Most observe in chapter 2, 38 percent of all wars fought between 1945 and 1976 were fought with foreign participation. Until the early 1970s, Western countries were the major interveners. However, as the hostilities in Central America, the Horn of Africa, and Lebanon demonstrate, Third World collaborative activity has increased substantially since then.

Finally, several analysts have concluded that because guerrilla wars pose particularly difficult policy challenges for governments and their supporters, they represent a new and different form of conflict. The indifferent performance of national forces in recent unconventional wars gives some credence to this judgment.

Although the jury is still out, however, some governments (including the superpowers) seem to be devising more effective counterinsurgency strategies—a development that may challenge the foregoing proposition. Perhaps Luvaas's longer view of military history offers insight here. It may be that today's defense planners—like the French, English, and Prussians before them, "smarting from their humiliating defeats"—have embarked upon a series of reforms in strategy, tactics, and organization to turn the tables on the next round.[4] Time and experience may have taught governments and their militaries how to respond better and more appropriately to the challenge of insurgencies. If so, is it possible that guerrilla warfare represents not a unique form of warfare but yet another phase of action and reaction in the historical struggle between the weak and the strong for tactical advantage?

Some support for this competing hypothesis can be found in our case studies. In chapter 8, for example, Sereseres points out that the insurrectionist model of revolution that worked for Fidel Castro in Cuba did not work in Venezuela, Peru, Bolivia, Colombia, and Argentina during the 1960s. More recently, the Nicaraguan model failed in Guatemala.[5] In Morocco, a similar picture has developed. After six indecisive years of war against the *Polisario* guerrillas, King Hassan devised a strategy of military consolidation and aggressive diplomacy that may be succeeding. Also, the Lebanon war can be interpreted as an Israeli tactical, if not strategic, victory over the PLO.

In Afghanistan, too, changes are occurring. The Soviets entered the war with an inappropriate force structure and inflexible tactics that were unable to cope with the military situation. Now, as Collins reports in chapter 9, the Russians are planning tactical adaptations. The question remains, of course, whether they and other governments fighting unconventional forces will be able to turn the lessons they have learned into a working doctrine before the guerrillas invent new combat techniques and the pendulum of tactical advantage begins swinging in the opposite direction again.

It might be added here that even if we had found unconventional war to be a permanent, intractable "policy challenge," such a finding would not necessarily have proved the unique character of such war. Conventional wars have also represented important, if different, policy challenges. The agonizing in the Kremlin and Washington over appropriate policy responses to the Iran-Iraq war has been well reported, and the dilemmas presented by the Horn war may have been only slightly less painful. Lewis's description in chapter 6 of the U.S. quandary over assistance to Morocco is another example. It is evident that wars in the Third World, whether conventional or unconventional, have posed new and difficult questions of doctrine and policy, particularly to the major powers, but whether unconventional conflicts have been more intractable remains open to question and further research.

Thus, the contributors to this volume have raised fundamental questions about the type of war being fought in the Third World. Based on their evidence, it may be that wars between Third World actors, whether governments or insurgents, have more in common with one another than with "modern" conventional warfare as it is known in the industrialized world.

Factors Determining How Wars Are Fought and Their Outcomes

Intriguing questions about the operations of recent wars and their outcomes have also been raised in the foregoing chapters. Although each war was fought in unique circumstances, many of the conclusions reached by the individual authors, at least by way of hypothesis, apply across most, if not all, of the wars examined here.

Without exception, for example, the contributors found that a preponderance in numbers and military equipment has not ensured victory in recent wars. They found this to be true for the superpowers (for example, the United States in Vietnam, the Soviets in Afghanistan) as well as for Third World powers (for example, Somalia, Iraq, China). In all cases, other factors were cited as decisive in determining outcomes.

Strategy and Tactics

In general, the authors point to strategy or tactics as key elements determining the outcomes of wars. In battles involving a modern army, the capability gap in this area has been most pronounced. For example, using his Quantified Judgment Model, Dupuy concludes in chapter 4 that the Israelis' employment of innovative tactics has put them at the cutting edge of modern warfare. The outcome of the wars over the Falklands and the Horn are also attributed to the superior strategy and tactics of Great Britain[6] and the Russians, respectively. Sereseres believes that, in Central America, it has not been technology or superior numbers, but the ability to move beyond a one-dimensional military approach to a broader strategy, that has determined victory in past wars and will decide the future of El Salvador.

Wars between Third World armies also reflect this general finding. Thus, according to Harlan Jencks (chapter 7), outmoded tactics, training, and techniques were largely responsible for China's limited military achievement in 1979. In the Gulf war, the tactical mistakes of the Iraqis—such as failing to retain critical terrain north of Ahvaz and Dizful during the early stages of the war—prevented them from realizing their strategic objectives. Likewise, the tactical clumsiness of the Syrians, particularly their inadequate electronics security, worked to the advantage of the Israelis during the Lebanon War.

Superior command and control and interservice cooperation were singled out as important assets in this regard. For example, in chapter 12, Carus gives credit to the coordination of Israel's ground and air forces for the success of the Israeli air defense suppression scheme. However, Israel's accomplishment is rare in the Third World, where interservice rivalries interfere with and negatively affect battlefield performance.

Argentina's command structure in the Falklands is a case in point. In chapter 11, Ullman reports that because of the great competition between service staffs and operational headquarters in Buenos Aires, Argentina's commander ashore in the Falklands was subjected to divided authority and apparently found himself without sufficient command authority to use effectively the forces that should have been under his operational control. In the air, the situation was not much better. Aside from two well-coordinated Exocet missions, there was virtually no sense of "joint" operations on Argentina's side. Ullman concludes: "If any lesson from the Falklands is appropriate, it is the requirement for the closest service cooperation in 'joint operations.' "

The same might be said for the Iran-Iraq conflict. Both sides have experienced serious command-and-control problems, which have had devastating effects on the progress of the war. Iran, for instance, has not been able to achieve unity of command because of the schism between the mullahs and the armed forces. According to Staudenmaier in chapter 10, the parallel chain of command that developed and the disunity this caused on the battlefield is one of the major reasons Iran has been unable to sustain an offensive that could end the war. Unlike Iran, which has suffered from a diffusion of authority, the Iraqi military organization is characterized by overcentralization. Military decisions are controlled by a small, cohesive group better known for its loyalty to Saddam Hussein than for its commitment to objective military goals. Thus, Iraq's command-and-control system has discouraged initiative at the front and has produced delays, indecision, and tactical errors on the battlefield.

Logistics

Historically, the ability to provide logistical support to fighting soldiers has served as the vital link between strategy, tactics, and operational capability. However, as the case studies in this volume demonstrate, for most recent combatants, sustaining troops in the field with sufficient food, ammunition, fuel, equipment, and spare parts has proved to be a severe problem.

A few examples should suffice. In the Vietnam-PRC engagement, despite the short duration of the war, the Chinese army, "ran short (or even ran out) of ammunition, fuel, and rations." Even transportation proved difficult, since there were not enough trucks or roads in southern China to get what supplies there were to the border. Similar difficulties faced Argentina's government, whose demoralized and underequipped ground troops ultimately surrendered to the British. And in Iran, the military, unable to find spare parts and other items to keep its American equipment operational, lost its ability to use airpower. Commenting on the Gulf war, Staudenmaier observes that a major operational-strategic lesson to be learned in logistics is that although it is possible to avoid losing when one does not control the wherewithal of war, it is nevertheless difficult to win without an adequate internal or external source of supply.

Apparently, this has been the general case in recent wars. Although less is known about the logistical difficulties facing the guerrillas, the elaborate web of suppliers upon which the Afghan rebels, the Contras and Sandinistas, and until recently the *Polisario* depend for training, equipment, and other services suggests the general applicability of Staudenmaier's conclusion.[7]

Internationalization of Conflict

A third factor, not unrelated to the second, that appears to have had an important impact on recent wars is the growing internationalization of Third World conflicts. Not only have outside parties actively intervened, but decisions made beyond the boundaries of the contenders have been increasingly responsible for their military success or failure.

The rising cost of war and the apparent willingness of more affluent friends and neighbors to provide assistance has reinforced this trend. Curiously, this pattern appears to hold across wars. Attrition rates and the associated costs of resupply have been higher than the combatants themselves can bear, regardless of the war's duration and who fights it.[8]

Harlan Jencks estimates, for instance, that the three-week invasion of Vietnam cost China $3.2 billion to 6.4 billion! The cost to Israel of the Lebanon war has been estimated to be $1 billion in direct costs between June 1982 and February 1985, which does not include the indirect costs of calling up reserves from the civilian economy.[9] Small wonder that LDC combatants have found themselves increasingly dependent on outside sources for assistance.

To cite only a few examples: Sereseres reports that, in Central America, both sides have been dependent on external actors for various forms of support. In his view, the combination of military and economic assistance from the United States to El Salvador and U.S. encouragement of major institutional changes in the military have helped create a more favorable environment for the government.

The Iran-Iraq war and the struggle in the Western Sahara are perhaps classic models of internationalized conflicts, and they provide the most vivid examples of the extensive role outside powers play in such conflicts. Until recently, Morocco was dependent on Saudi Arabia to underwrite 80 percent of its war effort. Now the International Monetary Fund (IMF) is playing a dominant role. Lewis starkly describes how King Hassan's effort to implement recommended IMF austerity measures have stimulated urban protests, which, if they continue, present a domestic security problem that may strain the resources of the armed forces. On the other hand, a decision to dispense with austerity measures would lead to curtailment of IMF support and a likely refusal by Saudi Arabia to reinstitute financial support. External assistance has been no less important to the opposition. According to Lewis, diminished support from Algeria and Libya, beginning in early 1983, has produced a potentially serious erosion of the *Polisario's* confidence and will to fight.

Syria's role in the Iran-Iraq war, as described in chapter 10, is only a small part of the vast web of indirect participants that are also involved. Nevertheless, even Syria's small contribution has had important consequences for the war. In 1982, for example, in response to Iran's request, Syria closed the Iraqi oil pipeline that traverses its territory, terminating at port facilities on the Mediterranean. This act, combined with Iran's naval blockade of the upper Persian Gulf, reduced Iraqi oil exports to 600,000 barrels a day (far below what was needed to finance the war) and increased Iraq's dependence on Soviet arms deliveries and the Gulf states' financial aid (reportedly about $1 billion per month).

Iran, on the other hand, unable to acquire new military equipment from the United States, has been forced to rely on a host of Soviet-bloc and Western states for military supplies. As a result, Iran's predominantly American inventory has grown increasingly diversified, creating servicing, maintenance, and training problems that have negatively affected Iran's operational capabilities.

Despite the overall internationalization of recent conflicts, the authors note the extensive influence—direct and indirect—the superpowers have wielded over their progress. Lewis, for example, implies that Soviet assistance, in combination with the policy paralysis of the United States during the Carter administration, turned the tide of the Horn war in favor of the Ethiopians.[10]

The PRC-Vietnam encounter also demonstrates the usefulness and involvement of superpower backing. Jencks believes that the threat of Soviet intervention served to limit and constrain the PRC's military goals. In addition, the Soviet Union provided signal intelligence and airlift capability, without which the redeployments of Vietnamese forces from the south to the battlefront could not have been accomplished.

In some wars (Afghanistan and Central America), the superpower presence has been more direct; in others, it has been more indirect. Even in the Iran-Iraq war, which has not lent itself to direct superpower intervention,[11] an argument can be made that much of the international assistance flowing into the Gulf has been orchestrated by the superpowers.

These factors stand out as recurrent themes in the foregoing chapters. Each of the contributors has found that they had an important influence on the conduct and results of recent wars. However, many other elements are singled out as equally significant by the individual chapter authors. Staudenmaier, for example, proposes several interesting hypotheses regarding the role of ethnic factors in the Gulf war. He suggests that such factors have constrained the Iraqis' ability to take casualties, have caused them to commit serious strategic errors, and have made it difficult for both sides to end the Gulf war.

Ethnic considerations apparently also influenced the tactics of the Moroccan government in its dealings with the Sahraoui peoples. However, it is not clear whether ethnic factors are substantially different from or more powerful than political factors. Do ethnic considerations have a more negative impact on Iraq's military capability than, for example, the political divisions that constrain Iran? And is the situation in the Gulf unlike that in Central America, where governments are struggling to win the allegiance of ethnically similar political opponents? These and many other related questions require further investigation.

Similarly, Seth Carus's discussion on the technological lessons learned—and his conclusion about the importance of electronic warfare, surveillance techniques, and real-time battlefield intelligence capabilities for future wars—raises but does not answer a series of provocative questions about the present and future character of war. Will Israel's military performance remain unique in the Third World context? Do the wars described in this volume represent a fundamentally different type of war, or are we witness to the early stages of a learning curve that will see modern techniques of warfare applied throughout the world? Will wars in the Third World come to resemble twentieth-century warfare, or, as suggested by one analyst, are they destined to be models of an earlier era, before the rise of national armies?[12]

Conclusion

This chapter has presented several of the general issues raised by the case studies in the preceding chapters. It cannot be considered, nor was it meant to be, a complete or final summary of those studies. Rather, it is offered merely as a point of departure for further research and synthesis. Many of the most interesting questions raised by the authors and their findings remain to be discussed, and some of them are the subject of volume II. As the introductory chapters in this volume suggest, however, this is a large, underresearched field, which will need the imagination and research talents of many people. There are many lessons to be learned. If any of our readers are moved to pursue, amend, expand, or disagree with what is written here, this project will have served its intended purpose.

Notes

1. The richness versus rigor controversy, which has plagued the social sciences for the past thirty years, may in fact be a nondebate. Rather than an either-or issue, it may be an if-then proposition. Different approaches may simply be required at different stages of a field's development. For example, *if* a field is young, *then* detailed case studies are necessary to build a data base for further testing. They provide the information and the initial, tentative insights that allow for more sophisticated qualitative and quantitative analyses. Thus, *if* sufficient data exist, *then* rigorous qualitative and quantitative methods are possible. For a discussion of the richness versus rigor debate as it relates to the field of Soviet foreign policy, see Jack Snyder, "Richness, Rigor, and Relevance in the Study of Soviet Foreign Policy," *International Security* 9, no. 3(Winter 1984–1985): 89–108. A recent study of deterrence demonstrates the importance of an existing body of data for macro-statistical analyses; see Paul Huth and Bruce Russett, "What Makes Deterrence Work? Cases from 1900 to 1980," *World Politics*, 1984, pp. 496–526 (see particularly footnote 15 for a list of data banks and case studies used by the authors to determine their universe of deterrence cases).

2. The use of conventional offensive tactics in the later stages of conflict is, of course, part of the guerrilla strategy of warfare, suggesting how narrow the differences are between the two types of war. It may be, as one U.S. Defense Department official remarked, that "revolutionary war presents a new justification for fighting, but as far as I can see, no new way of doing it."

3. Another exception—a case not covered in our study—is the Indian offensive in East Bengal in 1971.

4. In this connection, Luvaas quotes Frederick the Great, who observed that armies may learn more from defeat than from victory: "Good fortune is often more fatal . . . than adversity."

5. Sereseres is cautiously optimistic that the United States will be more successful in Central America than it was in Vietnam if it supports a more sophisticated total war strategy—one that incorporates a political and socioeconomic response along with the military effort.

6. In chapter 11, Ullman raises a fascinating question about the role of culture when he cites the ability of the British military to institutionalize innovation and imagination in its leadership as a major reason for the innovative strategy, tactics, and performance of the British in the Falklands. He suggests that the ability to nurture and encourage these qualities in all aspects of service life, training, and preparation is a particularly British cultural trait, one that tolerates idiosyncratic behavior and treats eccentricities as an art form.

7. Although supporting troops in the field is a challenge for all armies, it may be relatively less so for guerrillas, who are able to obtain food from local sources and can control the pace of war while waiting for supplies to arrive.

8. Some idea of the rate of attrition in recent wars can be gleaned from the materiel losses reported for the Soviet Union in Afghanistan and for Argentina and Great Britain in the Falklands. Ullman, for example, estimates that 37 of Great Britain's aircraft and helicopters were destroyed, either by enemy action or by other factors, such as bad weather. On the other hand, 7 Argentine ships were destroyed, including a cruiser and submarine, and 2 others were damaged; 103 Argentine aircraft and helicopters were destroyed, which amounted to 57 percent of its total airforce inventory; and approximately 14 aircraft were damaged beyond repair.

In Afghanistan, according to Collins, the rebels have shot down as many as 300 Soviet helicopters, and Soviet vehicle losses are estimated at 3,000 to 4,000.

According to Admiral Ahmed Madani, the first commander-in-chief under Khomeini, who defected to France, Iran's navy has lost about 20 percent of its warships and 80 percent of its helicopters (of which there were fifty). He described the Iranian army as "destitute," with ammunition rationed (*Milavnews*, September 1984).

9. *Jane's Defense Weekly*, April 14, 1984.

10. According to Lewis, the Soviet Union provided over $1 billion of military aid, injecting Cuban personnel into the war to train, gather intelligence, and serve as the cutting edge in military offensives, and dispatching Soviet Army General Vasily I. Petrov to oversee the tactical and strategic operations.

11. One important factor was Iran's promise to keep the Straits of Hormuz open, a declaration designed to reduce the U.S.'s incentive for direct intervention.

12. Brian Michael Jenkins, *New Modes of Conflict* R-3009-DNA (Santa Monica, Calif.: Rand Corporation, June 1983), believes that conventional war, guerrilla warfare, and international terrorism represent three components of a new mode of conflict deriving from a model that resembles warfare "in the Italian Renaissance or early seventeenth century."

Index

Page numbers in *italics* indicate figures.

About the Contributors

W. Seth Carus is the senior military analyst at the American Israel Public Affairs Committee.

Joseph J. Collins is a U.S. Army major who has commanded troops in Germany and South Korea. He has also served as an associate professor of international studies at the U.S. Military Academy, and on the faculty of the U.S. Army Infantry School. Major Collins's articles on the invasion of Afghanistan have appeared in the *Naval War College Review, Parameters, Conflict Quarterly,* and *Comparative Strategy*. He holds a doctorate in international relations from Columbia University and is currently a student in the Army's Command and General Staff College.

Trevor N. Dupuy is the author or coauthor of numerous books and articles on military history, including *Military Heritage of America*. A retired U.S. Army colonel, he is now the executive director of the Historical Evaluation and Research Organization (HERO) and president of Data Memory Systems, Inc. He was earlier professor of military science at Harvard University.

Harlan W. Jencks is an adjunct professor of national security affairs at the Naval Postgraduate School, Monterey, and research associate at the Center for Chinese Studies, University of California, Berkeley. He is the author of numerous articles on Chinese foreign and defense policy, as well as *From Muskets to Missiles* (1982) and coeditor of *Chinese Communist Politics* (1982).

Dr. William H. Lewis is director of the Security Policy Studies Program and a professor of political science at George Washington University. He served for a number of years in the U.S. Department of State, as well as in the Department of Defense. He is the coauthor of several books on political–military affairs, the most recent being *The Prevention of Nuclear War: An American Approach*.

Jay Luvaas is a professor of military history at the U.S. Army War College. He has taught history at Allegheny College, and was a visiting professor at the U.S. Military Academy in 1972–73. He has also lectured widely at service schools. Among his numerous works are *The Military Legacy of the Civil War* (1959) and *The Education of an Army* (1964).

Benjamin A. Most is associate professor in the Department of Political Science at the University of Iowa. His articles have appeared recently in *World Politics, The Journal of Conflict Resolution, The American Journal of Political Science,* and *Comparative Political Studies.*

Caesar D. Sereseres is an associate professor of political science, School of Social Sciences, University of California, Irvine, and is a research staff member at the RAND Corporation. His recent publications include "The Mexican Military Looks South," "The Guatemalan Highlands War, 1978–1982," and "The Management of U.S.–Mexico Relations." He holds a Ph.D. in political science from the University of California, Riverside.

Harvey Starr is professor and chair of political science at Indiana University. His most recent books are *Henry Kissinger: Perceptions of International Politics* (1984), and the second edition of Bruce Russett and Harvey Starr, *World Politics: The Menu for Choice* (1985).

William O. Staudenmaier is a Colonel in the U.S. Army and is the director of strategy for the Center for Land Warfare, U.S. Army War College. He is a graduate of the University of Chattanooga and Pennsylvania State University. Colonel Staudenmaier served in combat in Vietnam as a district advisor and in various staff assignments at the Department of the Army. He has contributed chapters to several books dealing with military strategy and defense policy. His articles have appeared in *Foreign Policy, Orbis, Naval War College Review, Military Review, Army,* and *Parameters.* He is coauthor of *Strategic Implications of the Continental-Maritime Debate* and coeditor of *Military Strategy in Transition: Defense and Deterrence.*

Dr. Harlan K. Ullman is senior fellow, The Center for Strategic and International Studies. He is currently involved in major studies concerning future U.S. continental force structure options. A former naval person, Dr. Ullman served in command assignments at sea and in the Office of the Secretary of Defense and the Chief of Naval Operations. He is the author of numerous articles and books including *Future Imperative: The U.S. Navy and National Security in the Next Decade* and *U.S. Conventional Force Structure Options* (forthcoming).

About the Editors

Robert E. Harkavy is a professor of political science at The Pennsylvania State University, specializing in national security policy, arms control, and U.S. foreign policy. He earlier served with the Atomic Energy Commission and the Arms Control and Disarmament Agency. He has been a senior research fellow at Cornell University, a visiting research professor at the U.S. Army War College, and an Alexander von Humboldt fellow at the University of Kiel, Germany. Professor Harkavy is the author of *The Arms Trade and International Systems* (1975), *Spectre of a Middle Eastern Holocaust* (1978), and *Great Power Competition for Overseas Bases* (1982). He is coeditor of several other books on national security. He is currently a consultant to the Office of the Secretary of Defense.

Stephanie G. Neuman is a senior research scholar at Columbia University's Research Institute on International Change, and the director of the Comparative Defense Studies Program. She was on the Graduate Faculty of the New School for Social Research from 1972 to 1983. Dr. Neuman's publications include: "International Stratification and Third World Military Industries," *International Organization,* winter 1984; "The Arms Trade and American National Interests," in *Power and Policy in Transition,* ed. Vojtech Mastny (1984); "Third World Military Industries and the Arms Trade," in *Arms Production in Developing Countries: An Analysis of Decision Making,* ed. James E. Katz (1984); and "Arms Transfers, Indigenous Defense Production, and Dependency: Implications for the Future," in *Security Issues in the Persian Gulf,* ed. Hossein Amirsadeghi (1981). Dr. Neuman has also coedited and contributed to *Arms Transfers in the Modern World* (1979) and has published articles in other academic and popular journals and newspapers.